My $50,000 Year at the Races

My $50,000

Year at the Races

Harcourt Brace Jovanovich

New York and London

Printed in the United States of America

Library of Congress Cataloging in Publication Data

Beyer, Andrew.
My $50,000 year at the races.

1. Horse race betting—United States.   2. Beyer, Andrew.
3. Gamblers—United States—Biography.
I. Title.
SF332.B49   798′.401   78–53918
ISBN 0–15–163693–1

First edition

B C D E

To Ann

ACKNOWLEDGMENTS

I am deeply indebted to the *Washington Star* and former sports editor David Burgin, who permitted (and even encouraged) me to combine my newspaper duties with my peripatetic gambling.

I also wish to thank David Obst and Dan Okrent, who conceived this book; Tom Stewart, who edited it; Dick White, who offered valuable comments on the manuscript; and the Kid, without whose assistance I would not have experienced a $50,000 year at the races.

Contents

My $50,000 Year
at the Races

1

Charting My Course

When I started playing the horses, I often dreamed about being a great professional gambler. This was more than a materialistic goal; it was a romantic vision. A man who could live by his wits at the racetrack would have the most independent, exhilarating, satisfying existence that I could imagine.

By the start of 1977, my fantasy had become a real possibility. I had already paid my tuition as a student of handicapping for many years. I had bet avidly, and lost consistently, while I grew up in Erie, Pennsylvania, attended Harvard, served in the Army, and worked as a sportswriter in Washington, D.C. Finally, in 1970, I achieved my first breakthrough. After making more than a hundred trips to the track, after devoting practically all of my mental energy to the *Racing Form*, after pushing nearly $20,000 through the betting windows, I showed a profit of $99.60. No matter that my hourly return was less than that of the average migrant farmworker; I could (and often did) proudly say that I beat the races.

Over the next few years I continued to beat them steadily enough so that I felt qualified to write a book on handicapping, *Picking Winners: A Horseplayer's Guide*. But my pride in my own modest accomplishments was beginning to turn into frustration. I thought that I should be able to win $50,000 in a year and prove that I could make a good living at the track. Instead, I had won slightly less than $10,000 in my very best year, which hardly certified me as a legendary high-rolling gambler and didn't even justify the enormous amount of time I invested in handicapping. I felt like a track star who can run a mile in 4:02 and knows that somewhere within himself he has the potential to break four minutes and join the elite. But how does he bridge that gap?

I wasn't sure, but I was determined to try. I wanted to make an all-out effort to realize my full potential as a horseplayer. And I would never find a more auspicious time to do it than 1977. I possessed a healthy bankroll; I was free of financial pressures and responsibilities; I had a job as the horse-racing columnist for the *Washington Star* which allowed me to go to the track wherever and whenever I wanted.

But before I could undertake this serious gambling venture, I had to understand the reasons why my past successes had been so limited. And I had to formulate an intelligent strategy for the year ahead. So I turned for guidance to the only gambler I knew who had achieved the goal for which I was striving.

Charlie had grown up in a lower-middle-class New York neighborhood where playing the horses was a way of life. He was probably not endowed with significantly greater intellectual gifts than the pals with whom he cut classes in order to play the daily double at Aqueduct. But Charlie had become a paragon of the professional horseplayer. Even in the jealous little world of the racetrack, he commanded the respect of everyone who had ever watched him operate.

"Is there anything," I asked him, "that you and all the other pros in New York have in common?" His answer was a revelation. "One thing," Charlie said. "We're all specialists. I know one guy who does nothing but bet horses who have been running in sprints on the main track and now are going a distance on the grass for the first time. He doesn't get many plays, but he wins enough of them to make money. There's another bettor here who only plays maiden two-year-old races according to the prices that the horses were sold for as yearlings. It sounds crazy, but he makes it work."

Charlie, too, was a specialist. He knew how to watch the post parade and tell which horses were ready for a maximum performance. He knew how to watch races and observe things that no one else could see. He would judge horses according to his own very subjective visual impressions. A few times a year, he would find a situation where a horse had impressed him in his previous races, looked good on the track, and was entered under optimal conditions. From these rare situations, Charlie would earn his livelihood. He had no desire to broaden his handicapping skills. "I've got a good thing going for me," he said, "and I don't want to tamper with it."

Charlie had become an extraordinarily successful professional gambler because he recognized his own narrow areas of expertise and capitalized on them. I had not. I had begun my handicapping career the way most people do, looking for some universal formula that would produce nine winners a day. And I never quite relinquished the hope that I could master every facet of the game. After *Picking Winners* was published, my ego was so inflated that I refused to acknowledge my own shortcomings as a horseplayer. I wanted to use every handicapping tool and master every type of race. I paid for my hubris. I was like a good singles hitter in baseball who suddenly gets delusions of grandeur, starts swinging in vain for the fences, and then finds that he can't even hit singles any more.

After my conversation with Charlie, I finally realized that there is nothing shameful about winning money with limited, specialized skills. So I took an inventory of my handicapping methods, looked back over my past triumphs and failures, and identified my own strengths. Obviously, I wasn't about to ignore the fundamentals of the game, but I wanted my serious bets to be grounded in one of the three areas of handicapping where I felt confident of my ability.

Speed Figures. I became a winning horseplayer when I discovered speed handicapping, a technique as intellectually stimulating as it is profitable.

I was enthralled by the mathematics involved in expressing a horse's performance as an unequivocal figure. I translated the time of his race into a numerical rating. To this I added the track variant—the product of some elaborate calculations—which indicated the inherent speed of the racing surface over which the horse had competed. The resultant figure gave me a whole new way of looking at the sport.

Never again would I have to judge a horse with such crude yardsticks as the class in which he competed and the number of lengths by which he was beaten. Now I could say that Horse A had earned figures of 82, 86, 84 in his last three starts. Horse B had run 79, 88, 78. So I would prefer Horse A unless I saw a reason why B was likely to duplicate his next-to-last performance.

When I started using figures I was dazzled by horses who had run extraordinarily well in their most recent race. But I soon found that speed handicapping is most effective when one horse has earned consistently higher figures than the other horses in the field. If I locate an animal whose last three or four performances are better than the last three or four races of all his opponents, I know from experience that he has a solid 70 or 80 percent probability of winning. There is no more reliable type of bet.

As I played horses like this in the early 1970s, I felt like a practitioner of an occult art. At that time most horseplayers were skeptical about the utility of speed handicapping; no book had ever explained how to make figures. So I was able to collect big prices on outstanding horses that the public overlooked.

Those glorious days are gone. *Picking Winners* and other books helped create a legion of new speed handicappers. Hucksters are advertising figures-by-mail services. And almost all horseplayers have increased their awareness of the importance of the times of races. This is unfortunate, because in order to win significantly a gambler has to stay a step ahead of the general public.

But while the payoffs on figure horses have decreased in recent years, I observed one common situation in which most speed handicappers went wrong. If a Maryland horse figured strongly in a race at Bowie, the people there would bet him accordingly. But if the same animal were shipped to Aqueduct and entered against a weak field, he would be overlooked. Speed handicappers can make figures for the horses at the track they follow, but they don't know how to evaluate an out-of-towner.

If I could calculate figures that were interchangeable from track to track, if I could predict how fast the Bowie horse was going to run at Aqueduct, I would possess a powerful handicapping tool. Its uses could be far-reaching. One of the most bewildering periods on the national racing calendar is the start of the midwinter Florida season, when the ranks of the local horses are suddenly invaded by stables from New York. Nobody knows how to compare the two groups with any precision, but with a sophisticated set of figures, I could. I did not know how I would calculate them, but I knew that if I could find the answer, I would not have to worry about making a profit in 1977.

Trainer Patterns.   Some of my most rewarding days as a bettor have come not from understanding horses, but from understanding the men who train them. The trainer always plays a fairly important role in the outcome of a race, but sometimes his methods are so overwhelmingly significant that they render every other handicapping factor irrelevant.

In *Picking Winners* I cited Allen Jerkens as a trainer who occasionally merits an automatic bet. Jerkens is astonishingly effective when he acquires a horse privately; he transformed Prove Out and Group Plan from run-of-the-mill allowance runners into stakes stars almost overnight. He is also a master at taking a sprinter and turning him into a distance runner. His sprinter Onion upset Secretariat at a mile and one-eighth; his speedster Beau Purple beat Kelso three times.

During the winter of 1976, I was enjoying a week's vacation at Hialeah when I encountered the archetypal Jerkens horse. Love Bird had been a nondescript sprinter under a different trainer the previous year, but now Jerkens had taken over his management. He gave the horse a pair of one-mile workouts, which suggested that he was aiming for a distance race. Next he entered Love Bird in a six-furlong race, which could not have been his principal objective, and the horse finished out of the money. After that, Jerkens worked him a mile again. And finally he entered Love Bird in a cheap allowance race at a mile and one-eighth on the grass. To a student of the *Racing Form* unfamiliar with the trainer, Love Bird was a horse with a dismal record and no prospects for any immediate improvement. But to an admirer of Jerkens, he was a fabulous betting opportunity. In view of the trainer's long-established record of success under similar circumstances, I thought that Love Bird had an even-money chance to win. After he led all the way at 13 to 1, I was flying to New York the next day for a shopping spree at Cartier's.

I knew only one other trainer whom I could bet with the same blind faith that I bet Jerkens. Although few horseplayers would recognize his name, the Fat Man is the most astute crook in American racing. He evidently devotes his life to executing one or two great betting coups a year, and he almost never fails. A horseplayer-sleuth could profit handsomely by following all of his intricate, larcenous machinations. I planned to follow the Fat Man very closely during 1977.

But there had to be other men who were similarly efficient with their own specialties. Trainers who score regularly with first-time starters. Trainers who win consistently with horses who have been laid off. Trainers who always win when they drop a horse in class sharply. It is not easy to identify these men. The only way to find out who they are and what they do is through hours of drudgery. I was going to have to burrow through stacks of old *Racing Forms*, look for horses who had won under interesting or unusual circumstances, and then analyze the overall record of their trainers to learn if they had a consistent method of operation. I would probably have to travel down a hundred blind alleys before I found one reliable trainer pattern. But if I could locate just one or two men who were as reliable as Jerkens—and, preferably, more obscure—I would be amply rewarded for my labors.

Track Biases. During August and September of 1976, I had an unparalleled opportunity to make a fortune. I did not take advantage of it.

I spent four weeks at Saratoga, where the racing surface was like two different tracks in one. The rail was so hard and fast that the horse who got the lead on the inside won almost automatically. Horses who tried to rally on the outside foundered in the deeper going. But when the New York horse population moved back downstate to Belmont Park, the game changed so drastically that one friend of mine suggested, "We ought to handicap here while standing on our heads." The inside part of the Belmont strip was a bog, and the track was so generally tiring that not a single front-runner won during the first week of the meeting. The horses who won at Saratoga could not win at Belmont, and vice versa.

Under such conditions, a perceptive handicapper ought to win easily and steadily. At Saratoga he should jettison all his usual methods and approach every race by looking for the horse who figured to get the lead on the rail. At Belmont, he should bet the horses who had been trying in vain to rally on the outside at Saratoga. I knew horseplayers who did just this and enjoyed the most profitable weeks of their lives while these unusual conditions prevailed.

At Saratoga I had quickly recognized the track bias, but I waited patiently for the perfect opportunity to capitalize on it. Toward the end of the meeting I finally found my horse. Introienne had earned superior speed figures while running on the outside part of the track. Now he was entered against a mediocre field, had drawn an inside post position, and figured to get the early lead along the rail. I made my biggest bet of the summer on Introienne, at 7 to 2, and watched in disbelief as he faded to finish out of the money. Evidently he hurt himself in that race, because he didn't run again for several weeks.

At Belmont I made an even worse mistake. I wasn't there. I was tired after four weeks of intensive gambling at Saratoga and I went back home to Washington instead. It was only after this period of track biases had ended, and my New York friends were telling me how they were planning to spend their winnings on new cars and fabulous vacations, that I realized how foolish I had been. I should have recognized that these track biases gave me the sort of rare opportunity that might not recur for months or years. I should have been taking advantage of the bias nine times a day at Saratoga instead of coyly waiting to put all my eggs in one basket. And I should have ignored my home, my job, and my cat in September in order to play nine races a day at Belmont Park.

Golden opportunities do not occur often. But when they do arise, a horseplayer has to be prepared to bet aggressively and to keep betting as long as the conditions are in his favor. There will be plenty of dull, unproductive periods on the racing calendar when he may rest. I would not make the same mistake again. In 1977 I would try to find a track bias as strong as the ones at Saratoga and Belmont, and if I did I would make the most of it.

I was confident that, with a few refinements, my handicapping methods would be good enough to produce a very profitable year. But I was much less sure of my betting skills. I knew that even brilliant students of the game are doomed to lose if they cannot handle their money properly, if they cannot select the right spots in which to make their serious wagers. Although I had been trying for years, I had never formulated a betting strategy with which I felt comfortable.

The classic approach, the one most horseplayers think of when they envision a professional gambler, is the one which Charlie had chosen. He wanted to bet only on winners, and he was willing to wait as long as necessary for horses who embodied his concept of perfection. "In my mind, a horse has to figure like a one-to-ten shot before I bet him," Charlie said. "And even that isn't enough. I've got to have the price, too. The horse has got to be at least five to one on the board. I don't see any reason why I should bother with races where everything isn't in my favor." Charlie waited for the right opportunities with superhuman patience. He could go to the track every day for weeks or months without making a move, allowing himself only the occasional indulgence of a $100 bet "to help me keep my sanity." Charlie could pass up a 4-to-1 shot whom he knew to be an absolute cinch because the horse's odds didn't quite meet his exacting standards. But when he did bet, Charlie was amply compensated for his weeks of forbearance. He could earn, on one winning bet, a sum which the average middle-class American would consider a decent annual income.

Ever since I aspired to be a gambler, I had accepted the premise that this was the proper way to play the horses, and I regretted the character weaknesses that prevented me from doing it. I am not endowed with the virtue of patience. And I like to gamble too much. I subscribe to the philosophy of the horseplayer who said, "You ought to make a bet every day or else you might be walking around lucky and not even know it." I will wager on the measurement of a snowfall or the size of the dinner check just for the sake of action. I cannot imagine sitting through an entire racing program without placing a bet.

So a few years ago I tried to formulate a betting system that would permit me to indulge in a few of my weaknesses—like a diet which allows its user an occasional chocolate sundae. The Beyer Money Management Plan called for me to place 5 percent of my total bankroll on any "prime bet," which I defined as a horse with at least a 50 percent chance of winning, at odds of 7 to 5 or greater. I allowed myself to venture a small, limited percentage of my bankroll on nonprime bets during the course of the day. I stuck with this formula, and I was miserable. Often I found a race where I thought I should take a bold gamble to win big money, but the system made me feel as if I were in a straitjacket. Often when the system told me to bet, say, $350 on a horse, my instincts told me that this sum was too much or too little. And my instincts were frequently right. When I finally couldn't stand it any more and abandoned the Beyer Money Management Plan, I felt horribly guilty.

I thought about reviving the Plan again as I began to map my strategy for 1977, but I finally came to my senses. There is no basis in fact for the notion that all professional gamblers are patient and selective, while only sickies yearn to play nine races a day. The winning horseplayers I know employ widely differing approaches. One of the most prosperous gamblers in New York treats every racing card as if there were going to be no tomorrow, and makes five or six $1000 bets every afternoon. Another man arbitrarily plays one race a day; two if he is riding a hot streak. I know a successful Marylander who uses an insane progression method of betting. If he wins on the early races, he escalates his wagers. If he keeps winning, he often finds himself making his biggest plunge of the day on one of his weaker selections, just because it happens to be running in the ninth race. "I know it's stupid," he conceded. "But every time I try to play the horses any other way I wind up losing my shirt."

As illogical as his method is, my friend had hit upon the real key to intelligent betting. A horseplayer cannot operate according to some theoretical textbook notion of what is right and wrong. He has to adapt his approach to suit his own temperament and personality. So instead of forcing myself to use a system with which I felt uncomfortable, I decided that in 1977 I would do what came naturally. I would gamble aggressively, frequently, and enthusiastically. Instead of constricting myself with rigid rules, I would merely formulate some general guidelines that would help me operate most intelligently and profitably, and would prevent my aggressiveness at the betting windows from turning into lunacy.

Whether a horseplayer employs a very patient or a very active approach to betting, he still must know how to identify the optimal situations in which he should place his largest wagers. I knew that I was going to make my serious moves on the basis of speed figures, track biases, and trainer patterns, but there was one other factor that had to be taken into the calculations: price. At one time I would happily take 7 to 5 on horses with impeccable credentials, until I realized that I was not making much money in the long run on these obvious, conservative selections. It is difficult to grind out a slow, steady profit at the track. While I tended to overbet short-priced standouts, I consistently underbet horses like Love Bird, who couldn't be defined as a sure thing but who offered a great opportunity for a financial windfall. I did not want to trap myself by setting a minimum price that I would take on any horse; there would still be times when I wanted to bet my lungs on a 7-to-5 shot. But I vowed that I would be generally more demanding about odds, and that I would always weigh a horse's chances of winning against his price while I was deciding how strongly to bet him.

In order to manage money intelligently, every horseplayer must maintain a proper balance between his prime bets and his more routine wagers. He has to avoid those days when he comes home from the track disgusted because he cashed a small bet on the horse he liked most and then lost a large bet on a race where he was stabbing. A man whose maximum wager is $100 shouldn't risk more than $10 or $20 on the races he is playing largely for action and entertainment. If I was prepared to invest $1000 on my prime selections, I thought I could rationally venture $100 or $200 on races where I was gambling.

Conservatives might be appalled by the notion that I would bet $200 on a race, or perhaps as much as $1000 during the course of a day, when I didn't even have a horse I considered a standout. But such purists are living in the past and failing to recognize that a profound change has swept the parimutuel world in the last decade. For centuries, the only way to play the races has been to look for the superior horse in a field and bet him to win, place, or show. But now that almost every track offers "gimmick" bets—most notably the exacta—horseplayers have greater opportunities for profit and entirely new types of valid betting situations. There are, for example, many times when a handicapper will narrow a race to two contenders at decent odds—say, 4 to 1. In the past, this handicapper had limited and unappealing choices. He could bet both horses and get a modest return on his total investment. He could flip a coin, bet one horse, and pray. Or, more likely, he could pass the race. But now a bettor can play both horses back and forth in the exacta. If he is right, he will be getting a return of about 10 to 1. Exactas give a bettor the opportunity to collect a substantial payoff on a logical, predictable outcome of a race. I wanted to use them to my advantage as much as possible.

While I had decided on the general style of betting I would employ in 1977, I still did not know how much I would be betting. With a starting bankroll of $8000, I thought I could afford to put $800 or $1000 on my top selections, with my other wagers scaled down from there. But I wanted to be flexible and adjust the level of my betting as circumstances dictated.

In particular, I planned to show some uncharacteristic restraint at the outset of the year. I remembered too vividly the first few days of one painful season at Saratoga. On opening day I found a horse who qualified for a prime bet and saw no reason to hesitate. I bet heavily, and lost. The next day I saw another standout, bet heavily again, and lost again. By the third day of the meeting I was $2700 in the red and my equilibrium was seriously disturbed. At a time when I still should have been getting my feet wet, I was drowning. I realized then that it makes sense to go slow at the start of a new season or a new year, to make a few moderate bets before getting serious. If I am going to make $1000 bets on my top selections, I would like to be $1000 ahead for a season before I make the first one.

One of the traits of any successful gambler—whether he bets the horses, shoots craps, or speculates on commodity futures—is the tendency to increase his stakes when he is winning and pull back when he is losing. If a day starts to go badly for me, I prefer to cut down my bets on the later races so I don't have to risk a disaster that will plunge me into gloom and sap my self-confidence. If I am hot, I will escalate my wagers a bit; I want the days when I pick six or seven winners to be blockbusters.

This principle applies to a bettor's long-term fortunes even more than it does to his performance on a single day. Any man who calls himself a gambler has experienced the thrill of dizzying winning streaks and suffered through the despair of protracted losing streaks. His ability to cope with these streaks—to maximize his profits during the good times and minimize his losses during the bad times—may largely determine his ultimate success or failure.

Throughout most of my life I have been fascinated and mystified by the phenomenon that luck runs in streaks. I could use unvarying methods of handicapping, deal with the same horses and the same trainers at the same tracks, but I would never achieve anything close to a steady, consistent rate of success. I was always riding a roller coaster. Evidently, it wasn't my handicapping that determined my fortunes. But what did? I had to endure a $10,000 losing streak before I found the answer, but when I did, I had the most valuable piece of information that a horseplayer could ever want. I knew what made me win and lose.

At the start of 1975 I was bursting with self-confidence. I was winning at the track and looking forward to becoming an author, which I thought would officially certify me as an expert handicapper. But by the time *Picking Winners* was published, I found myself mired in a losing streak for which there seemed to be no explanation and no escape. By autumn I was so depressed that I was ready to quit the game I loved. Why, I asked myself, should I let my own happiness and self-esteem be solely determined by the performance of a bunch of dumb animals? I told my editor at the *Star* that I wanted to abandon the racing beat and write a Wall Street column instead.

Fortunately, a 5-to-2 shot at Belmont Park ended my slump, reversed my luck, and rescued me from a life with municipal bonds. But I had been so affected by the agony of that losing streak that I wanted to understand it and avoid any repetition of it. I realized that my own mental state probably had a lot to do with the streak. My cocky overconfidence might have triggered it, and my utter despair surely prolonged it. As I reviewed other streaks in my gambling career, I saw for the first time that this was all part of a pattern. My fortunes at the track regularly passed through stages that were as predictable and immutable as the cycle of the seasons.

I always began the pattern with my back to the wall. I would be short of money, facing the uncomfortable realization that I couldn't afford to lose. So I would concentrate intensely on my handicapping, bet moderate sums on solid, conservative horses—and start to win. With my self-confidence resuscitated, I would bet more boldly and win more heavily. Success would beget further success. I would hit such a smooth, comfortable stride that I dared to think I had made the ultimate breakthrough, and that I would never lose at the track again. And then one of two things would disrupt my dreams of infallibility.

Sometimes a single dramatic disaster—a disqualification, a photo finish, a bet that wasn't made—would knock me completely off stride. I would subconsciously start betting in order to recoup the winnings I rightfully deserved. I would gamble too heavily, too impatiently, altering the routine which had brought me my success.

Other times a winning streak would end for much more subtle reasons. My self-confidence would change imperceptibly into over-confidence. I would develop sloppy habits because I was sure that success was inevitable anyway. I would bet horses merely because I was convinced of my own infallibility.

When the tide turned, I would not notice it at first, thinking that my losses were temporary setbacks. I would continue to bet aggressively. As the losses mounted, I might finally acknowledge that the streak was over, but I could rarely force myself to make a tactical retreat from the track. I was still clinging to the notion that I was infallible and trying to recoup my recent losses. As I kept pressing and kept losing, my judgment would be warped. Failure would beget more failures, and soon I would be trapped in a losing streak from which I could not extricate myself. It would last until some climactic disaster left me with my back to the wall, ready to start the whole cycle over again.

My mental state determined my fortunes at the track. I won when I maintained an air of calm self-confidence. I lost because of my emotional excesses. So I knew what I had to do in order to make 1977 the best year of my life. I was going to have to monitor my own emotions as carefully as a cardiologist monitors a patient's heartbeat. During the good times I had to watch myself closely and resist delusions of grandeur. At the onset of bad times I had to pull back before my attitude was poisoned and my confidence was wrecked. Nor could I let isolated instances of adversity faze me. If in 1977 (as had happened in 1975) the Metroliner to New York broke down outside Newark, and I didn't get to Aqueduct until after the fifth race, and I learned that my cinch had won by ten lengths, I would have to shrug off the disappointment. I could not let my frustration affect the way I handicapped and bet the next day.

I did not know if I would be able to muster such stoicism. I had never displayed a notable degree of even-temperedness at the track before, and telling myself to do it now might be as futile as ordering a nine-year-old to start behaving maturely. Human nature and emotions are hard to control. But I had to try.

As 1977 approached I drew up a tentative battle plan. I wanted to concentrate my efforts at a few tracks where I could exploit my own strengths as a handicapper. I wanted the race meetings spaced a few weeks apart so I would be able to rest and recuperate between each. And I wanted to spend my time in congenial atmospheres. So I decided to start my year of gambling at Miami's Gulfstream Park, where I thought I could profit from a set of speed figures which enabled me to compare the Florida horses with the New York shippers. In the spring I would bet at Pimlico Race Course in Baltimore, where I had often been able to capitalize on a track bias favoring horses with early speed and inside post positions. In August I would go to Saratoga, partly because I might find another track bias, partly because I know the New York trainers well, and partly because it is the finest racetrack in America. If a track bias did exist at Saratoga, I would probably follow the New York horses to Belmont Park in September.

By the end of September, I would know whether I had succeeded or failed in the ultimate test of myself as a horseplayer. There would be no ambiguity; there could be no rationalizations. My intelligence, my judgment, my maturity, my character would be measured by one unequivocal figure on the bottom line. The prospect was as frightening as it was exciting.

Gulfstream:
Palmy Days

A month before Gulfstream Park was scheduled to open its 1977 season, I was already becoming obsessed. I scrutinized stacks of old, yellowing copies of the *Daily Racing Form* to learn all I could about the track. I thought incessantly about betting strategy. I felt as motivated as a football player preparing for the Super Bowl. But as important as this assault on Gulfstream was for me, it was even more crucial for a twenty-three-year-old horseplayer who was going to be my companion and protégé in Miami.

The Kid had discovered the intellectual stimulation of handicapping while he was an undergraduate, but at first he didn't let his new passion disrupt the life for which he had been programmed. He received his diploma, attended graduate school at the University of Chicago, and then came back home to Washington to write the paper that would bring him his master's degree. Every morning he would pack his briefcase and say goodbye to his parents, telling them he was going to the Library of Congress. Usually he wound up at Bowie Race Course instead.

When the Kid introduced himself one night in a Washington bar, told me about his background, and described his growing interest in the sport, I felt as if I were seeing a flashback of my own life. I, too, had gone through an agonizing period of disenchantment with academia while I was becoming a horseplayer. Because of this sense of kinship, I started going to the track with the Kid, playing the role of the wise old handicapper. But within a few months, the Kid had ceased to be a mere understudy; he was my partner. At the 1976 Saratoga meeting, his exhaustive, brilliant research on trainers paid off handsomely for both of us and convinced him that he had the ability to make his living at the track.

This realization, which should have delighted any aspiring horseplayer, plunged the Kid temporarily into a black depression. He spent his last night in Saratoga sitting almost catatonically in a darkened room, chain-smoking and groping with the crisis he had created for himself. He had to make the first crucial decision of his adult life. He could take a respectable job and let racing be his chief form of recreation. Or he could devote himself entirely to the track, while horrifying his parents and defying all the dictates of society. He continued to wrestle with his dilemma when he returned home to Washington. One night his parents discreetly inquired, over the dinner table, "Don't you think it's about time you got a job?" The Kid answered, "I have one. I'm going to be a professional gambler."

Gulfstream Park would be the first assignment in the Kid's chosen career, so he enthusiastically joined me in my study of the racing there. An outsider who watched us work throughout December might have wondered how any human being could tolerate such tedium. But we were motivated and stimulated by the knowledge that any obscure scrap of information might be worth thousands of dollars in the weeks ahead.

Because our handicapping methods are very similar, and because we trust each other, the Kid and I could divide our work load. I spent most of my time constructing sets of speed figures for Gulfstream and for Calder, the track which preceded it on the Florida racing schedule. I analyzed the times of hundreds of races and grappled with problems which were ridiculously arcane. At one point I found that a horse who runs six furlongs in 1:13 at Gulfstream will run seven furlongs in 1:26⅕, while a 1:13 horse at Calder will run seven-eighths of a mile in 1:26⅘. Those mysterious three-fifths of a second had me perplexed and preoccupied for days. The whole process was intricate and laborious (and, to spare the reader temporarily, I have postponed an explanation of speed figures until a later chapter). But when I was finished, I had a set of numbers which would enable me to evaluate horses with precision, whether they had been running at Calder, Gulfstream, Aqueduct, or Belmont.

Meanwhile the Kid was practicing his specialty, studying the trainers who would be at Gulfstream. He maintained an index card for each of them, and as he reviewed all of the previous season's races, he wrote down the interesting characteristics of their winners. He noted when a trainer won with a horse stepping up in class, with a jockey switch, with a move from grass to dirt, with a first-time starter. After accumulating all the data, he tried to identify men who won frequently under similar circumstances. He also paid special attention to the trainers with the highest percentage of winners. And he discovered two patterns which promised to make all of this work worthwhile.

Warren A. "Jimmy" Croll has been one of the most successful horsemen in Florida and New Jersey for many years, and he has a reputation for skill with two-year-olds. The Kid saw that he had saddled three winning first-time starters at Gulfstream the previous year. To get a better understanding of Croll's methods and reliability, the Kid rummaged through old *Racing Forms* in my basement and found twenty of the trainer's first-time starters. Excitedly, he showed me this summary:

Horse	Best Workout	Odds	Finish
Double Ack	5 fur., 1:00⅗	9–1	third
Gay Jitterbug	5 fur., 1:01	6–1	won
Phoney	4 fur., :48	4–1	won
I Luv Dragons	5 fur., 1:02	12–1	out
Holmes Shore	6 fur., 1:15⅖	10–1	out
Bold Kit	4 fur., :49	17–1	third
Veroom Maid	4 fur., :49	5–2	out
Gold Streak	4 fur., :48⅖	2–1	won
Lil King	5 fur., 1:02⅖	8–1	out
Like a Julep	3 fur., :35⅘	12–1	out
Cheeky Cheetah	5 fur., 1:01	3–5	won
Noble Madame	5 fur., 1:01⅗	2–1	won
Herecomesthebride	6 fur., 1:15	9–10	won
Ali Oop	5 fur., 1:01	2–1	won
Lady Lib	3 fur., :36⅖	5–2	out
Lady Larida	4 fur., :48⅕	7–5	third
Jake Piccozzi	5 fur., :59	1–1	out
Nashver's Omega	4 fur., :49⅗	3–1	out
Royal Fleece	—	5–2	won
Exerene	5 fur., 1:01	5–2	won

Nine of Croll's twenty first-time starters had won, but their workouts gave few clues to their ability. Brilliantly fast stakes horses like Herecomesthebride, Exerene, and Ali Oop had shown little speed in published workouts before their racing debuts. But somebody knew how good they were anyway. Herecomesthebride had won as an odds-on favorite. Exerene had been bet down to 5 to 2, Ali Oop 2 to 1. Croll or his clients obviously went to the high denomination windows when they thought they had a promising young horse, and they were usually right. Of the Croll first-timers at odds of 6 to 1 or less, nine out of fourteen had won—an incredible 64 percent. Although betting unraced two-year-olds is usually a risky proposition, the Kid and I knew we could play Croll's horses with confidence—as long as we saw evidence that Croll was doing the same.

Like Croll, Jack Weipert was a trainer I had always respected without realizing how good he was at his own specialty. But after studying his record, the Kid and I saw that Weipert won consistently with horses who seemed to defy the fundamentals of handicapping. Thoroughbreds are usually not ready to win a distance race unless they have had the benefit of recent competition. But Weipert was obviously a very skillful conditioner, because he would win with horses who had been laid off for several months, who showed no strong evidence of fitness in their workouts, and who were entered at a mile or longer. In 1976 his colt Archie Beamish won the first start of his career at a mile and one-eighth, paying $15.60. Summer Wind II won a route after a three-month layoff early in the Florida season, and later scored again after a two-month rest. Arctic Quill made his first start of the year in a $1\frac{1}{16}$-mile grass race and lost a photo finish at 19 to 1. Because Weipert's horses often paid such generous prices, I thought he might be the key to a profitable winter.

By early January I felt thoroughly prepared, and I was practically counting the hours until post time for the first race of the Gulfstream Park season. On January 14 I said goodbye without regrets to the most bitter weather of the century, flew to Miami, and (unable to resist temptation) joined the Kid and Charlie for an evening at the Hollywood Dog Track. The next morning the Kid and I drove from our apartment to Gulfstream for the first time, and our breath was taken away as we passed between rows of palm trees and saw the track silhouetted against the azure sky. We immediately inspected all the facilities, found an ideal section in the grandstand from which to watch the races, located the high-denomination betting windows, and also spotted a grassy area by the paddock where we could absorb some sunshine between races. For two horseplayers who had spent previous winters in the cavernous gloom of Bowie Race Course, this was like a vision of heaven.

The sky didn't stay blue for long. Light rain started to fall during the first race, and by midafternoon it had turned into a driving thunderstorm. But while the downpour may have spoiled the day, it created a betting situation that was as instructive as it was profitable.

The eighth race had been scheduled to be run at one mile on the grass. But with the turf course waterlogged, it was belatedly switched to seven furlongs on the sloppy main track. These were the past performances* of the two principals in the ten-horse field:

* Appendix A, p. 155, explains how to read past performances.

Cinteelo ✻ — B. c. 4, by Jacinto—Teela, by Cockrullah — Br.—Schiff J M (Ky) — Tr.—Kelly Thomas J — Own.—Schiff J M

112 — Turf Record: St. 7, 1st 1, 2nd 2, 3rd 0 — 1976: St. 14, 1st 3, 2nd 3, 3rd 2, Amt. $70,885 — 1975: St. 7, 1st 2, 2nd 0, 3rd 1, Amt. $13,260

20Oct76- 8Bel fst 1 1/16 :46 1:09⅘ 1:40⅗ 3↑Handicap 3 2 21 3½ 21 22¼ Cordero A Jr b 114 *1.50 97-12 Distant Land 1132¼ Cinteelo 1142 Northerly 113¾ Gamely 8

7Oct76- 8Bel yl 1 1/16 Ⓣ:47 1:11⅕ 1:43⅘ 3↑Handicap 3 3 2½ 2½ 1½ 21¼ Day P b 115 9.00 80-19 Silver Prince 1121¼ Cinteelo 1153¾ I'm On Top 116hd Gamely 8

29Aug76- 8Del fm 1 1/16 Ⓣ:47⅕ 1:11⅖ 1:43⅖ L. Richards 12 1 12 12 1½ 1nk Thornburg B b 117 4.40e 87-16 Cinteelo 117nk Chati 1171 Babas Fables 1142½ Driving 12

5Aug76- 8Sar fm 1 1/16 Ⓣ:47⅕ 1:10⅘ 1:40⅘ 3↑Handicap 3 3 41½ 44 46½ 57½ Velez R I b 108 3.70e 85-07 Clout 117¾ Teddy's Courage 1124¼ Co Host 1112 Tired 7

17Jly76- 6Mth fm 1 1/16 Ⓣ:47⅕ 1:11⅖ 1:43⅗ Lamplightr H 1 4 43½ 42½ 46 46¼ Thornburg B b 118 5.30 82-12 Chati 1172¼ Family Doctor 1133¼ Fighting Bill 115¾ Bore out 9

17Jly76-Run in two divisions 6th & 8th Races.

4Jly76- 8Del sf 1 1/16 Ⓣ:48 1:13 1:45⅗ C. Rodney 3 1 11 1½ 11 2no Thornburg B 117 *1.60e 76-24 Quick Card 120no Cinteelo 117¾ No Link 1231 Just missed 11

4Jly76-Run in two divisions 7th and 8th races.

20Jun76- 8Bel fm 1 1/16 Ⓣ:46⅗ 1:10⅖ 1:41⅕ Hill Prnce H 1 2 2½ 1hd 31 54½ Velez R I b 112♦ 2.80e 90-05 Fifth Marine 1263 Quick Card 120½ Drovers Dawn 1121 Weakened 9

20Jun76-Dead heat

5Jun76- 8Bel fst 1 1/16 :45⅖ 1:10 1:42⅕ Allowance 5 1 2½ 77 724 731 Velasquez J b 119 10.20 60-15 Quiet LittleTable1192¾KirbyLane1154¼Sawbones115½ Speed, tired 7

19May76- 8Bel sly 1 1/16 :46⅖ 1:11⅗ 1:43⅕ 3↑Allowance 3 1 12 11½ 15 17½ Velez R I5 b 106 *.70 86-17 Cinteelo 1067½BabyFaceBeau120nkGreenAsGrass1201¼ Ridden out 8

LATEST WORKOUTS Dec 26 Hia 5f gd 1:06 b — Dec 18 Hia 5f fst 1:03 b — Dec 11 Hia 5f fst 1:04 b — Dec 6 Hia 5f fst 1:02 h

***Sabinal** — B. h. 5, by Francis U.—Saette, by Gulf-Weed — Br.—Haras America (Arg) — Tr.—Azpurua Leo — Own.—Aquiar & Gonzalez

112 — Turf Record: St. 1, 1st 1, 2nd 0, 3rd 0 — 1976: St. 5, 1st 4, 2nd 1, 3rd 0, Amt. $23,728 — 1975: St. 3, 1st 1, 2nd 1, 3rd 0, Amt. $2,964

1Aug76♦5LaGavea(Brazil) fm*1 1:34 Ⓣ Gr Pr Presidente d'Rep 11¾ Centeno V R 128 *1.00 — — Sabinal 1821¾ Suarelo 1281¼ Povorino 128½ Well up,driving 16

9Jly76♦7Palermo(Arg) fst*1⅜ 2:14 Clasico Independencia Hcp 26 Centeno V R 132 3.10 — — Patron 1136 Sabinal 132no Rail 1201½ Well up thruout 11

13Jun76♦5Palermo(Arg) gd*1⅛ 1:50⅖ Clasico Peru 1¾ Centeno V R 127 *.70 — — Sabinal 127¾ Stein 1321½ Povorino 12712 Led most of way 5

16May76♦6Palermo(Arg) fst*1 1:36⅕ PreFragata 25 de Mayo Hcp 15 Centeno V R 115 5.65 — — Sabinal 1155 Rodesiano 1192 Sheraton 1192 Well up,drew away 9

7Mar76♦10Palermo(Arg) fst*1 1:36⅘ Premio Circinus(Alw) 11½ Alvis J 123 2.45 — — Sabinal1231½ FightingIndian123¾ NightWtch1177 Well up,dr.clear 10

14Dec75♦2Palermo(Arg) fst*1 1:36⅖ Premio Ligero(Alw) 411 Alvis J 123 *1.95 — — MickeyBluff 1239 Azulado 115¾ Calbally 1231½ Well up to str 7

26Oct75♦6Palermo(Arg) hy*1 1:39 Premio Siempre Lindo(Mdn) 1hd Alvis J 123 *1.85 — — Sabinal 123hd Saldano 1231 Preview 1151 Saved ground,up 11

5Oct75♦5Palermo(Arg) fst*1 1:36⅗ Premio Tai(Mdn) 23 Alvis J 123 23.50 — — Provinciano 1233 Sabinal 1239 Prospero 123½ Well up,led 18

LATEST WORKOUTS ●Jan 13 Crc 4f fst :47⅗ h — Jan 11 Crc 5f fst 1:03⅕ bg — Jan 6 Crc 5f fst 1:02 b

Cinteelo was a consistent, capable runner under almost any conditions, but on a wet track he became as good as any horse in America. The bottom line of his past performances showed that he had won by 7½ lengths on a sloppy track. I remembered that he had captured his two previous starts in the slop by margins of 8½ and 6 lengths. Although he had not raced for nearly three months, Cinteelo had been training steadily, and he deserved to be a heavy favorite against the average allowance horses he was now facing.

Sabinal, an invader from Argentina, was the mystery horse in the field. As far as most American handicappers could tell, he might be anything from a $1500 claimer to a stakes horse. He was 10 to 1 in the morning line, but money poured in on him from the opening bell. He was 5 to 1 when he came onto the track for the post parade, and 7 to 2 as he approached the starting gate. With Sabinal's odds plummeting, Cinteelo's price crept up to 2 to 1.

I had not anticipated betting this race, but now I had to make a hasty judgment. The public at large could not have been making Sabinal 7 to 2; insiders had to be betting him heavily. And such "smart money" can be very significant, especially when it shows for an unknown quantity, like a first-time starter or a foreign import. Obviously, trainer Leo Azpurua knew that Sabinal was a top-quality animal in sharp condition.

But I had to conclude also that Azpurua could not know what kind of opposition he was facing. I did not think that the trainer of any horse in the world could rationally bet heavily against Cinteelo in the slop. There are times when a trainer can be certain that his horse is going to win, but this was not one of them. Azpurua was gambling.

He probably had committed himself to a course of action when he entered Sabinal in the grass race, and now was imprudently sticking to his plans in spite of the sloppy track.

I was willing to bet on Cinteelo and against the remote possibility that Sabinal was a superhorse. I regretted that this race was not occurring at a stage of the season when I was winning substantially and feeling loose with my money. But I did not want to risk digging myself into a deep hole on opening day, so I cautiously ventured $200 to win on Cinteelo. He stalked the leaders on the backstretch, took command on the turn, and then held off Sabinal's late rally to score by 2½ lengths.

Delighted as I was, I felt a twinge of sympathy for Azpurua, who had been robbed by fate (and rain) of a fabulous betting opportunity. I sought out the trainer and offered my condolences, but he seemed calm and philosophical about it all. He told me that Sabinal had won an invitational race that was South America's equivalent of the Washington, D.C., International, prompting his two Argentine owners to send him to the United States. Sabinal trained exceptionally well here, and Azpurua notified the owners that he was ready to run. They flew to Miami on the morning of the race—just before the rains came.

Azpurua told the owners that the sloppy track would almost certainly hurt the horse's chances. He said he would like to scratch, but he needed a prep race before a stake the next weekend. The owners had been warned. But it would have been contrary to human nature for men to make an intercontinental trip to bet on a horse race and then decide at the last moment to pass it. They bet anyway, and they would have won, except for the presence of Cinteelo in the field.

There was a valuable lesson in the eighth race at Gulfstream. A handicapper should always try to recognize when a stable seems to be betting its horse with confidence. But there are times when the handicapper must stand by his own convictions and conclude that the stable is wrong. Having done so, I had started the season modestly in the black.

Better things lay ahead. When I opened the next day's *Racing Form*, I was excited to discover that the most promising young horse in Jack Weipert's barn was entered in the seventh race. Rich Soil had run a brilliantly fast race at Belmont Park in September, earning a bigger speed figure than any other two-year-old filly in the country. But a minor injury cut short her campaign and prevented her from proving her ability in stakes competition. Now she was making her first start after a layoff and, with Weipert training her, she figured to be in peak condition. Rich Soil's opposition was so mediocre that she was going to be a short price, but I didn't care. I knew she couldn't lose.

I hit the daily double and an exacta with small bets early in the program, putting me a few hundred dollars ahead and enabling me to bet the seventh race aggressively. With Rich Soil the even-money favorite, I elected to put all my money into exactas, betting a pair of $200 combinations with her on top of the chief contenders, Wave in Glory and Mary L. For a while, everything looked perfect. Wave in Glory and Mary L. were battling for the lead, with Rich Soil positioned in the middle of the pack, within easy striking distance. Rich Soil started to advance quickly along the rail, but on the turn she found a wall of horses in her path. Jockey Miguel Rivera stood up in the irons, looked for a place to go, and then swung five horses wide in the turn. By the time Rich Soil had regained her momentum, it was too late. She finished three-quarters of a length behind Mary L. Bad luck had cost me more than $2000 and robbed the Kid of a substantial sum as well. That night he was staring silently at the wall of our apartment and chain-smoking Camels, which he does only in times of extreme distress. I believe in responding more actively to gambling misfortunes, so I accompanied two racetrack cronies from Washington on an evening of dining and drinking that helped us forget Rich Soil. My friend Carlos spent $12 on dinner and $274 on drinks, a feat we would have considered incredible until we learned that when a girl at the Backstage Lounge asks you to buy her a drink, she is talking about a $33 bottle of champagne and not a 95-cent draft beer.

Even though a fog enveloped me the next afternoon at Gulfstream, I saw that there was a fitting way to redress the injustice of Rich Soil's defeat. Weipert was starting another filly, New Scent, who had shown considerable promise the previous summer and now was making her first start in six months. I bet $300, and this time there were no excuses. New Scent finished sixth. The next day I bet a Weipert colt who was making his first start after a layoff, and he ran last all the way. I didn't even like him much, but I was sure that the first time I disregarded a Weipert horse, he would win and I would feel miserable.

All gamblers tend to think along these lines. The man who loses on the same number fifty straight times at roulette cannot tear himself away from the wheel, because he knows the number will come up as soon as he leaves. The owners of Sabinal could not abstain from betting, even though that would have been prudent, because they knew they would feel ridiculous if their horse won anyway. But a professional cannot afford to think like this. He has to be flexible, not bound to a fixed course of action. He has to evaluate his handicapping methods constantly and coldly jettison the ones which are not working. In order to do this, he has to be willing to let an occasional winner go by. I would cross Weipert's name off my list until he started winning.

But there was another name on the list, and on January 21 I encountered a Jimmy Croll first-time starter in the past performances for the fourth race.

4 GULFSTREAM — 6 FURLONGS (GULFSTREAM; Start, Finish)

6 FURLONGS. (1.07⅘) MAIDEN CLAIMING. Purse $6,000. 3-year-olds. Weights 120 lbs. Claiming Price $40,000 for each $2,500 to $35,000 allowed 2 lbs. (Preference to hoses which have not started for $1,000 or less).

Dad's Sugar — B. f. 3, by My Dad George—Gentle Mollie, by Gentle Art — $35,000 — Br.—Beardsley Mollie J (Fla) — Tr.—Simmons John P — **111**
Own.—Beardsley Mrs M & Pillsbury J
St. 1st 2nd 3rd Amt. — 1977 0 M 0 0 — 1976 0 M 0 0
LATEST WORKOUTS Jan 13 Crc 6f fst 1:18 b Jan 7 Crc 6f fst 1:19 bg Jan 3 Crc 5f fst 1:06 b Dec 29 Crc 4f fst :51 b

Indian Mountain — Ch. c. 3, by Jim J—Lorgnette II, by High Hat — $40,000 — Br.—Moore Marie A (Ky) — Tr.—Richards Robert J Jr — **120**
Own.—Lake Don
St. 1st 2nd 3rd Amt. — 1976 2 M 0 0 $300
22Dec76- 2Crc fst 6f :22⅗ :46⅖ 1:13⅗ Md Sp Wt 3 9 32½ 32½ 45 54¼ St Leon G 118 5.60 82-14 Be Gallant 118^1 G's Brandy 118^{nk} Mills Bill 118^2 Weakened 11
13Dec76- 4Crc fst 7f :23⅗ :47⅕ 1:27 Md Sp Wt 3 3 12 11½ 1½ 44¼ Bohenko P 118 41.10 77-17 Highland Jim 118^{1}PoorMan'sBluff118^{nk}Satan'sThunder118^3 Tired 12
LATEST WORKOUTS Jan 11 GP 6f fst 1:16⅖ b Dec 30 GP 4f fst :49⅖ b Dec 1 GP 3f fst :37⅗ bg

Never Guilty — Ch. c. 3, by No Robbery—Case Dismissed, by Traffic Judge — $35,000 — Br.—Walden BenP (Ky) — Tr.—Merrill Frank H — **116**
Own.—Wilson M
St. 1st 2nd 3rd Amt. — 1977 0 M 0 0 — 1976 0 M 0 0
LATEST WORKOUTS Jan 11 GP 6f fst 1:16⅗ b Jan 5 GP 6f gd 1:18 bg Dec 28 GP 5f fst 1:05 b Dec 20 GP 5f fst 1:04⅖ bg

Cash Or Credit — Ch. c. 3, by Restless Wind—Winging Lark, by Bold Lark — $40,000 — Br.—Stoll Mr-Mrs J F (Ky) — Tr.—Bond J Bowes — **120**
Own.—Stoll Mr-Mrs J
St. 1st 2nd 3rd Amt. — 1977 0 M 0 0 — 1976 0 M 0 0
LATEST WORKOUTS Jan 18 GP 4f fst :49 bg Jan 8 GP 6f fst 1:18⅗ b Jan 3 GP 5f fst 1:04 b Dec 28 GP 4f fst :49 b

Sir Judge — Ch. c. 3, by Delta Judge—Miss Remaid, by Reneged — $40,000 — Br.—Nuckols Brothers (Ky) — Tr.—Kelley Walter A — **120**
Own.—S & F Farm
St. 1st 2nd 3rd Amt. — 1977 0 M 0 0 — 1976 0 M 0 0
LATEST WORKOUTS Jan 15 Hia 7f fst 1:28 hg Jan 10 Hia 5f fst 1:01 hg Jan 6 Hia 6f fst 1:15⅗ h Dec 31 Hia 5f fst 1:04⅖ b

Bio Grey — B. c. 3, by Tudor Grey—Lady Bio, by Crimson Satan — $35,000 — Br.—Crimson King Farm (Ky) — Tr.—Salmen Peter W Jr — **116**
Own.—Crimson King Farm
St. 1st 2nd 3rd Amt. — 1977 0 M 0 0 — 1976 0 M 0 0
LATEST WORKOUTS Jan 7 GP 6f fst 1:15⅖ h Dec 28 GP 6f fst 1:16⅗ b Dec 18 GP 5f fst 1:02 b Dec 11 GP 5f fst 1:02 b

Squadron Castle — Ch. c. 3, by Road At Sea—Cherie Rose, by Peter Flower — $35,000 — Br.—Wettach M (Md) — Tr.—Field Kenneth — **116**
Own.—Wettach M
St. 1st 2nd 3rd Amt. — 1976 0 M 0 0
LATEST WORKOUTS Jan 11 Hia 4f fst :50 b Dec 18 Pim 6f fst 1:16⅘ h Dec 6 Pim 5f fst 1:07 b

Mohawk Drive — Dk. b. or br. g. 3, by U Bearcat—Red Pilot, by Pilot — $40,000 — Br.—Thomas Elmer W (Ind) — Tr.—Gallagher R J — **120**
Own.—Horner Earl & Ellie
St. 1st 2nd 3rd Amt. — 1977 0 M 0 0 — 1976 0 M 0 0
LATEST WORKOUTS Jan 19 GP 4f fst :49 b Jan 15 GP 6f fst 1:15⅖ b Jan 10 GP 6f fst 1:16 bg Jan 4 GP 6f sly 1:17 b

Speedy Catch — Ch. g. 3, by Pass Catcher—Bibijagua, by Tarik — $35,000 — Br.—Hoffman Mrs Georgia E (Fla) — Tr.—Prater R W — **116**
Own.—Hoffman Mrs P B
St. 1st 2nd 3rd Amt. — 1977 1 M 0 0 $36 — 1976 0 M 0 0
17Jan77- 3GP my 6f :22⅗ :46⅗ 1:12⅕ Md Sp Wt 10 10 128¾ 1115 1217 1118 Saumell L 120 4.70 60-25 My Son Howard 120^2 RealFlyer120^{1}ForwardCharger120^{2½} Outrun 12
LATEST WORKOUTS Jan 10 Hia 3f fst :36⅗ hg Jan 9 Bel tr.t 4f fst :50⅘ b Dec 29 Hia 6f fst 1:14 h Dec 21 Hia 5f sly 1:01⅖ h

East Union — Ch. c. 3, by Sensitivo—Dearest Mommy, by Summer Tan — $35,000 — Br.—Delray Training Center (Fla) — Tr.—Kelley Thomas W — **116**
Own.—Bromagen G S & W
St. 1st 2nd 3rd Amt. — 1976 7 M 0 0
11Nov76- 4CD fst 6½f :23⅖ :47⅖ 1:21⅘ Md Sp Wt 12 1 3½ 3^1 3^5 56¼ Gavidia W b 122 6.80 65-23 Picarro 122^2 Rouleit 122½ Beau Dustin 122¾ Tired 12
4Nov76- 5CD fst 6½f :22⅘ :46⅖ 1:19⅖ Md Sp Wt 7 2 1^4 12½ 1hd 57¾ Turcotte R L b 122 72.50 75-23 Kodiack 122^{2¾} Beau Dustin 122^{4½}MisterWiggle122^{nk} Speed; tired 12
11Oct76- 4Kee fst 6f :22⅗ :46 1:11⅘ Md Sp Wt 12 6 32½ 10^{14} 8^{13} 12^{21} Melancon L b 118 34.40f 62-17 Coined Silver 118^{2¼} Rouleit 118no Coldwater 118^{2½} Tired 12
31Aug76- 1AP fst 6f :21⅘ :45⅕ 1:12⅕ Md Sp Wt 4 2 31½ 33½ 10^{13} 10^{20} Cauthen S^5 b 114 17.10 62-17 Cornucopian 119^1 Promising Dream 119^{1¼} Ruff Mark 119^{1¾} Tired 10
23Aug76- 3AP fst 6f :22⅖ :46⅖ 1:11⅘ Md Sp Wt 4 2 12 12½ 31½ 79½ Powell J b 119 17.20 74-14 WindyCityButch119^{nk}Cornucopian119^{1½}Hinkston119^5 Speed, tired 9
6Aug76- 4AP gd 6f :22⅗ :47 1:12⅖ Md Sp Wt 8 4 1½ 1½ 33½ 7^{12} Sibille R 119 40.50 69-19 Smiley's Dream 119^1 Iron Crow 119^2 Humor Me119^4 Speed, tired 10
13Jly76- 2AP fst 5½f :22⅕ :46⅕ 1:05 Md Sp Wt 8 3 43½ 6^5 106¼ 11^{16} Breen R 118 15.10 74-13 Bob's Dusty 118^5 Bask 118^{1¼} Iron Crow 118^{nk} Brief speed 11
LATEST WORKOUTS Jan 15 GP 3f fst :37⅖ b

White Rammer — Ch. c. 3, by Jim J—Been Taken, by Tom Fool — $40,000 — Br.—Bryand Mr-Mrs J C H (Va) — Tr.—Croll Warren A Jr — **120**
Own.—Bryant J C H
St. 1st 2nd 3rd Amt. — 1977 0 M 0 0 — 1976 0 M 0 0
LATEST WORKOUTS Jan 19 GP 4f fst :48 h Jan 14 GP 4f fst :48 hg Jan 10 GP 5f fst 1:01 hg Jan 6 GP 4f fst :49 b

Lugano — B. c. 3, by Templario II—Hellio Valentine, by Maribeau — $40,000 — Br.—Imbesi Anthony (NJ) — Tr.—Armstrong K D — **120**
Own.—Briardale Farm
St. 1st 2nd 3rd Amt. — 1977 0 M 0 0 — 1976 0 M 0 0
LATEST WORKOUTS Jan 19 GP 3f fst :38 b Jan 6 GP 5f fst 1:05 b Dec 29 GP 4f fst :51 b Dec 18 GP 5f fst 1:02 b

White Rammer's breeding and workouts suggested that he had ability, but I was going to let the tote board dictate my course of action. If Croll bet, I would bet. White Rammer was the 3-to-1 favorite in the morning line, and he remained that price through most of the wagering. This was ambiguous. In a field where none of the horses had proven credentials, the public could be responsible for all the money on White Rammer. But in the last few minutes before post time, the colt's odds plunged suddenly and emphatically to 9 to 5. I had been hovering by the windows waiting for this, and now I played $30 exactas with White Rammer on top of Indian Mountain, the only horse with established form, and on top of three first-time starters whose trainers I respected: Cash Or Credit, trained by Bowes Bond; Sir Judge, trained by Walter Kelley; and Bio Grey, trained by Peter Salmen. I had never heard of Salmen until two days earlier, when I collected a token bet on a 20-to-1 shot who proved that he is a skilled, patient horseman. The animal had won his only start a year earlier, had obviously been beset by physical problems, but came back from his long absence to win by six lengths. After playing my exactas, I timidly bet only $100 to win on White Rammer, perhaps because I was still feeling a bit shaky about trainer patterns after my Weipert experiences. But the inadequacy of this wager didn't matter much.

FOURTH RACE

Gulfstream

JANUARY 21, 1977

6 FURLONGS. (1.07⅘) MAIDEN CLAIMING. Purse $6,000. 3-year-olds. Weights 120 lbs. Claiming Price $40,000 for each $2,500 to $35,000 allowed 2 lbs. (Preference to horses which have not started for $15,000 or less).

Value of race $6,000, value to winner $3,732, second $1,140, third $540, fourth $300, balance of starters $36 each. Mutuel pool $65,161. Perfecta Pool $81,509.

Last Raced	Horse	Eqt.A.Wt PP St	¼	½	Str	Fin	Jockey	Cl'g Pr	Odds $1
	White Rammer	3 120 11 2	4¹½	2hd	2⁵	1¹	Saumell L	40000	1.90
	Bio Grey	3 116 6 4	1¹½	11½	1½	2⁹	Manganello M	35000	16.80
	Never Guilty	3 116 3 5	5³	4²	3²	3³	Gomez A	35000	14.60
	Sir Judge	3 120 5 9	7½	6hd	5³	4¹½	Aviles O B	40000	7.30
	Cash Or Credit	3 120 4 6	2¹	3²	4²	5²	Perret C	40000	5.70
	Squadron Castle	3 116 7 11	9²	8¹½	6¹½	6²	Salinas S	35000	45.10
17Jan77 3GP11	Speedy Catch	3 116 9 10	10⁸	10¹⁰	8½	7¹	Solomone M	35000	11.10
22Dec76 2Crc5	Indian Mountain	3 120 2 7	6½	7³	9³	8¹	MacBeth D	40000	4.00
11Nov76 4CD5	East Union	b 3 116 10 1	3hd	5³	7¹	9³	Gavidia W	35000	8.50
	Mohawk Drive	3 120 8 8	8³	9¹½	10¹⁴	10¹¹	Cedeno M	40000	37.70
	Lugano	3 120 12 3	12	12	12	11⁷	Miceli M	40000	80.20
	Dad's Sugar	3 116 1 12	11¹⁰	11¹⁸	11²	12	Barrow T	35000	28.80

OFF AT 2:38 1/2 EST. Start good, Won driving. Time, :22, :46⅕, 1:11⅗ Track fast.

$2 Mutuel Prices:

11-WHITE RAMMER	5.80	4.00	3.00
6-BIO GREY		12.20	9.20
3-NEVER GUILTY			6.00

$2 PERFECTA 11-6 PAID $99.00.

Ch. c, by Jim J—Been Taken, by Tom Fool. Trainer Croll Warren A Jr. Bred by Bryand Mr-Mrs J C H (Va).

WHITE RAMMER well placed early improved position from the outside on the turn to challenge in midstretch and under brisk left handed pressure was drawing clear at the finish. BIO GREY sprinted to a clear lead early responded when challenged in midstretch but was outfinished. NEVER GUILTY prominent early had no apparent mishap. SIR JUDGE was outrun. CASH OR CREDIT had speed to head of stretch. INDIAN MOUNTAIN showed little. EAST UNION was finished after a half. LUGANO bore out badly along the backstretch.

Owners— 1, Bryant J C H; 2, Crimson King Farm; 3, Wilson M; 4, S & F Farm; 5, Stoll Mr-Mrs J; 6, Wettach M; 7, Hoffman Mrs P B; 8, Lake Don; 9, Bromagen G S & W; 10, Horner Earl & Ellie; 11, Briardale Farm; 12, Beardsley Mrs M & Pillsbury J.

Trainers— 1, Croll Warren A Jr; 2, Salmen Peter W Jr; 3, Merrill Frank H; 4, Kelley Walter A; 5, Bond J Bowes; 6, Field Kenneth; 7, Prater R W; 8, Richards Robert J Jr; 9, Kelley Thomas W; 10, Gallagher R J; 11, Armstrong K D; 12, Simmons John P.

Overweight: Dad's Sugar 5 pounds.

Scratched—Real Flyer (17Jan77 3GP2); Pac; Joe Gural (7Jan77 2Crc2); No Bluffing; Back First; Senate.

Croll's horse caught Salmen's horse in the stretch and beat him by a length, with the rest of the field nine lengths behind. The winner paid $5.80, the exacta returned $99, and I collected nearly $1800. I was rolling.

I was developing the confident, positive mental attitude that mysteriously enables horseplayers to make all the marginal decisions correctly. I was stabbing with inspiration on daily doubles and exactas that I never would have hit in ordinary times. As my profits for the season climbed past the $3000 mark, I was afflicted by a virulent case of betting fever, and a man in the clutches of that disease can find few places better than Miami for the proper therapy.

After spending an afternoon at Gulfstream, I had to choose among two jai-alai frontons, two dog tracks, and a harness track for my evening entertainment. I could also take a short nocturnal plane trip to the casinos in Freeport. And as if this weren't action enough, my broker had advised me to keep an ear cocked for all the hot stock-market tips that circulate around Miami at the height of the tourist season. There were days when all this activity amounted to an emotional overload. Days like January 26.

I spent the afternoon sitting in the Gulfstream grandstand with the Kid and Charlie, and in the seventh race we all liked a Maryland invader named Flashy Guy. The Kid and I bet with enthusiasm but Charlie, displaying his usual forbearance, passed. Flashy Guy was not a "three-star horse," his designation for the ultimate betting opportunity, and therefore not worth a bet. Flashy Guy was parked four-wide on both turns, came into the stretch with a narrow lead, but weakened in the last sixteenth of a mile.

The Kid and I were cursing our fate when Charlie consoled us. "Don't worry," he said. "I've got a three-star dog tonight." He was absolutely straightfaced. "I went to the dog track for fun a few nights ago, and I saw this dog named Dark Special run. Everything bad that could happen to a dog happened to him, but he still showed such courage, such determination that he finished second. He's three stars."

That night the Kid and I joined Charlie and his wife Lana at the Hollywood Kennel Club. "I can't believe I'm here getting ready to bet three hundred dollars on a dog," I said in my last moment of lucidity.

"I don't know what I'm doing here either," Lana said. "I was at the jai-alai the other night and a very well-connected man told me that the four-five-one trifecta is going to win tonight. He didn't tell me what game, but he said it's a sure thing."

Much as I am willing to believe inside information when all the competitors speak a foreign tongue, I was still glad I was at Hollywood. I was, at least, until the three-star dog finished next to last with no excuses. We all went to a bar and took an overdose of Jack Daniel's and then, on the way home, bought a morning paper and saw the inevitable. The Olea-Ochita team had won the seventh game at Dania Jai-Alai, with Larrea-Azpizu second and Guardino-Arregui third, and the 4–5–1 trifecta had paid $1155. I had one last shot to salvage the day. I turned to the American Stock Exchange tables and breathed a sigh of relief. My red-hot little pantyhose company had skyrocketed from 5⅞ to 6⅞. I had just about broken even for the day, but I didn't know how many more such days my constitution could stand.

While Miami was offering me an abundance of action, Gulfstream was not yielding many high-quality bets, a problem which affected the Kid more than me. With a limited bankroll and no outside income, he could not afford to take excessive risks, and so he had adopted an approach to the game very much like Charlie's. For the Kid to make a serious bet, everything had to be right, especially the price. He did not want to take less than 3 to 1. Unfortunately, all the standouts at Gulfstream—like Cinteelo and White Rammer—had gone off at short prices. What should a handicapper do when he finds a horse who looks like a certain winner but whose odds are inadequate? What does he do with a horse like Stutsmanville in the fourth race on February 2?

4 GULFSTREAM 1 1-16 MILES GULFSTREAM Start Finish

1 1/16 MILES. (1.40⅕) MAIDEN CLAIMING. Purse $6,000. 3-year-olds. Weights 120 lbs. Claiming Price $30,000 if for $25,000 allowed 3 lbs. (Preference to horses which have not started for $15,000 or less.)

Bosoni
Own.—Chianelli A
Ch. g. 3, by High Tribute—Ship Romance, by Count of Honor
$25,000 Br.—Karutz W S & Milange Farm (Ky) Tr.—Mullin William
117
St. 1st 2nd 3rd Amt. 1977 1 M 0 0 $36 1976 0 M 0 0
21Jan77- 2GP fst 6f :23 :47⅘ 1:13⅘ Md 35000 10 12 129¾ 1213 1217 1223 Solomone M b 116 34.70 47-29 G's Brandy 1161 Bobs A Prince 116½ Li'l Indian 1205 Trailed 12
LATEST WORKOUTS Feb 1 GP 3f fst :37 b Jan 20 GP 3f fst :38⅖ b Jan 17 GP 4f sly :52 bg Jan 12 GP 5f fst 1:03 b

Never Guilty
Own.—Wilson M
Ch. c. 3, by No Robbery—Case Dismissed, by Traffic Judge
$25,000 Br.—Walden B P (Ky) Tr.—Merrill Frank H
117
St. 1st 2nd 3rd Amt. 1977 1 M 0 1 $540 1976 0 M 0 0
21Jan77- 4GP fst 6f :22 :46⅕ 1:11⅗ Md 35000 3 5 54 43½ 35½ 310 Gomez A 79 116 14.60 71-29 White Rammer 1201 Bio Grey 1169 Never Guilty 1163 No mishap 12
LATEST WORKOUTS Jan 28 GP 7f fst 1:28 hg Jan 11 GP 6f fst 1:16⅗ b Jan 5 GP 6f gd 1:18 bg Dec 28 GP 5f fst 1:05 b

Brach's Luv
Own.—Brach Helen
B. c. 3, by I'm For More—Trijugate, by Arrogate or Luminary II
$25,000 Br.—Durkin Mrs J T & O'Farrell Jr (Fla) Tr.—Divito Peter J
117
Turf Record St. 1st 2nd 3rd 2 0 0 0
St. 1st 2nd 3rd Amt. 1977 2 M 0 0 $101 1976 0 M 0 0
27Jan77- 3GP fm *1 1/16 Ⓣ 1:47⅖ Md Sp Wt 1 6 78 69½ 614 715 MacBeth D b 120 181.70 55-24 That's A Nice 1153½ SilverGreek 1201½ OvertheBridge 120no Outrun 10
10Jan77- 4Crc fm 1 1/16 Ⓣ:47⅘ 1:12⅖ 1:44⅘ Md Sp Wt 9 11 1119 1118 1020 927 MacBeth D b 120 52.90 57-18 Poor Man's Bluff 1203 Ramacette 120hd LiegeLord 1206 No factor 11
LATEST WORKOUTS Jan 25 GP 3f fst :37⅗ bg Jan 20 GP 4f fst :50⅖ b Jan 15 GP 3f fst :36⅗ b Jan 7 GP 4f fst :50 bg

***Arezzo**
Own.—Batthyany Countess Margit
Dk. b. or br. c. 3, by Frontal—Abricotine, by Janitor
$25,000 Br.—Leisten Mrs H (Ger) Tr.—Sarmiento Guillermo
117
St. 1st 2nd 3rd Amt. 1977 1 M 0 0 $36 1976 5 M 0 0 $805
26Jan77- 4GP fst 7f :22⅖ :45⅗ 1:23⅕ Md Sp Wt 9 10 1112 1116 1220 1223 Lopez R D 120 73.10 65-14 Baldski 1204 Dress Extra 1206 Capitanus 1205 Outrun 12
16Oct76- 3Crc fst 7f :23⅕ :46⅖ 1:26⅖ Md Sp Wt 8 2 89 813 89½ 56½ Lopez R D 118 19.20 77-15 Sonny Collins 1182 Mark Four 118hd Mini Styls 1184 No mishap 9
1Oct76- 3Crc sly 1 :48⅕ 1:15⅖ 1:42⅗ Md Sp Wt 9 9 914 710 77¾ 43 Lopez R D 118 78.20 73-18 Breton Sailor 118hd Mark Four 1181½ Here Here 1151½ Stride late 10
18Sep76- 3Crc fst 6f :23⅗ :47⅕ 1:13⅗ Md Sp Wt 11 2 83¼ 911 1114 1110 Baltazar C 118 34.10 75-13 FameInternational 1183 NativeVelvet 118no MiniStyls 118¾ No factor 11
1Sep76- 3Crc fst 6½f :24 :48 1:20 Md Sp Wt 7 6 41 52¼ 66½ 57¾ Lopez R D 118 16.10 83-15 Blazing Judge 118½ Poor Man's Bluff 1186 Mark Four 118½ Tired 8
25Aug76- 5Crc fst 7f :24⅖ :48⅖ 1:28 Md Sp Wt 3 4 2½ 1hd 42½ 46¼ Astorga C 118 35.50 70-17 Millwood Road 118¾ Shape Of Fame 1184 Sir Sir 1181½ Tired 7
LATEST WORKOUTS Jan 31 Crc 4f fst :49 b Jan 22 Crc 5f fst 1:02 b Jan 19 Crc 3f fst :39⅗ b Jan 14 Crc 3f fst :38 bg

Tieayellowribbon
Own.—Adams Andrew
Ch. c. 3, by Gallant Man—My Ideal, by My Babu
$25,000 Br.—Power Mr-Mrs A M (Ky) Tr.—Kassen David
117
St. 1st 2nd 3rd Amt. 1977 1 M 0 0 $240 1976 3 M 0 0
6Jan77- 5Crc fst 6f :23⅕ :46⅗ 1:12 Md Sp Wt 2 10 84¾ 66½ 48 412 Brumfield D 68 120 20.80 81-17 Gonzago 120½ That's A Nice 1157 Dress Extra 1204 No threat 12
28Nov76- 3CD fst 6f :22⅕ :46⅕ 1:12⅖ Md Sp Wt 2 7 46½ 56½ 512 612 Brumfield D 122 9.90 72-25 Maple Mousse 1222¼ Silk Heriz 1223¼ Chrisy Mac 1224 No factor 12
4Nov76- 5CD fst 6½f :22⅘ :46⅖ 1:19⅖ Md Sp Wt 12 8 813 69½ 66½ 88¼ Brumfield D 122 23.30 75-23 Kodiack 1222¾ Beau Dustin 1224½ Mister Wiggle 122nk No factor 12
29Jly76- 6Mth fst 5½f :22⅕ :45⅗ 1:05 Md Sp Wt 6 6 712 712 612 615 Brumfield D 118 13.60 77-16 Happy Fleet 1185 Prunum 113¾ Tuxson 1184½ No factor 7
LATEST WORKOUTS ●Feb 1 Hia 3f fst :36⅖ b Jan 26 Hia 5f fst 1:02 b Jan 20 Hia 5f fst 1:03 b Jan 15 Hia 4f fst :53 b

Marnesian's Sun
Own.—D'Allesandro A Jr
Dk. b. or br. c. 3, by Sun Cross—Marnesian, by Boldnesian
$30,000 Br.—DiLibero C (Ky) Tr.—Stuckey Alexander P
120
Turf Record St. 1st 2nd 3rd 1 0 0 0
St. 1st 2nd 3rd Amt. 1977 1 M 0 0 $36 1976 0 M 0 0
27Jan77- 3GP fm *1 1/16 Ⓣ 1:47⅖ Md Sp Wt 10 8 89½ 712 815 816 Crews W 120 95.00 54-24 That's A Nice 1153½ SilverGreek 1201½ OvertheBridge 120no Outrun 10
LATEST WORKOUTS Jan 22 Crc 5f fst 1:02⅖ bg Jan 13 Crc 5f fst 1:04 b Dec 20 Crc 4f fst :51⅕ bg Dec 15 Crc 5f fst 1:04⅖ bg

```
Frank's Catch                    Dk. b. or br. c. 3, by Pass Catcher—Candy Belle, by Beau Gar        Turf Record        St. 1st 2nd 3rd   Amt.
                                 $25,000  Br.—Rodgers W J Jr (Fla)                          117   St. 1st 2nd 3rd   1977  2  M  0  0     $125
   Own.—Hillier J F                       Tr.—Patterson Pat                                       1   0   0   0    1976  5  M  0  0     $106
10Jan77- 4Crc fm 1 1/16 (T):47⅖ 1:12⅖ 1:44⅖  Md Sp Wt   10 3 34 912 9181028 Thornburg B   b 120 159.90  56-18 Poor Man's Bluff 1203Ramacette120hdLiegeLord1206 Early speed 11
 6Jan77- 5Crc fst 6f   :23⅕  :46⅗ 1:12      Md Sp Wt    7 8 107 11141220 1225 Thornburg B    120  99.90  68-17 Gonzago 120½ That's A Nice 1157 Dress Extra 1204        Outrun 12
22Dec76- 4Crc fst 6f   :22⅖  :45⅘ 1:12⅖     Md Sp Wt    4 11 11101115 1223 1219 Thornburg B b 118  55.70  72-14 Julian 1185½ Gonzago 1182 Jungle Adam 118hd           No factor 12
10Dec76- 5Crc fst 6f   :23⅖  :47  1:13⅕     Md 18000    7 2 32½ 44½ 59½ 613 Thornburg B     b 118  56.90  74-14 T. V. Station 118nk Janco's Jim 1161½ On The Rib 1142     Tired 8
14Oct76- 6Mth fst 6f   :22⅖  :46  1:11⅖     Md Sp Wt    7 9 811 816 816 822 Gomez M A       b 118  75.80  61-23 Fed Funds 118½ Michael's Charge 1188 Dr. Kim 1181½   No factor 9
 4Oct76- 1Mth my  6f   :22⅗  :46⅕ 1:11⅗     Md Sp Wt    2 5 72¾ 815 925 930 Saumell L       b 118  47.50  52-24 Seranic 113¾ Fed Funds 1188 El Exigente 1182           Outrun 9
27Aug76- 9Mth fst 6f   :22⅕  :45⅖ 1:11⅖     Md Sp Wt    7 11 1121 1123 1127 1128 Lovato F     118  35.10  55-19 Polemicist 1185ProudCabildo1184LaughingHolme118nk No factor 11
  LATEST WORKOUTS   Jan 21 Hia  4f fst :49  b         Dec 18 Hia  4f fst :49⅕ h
L'Artiste                        Ch. g. 3, by Tobin Bronze—Belle Riviere, by Lebeau Prince            Turf Record        St. 1st 2nd 3rd   Amt.
                                 $30,000  Br.—Penbanx Jacqueline (Ky)                       120   St. 1st 2nd 3rd   1977  1  M  0  0     $325
   Own.—Anaka Mel                         Tr.—Plesa Edward Sr                                     1   0   0   0    1976  1  M  1  0     $792
10Jan77- 4Crc fm 1 1/16 (T):47⅖ 1:12⅖ 1:44⅖  Md Sp Wt    6 7 812 812 89¾ 49 Capodici J      120   8.30  75-18 Poor Man's Bluff 1203 Ramacette 120hdLiegeLord1206 No factor 11
31Dec76- 1Crc fst 6f   :23⅕  :47⅖ 1:14⅕     Md c-15000  6 12 107¾ 96½ 73¾ 21½ Cruguet J 64 118  7.60  80-22 Cool Coco 1141½ L'Artiste 118no Morlaine 118½       Wide, rallied 12
  LATEST WORKOUTS   Jan 17 Crc  5f fst 1:02⅘ bg     Jan 8 Crc (T) 4f fm :50  b     Dec 28 GP  5f fst 1:02  h     Dec 18 GP  7f fst 1:29  h
Stutsmanville                    B. g. 3, by Grand Central—Forelass, by Miss Guide                    Turf Record        St. 1st 2nd 3rd   Amt.
                                 $30,000  Br.—Polk A F (Ohio)                               120   St. 1st 2nd 3rd   1977  2  M  1  0   $1,116
   Own.—Polk A F                          Tr.—Gomez Frank                                         1   0   0   0    1976  0  M  0  0
27Jan77- 3GP  fm *1 1/16 (T)      1:47⅖     Md Sp Wt    6 4 45½ 43 55½ 57½ Brumfield D      120   3.60  62-24 That's A Nice 1153½ Silver Greek 1201½ OvertheBridge120no Tired 10
14Jan77- 3Crc fst 6½f  :23⅘  :47⅖ 1:19⅗     Md Sp Wt    1 10 95¾ 88¼ 53 21½ Brumfield D 89 120 *2.40e 91-13 Time Call 1201½ Stutsmanville 1203 Gun Blast 1202   Best others 10
  LATEST WORKOUTS   Jan 31 Crc  3f fst :39⅖ bg      Jan 20 Crc  4f fst :52  b      Jan 10 Crc  4f fst :50⅘ bg     Jan 4 Crc  5f fst 1:08  b
Idle Ruler                       Dk. b. or br. c. 3, by Fair Ruler—Pattie I Will, by I Will                               St. 1st 2nd 3rd   Amt.
                                 $25,000  Br.—Guttridge Mr-Mrs H B (Fla)                    117                      1977  1  M  0  0      $60
   Own.—Idle Hour Farm                    Tr.—Cantanese Joseph                                                     1976  3  M  0  0     $240
 6Jan77- 5Crc fst 6f   :23⅕  :46⅗ 1:12      Md Sp Wt   10 1 3nk 55½ 611 718 Suarez J H       120 108.10  75-17 Gonzago 120½ That's A Nice 1157 Dress Extra 1204         Tired 12
22Dec76- 4Crc fst 6f   :22⅖  :45⅘ 1:12⅖     Md Sp Wt    1 9 98 1014 1019 1015 Suarez J H    b 118  21.90  76-14 Julian 1185½ Gonzago 1182 Jungle Adam 118hd           No factor 12
19Jly76- 4Rkmfst 5f    :22⅘  :47⅕  :59⅘     Md Sp Wt    8 4 43½ 53½ 58½ 68¼ Suarez J H      b 118  10.20  77-16 New Cesere 118no Guess Again 115no Dollar Value 1181½      Tired 8
 6Jly76- 6Rkmfst 5f    :21⅘  :45⅖  :58⅕     Allowance   1 7 713 714 715 613 Riera R Jr      b 112  19.80  80-11 Mystery Power 1202 Super'sPet1127½VikingWeather107hd   Outrun 7
  LATEST WORKOUTS   Jan 29 Crc  5f sly 1:03  b      Jan 21 Crc  5f fst 1:04  b      Jan 12 Crc  4f fst :50⅗ b      Dec 31 Crc  4f fst :50⅗ b
My Trip                          B. c. 3, by Sunny Tim—Blazing Treasure, by Treasury Note                                 St. 1st 2nd 3rd   Amt.
                                 $30,000  Br.—Twin W W Stable (Ill)                         120                      1976  1  M  0  1     $924
   Own.—Von Sydow Walter                  Tr.—Namen Robert
      Entered 1Feb77- 6 GP
25Nov76- 3Spt fst 6f   :23⅖  :48⅗ 1:16⅖  [S]Md Sp Wt    6 8 65½ 47 45½ 31¼ Gallitano G     b 119  *2.20  68-30 Frosty Kilometer 116hd Mr. British 1191½ My Trip 119hd    Rallied 10
  LATEST WORKOUTS   Jan 24 Hia  3f fst :36  hg      Jan 19 Hia  6f fst 1:15  h      Jan 14 Hia  5f fst 1:02⅖ b     Jan 9 Hia  3f fst :37  b
```

Stutsmanville had made his racing debut at Calder on January 14 and had finished 1½ lengths behind Time Call, who subsequently ran a strong second in allowance company. A handicapper did not need speed figures to recognize that this was a good performance, but mine said that Stutsmanville had earned a rating of 89—an edge of ten points over his nearest rival, Never Guilty. In my system, this translates into a superiority of six lengths.

Two weeks later, Stutsmanville ran a mile and one-sixteenth on the grass and finished fifth. I do not make figures for turf races, but I knew the horses in that field were very promising three-year-olds. Now Stutsmanville was dropping into a $30,000 maiden claiming race where his opposition was dismal. Everything about him was perfect, except his price. He was the 6-to-5 favorite. I could reasonably make a moderate win bet on Stutsmanville, or pass the race entirely, but I thought that this was a case where the exacta opened the possibility for an aggressive, creative bet.

I narrowed the possible exacta combinations by summarily eliminating six horses who didn't have a chance: Bosoni, Brach's Luv, Marnesian's Sun, Frank's Catch, Idle Ruler, and My Trip. The first five had never been close. My Trip had lost the only start of his career by a length, but he had been running against abysmal Illinois-bred maidens. The time of the race was 1:16⅖ for six furlongs. Checking the result charts in a back issue of the *Racing Form*, I saw that a field of $2500 claiming horses had run the same distance on the same day in 1:14⅕. If My Trip was so much slower than $2500 animals, he had no business in a $30,000 race.

I was willing to proceed under the assumption that only four horses could run second to Stutsmanville. Never Guilty had the second-best speed figure in the field, but when he came onto the track for the post parade, he ran off with his jockey for a quarter of a mile. That is usually a negative omen.

Arezzo had shown some stretch-running ability in the fall, but had finished last in his only Gulfstream start, against superior horses on a speed-favoring track. Now he was dropping into a claiming race for the first time.

Tieayellowribbon had broken tenth and finished fourth in his only Florida race, earning a speed figure six points below that of Never Guilty. Now he was running a distance for the first time, and as a son of the long-winded Gallant Man, he figured to like it.

L'Artiste impressed me as a very marginal contender. He had finished second in the initial start of his career, but he had been running against weak $15,000 company and his speed figure was inferior.

Gulfstream's closed-circuit television monitors flash the probable payoffs for exacta combinations, and with five minutes to post time these were the prices for Stutsmanville and my four contenders:

Stutsmanville–Never Guilty	$16
Stutsmanville–Arezzo	$80
Stutsmanville–Tieayellowribbon	$41
Stutsmanville–L'Artiste	$18

I saw that I could make a substantial profit if either Arezzo or Tieayellowribbon ran second. And I could weight my bets to get a decent return with Never Guilty, even though the odds on that combination were puny. If L'Artiste finished second, I would settle for breaking even on the race. So I invested $450 in exactas in this fashion:

Second Horse	Probable Payoff	Bet	Possible Return
Never Guilty	$16	$150	$1200
Arezzo	80	100	4000
Tieayellowribbon	41	150	3075
L'Artiste	18	50	450

(*Note:* The return on a bet is, of course, calculated by multiplying the payoff by the size of the wager, and then dividing by 2. A $100 bet on an $80 exacta is actually fifty $2 tickets which return $80 each, for a total of $4000.)

FOURTH RACE

Gulfstream

FEBRUARY 2, 1977

1 $\frac{1}{16}$ MILES. (1.40½) MAIDEN CLAIMING. Purse $6,000. 3-year-olds. Weights 120 lbs. Claiming Price $30,000 if for $25,000 allowed 3 lbs. (Preference to horses which have not started for $15,000 or less.)

Value of race $6,000, value to winner $3,768, second $1,140, third $540, fourth $300, balance of starters $36 each. Mutuel pool $71,206. Perfecta Pool $97,241.

Last Raced	Horse	Eqt.	A.	Wt	PP	St	¼	½	¾	Str	Fin	Jockey	Cl'g Pr	Odds $1
27Jan77 3GP5	Stutsmanville	b	3	120	9	5	4hd	42	21	13	13½	Vasquez J	38000	1.30
6Jan77 5Crc4	Tieayellowribbon		3	117	5	7	63	5½	33	21½	22	Brumfield D	25000	8.50
21Jan77 4GP3	Never Guilty		3	117	2	2	11½	11½	11	36	36	Gomez A	25000	2.80
10Jan77 4Crc4	L'Artiste	b	3	120	8	9	103	11	7hd	43	42½	Capodici J	30000	4.50
26Jan77 4GP12	Arezzo		3	117	4	11	11	10hd	8hd	51½	53	St Leon G	25000	13.90
27Jan77 3GP7	Brach's Luv	b	3	117	3	3	8hd	7hd	51½	61	6¾	MacBeth D	25000	38.90
25Nov76 3Spt3	My Trip	b	3	120	11	8	91½	8½	61	71½	74	Gell V D	30000	8.30
10Jan77 4Crc10	Frank's Catch	b	3	117	7	4	52	61	9hd	83	81½	Thornburg B	25000	79.10
27Jan77 3GP8	Marnesian's Sun		3	120	6	10	7hd	93	10hd	91	9nk	Crews W	30000	98.40
6Jan77 5Crc7	Idle Ruler		3	117	10	6	3½	31½	11	102	108	Delguidice R Jr	25000	76.10
21Jan77 2GP12	Bosoni	b	3	117	1	1	2¹	2½	4hd	11	11	Perret C	25000	75.60

OFF AT 2:36 EST. Start good, Won ridden out. Time, :23⅗, :48⅕, 1:13⅗, 1:38⅖, 1:45⅕ Track fast.

$2 Mutuel Prices:

9-STUTSMANVILLE	4.60	3.00	2.40
5-TIEAYELLOWRIBBON		6.20	3.80
2-NEVER GUILTY			3.00

$2 PERFECTA 9-5 PAID $30.20.

B. g, by Grand Central—Foreless, by Miss Guide. Trainer Gomez Frank. Bred by Polk A F (Ohio).

STUTSMANVILLE, well placed and racing in hand early, moved to command at the head of stretch, drew clear and won with authority.TIEAYELLOWRIBBON raced forwardly, reached attending position in early stretch but could not gain on winner. NEVER GUILTY set the pace to head of the stretch then gave way to winner. L'ARTISTE outfinished the others. MY TRIP was outrun.

Owners— 1, Polk A F; 2, Adams Andrew; 3, Wilson M; 4, Anaka Mel; 5, Batthyany Countess Margit; 6, Brach Helen; 7, Von Sydow Walter; 8, Hillier J F; 9, D'Allesandro A Jr; 10, Idle Hour Farm; 11, Chianelli A.

Trainers— 1, Gomez Frank; 2, Kassen David; 3, Merrill Frank H; 4, Plesa Edward Sr; 5, Sarmiento Guillermo; 6, Divito Peter J; 7, Namen Robert; 8, Patterson Pat; 9, Stuckey Alexander P; 10, Cantanese Joseph; 11, Mullin William.

Scratched—Lugano (21Jan77 4GP11).

By the time the race was half over, I knew I could walk to the cashiers' windows. Stutsmanville was surging to the lead, and Tieayellowribbon was wearing down Never Guilty for second place. The exacta combination had been bet down in the last five minutes, but it still paid $30.20. I collected $2265, making an $1815 profit on a race which wouldn't have offered much money-making potential without the exacta.

Because an exacta bet like this does involve so many more pitfalls than a straight win wager, a conservative gambler who demands near-perfection could not make it. But the Kid recognized the virtues of Stutsmanville and wanted to give himself some inexpensive entertainment, and he announced to Charlie and me, "I'm going to bet a three-race parlay. I'm going to play three $10 exactas with Stutsmanville on top. I'm going to let all the winnings ride onto Gonzago in the fifth. Then I'm going to let everything ride onto a White Rammer—Be Gallant exacta in the seventh. And I'll be rich."

At the age of twenty-three, the Kid was too young and inexperienced to know that parlays occupy a special niche in the lore of the turf because they offer such tremendous potential for agony. The classic parlay story is the one about the horseplayer who bets $2 on the first race every day with the intention of letting his profits ride onto all the subsequent races. One day he picks the first eight winners, builds his stake up to $10,000, and bets it all on the favorite in the ninth race. He loses by a nose. The horseplayer goes home and his wife asks him, "How did it go today?"

"Same old story," he says. "I lost two bucks."

Implicit in this tale is the principle that a parlay is a commitment as well as a bet. A self-respecting horseplayer wouldn't have considered taking his $10,000 home after the eighth race. He had to stick to his plan and take the consequences philosophically. But the Kid hadn't considered all these ramifications when he decided he was going to bet a parlay.

When Stutsmanville and Tieayellowribbon ran one-two in the fourth race, the Kid collected $151 for his $10 ticket and bet it immediately on Gonzago, who had the top figure in the next event. Gonzago battled head-and-head through the stretch, won by a neck, and paid $8.80. The Kid collected $660, and it was only then that he realized what he had done. He was now supposed to make the biggest wager of his life, and although he liked his horses in the seventh race, they weren't worth a $660 investment. What should he do? He looked at his two gurus, Charlie and me.

Charlie eyed the Kid sternly. "If you back out of this," he said, "I'll lose all respect for you. One of the most important things about gambling is that the betting part of it has got to be automatic. You can't second-guess yourself. If you say you're going to bet a parlay, you bet a parlay."

"Hold it!" I interjected. "Kid, you got involved in this without thinking through the consequences. There's no point making a stupid bet just so you can be consistently stupid. This race doesn't justify this kind of money."

With contradictory advice swirling around him, the Kid sat brooding in silence, until ten minutes before the seventh race. His top choice, White Rammer, was the 6-to-5 favorite. His second horse, Be Gallant, was 7 to 2. The combination was logical, but no exacta is ever unbeatable. Slowly, the Kid got up from his seat and walked to the betting area. A minute before post time he came back. Charlie and I stared at him. "I didn't bet," the Kid announced.

A speedball named Golden Gossip busted out of the gate and opened a five-length lead but started weakening on the turn when White Rammer challenged him. The favorite surged to a commanding lead in midstretch, just as Be Gallant was rallying to finish second. The Kid didn't flinch when he saw the result. When the race was official and the exacta returned $14.60, I calculated that the Kid's parlay would have been worth $4818—the biggest score of his life. He shrugged. "I looked at those exacta prices and I decided that at the odds, this wasn't a good bet. I did the right thing."

I admired the Kid's attempt to maintain a stoical front in the face of such adversity, because I had been struggling to do the same. Even though I was winning at the meeting, I kept experiencing traumas that threatened to wreck my equilibrium.

The little men who rode my horses were often the cause of my woes. Most good jockeys were competing for the larger purses in New York and California, so Gulfstream had attracted such an untalented jockey colony that it was practically impossible to avoid betting bad riders. One day I wagered heavily on a horse named Royal Swirl because he had been ridden recently by Daniel Harbacek, whom I loathed, and now was getting the services of Jeffrey Fell, whom I merely disliked. I figured that the horse would get the early lead on the rail, where even Fell couldn't get him into trouble. But the jockey somehow managed to position himself next-to-last, five horses wide, by the time he hit the first turn. I cursed the heavens, and I cursed Jeffrey Fell.

On another day I made a last-minute decision to take a $10 flyer on a longshot, dashed to the betting area, and found myself in a slow-moving line of senior citizens. As I reached the window and opened my mouth to form the words "Number three . . ." the bell rang. Number three paid $167 to win. A few minutes later I bumped into an amiable press-box colleague who asked, cheerfully, "Did you have that big one?" I turned purple, crumpled my *Racing Form*, muttered a string of expletives, and stomped away from my bewildered friend.

Despite the frequency of these annoyances, I managed to shake off their effects quickly and regain my composure. I was maintaining a comfortable stride, betting rationally rather than emotionally, and keeping my profits around the $3000 level. I was doing so, at least, until February 7. A gaping, jagged hole in the wall of the Gulfstream press box still exists as a monument of sorts to the enormity of that day's events.

I had gone to the track with no particular interest in the eighth race. The event had two obvious, evenly matched contenders and no exacta wagering. It figured to be unbettable.

8 GULFSTREAM

6 FURLONGS GULFSTREAM (Start / Finish)

6 FURLONGS. (1.07⅘) CLAIMING. Purse $8,000. 4-year-olds and upward. Weight, 122 lbs. Non-winners of two races since December 20 allowed 2 lbs. Two races since November 5, 4 lbs. A race since January 15, 6 lbs. Claiming price $25,000; for each $2,500 to $20,000 allowed 2 lbs. (Races where entered for $18,000 or less not considered.)

Yon Dan

Ch. c. 4, by Fouquier—Chinese Chick, by Chinese Sun
$20,000 Br.—Irish Acres Farm Inc (Fla) Tr.—Blengs Vincent
Own.—Grimmo C F
112 Turf Record St. 1st 2nd 3rd: 1 0 0 0
St. 1st 2nd 3rd Amt.: 1977 1 0 0 0 $36; 1976 15 2 2 2 $14,595

19Jan77-10GP fm *1 1/16 Ⓣ 1:48⅗ Clm 25000 5 2 22 34½ 810 1012 Perret C 116 30.30 52-33 Waggish 116no Silverbatim 114no Black Crow 1164½ Tired 10
15Dec76- 8Crc fst 6f :22⅘ :45⅘ 1:11⅘ Allowance 5 2 55½ 814 812 912 Riera R Jr 119 48.00 82-15 Coverack 1163 Flashy Image 1161 Seraphic 113nk Tired 9
11Nov76- 8Suf fst 170 :46 1:11⅘ 1:43⅗ Vet. Day H 9 2 2hd 65 1120 1124 Cotrone F Jr 110 50.60 58-26 In a Trance 124½ Super Boy 113hd Lark's Tune 1154 Stopped 11
30Oct76- 8Suf fst 6f :22⅖ :45⅗ 1:11 3↑Allowance 3 1 1hd 2hd 1½ 31¾ Casey R 114 2.30 84-17 Royal Reality 1191½CallThePlumber116nkYonDan1141½ Weakened 8
11Oct76- 9Suf fst 1 :46⅖ 1:10⅗ 1:37⅕ 3↑Allowance 3 1 11 2hd 21 34 Casey R 114 4.80 87-20 Lil's Luck 117½ Little Watermellon 1193½ Yon Dan114½ Weakened 9
25Sep76- 9Suf fst 6f :22⅖ :45⅘ 1:12 Handicap 2 3 31 41¼ 3½ 1¾ Casey R 112 4.80 81-22 Yon Dan 112¾ Can Slam 1111 Kick 'n Run 114¾ Driving 8
17Sep76- 7Rkmfst 6f :22 :45⅖ 1:11 3↑Allowance 1 4 34 21 21 2nk Casey R 112 5.90 89-20 Cheryl Lisa 112nk Yon Dan 1122¼ Prince Alto 1141 Just missed 8
13Aug76- 8Rkmfst 6f :22 :45 1:11⅕ 3↑Allowance 1 4 43½ 45 43½ 43½ Casey R 113 2.70 84-20 Caribbean Heart 1121¼ Keep The Oath 1141 Ricer 1141¼ Evenly 7
1Aug76- 9Rkmmy 6f :22⅖ :46⅘ 1:13⅕ 3↑Allowance 4 8 712 712 79½ 714 Casey R 112 *2.30 64-30 Tom Who 1143 Spanish Bag 1171½ Ribot's Drink 1222¼ No factor 9
23Jly76- 8Rkmfst 6f :22⅗ :46 1:11⅕ 3↑Allowance 4 2 31½ 1hd 1hd 21¼ Casey R 111 *1.70 87-18 Call The Plumber 1161¼ Yon Dan 1111½ Durbin 1091 Gamely 7
LATEST WORKOUTS Jan 29 Hia 3f fst :36 b Jan 13 Hia 5f fst :59 h Dec 27 Hia 4f fst :48⅗ h Dec 14 Hia 3f fst :36 h

Judge's Fee

Dk. b. or br. g. 5, by Barbizon—Sandy Lora, by One Sub
$22,500 Br.—Brothers Thomas (Ky) Tr.—Winick Neal J
Own.—Schoninger B
114 St. 1st 2nd 3rd Amt.: 1976 18 4 5 2 $30,950; 1975 10 1 2 0 $4,842

24Dec76- 9Crc sly 7f :23⅗ :46⅘ 1:25⅖ 3↑Allowance 2 4 31 22 11 12 Bailey J D 116 *1.20 89-21 Judge's Fee 1162 Lumpose 106nk Royal Knave 1132 Driving 7
14Dec76- 8Crc sly 6f :22⅘ :45⅗ 1:11⅘ 3↑Clm 22000 6 9 86¼ 911 96½ 64¾ Bailey J D 116 *1.10 89-17 PrinceRoMr1111BrillintBehvior110nkKnowItAllJms1171½ Blocked 12
17Nov76- 6Crc fst 6f :23⅖ :47 1:12⅖ 3↑Allowance 4 4 4¾ 45½ 42¼ 31 Bailey J D b 119 2.60 90-17 Lightning Bob 119½ Mr. Aviator 114½ Judge's Fee 119no Rallied 6
18Sep76- 4AP fst 7f :22 :44⅘ 1:22⅕ 3↑Clm 30000 6 6 66 54½ 67¾ 817 Bailey J D b 122 5.00 74-08 Royal Legacy 1162 Money Flow 1162½ Ky. Cad 1171½ Tired 8
4Sep76- 6AP fst 6f :22⅕ :45⅕ 1:09⅘ 3↑Clm 30000 8 7 42 1hd 1hd 23½ Bailey J D b 119 *1.90 90-11 Right Key 1223½ Judge's Fee 119¾ Ky. Cad 119¾ Sharp 9
25Aug76- 7AP fst 6f :22⅕ :45⅗ 1:09⅘ 3↑Clm 30000 3 8 87¼ 62¾ 2½ 14 Bailey J D b 114 4.00 94-13 Judge's Fee 1144 EasterIsland119hdStoneCoolFox1201 Drew clear 8
14Aug76- 6AP sly 6f :22⅘ :46 1:10⅗ 3↑Clm 25000 9 3 44½ 22 1hd 22 Bailey J D b 116 *2.20 88-20 Ky. Cad 1162 Judge's Fee 1162 DH Gay Romeo 116 Gamely 9
23Jly76- 6AP fst 6f :21⅘ :44⅘ 1:09⅕ Clm 25000 8 6 86¾ 55 32 21 Bailey J D b 114 7.00 96-11 Right Key 1191 Judge's Fee 114nk Greencash 1144 Closed well 9
3Jly76- 9AP fst 6f :22⅘ :46⅗ 1:11⅗ Clm 18500 1 8 31 3nk 12 12 Bailey J D b 114 11.10 85-16 Judge's Fee 1142 Untangle 1191½ Moon Orbitor 1141½ Driving 11
23Jun76- 6AP sly 6f :22⅗ :46⅕ 1:11⅕ Clm 14500 10 4 3nk 3nk 1hd 2hd Espinoza J C b 114 4.40 87-18 Milldale 114hd Judge's Fee 1142 Semi Royal 1141¾ Gamely 11
LATEST WORKOUTS Jan 31 Crc 4f fst :49 b Jan 24 Crc 4f fst :50 b Jan 3 Crc 4f fst :50 b Dec 22 Crc 3f fst :36⅕ h

Captain Mitch

B. g. 4, by Captain Nash—Sunny David, by Sun David
$25,000 Br.—Royal Way Farm (Fla) Tr.—Mullin William
Own.—Flying W Stable
116 Turf Record St. 1st 2nd 3rd: 2 0 0 0
St. 1st 2nd 3rd Amt.: 1977 2 0 0 1 $1,141; 1976 22 6 2 3 $29,168

15Jan77- 5GP sly 6f :22⅕ :45⅕ 1:10⅗ Clm 32500 5 5 98 910 711 53¾ Solomone M 114 4.70 82-12 Cissie's Song 1181¾ Full Catch1131StarkRibot116no Finished well 9
7Jan77- 9Crc fst 6f :23 :46⅗ 1:11⅘ Clm 35000 7 1 32 21½ 21½ 34 Bohenko P 112 6.00 90-15 Cissie'sSong1133½StickySituation116½CaptinMitch112½ Weakened 7
4Dec76- 6Crc fst 6f :22⅗ :45⅘ 1:10⅘ 3↑Allowance 4 6 67 711 79¼ 49 Solomone M 119 10.70 90-12 Buena Shore 1193 Tumble Gar 1164 CanYouBeatThat1222 Rallied 7
27Oct76- 8Mth gd 6f :22⅖ :46⅕ 1:11⅗ 3↑Clm 27500 2 7 64½ 65¼ 32 11 Solomone M b 118 6.40 82-26 Captain Mitch 1181 Cissie's Song 117no Colored T.V.1152 Driving 8
18Oct76- 8Mth fst 6f :22⅕ :45⅖ 1:10⅘ 3↑Clm 27500 8 9 96¾ 58 57 66¼ McCauley W H b 118 7.60 80-22 BrntwoodPrnc120hdClrdT.V.1151Css'sSng1174 Crowded, stumbled 10
29Sep76- 6Mth fst 6f :21⅗ :44⅗ 1:10⅕ Clm 25000 2 5 54½ 57 43 1nk Solomone M b 119 7.40 89-17 Captain Mitch 119nk Party King117¾EveningAssault1171½ Just up 9
9Sep76- 8Rkmfst 6f :22⅕ :45⅖ 1:10⅗ 3↑Allowance 7 1 34 33½ 33½ 25½ Mercier N b 114 14.60 85-22 I Think No Evil 1175½ Captain Mitch114¾BeKnighted114½ Gamely 7
21Aug76- 9Rkmfst 6f :21⅘ :45⅖ 1:11⅗ 3↑Allowance 3 6 52¾ 31½ 2hd 1nk Mercier N b 114 2.60 86-16 Captain Mitch 114nk He Man Jr. 112no Bevron 1092 Driving 9
14Aug76- 9Rkmsly 6f :22⅕ :46 1:12⅖ 3↑Allowance 5 6 67¼ 69½ 714 711 Mercier N b 114 8.70 71-24 Lil's Luck 117hd Bevron 109no Scottie's Babe 1144½ No threat 8
24Jly76- 7Rkmgd 6f :22⅕ :45⅖ 1:11⅕ 3↑Allowance 8 3 64¼ 74¾ 76 811 Mercier N b 116 5.70 77-16 Rebelling 1131 Can Slam 114½ Bridget O. 1121¼ Outrun 8
LATEST WORKOUTS Feb 1 GP 4f fst :51⅖ b Dec 30 GP 4f fst :50 b

Full Catch

Dk. b. or br. c. 4, by Forward Pass—Fish Net, by Dotted Swiss
$25,000 Br.—Whitney C V (Ky) Tr.—Kelley Walter A
Own.—Kelley Mrs W A
116 Turf Record St. 1st 2nd 3rd: 2 0 0 0
St. 1st 2nd 3rd Amt.: 1977 2 0 1 0 $1,736; 1976 15 2 1 2 $19,160

29Jan77- 6GP gd 7f :22⅗ :45⅗ 1:23⅕ Clm 27500 4 8 75 75½ 76½ 89½ Hernandez R 114 *1.80 78-11 Prince Ro Mar 1144 Jet Jumper 1161 Black Balled 1162 Bumped 10
15Jan77- 5GP sly 6f :22⅕ :45⅕ 1:10⅗ Clm 30000 9 6 53½ 24 33½ 21¾ Hernandez R 113 11.70 84-12 Cissie's Song 1181¾ Full Catch 1131 Stark Ribot 116no Wide 9
15Dec76- 3Aqu fst 6f ⊡:22⅗ :46 1:11⅖ Clm 30000 7 5 73 85½ 99¾ 98½ Vasquez J b 117 9.40 — — Kaiser Fluff 112¾ Itsagoodlife 115hd Amber Spy 1101¼ No factor 10
6Dec76- 5Aqu fst 6f :22⅖ :45⅗ 1:10⅗ Clm 35000 1 8 73¼ 63¼ 52 61½ Hernandez R b 117 15.30 88-21 Tex's Chaps 114nk Bonge 119hd Itsagoodlife 115nk No mishap 9
12Nov76- 4Aqu fst 7f :23⅗ :47 1:24⅕ Clm 40000 2 8 73¾ 74 77 78½ Vasquez J b 118 5.30 71-24 Bonge 117½ Salim Alicum 1152½ Itsagoodlife 113nk Outrun 8
28Oct76- 5Aqu fst 7f :23⅕ :46⅕ 1:23⅗ Clm 37500 4 7 53 52 21½ 1hd Vasquez J b 115 4.90 82-21 Full Catch 115hd Gaitor Ratten 1123½ Salim Alicum 1221 Driving 9
16Oct76- 2Bel fst 6½f :23 :46⅖ 1:17⅖ Clm 35000 6 5 54¾ 54¾ 44 23¾ Vasquez J b 117 3.70 85-13 SalimAlicum1173¾FullCtch1173PeerlessMcGrth117nk Second best 7
6Oct76- 7Bel fst 1 1/16 :45⅖ 1:09⅘ 1:42 3↑Allowance 7 5 53¾ 33 22 41¼ Vasquez J b 114 7.70 91-08 Equation 117nk Expletive Deleted 109nk Bakor 114¾ Weakened 8
18Sep76- 6Bel fst 7f :22⅖ :44⅘ 1:22⅕ 3↑Allowance 8 4 45½ 49½ 59½ 612 Montoya D b 115 9.70 79-10 Little Riva 113nk Private Thoughts 1133¾ Finger Paints1133 Tired 8
14Aug76- 5Sar fst 6f :22 :45 1:10⅕ 3↑Allowance 3 9 97¼ 96½ 911 912 Turcotte R b 117 9.00 77-11 Big Z. 1171 Magnetizer 1141 Introienne 1143 No factor 9
LATEST WORKOUTS Jan 24 Hia 4f fst :50⅖ b Jan 12 Hia 3f fst :36 h Jan 7 Hia 4f fst :50 b Jan 2 Hia 3f fst :36⅖ b

Custom

Dk. b. or br. h. 5, by Info—My Mistletoe, by Day Court
$25,000 Br.—Brisbine Elizabeth (Ky) Tr.—Bollero Joseph M
Own.—Brisbine Mrs E J
116 Turf Record St. 1st 2nd 3rd: 3 0 1 0
St. 1st 2nd 3rd Amt.: 1977 1 0 0 0 $36; 1976 19 2 6 3 $18,204

18Jan77- 9GP fst 6f :22⅘ :46 1:11 Allowance 3 4 63½ 65¼ 76 68¾ Fires E b 112 5.70e 75-22 Swinging Hal 112¾ Fiacun 112½ Justa Bad Boy 1152 No factor 8
11Dec76- 6Crc fst 6½f :23 :46 1:18⅕ 3↑Allowance 6 4 53½ 99 97¾ 99¾ Fires E b 119 22.10 90-11 Beau Claire 1192½ Peaceful Hour 1131½ Helixiv 116nk Tired 10
28Oct76- 6Kee fst 6½f :23 :45⅘ 1:17⅖ 3↑Allowance 1 / 45½ 56 52½ 32¾ Gavidia W b 114 2.20 87-21 Brave Scout 1172 Second Term 114¾ Custom 1141¼ Rallied 7
19Oct76- 5Kee fst 6f :21⅘ :44⅘ 1:09⅘ 3↑Allowance 4 4 59 57 34½ 21½ Gavidia W b 118 13.20 91-14 Sir Bell 1151½ Custom 118hd Windy Thistle 113nk Gamely 8
2Oct76- 5AP fm 1 1/16 Ⓣ:48⅗ 1:13 1:44⅖ 3↑Allowance 7 4 43 45 78¾ 715 Fires E b 116 5.80 72-15 Native Praise 1131 Duke Ricer 1121¼ Noble Lark 1191½ Tired 7
7Sep76- 8AP fst 6f :22⅗ :45⅖ 1:10⅕ 3↑Allowance 2 6 33 35 34½ 33¾ Fires E b 119 5.40 88-15 Khyber King 1111¼ Ruling Eagle 1142½ Custom 1191 No mishap 7
28Aug76- 9AP gd 1 1/16 Ⓣ:49⅘ 1:14⅗ 1:47 3↑Allowance 3 3 31 41½ 42 54½ Gavidia W b 119 6.50 69-25 Fair Evar Bart 116½ Silent Dictator 1131¼ Henry Clay 1131 Tired 8
17Aug76- 8AP fst 6½f :23⅖ :46⅕ 1:16⅗ 3↑Allowance 6 3 42½ 55½ 67¾ 612 Fires E b 122 5.80 80-19 Flying Kansu 110¾ Whirlawhile 1103 Henry Clay 1164½ Tired 9
4Aug76- 5AP fst 7f :22⅗ :45⅖ 1:23 3↑Allowance 1 7 62¾ 52¼ 1hd 11¾ Fires E b 116 4.50 87-15 Custom 1161¾ Our Doctor 1165 Golden Era 1101¼ Driving 9
27Jly76- 8AP fm 1 1/16 Ⓣ:50⅖ 1:14⅘ 1:46⅕ 3↑Allowance 5 3 2½ 2½ 3nk 21½ Fires E b 117 9.30 76-22 Noble Lark 1171½ Custom 1171 Doric Type 117hd Gamely 10
LATEST WORKOUTS Feb 3 GP 5f fst 1:02⅖ b Jan 29 GP 4f sly :53 b Jan 24 GP 5f fst 1:03⅗ b Jan 17 GP 3f sly :37⅖ b

Ardent Student

B. g. 4, by Francis S—Peg The Cat, by Iron Peg
$20,000 Br.—Harbor View Farm (Ky) Tr.—Jennings Lawrence W
Own.—Heather R M
112 Turf Record St. 1st 2nd 3rd: 1 0 0 0
St. 1st 2nd 3rd Amt.: 1976 23 3 5 1 $23,540; 1975 0 M 0 0

9Nov76- 7Mth fst 6f :21⅘ :44⅖ 1:10⅕ 3↑Clm c-20000 3 1 1½ 22½ 43 66¾ Drury M A b 119 13.40 82-20 Dugkworth Dilema 1152 Tudor Spook 120¾ SlowJoe1154 Bore out 8
3Nov76- 7Key fst 6f :22⅕ :45⅖ 1:10⅖ 3↑Allowance 5 2 31½ 31 34 44½ Kimball R b 115 12.00 85-22 Ace's Harlequin1081SharpKid1172¼GentlemanJ.G.1191¼ Weakened 6
5Oct76- 7Key fst 6f :23⅕ :46⅕ 1:12 Clm 19000 4 2 12 13 12 11 Black A S b 116 6.40 82-25 Ardent Student 1161 Lucky Fling 112no Soulange 112hd Driving 6
30Sep76- 8Key sly 6f :22⅗ :45⅘ 1:11⅘ 3↑Allowance 7 3 2½ 32 46 57 Drury M A b 115 5.00 76-27 Noyoudaunt 110hd Something Gold1126Nige'sNail112½ Weakened 9
19Sep76- 6Pen fst 6f :22⅕ :45⅗ 1:11⅖ 3↑Clm 22500 7 2 2hd 3½ 85 89¼ Drury M A b 112 *1.20 80-18 Sid Said 110½ Regimentation 1151 Green Beret 119½ Tired 8
7Sep76- 7Atl fst 6f :22⅕ :45⅖ 1:10⅕ 3↑Allowance 8 1 12 14 14 15 Drury M A b 113 2.70 91-17 Ardent Student 1135 Amatwin 1131½ Day OfPleasure1121 Handily 8
2Sep76- 9Mth fst 6f :22 :45⅖ 1:10⅖ 3↑Allowance 7 2 1½ 1½ 1½ 2¾ Drury M A b 117 12.50 87-19 Ocalahand 117¾ Ardent Student 1171½ Larry's Lark 1172 Gamely 10
25Aug76- 9Mth fst 6f :22 :44⅖ 1:09⅕ 3↑Allowance 7 1 2½ 36 36 48 Drury M A b 117 8.90 86-13 Taylor's Falls 1172 Donald Young 1144 Larry's Lark 1172 Tired 9
9Aug76- 6Mth sly 6f :22⅕ :45⅗ 1:12 3↑Allowance 6 1 1hd 1hd 1hd 2no Drury M A b 117 9.50 80-24 Rebel Roche 120no ArdentStudent1171¼PatronFair1152½ Bore out 7
4Aug76- 5Mth fst 6f :21⅘ :44⅗ 1:10 Clm 20000 8 1 1½ 1hd 2½ 510 LeBlanc K b 116 7.00 80-14 Around Dark 1165 Princely Glow 118¾ Makoo Tan 1163 Tired 8
LATEST WORKOUTS Feb 5 GP 3f fst :37⅖ b Jan 31 GP 6f fst 1:13⅖ h Jan 19 GP 5f fst 1:03 b Jan 12 GP 4f fst :48⅗ h

Larry's Lark

Ch. c. 4, by Bold Lark—Anxious Ema, by Phalanx
$25,000 Br.—Young Tollie (Ky) Tr.—Jennings Lawrence W
Own.—Jennings L W
116

	St.	1st	2nd	3rd	Amt.
1977	2	0	0	0	$461
1976	18	2	2	4	$17,394

22Jan77- 4GP	fst	6f	:22⅘ :46⅘ 1:12	Clm 35000	1 12 77 1010 1111 1111	Brumfield D	114	7.00	68-23	Frohlich 1143 Lightning Bob1201RoyalLegacy1201½	Showed little	12
15Jan77- 5GP	sly	6f	:22⅕ :45⅕ 1:10⅘	Clm 35000	4 8 74½ 56½ 45 42¾	Brumfield D	116	10.10	83-12	Cissie's Song 1181¾ Full Catch 1131 Stark Ribot 116no	Rallied	9
12Oct76- 8Mth	fst	6f	:22 :45⅗ 1:10⅗	3↑Allowance	6 3 35 22 32 37	Nemeti W	116	4.40	80-22	PoliticalCoverup1203CaptivePrince1164Larry'sLrk1164	Weakened	6
25Sep76- 6Mth	fst	6f	:22⅖ :45 1:09⅕	3↑Allowance	7 4 41½ 75¾ 75½ 610	Nemeti W	115	4.90	84-15	In Good Tune 1153 Astaire 1182 Donald Young 1151½	Wide	7
10Sep76- 7Mth	fst	6f	:22⅖ :46 1:10⅗	3↑Allowance	3 3 33 3½ 1hd 11½	Nemeti W	116	8.00	87-18	Larry's Lark 1161½ Hard Sell 1163 Donald Young 1142	Driving	7
2Sep76- 9Mth	fst	6f	:22 :45⅗ 1:10⅖	3↑Allowance	6 9 86¾ 56 45 32¼	Nemeti W	117	5.00	86-19	Ocalahand 117¾ Ardent Student 1171½ Larry's Lark 1172	Rallied	10
25Aug76- 9Mth	fst	6f	:22 :44⅖ 1:09⅕	3↑Allowance	5 6 65 59 58½ 36	Nemeti W	117	15.30	88-13	Taylor's Falls 1172 Donald Young 1144 Larry's Lark 1172	Rallied	9
9Aug76- 6Mth	sly	6f	:22⅕ :45⅗ 1:12	3↑Allowance	7 6 68 711 79 66¼	Wilson R	117	4.10	74-24	Rebel Roche 120no Ardent Student 1171½ PatronFair1152½	Outrun	7
31Jly76- 9Mth	fst	6f	:21⅘ :44⅗ 1:09⅗	3↑Allowance	3 9 76½ 710 57½ 511	Wilson R	115	10.20	81-17	Chief Tamanaco 11510 Tom Mann113nkMightyMoon115hd	Outrun	9
16Jly76- 7Mth	fst	6f	:21⅗ :44⅘ 1:10⅖	3↑Allowance	1 7 52½ 44½ 34½ 47	Saumell L	115	7.10	81-15	StickySituation1131½TomMann1145½PleasureisWest115nk	No rally	9

LATEST WORKOUTS Feb 2 GP 4f fst :48 b Jan 13 GP 3f fst :36 hg Jan 8 GP 6f fst 1:16⅗ b Jan 2 GP 5f fst 1:02 b

Henry Edward

B. g. 6, by Bold Sultan—Flying Start, by Whirlaway
$22,500 Br.—Curry & Wilson (Ky) Tr.—Green Newcomb
Own.—Green R I
120

Turf Record: St. 4, 1st 0, 2nd 0, 3rd 0

	St.	1st	2nd	3rd	Amt.
1977	3	1	0	1	$4,980
1976	23	6	4	5	$39,075

22Jan77- 5GP	fst	7f	:23 :46⅘ 1:25⅕	Allowance	6 1 2hd 1hd 3½ 37½	Lopez R D	b 114	3.10	70-23	OneMoreJump1145½PeacefulHour1142HenryEdwrd114no	Faltered	9
13Jan77- 8Crc	fst	6½f	:23⅕ :45⅘ 1:18⅖	Clm 25000	5 6 61¾ 42½ 64½ 82¼	Lopez R D	b 119	3.70	97-17	Last Flute 114no Black Balled 116noMangoright112¾	No response	10
5Jan77- 8Crc	fst	1	:48⅕ 1:13⅖ 1:40⅗	Allowance	8 1 12 13 15 11½	Lopez R D	b 116	2.10	86-14	Henry Edward 1161½ Fighting Time119½Pidge'sBoys116hd	Driving	8
25Dec76- 8Crc	fst	7f	:23⅖ :46⅖ 1:25⅕	3↑Clm 19000	6 1 1hd 11½ 14 13	Lopez R D	b 113	5.70	90-16	Henry Edward1133KnowItAllJames1191NativeCousin1061	Driving	9
18Dec76- 5Crc	fst	6f	:22⅘ :46 1:12	3↑Clm 20000	2 2 33 43 34½ 31½	Lopez R D	b 112	5.00	91-14	Mangoright 116no Native Cousin 1041½ Henry Edward1121	Evenly	10
6Dec76- 6Crc	fst	7f	:23⅖ :46⅘ 1:25⅘	3↑Clm c-15000	9 1 41 2hd 13 14	Lopez R D	b 122	*1.50	87-16	Henry Edward 1224 Solid Performer117½AtractivoII1161½	Handily	10
27Nov76- 7Crc	fst	6f	:23⅕ :46⅗ 1:12⅖	3↑Clm 15000	7 6 72 52¾ 3nk 11½	Lopez R D	b 119	3.10	91-15	HenryEdwrd1191½SwingLbrSwing116¾[DH]BrillintBhvior116	Driving	10
16Nov76-10Crc	fst	6f	:23⅕ :47 1:12⅗	3↑Clm 15000	4 5 51½ 31½ 31 3¾	Lopez R D	b 119	7.80	89-16	Cudco 114¾ Wayme 112no Henry Edward 119nk	Held well	8
23Sep76- 7AP	fst	6f	:22⅗ :45⅗ 1:10⅖	3↑Clm 18500	6 4 62½ 76 53 34½	Arroyo H	b 122	5.60	86-15	Lucky Meeting 1162 Classic Donut1162½HenryEdward122½	Rallied	8
2Sep76- 6AP	fst	7f	:22⅘ :45⅘ 1:23⅕	3↑Clm 16500	4 1 42½ 41½ 21 11½	Viera H	b 114	8.20	86-16	HenryEdward1141½YoungNoblemn116¾TheAstonisher116½	Driving	9

LATEST WORKOUTS ●Feb 2 Crc 5f fst 1:00⅖ h ●Jan 3 Crc 4f fst :48⅖ h Dec 15 Crc 4f fst :49 b

Mr. Door

Ch. g. 6, by Lurullah—Girl Next Door, by Windy City II
$22,500 Br.—Partee W C (Ky) Tr.—Kelley Thomas W
Own.—Bromagen Glen
114

Turf Record: St. 4, 1st 1, 2nd 0, 3rd 2

	St.	1st	2nd	3rd	Amt.
1976	5	0	0	0	
1975	17	2	3	3	$68,460

28Aug76- 5AP	fst	6f	:22 :44⅘ 1:09⅗	3↑Allowance	4 8 810 811 815 816	Sibille R	113	28.80	79-15	WhisperKing122nkHndsomeProfit1193½BoldDun-Cee1192¼	Trailed	8
12Aug76- 8AP	fst	6f	:22 :44⅘ 1:09⅖	3↑Allowance	4 6 67½ 69½ 613 617	Sibille R	113	8.90	79-14	Bold Dun-Cee 1133½ Dashboard 1194 Easabaya 119nk	Trailed	6
30Jly76- 9AP	fst	1	:44⅘ 1:09⅖ 1:35⅕	3↑Allowance	2 5 53½ 914 921 923	Breen R	b 113	5.10	62-14	Sr. Diplomat 113hd Rocket Force 115nk Money Flow 1192½	Tired	9
13May76- 8CD	fst	6f	:22 :45⅕ 1:11	Allowance	6 6 44½ 54½ 55½ 55½	Patterson G	119	2.60	85-15	Fun To Dance 1171 Mr. Ralph 119¾ Just a Wonder 119¾		6
1May76- 9CD	fst	6f	:22⅕ :45 1:10⅖	Allowance	4 8 814 913 89¾ 712	Valdizan F	119	3.50e	82-11	Jazziness 1151½ Fashion Sale 1191½ Mr. Barb 1223¼	No factor	9
29Nov75- 8CD	my	1⅛	:48⅗ 1:14 1:54⅖	3↑Clark H.	2 2 22½ 32½ 54½ 78¼	Gavidia W	115	2.60	62-27	Warbucks 124¾ Silver Badge 1181 Shoo Dear 111½	Bid, tired	7
15Nov75- 8Haw	fst	1¼	:48⅕ 1:11⅘ 2:02⅕	3↑Haw Gold Cup	5 1 1hd 44½ 510 513	Gavidia W	113	6.80	70-09	Royal Glint 1243½ Buffalo Lark 1233 Group Plan 126½	Stopped	5
5Nov75- 8Haw	fst	1⅛	:46⅗ 1:11 1:48⅗	3↑Chas Bidwill	9 1 11 11 14 13	Gavidia W	113	*2.60	90-17	Mr. Door 1133 Super Sail 1153 Boonesborough 1151½	Ridden out	10
27Oct75- 8CD	fst	1 1/16	:48⅖ 1:13⅖ 1:46⅕	3↑Allowance	7 4 31½ 5¾ 22½ 43¼	Gavidia W	119	2.90	74-25	Warbucks 117nk Super Sail 112hd Silver Badge 1193		8
11Oct75- 7Kee	fst	1 1/16	:47⅕ 1:11⅗ 1:44⅖	3↑Fayette	8 4 35 44 43 32	Delahoussaye E	114	9.00	82-27	Warbucks 120no Hasty Flyer 1192 Mr. Door 114hd	Rallied	11

LATEST WORKOUTS Feb 4 GP 5f fst 1:00⅗ hg Jan 31 GP 4f fst :49⅘ b Jan 29 GP 4f sly :48⅖ b ●Jan 25 GP 3f fst :35 h

Big Star

B. c. 4, by Decathlon—Tusis, by Tournoi
$25,000 Br.—Wallace Farm (Fla) Tr.—Mayberry Brian A
Own.—Nordham Elizabeth
116

Turf Record: St. 2, 1st 0, 2nd 0, 3rd 0

	St.	1st	2nd	3rd	Amt.
1977	2	2	0	0	$7,500
1976	15	3	2	1	$16,012

25Jan77- 6GP	fst	6f	:22⅕ :45⅗ 1:09⅗	Clm 17000	12 6 56 2½ 13 16	Bailey J D	116	*1.70	91-19	Big Star 1166 Che Che's Pride 1163 Tailor's Tack 112½	Easily	12
15Jan77- 1GP	fst	7f	:22⅖ :44⅘ 1:22⅗	Clm c-13000	10 1 1hd 13 12 13½	MacBeth D	116	3.20	91-15	Big Star 1163½ Salvamento 1144½ Midnite Romeo1161	Ridden out	11
11Dec76- 2Crc	fm	*1 1/16 ⓣ	1:46⅕	3↑Clm 16000	7 1 1½ 33 45 76	MacBeth D	b 112	11.60	78-13	ForemostPlesure1141BeuBronze111hdRoylSwirl105nk	Speed; tired	10
25Nov76- 6Crc	fst	6f	:23 :46⅕ 1:11⅗	3↑Clm 19000	4 7 31½ 31 44½ 68¼	MacBeth D	b 112	4.40	87-13	PatrickO'Hara1161½YoungNobleman1163½NtiveCousin1092½	Tired	7
6Nov76- 7Crc	fst	7f	:23⅗ :47⅕ 1:25⅖	3↑Clm 20000	2 10 104 95¼ 89½ 66¼	Brocklebank J	b 113	41.00	83-18	Rule Out 1121 Patrick O'Hara 116½ Six Foot Power 1161½	Outrun	10
27Oct76- 6Crc	fst	6f	:23 :46⅖ 1:11⅗	Clm 22000	5 7 54½ 55 68½ 510	Marquez C	b 116	4.30	85-15	Lightning Bob 1171 Governor's Lad 1162½ Dr. J.V.1162½	No factor	7
7Oct76- 6Mth	gd	6f	:22⅕ :45⅘ 1:11⅗	Clm 22000	6 2 42¾ 67 64¾ 56¼	Brocklebank J	b 115	8.10	75-23	BrentwoodPrinc1171½Wingwy115¾AroundDrk1173½	Disliked going	8
24Sep76- 8Atl	fst	6f	:22 :45 1:10	Clm 25000	4 7 711 713 715 711	Barrow T	b 116	4.00e	81-15	Princely Glow 113no Revson 109¾ Super Starter 1204½	Trailed	7
7May76- 8GP	fst	6f	:21⅘ :44⅘ 1:10⅖	3↑Allowance	2 4 33½ 21½ 2hd 1hd	Barrow T	b 114	2.40	87-22	Big Star 114hd Daylight Prince 1111 Cowichan Bay 1071½	Just up	8
23Apr76- 9GP	fst	7f	:22⅕ :44⅘ 1:23⅕	3↑Allowance	3 3 21½ 21½ 1½ 2½	Barrow T	b 116	4.10	87-17	Noble Surviver 110½ Big Star 1165½ Proponent 1161	Second best	5

LATEST WORKOUTS Jan 22 Hia 4f fst :48⅖ h Dec 28 GP 6f fst 1:16 b Dec 10 GP 3f fst :37 b

Peaceful Hour

B. g. 4, by Salem—Magic Me, by Like Magic
$25,000 Br.—Quiet Winter Farm (Md) Tr.—Arcodia Anthony
Own.—Miami Lakes Ranch
116

Turf Record: St. 1, 1st 0, 2nd 0, 3rd 1

	St.	1st	2nd	3rd	Amt.
1977	2	0	1	0	$1,775
1976	13	4	2	3	$24,780

22Jan77- 5GP	fst	7f	:23 :46⅘ 1:25⅕	Allowance	7 2 1hd 2hd 2hd 25½	Rivera M A	114	4.70	72-23	OneMoreJump1145½PecfulHour1142HnryEdwrd114no	Second best	9
15Jan77- 7GP	sly	1 1/16	:47 1:11⅖ 1:43⅗	Allowance	6 2 25 33 38 416	Solomone M	117	2.50	67-12	Meritable 1147 Notably Different 1149 Native Cousin 107nk	Tired	8
30Dec76- 9Crc	fst	6f	:22⅕ :45⅖ 1:12	3↑Allowance	2 4 34 55½ 47 49½	Jimenez C	116	7.20	83-19	Lord Arlen 1163 L'Natural 1134½ Hosiery 1162	No mishap	8
11Dec76- 6Crc	fst	6½f	:23 :46 1:18⅕	3↑Allowance	2 5 21½ 31½ 22 22½	Jimenez C	113	39.40	97-11	Beau Claire 1192½ Peaceful Hour 1131½ Helixiv 116nk	Gamely	10
2Dec76- 9Crc	sly	1	:48⅖ 1:13⅖ 1:39⅘	3↑Allowance	9 1 11 11 11 2no	Jimenez C	118	4.20	90-13	Billy Frank 115no Peaceful Hour 1182 Di Qualita 1164	Gamely	9
22Nov76- 9Crc	fm	*1 1/16 ⓣ	1:46	3↑Allowance	1 1 11 11 2½ 35½	Jimenez C	114	39.30	79-15	Hasty Tudor1244HallofReason1171½PeacefulHour114no	Weakened	6
30Oct76- 6Mth	fst	1	:48 1:12⅕ 1:38⅘	Clm c-22000	6 1 11½ 12½ 12½ 11¼	Dowd M Jr7	112	*1.70	79-20	Peaceful Hour 1121¼ Savage Moon 115½ Royaccord 1115	Driving	6
21Oct76- 7Mth	gd	6f	:22⅕ :46 1:12⅕	3↑Allowance	1 3 1hd 1½ 1½ 14	Dowd M Jr7	111	6.10	79-26	Peaceful Hour 1114 Growler 1182½ Statement 118no	Driving	8
15Oct76- 9Mth	fst	6f	:21⅗ :44⅖ 1:10⅗	Clm 20000	12 1 24 23 23½ 34	Dowd M Jr7	108	15.60	83-16	Makoo Tan 1153 Feast or Fast 1191 PeacefulHour1084	Weakened	12
24Sep76- 5Mth	fst	1	:47⅖ 1:12 1:37⅖	Clm 25000	3 2 21 2½ 21½ 52¾	Barrera C	111	15.90	83-17	Sellin' Barry 117hd Quick Marine 119¾ Minnie Buss1151½	Steadied	8

LATEST WORKOUTS Feb 1 Hia 4f fst :50 b Jan 8 Hia 4f fst :50 b Dec 26 Hia 4f gd :47⅗ h Dec 10 Hia 3f fst :36 h

What A Lucky Star

B. h. 5, by What A Pleasure—Bright Starlite, by Rough'n Tumble
$25,000 Br.—Meadowbrook Farm Inc (Fla) Tr.—Bracken James
Own.—LaCroix J W
116

	St.	1st	2nd	3rd	Amt.
1977	3	1	0	0	$4,467
1976	5	0	0	0	$650

22Jan77- 2GP	fst	6f	:22⅖ :46⅖ 1:11⅖	Clm 16000	8 6 52½ 43½ 3½ 15	Fieselman	b 116	6.70	82-23	What A Lucky Star 1165PrinceCrozier116noLePunch1161½	Driving	12
13Jan77- 8Crc	fst	6½f	:23⅕ :45⅘ 1:18⅖	Clm 22500	6 9 107¾ 1013 1011 106	Fieselman	b 114	49.70	93-17	Last Flute 114no Black Balled 116no Mangoright 112¾	No factor	10
3Jan77- 8Crc	sly	6f	:23⅕ :46⅘ 1:13⅕	Clm 20000	12 1 32½ 32½ 32 42¾	Fieselman	b 116	107.30	84-23	Satan's Sentry 115¾ Unchallenged 1221 Chic Ruler 1191	No rally	12
18Dec76- 5Crc	fst	6f	:22⅘ :46 1:12	3↑Clm 25000	7 5 43 33 67½ 88½	Baltazar C	b 116	27.10	84-14	Mangoright 116no Native Cousin 1041½ Henry Edward 1121	Tired	10
30Aug76- 2Bel	fst	6f	:23⅕ :47⅕ 1:11⅘	3↑Clm 20000	10 5 1½ 913 1026 1030	Velez R I	b 117	30.10	53-18	Cane Pole 113nk Snappy Chatter 1133 Bullyrag 1191½	Stopped	10
21Aug76- 3Sar	fst	6f	:21⅘ :44⅗ 1:09⅘	3↑Clm 20000	6 1 2hd 33 56½ 814	Day P	b 117	14.90	77-12	Gabilan 1173 Rare Joel 117hd Snappy Chatter 117¾	Stopped	8
7Aug76- 4Sar	sly	6f	:22⅕ :46 1:11⅗	3↑Clm 20000	3 2 1½ 1½ 32½ 48½	Day P	b 117	9.00	73-17	Irish Fun 1144¾ Native Blend 1193 Jumbolaka 117¾	Speed, tired	9
22Jly76- 5Aqu	fst	6f	:22⅗ :46 1:10⅗	3↑Clm 35000	7 3 1½ 2hd 33½ 1014	Turcotte R	117	16.60	76-22	Checkerhall 1193 Divine Royalty 1221½ Russ Miron 1131½	Tired	10
14Sep75- 9Bel	fst	6f	:22⅘ :45⅘ 1:10⅗	Clm 35000	7 3 2hd 2hd 109¾ 108	Vasquez J	b 116	9.20	81-14	Real George 114hd Jack Sexton 116nk Cornishman 116¾	Tired	12
4Sep75- 4Bel	fst	6f	:23⅗ :46⅗ 1:11	3↑Allowance	4 5 31½ 22 38 615	Maple E	b 113	3.70	72-18	Hole in thePants1172BoldandStormy1135½DancingGun1062½	Tired	6

LATEST WORKOUTS Jan 28 Crc 6f fst 1:15 h Jan 20 Crc 4f fst :51 b Jan 9 Crc 5f fst 1:02⅕ b Dec 30 Crc 5f fst 1:02⅖ b

Big Star and What A Lucky Star towered over this field. Big Star had won his last start by six lengths, easily, in the spectacular time of 1:09⅗ for six furlongs. He covered the distance more than two seconds faster than any of the other winners that day. What A Lucky Star had captured his most recent race by five lengths in 1:11⅖, a time which was deceptively slow because the track over which he competed was slow. On the same afternoon, $40,000 claiming horses ran in 1:12, good allowance horses ran in 1:12⅕, and some of the best sprinters in Florida went in 1:11. Obviously, a horse who can run faster than $40,000 claimers and almost as fast as stakes-class animals figures to be a strong contender in a $25,000 claiming race.

Speed figures are based on such comparisons of the times of races. They reflect the time of a horse's performance, as well as the times of other races on the same day which indicate the inherent speed of the track. They put this information in a convenient numerical form rather than a crude observation of who is faster than whom. My figures said that Big Star had run a 109, making him about one length faster than What A Lucky Star, with a 106. I regretted that these two exceptional horses had wound up in the same field, but I saw no possibility for a bet.

And then I looked with disbelief at the odds board. While Big Star was the favorite in the early wagering, What A Lucky Star was 20 to 1. His odds began to drift downward slowly, but two minutes before post time he was still an incredible 9 to 1. I had to capitalize on this value somehow. Although I rarely bet to win and place, preferring to sink or swim with my opinion, this seemed to be an occasion where the move was justified. I bet $300 to win and $300 to place on What A Lucky Star, shooting for my biggest score of the season without taking a great risk of losing my whole investment.

What A Lucky Star surged to the lead on the backstretch and opened a two-length advantage turning for home, when Big Star advanced along the rail and challenged him. The moment of truth lasted for a few seconds. Then What A Lucky Star repulsed the bid, and led his rival to the finish line by a length. Just as they reached the wire, I thought I saw Big Star's jockey stand up in the irons. Aware of the possibility of a disqualification, I deferred my celebrating and dashed from the stands to the press box, where a television monitor shows the same film-patrol replays that the stewards watch.

The films showed that What A Lucky Star crossed into Big Star's path a few yards before the finish line. But he had a clear lead at the time and caused no interference. Jockey Donald MacBeth, on Big Star, knew that his only chance to win the race was through a disqualification, so he stood straight up in the irons, pretending to be the victim of a heinous foul. Nobody was fooled. I hadn't seen such blatant overacting since my high school's senior-class play, and the stewards didn't bother to post the INQUIRY sign.

So when MacBeth filed his desperate claim of foul, I calmly sipped a Coke and pondered whether I should fly to Nassau for my celebration that evening. I did not know at the time that the stewards had a vendetta against the trainer of What A Lucky Star. Nor did I know, as a colleague later told me, that "only one of these stewards knows anything about racing, and his brain is the size of a gnat."

As I watched the television monitor, I saw that the stewards were looking at the final yards of the race, over and over again. Then they started scrutinizing the action on the stretch turn. Then they looked at the start of the race. I had seen the officials in Maryland operate in such a fashion often enough to know what was happening: the stewards were trying to find a reason to disqualify What A Lucky Star. Suddenly the tote board went blank, the crowd roared, and Big Star's number was put up as the winner. I had just been robbed of $3000.

EIGHTH RACE
Gulfstream
FEBRUARY 7, 1977

6 FURLONGS. (1.07$\frac{4}{5}$) CLAIMING. Purse $8,000. 4–year–olds and upward. Weight, 122 lbs. Non–winners of two races since December 20 allowed 2 lbs. Two races since November 5, 4 lbs. A race since January 15, 6 lbs. Claiming price $25,000; for each $2,500 to $20,000 allowed 2 lbs. (Races where entered for $18,000 or less not considered.)

Value of race $8,000, value to winner $5,072, second $1,520, third $720, fourth $400, balance of starters $36 each. Mutuel pool $163,256.

Last Raced	Horse	Eqt.	A.	Wt	PP	St	¼	½	Str	Fin	Jockey	Cl'g Pr	Odds $1
22Jan77 ^{2}GP^{1}	[D]What A Lucky Star	b	5	116	12	1	2^{1}	$1^{1\frac{1}{2}}$	1^{2}	1^{1}	Fieselman J	25000	9.30
25Jan77 ^{6}GP^{1}	Big Star	b	4	116	10	6	$3^{\frac{1}{2}}$	3^{4}	2^{2}	$2^{4\frac{1}{2}}$	MacBeth D	25000	1.70
22Jan77 ^{5}GP^{3}	Henry Edward	b	6	120	8	3	$9^{\frac{1}{2}}$	9^{3}	6^{2}	3^{2}	St Leon G	22500	13.80
9Nov76 ^{7}Mth^{6}	Ardent Student	b	4	113	6	2	1^{hd}	2^{hd}	3^{2}	$4^{\frac{3}{4}}$	Thornburg B	20000	21.90
15Jan77 ^{5}GP^{5}	Captain Mitch	b	4	116	3	4	$7^{\frac{1}{2}}$	$5^{1\frac{1}{2}}$	5^{2}	5^{1}	Brumfield D	25000	5.90
22Jan77 ^{4}GP^{11}	Larry's Lark		4	116	7	11	12	$10^{\frac{1}{2}}$	$7^{1\frac{1}{2}}$	$6^{1\frac{1}{2}}$	Fell J	25000	18.30
18Jan77 ^{9}GP^{6}	Custom	b	5	116	5	8	$4^{\frac{1}{2}}$	4^{1}	4^{hd}	7no	Fires E	25000	36.00
29Jan77 ^{6}GP^{8}	Full Catch	b	4	116	4	12	11^{1}	11^{3}	10^{1}	$8^{\frac{1}{2}}$	Hernandez R	25000	7.20
22Jan77 ^{5}GP^{2}	Peaceful Hour		4	116	11	7	$8^{1\frac{1}{2}}$	6^{1}	8^{1}	9^{2}	Rivera M A	25000	7.80
28Aug76 ^{5}AP^{8}	Mr. Door		6	114	9	5	10^{2}	12	12	$10^{\frac{1}{2}}$	Gavidia W	22500	21.00
24Dec76 ^{9}Crc^{1}	Judge's Fee	b	5	114	2	9	6^{hd}	7^{hd}	11^{1}	11^{1}	Bailey J D	22500	7.50
19Jan77 ^{10}GP^{10}	Yon Dan		4	114	1	10	5^{hd}	$8^{\frac{1}{2}}$	9^{hd}	12	Perret C	20000	49.40

[D]–What A Lucky Star Disqualified and placed second.

OFF AT 4:35, EST. Start good, Won driving. Time, :22$\frac{1}{5}$, :44$\frac{4}{5}$, 1:09$\frac{4}{5}$ Track fast.

$2 Mutuel Prices:				
	10–BIG STAR	5.40	3.60	3.00
	12–WHAT A LUCKY STAR		8.20	6.00
	8–HENRY EDWARD			5.80

Big Star—B. c, by Decathlon—Tusis, by Tournoi. Trainer Mayberry Brian A. Bred by Wallace Farm (Fla).

WHAT A LUCKY STAR dueled for command early, moved to a clear lead approaching the head of the stretch, drifted out in front of BIG STAR in early stretch, and then bore in in the closing yards causing BIG STAR'S rider to take up sharply. WHAT A LUCKY STAR was disqualified and placed second for interference in the stretch run. BIG STAR raced forwardly, moved to challenge from the outside at the head of the stretch, altered course inside when the winner crossed over in front of him and then was taken up sharply in the closing strides when WHAT A LUCKY STAR bore in. HENRY EDWARD steadily improved position in the drive. ARDENT STUDENT raced on or near the pace to midstretch, then weakened. CAPTAIN MITCH raced forwardly, but failed to respond sufficiently in the stretch run. FULL CATCH failed to reach contention. PEACEFUL HOUR was outrun. JUDGE'S FEE was finished after a half.

Owners— 1, LaCroix J W; 2, Nordham Elizabeth; 3, Green R I; 4, Heather R M; 5, Flying W Stable; 6, Jennings L W; 7, Brisbine Mrs E J; 8, Kelley Mrs W A; 9, Miami Lakes Ranch; 10, Bromagen Glen; 11, Schoninger B; 12, Grimmo C F.

Trainers— 1, Bracken James; 2, Mayberry Brian A; 3, Green Newcomb; 4, Jennings Lawrence W; 5, Mullin William; 6, Jennings Lawrence W; 7, Bollero Joseph M; 8, Kelley Walter A; 9, Arcodia Anthony; 10, Kelley Thomas W; 11, Winick Neal J; 12, Blengs Vincent.

Overweight: Ardent Student 1 pound; Yon Dan 2.

Scratched—Our Count (15Dec76 ^{7}Spt^{3}); Parc Forillon (1Feb77 ^{7}GP^{5}); Ky. Cad (1Feb77 ^{7}GP^{1}).

As I watched the replay one more time, and saw the nonexistent foul again, I was overwhelmed by the injustice of it all. Fortunately I remembered the cautionary advice of a friend who had almost set his house on fire by smashing his television set after losing a football bet. So I vented my rage by driving my fist through the plasterboard wall of the press box, regretting only that the stewards weren't standing between me and it. I walked to the clubhouse, where I saw other losers standing in stunned disbelief by the television monitors, and then went to the window to redeem my place tickets. The $50 cashier, who ought to be the most blasé man at the racetrack, apologized when he saw my tickets. "They robbed you," he said.

Early the next morning I went to the track to commiserate with Jim Bracken, the trainer of What A Lucky Star. "Every time I've ever seen a disqualification like this," I told him, "there's something behind it. Usually the stewards have got something against the jockey or the trainer. What's the story?" Bracken related a complicated tale about a disputed contract between him and an apprentice jockey. The bottom line was that Bracken had been threatening the stewards with legal action. That explanation made me feel even worse. I had been such an innocent victim of circumstances.

That afternoon I squandered nearly $1000 on a program where I didn't like anything. I believe that the gods who oversee horse racing will even out a bettor's good and bad luck in the long run, and I was trying to accelerate the process. Two days later I worked up some genuine enthusiasm for an animal named Winged Brook, whose next-to-last figure was excellent and whose bad last race was probably excusable because of an unfavorable distance and track bias. At 9-to-1 odds he was worth a stab of moderate proportions. I plunged $1000 and watched without surprise as he finished out of the money. I went home feeling that Gulfstream had beaten me.

I knew only one proven remedy for such a decline. Usually I would make a tactical retreat from the track, wait until I found a solid, conservative standout, and then try to cash a moderate bet that would help restore my self-confidence. But at Gulfstream I now found myself facing the same problem with which the Kid had been wrestling for the whole season. Outstanding bets never seemed to materialize.

We were the victims of politics, economics, and Reuben Askew. Under the moralistic, antigambling governor, Florida was taxing its racing industry to death. The tracks were in such shaky financial condition that they could not offer adequate purses. Horses who competed for $16,000 purses in New York were running for $8000 at Gulfstream. Like the good jockeys, the good northern stables that traditionally migrated south were staying at Aqueduct or going to California instead. There simply weren't many good horses in Florida.

As a result, the higher-grade races, which usually provide the best gambling opportunities, were uncompetitive, unbettable affairs with small fields and short-priced favorites.

As he passed these races day after day and week after week, the Kid was learning in a painful fashion about the difficulty of being a professional gambler. He knew he could not afford to risk his money under less-than-optimal conditions. But at the same time, with high living expenses in Miami and no other source of income, he couldn't afford not to bet. The tension produced by these two conflicting pressures was almost too much for the Kid to bear. Even when a day's races were over, he couldn't escape. Betting was his job, his hobby, his love, his whole life. So his happiness and self-esteem depended almost entirely on his performance at the track. As the Gulfstream meeting progressed, he became increasingly sullen, withdrawn, and pessimistic until one midnight when he looked up from his *Racing Form* and announced, "I've got my horse."

After weeks of waiting, the Kid had finally found an animal who met all of his important handicapping standards. One Moment had earned consistently superior speed figures while running against some of the best horses in Florida. He was trained by a competent man. Now he was entered against an unimposing group of allowance horses. And he had drawn the favorable inside post position at a mile and one-sixteenth.

When One Moment went off at 7 to 2, the Kid made his major bet of the meeting and I wagered enthusiastically, too. We watched with a mixture of pain and bewilderment as the horse failed to reach contention and struggled home fourth. The Kid was finished. He couldn't bear the thought of waiting weeks at Gulfstream for another serious betting opportunity. He went home and packed his bags.

As I drove the Kid to the airport the next day, I assured him that this was only a temporary setback. He had already proved conclusively that he had the handicapping skills to be a winner. But I hoped that he had learned—as I had been reminded—about the tremendous importance of the psychological side of betting. He had allowed Gulfstream to defeat him mentally. He had let pressure and adversity wreck his spirits and plunge him into a state of depression that almost certainly impaired his judgment.

I was struggling to avoid the same fate, still trying to shake off the effects of What A Lucky Star's disqualification. If I looked at my ledger for the season and saw I was $2000 ahead, I thought immediately that I deserved to be winning $5000. My eagerness to boost my profits to that rightful figure would distort my handicapping and my betting. But finally I found an animal who did merit a fairly serious wager.

GULFSTREAM

1 1-16 MILES GULFSTREAM

1 1/16 MILES, (1.40½) ALLOWANCE. Purse $7,000. Fillies and Mares, 4-year-olds and upward which have not won two races. Weight, 122 lbs. Non-winners of $6,300 allowed 3 lbs. $5,400, 5 lbs. Maidens, 8 lbs. (Winners preferred)

Satan's Hen
Ch. f. 4, by Crimson Satan—Platypus, by Destino
Br.—Crimson King Farm (Ky)
Tr.—Salmen Peter W Jr
Own.—Crimson King Farm

117

	St.	1st	2nd	3rd	Amt.
1977	1	0	0	0	$36
1976	7	1	2	0	$3,756

8Feb77- 6GP fst 1¼ :48½ 1:13¾ 1:44	⑤Allowance	8 2 2nd 42½ 67 719 Manganello M	114 55.90	62-19 KlassyReason114⁸SweetLiznne119¹¼DungreeDoll114² Speed, tired 9
16Nov76- 6CD fst 6f :23½ :47 1:12¾ 3↑⑤Allowance	5 7 78 71½ 718 72¹ Manganello M	116 34.90	61-30 Fleeting Echo 116²½ Name Me Not 119⁵ Pakua 116²½ Outrun 7
9Nov76- 7CD fst 6f :22½ :46 1:12¾ 3↑⑤Allowance	11 12 1118¹019 918 713 Manganello M	116 59.60	70-28 Airman'sLassie116¹½LeighSimms116¼NameMeNot119¹ Slow start 12
31Aug76- 5Det fst 1 :49 1:15 1:41½ 3↑Md Sp Wt	4 4 32½ 1hd 1½ 1³ Manganello M	113 *.70	70-28 Satan's Hen 113³ Crossed Countess 112⁴ Contado 110nk 8
12Aug76- 4Det fst 6f :22½ :45½ 1:13½ 3↑ Md Sp Wt	2 7 510 411 49 2² Manganello M	112 *1.30	66-31 Henrietta Louella 1112 Satan's Hen 112² Space Folly 1152½ 7
5Aug76- 9Det fst 6f :22½ :46½ 1:13½ Md Sp Wts	1 4 95½ 97½ 89 26 Manganello M	115 3.20	68-27 Broken Contract 120⁶ Satan's Hen 115¹ Im Realistic 110nk 12
21Jun76- 4CD fst 6f :22½ :46½ 1:12¾ 3↑Md Sp Wt	2 8 75½ 76½ 56 56½ Manganello M	113 28.70	77-20 Prolific Princess 114nk Sea Dollie 113no Fleeting Echo 116hd 8
14Jun76- 5CD fst 6f :24½ :45¾ 1:12 3↑Md Sp Wt	4 8 96½108 97½ 911 Manganello M	113 29.60	75-16 Ruby River 114¹½ Real Happy 108² Fleeting Echo 113hd 12
LATEST WORKOUTS	Feb 16 GP 3f sly :37¾ b	Feb 2 GP 5f fst 1:02 b	Jan 25 GP 4f fst :48½ b	Jan 21 GP ⑦ 7f fm 1:36 b

---

Fast Freedom
Ch. f. 4, by Vertex—Freedom At Last, by Needles
Br.—Meadowbrook Farm Inc (Fla)
Tr.—Bracken James
Own.—Lacroix J W

117

Turf Record					St.	1st	2nd	3rd	Amt.
St. 1st 2nd 3rd	1977	2	0	0	0	$386
2 0 0 0	1976	16	1	0	3	$7,535

19Jan77- 7GP fst 6f :22½ :46½ 1:11¾	⑤Allowance	2 12 1212¹013 612 510 St Leon G	117 7.60	72-30 Silent Echo 117⁵ Action Street 117¹ Klassy Reason 117¹ Outrun 12
7Jan77- 8Crc fst 1 :49½ 1:14¾ 1:40¾	⑤Allowance	5 5 31½ 53½ 53½ 42½ Fieselman J	118 6.90	83-15 Playin'Footsie118³Platitude118²CasualAquaintnce122¹ Bid, tired 7
11Dec76- 7Crc fst 6f :22½ :45½ 1:12¾ 3↑Allowance	5 9 88½ 811 66½ 36 Fieselman J	119 8.20	85-11 Ada Potatoe 115¹ Action Street 115⁵ Fast Freedom 119nk Rallied 11
27Nov76- 5Crc fst 7f :23½ :46½ 1:25¾ 3↑Allowance	8 8 88 811 511 Baltazar C b 119	70.70	77-15 Record Hop 113⁶ Compote 116³½ Fleet Wind 119½ No mishap 8
19Nov76- 8Crc fm *1 ⑦ 1:39½ 3↑Allowance	2 8 89½ 613 59½ 55 Baltazar C b 118	*1.60	86-07 Princess Belvane 118² Spec Gal 122³ Totie Fields 118½ No factor 8
10Nov76- 9Crc fst 6f :23 :46½ 1:12½ 3↑Allowance	3 7 78¼ 812 89½ 66¼ Baltazar C b 116½	9.60	84-18 JustForPlesur116noBornBrillint115²DiplomtPrinc108¹½ No factor 8
10Nov76-Dead heat			
15Oct76- 9Crc fm *1½ ⑦ 1:45 3↑Allowance	5 6 57 53 63½ 42½ Baltazar C b 116	70.00	87-12 Suzy Creamcheese 116¹FullSpringII118¹SpecGal122½ Good effort 8
24Sep76-10Crc fst 1 :48½ 1:14¾ 1:43¾ 3↑Md Sp Wt	3 6 53 1hd 1½ 42½ Baltazar C b 116	3.40	42-17 FstFrdom1134²FightingTim1112¼ForgivAForgt116⁴½ Ridden out 10
20Aug76- 5Crc fst 1 :48½ 1:15 1:42½ 3↑Md Sp Wt	1 4 56 54 42½ 32 Baltazar C b 115	2.10	76-21 Frond 122¹ Full Spring II 122¹ Fast Freedom 115½ Late rally 7
6Aug76- 4Crc fst 6f :23½ :46½ 1:13½ 3↑Md Sp Wt	12 1 64 85½ 76½ 57 Baltazar C b 114	5.90	79-19 KickapooCreek112½SydeBord117⁴¼FightingTime110hd No factor 12
LATEST WORKOUTS	● Feb 15 Crc 4f sly :50½ b	Feb 4 Crc 4f fst :48 h	Jan 31 Crc 3f fst :36½ h	Jan 16 Crc 4f sly :50¾ b

---

Sweet Lizanne
B. f. 4, by Sea-Bird—Lizanne Dear, by Bold Ruler
Br.—Galbreath D M (Ky)
Tr.—Rondinello Thomas L
Own.—Galbreath D M

119

Turf Record					St.	1st	2nd	3rd	Amt.
St. 1st 2nd 3rd	1977	1	0	1	0	$1,400
2 0 0 1	1976	12	1	1	4	$12,160

8Feb77- 6GP fst 1¼ :48½ 1:13¾ 1:44	⑤Allowance	4 8 74½ 52¾ 45 28 Rivera M A	b 119 4.10	73-19 KlassyReason114⁸SweetLiznne119¹¼DungreeDoll114² Second best 9
16Nov76- 7Aqu fm 1½ ⑦:47¾ 1:12½ 1:43½ 3↑Allowance	3 4 69 54½ 53¼ 42½ Velasquez J b 115	2.10	85-12 Tmp'sDrm115noPlyin'Footsi115¹¼MissRitz115½ Bothered, steadied 6
9Nov76- 8Aqu fm 1½ ⑦:48 1:12½ 1:45 3↑Allowance	6 4 510 57 42 32½ Velasquez J b 119	8.50	79-19 ImogeneII115¹¼Tamp'sDrem115½SweetLiznne115¹½ Finished well 8
25Oct76- 4Aqu fst 6f :22½ :46¾ 1:11¾ 3↑Md Sp Wt	1 7 71½ 55 21 1½ Velasquez J b 119	7.70	84-13 Sweet Lizanne 119³ D. J. Debs119nk AmAvailable119⁴½ Ridden out 7
17Sep76- 1Bel sly 7f :22½ :46½ 1:25½ 3↑Md Sp Wt	4 8 74½ 96½ 816 813 Gustines H b 118	6.50	43-15 Floral Empress 118¹½ Like For Like 118⁴½AmAvailable119¼ Lost whip 8
8Sep76- 5Bel fst 1 :22½ :46 1:11 3↑Md Sp Wt	5 7 83½ 77 54¼ 58½ Maple E b 118	6.80	79-13 Sour Orange 118⁴½ Skater's Waltz118½CornishPet1132½ Lost whip 8
23Jun76- 5Mth fst 1½ :49½ 1:14¾ 1:47¾ 3↑Allowance	5 9 84½ 75½ 73½ 63½ Solomone M b 115	*2.00	62-21 Native Lou 115¹ Court Accountant 115½CoinSilver115hd Bore out 5
29May76- 2Bel- fst 1 :46½ 1:11¾ 1:45¾ 3↑Allowance	3 9 87½ 54 35 35½ Cordero A Jr b 115	*1.80	72-19 LaughingKeys1154½TbleHopper1154½SweetLiznne1152½ Lost whip 9
28Apr76- 4Aqu fst 1 :48½ 1:13½ 1:38¾ 3↑Allowance	8 8 65 53¾ 42½ 44½ Cordero A Jr b 114	*1.80	70-19 PlaceDauphine1072DonaMaya112noDzzlingDisply122½ No excuse 8
12Apr76- 4Aqu fst 1 :48½ 1:14½ 1:40½ 3↑Allowance	3 7 62½ 65 43 42 Cordero A Jr b 114	2.50e	64-24 Weatherwise 113hd Forwardly 112½ Cuvee 112nk Blocked 7
LATEST WORKOUTS	Feb 15 Hia 4f sly :51 b	Feb 7 Hia 3f fst :38½ b	Feb 2 Hia 6f fst 1:18 b	Jan 28 Hia 5f fst 1:05¾ b

---

Linda M. P.
Ch. f. 4, by Fiddle Isle—Chappaquiddick, by Relic
Br.—Claiborne Farm & Perry (Ky)
Tr.—Hickey P Noel
Own.—Irish Acres Stable

112⁵

Turf Record					St.	1st	2nd	3rd	Amt.
St. 1st 2nd 3rd	1977	3	1	0	0	$3,672
1 0 0 0	1976	0	M	0	0	

27Jan77- 7GP fm *1 ⑦ 1:40½	⑤Allowance	1 2 63½ 74½ 63½ 52½ Harbacek D⁵	109 5.90	76-24 Platitude 114hd Klassy Reason 114¹ Positive Attitude 114½ Tired 10
19Jan77- 7GP fst 6f :22½ :46½ 1:11¾	⑤Allowance	10 4 1112¹11611¹1170¹7 Harbacek D⁵	112 4.90	65-30 Silent Echo 117⁵ Action Street 117¹ Klassy Reason 117¹ Outrun 12
6Jan77- 3Crc fst 7f :23½ :47½ 1:26½	⑤Md Sp Wt	5 2 2hd 11 12 1³ Harbacek D⁵	117 20.00	85-17 Linda M. P. 117³MademoiselleMolly1222½LadyJudybee122½ Driving 8

Dungaree Doll
Dk. b. or br. f. 4, by Francis S—Miss Rossean, by Intentionally
Br.—Hooper F W (Fla)
Tr.—Metcalf Raymond F
Own.—Hooper F W

117

Turf Record					St.	1st	2nd	3rd	Amt.
St. 1st 2nd 3rd	1977	2	0	0	1	$736
3 0 0 0	1976	17	1	2	3	$11,530

8Feb77- 6GP fst 1¼ :48½ 1:13¾ 1:44	⑤Allowance	9 3 3½ 7hd 3³ 39½ Brumfield D	b 114 21.70	71-19 KlassyReason114⁸SweetLiznne119¹¼DungareeDoll114² Weakened 9
19Jan77- 7GP fst 6f :22½ :46½ 1:11¾	⑤Allowance	8 9 1011 911 712 715 Hernandez R	117 38.10	67-30 Silent Echo 117⁵ Action Street 117¹ Klassy Reason 117¹ Outrun 12
21Oct76- 6Kee gd 6½f :23½ :46 1:17¾ 3↑Allowance	8 10 1027 1029 — — Turcotte R L	114 36.50	— — Romeo's Coquette115⁴PlayOnWords112²MissKahuna1131½ Eased 10
14Oct76- 6Kee fst 7f :23 :45½ 1:23½ 3↑Allowance	5 11 97 85½ 54½ 48½ Turcotte R L	114 29.80	80-16 Bold Express 112⁶ Happy Quote 114¹½ HadToBuy114½ Stride late 12
30Sep76- 8AP fm *1 ⑦:48 1:14 1:39½ 3↑Allowance	5 6 86½ 84½ 52½ 63¼ Powell J	110 4.80e	74-22 Positioning 118hd Platitude 118¹¼ Jay Bar Fancy112¹½ No mishap 10
31Aug76- 7AP fst 1 :45½ 1:10½ 1:36½ 3↑Allowance	2 8 710 44½ 31 22 Powell J	110 6.90e	78-17 Lady Deb 113¹ Dungaree Doll 110½ Julie O. 113¹½ Gamely 8
26Aug76- 7AP fst 7f :23 1:12½ 3↑Allowance	5 8 811 811 67 511 Powell J	110 20.00	78-13 Dncer'sVixen110⁶Bickie'sDncer1131½FmdPrincess110hd Slow early 8
19Aug76- 9AP fst 6f :22½ :46½ 1:11¾ 3↑Allowance	10 8 813 89½ 78½ 96 Patterson A	114 61.00	78-16 SpringtownTex110¾PleasureIsMine116¾AuntieGay116¹½ No factor4 10
28Jly76- 6AP fst 6f :22½ :46¾ 1:12¼ 3↑Allowance	4 7 75½ 810 812 816 Patterson A	114 88.00	68-16 MajesticMedallion117⁴PlesureIsMine117¾AuntieGay107½ Outrun 8
26Jun76- 6AP fst 6f :22½ :45 1:10 3↑Allowance	7 1 85½ 77½ 57 55½ Patterson A	113 8.90	80-16 My Fair Maid 113¹ Little Divy 1131½ Miss Strate1131½ No mishap 9
LATEST WORKOUTS	Feb 15 Hia 3f sly :36 h	Jan 24 Hia 4f fst :49¾ b	Jan 13 Hia 5f fst 1:01 b	Jan 8 Hia 5f fst 1:01 h

---

Singing Monarch
Ch. f. 4, by Northern Monarch—Song of Sixpence, by Indian Hemp
Br.—Clearbrook Stock Farm (Can)
Tr.—Moerman Gerald C
Own.—Shefry Farms

110⁷

Turf Record					St.	1st	2nd	3rd	Amt.
St. 1st 2nd 3rd	1977	2	0	0	0	$288
12 1 0 1	1976	16	0	1	3	$5,319

5Feb77- 3GP fst 1⅟₁₆ :47½ 1:12½ 1:46½	⑤Clm 10000	3 6 68½ 67 65½ 86 Gomez A	116 18.10	64-18 Second Daughter 116¾ Flora 116¹¼FlowersInMay113⁴ Wide 12
27Jan77- 7GP fm *1 ⑦ 1:40½	⑤Clm 12500	10 9 89½ 97½ 86½ 86½ Duffy L	116 64.20	72-24 Platitude 114hd Klassy Reason 114¹ Positive Attitude114½ Outrun 10
19Nov76- 8Crc fm *1 ⑦ 1:39½ 3↑Allowance	3 7 78½ 815 712 67½ Gomez A	112 24.00	84-07 Princess Belvane 118² Spec Gal 122³ Totie Fields 118½ No factor 8
22Oct76- 6Mth fst 1 :47 1:13¼ 1:39½ 3↑⑤Clm 15000	4 4 68 810 79½ 714 Drury M A	112 17.40	63-23 Pal Joey 113⁶ Princess Free 116¹½ Instant Justice 115² Tired 9
27Sep76- 5Mth fst 1 :47 1:12½ 1:45½ 3↑⑤Clm 15000	6 6 86½ 86½ 812 812 Thomas D B	113 10.40	68-16 SecondDaughter119¹¾AurofGlory117nkLonny'sEvent111½ Outrun 10
9Sep76- 4Mth fm 1⅟₁₆ ⑦:48 1:12½ 1:45½ 3↑⑤Clm 15000	5 8 810 86½ 79½ 68 Solomone M	114 *2.90	72-21 Ruling All 111nk Lonny's Event 115¹ AmazingSafety115¹½ Outrun 9
27Aug76- 5Mth fst 1⅟₁₆ :47½ 1:12½ 1:45½ 3↑⑤Clm 15000	4 3 42 31½ 34½ 31 Solomone M	113 3.20	72-19 SecondDughter115nkRobinsFvor1192SingingMonrch114³ No mishap 7
18Aug76- 5Mth fst 1⅟₁₆ :47½ 1:12½ 1:45½ 3↑⑤Clm 15000	3 4 42½ 32½ 34 42 Solomone M	115 3.70	81-13 TwiceAMonth115nkSingingMonrch116hdAdvnturLyric116³ Gamely 9
24Jly76- 8FE fst 1 :47 1:12½ 1:46 3↑Allowance	1 6 78½ 35 3½ 2nk Gomez A	115 3.00	80-16 Likes O' Lori 121½ Gallant Herod 115³ Natalba 111½ Outrun 10
18Jly76- 4FE fst *7f ⑦:22½ :46½ 1:26 3↑⑤Allowance	5 6 66½ 79 64 54 Turcotte R J	113 10.90	
LATEST WORKOUTS	Feb 14 GP 4f fst :50 b	Jan 18 GP 3f fst :39 b	Jan 10 GP 3f fst :38 b	Jan 6 GP ⑦ 7f fst 1:06¾ b

---

Uh Oh
B. f. 4, by T V Commercial—True, by Bold Bidder
Br.—Bate N P (Md)
Tr.—Viera Christine
Own.—Bate N

117

	St.	1st	2nd	3rd	Amt.
1977	1	0	0	0	$350
1976	16	1	0	0	$4,135

8Feb77- 6GP fst 1¼ :48½ 1:13¾ 1:44	⑤Allowance	7 1 1hd 3nk 35 412 Lopez R D	114 10.30	69-19 Klassy Reason 114⁸ Sweet Lizanne 119¹¼ DungareeDoll114² Tired 9
20Jly76- 9AP fst 6f :22½ :46½ 1:13½	⑤Clm 16500	3 10 1011¹107½ 66 612 Viera H	114 9.90	83-16 Shelly's Star 112nk Zippy Dream 114nkPagoFlyer117nk Stride late 10
4Jun76- 2Hol fst 6½f :22½ :45 1:17¾	⑤Clm 16500	4 8 88½ 88 611 43¼ Pierce D	116 37.70	80-12 MyLittleMargie116³CactusValleyReg109noBylineGirl116½ Rallied 12
21May76- 1Hol fst 6f :22 :45½ 1:12½	⑤Clm 20000	1 11 1114¹113¹010½107½ Martini V⁵	b 111 23.80	74-17 Never Promised 116¹ Sing Back116¹¼ThirteenthHope116hd Outrun 11
26Mar76- 2SA fst 1⅟₁₆ :47½ 1:11½ 1:38	⑤Clm 25000	5 9 85¾ 89½ 77½ 89¼ Martini V⁵	b 111 21.00	69-18 Silver Slip 116⁵ Deep Valley 116¼ Rafaga 115¹ No factor 10
3Mar76- 7SA sl 1 :47½ 1:11½ 1:38	⑤Clm 30000	4 8 96½ 913 912 817 Martini V⁵	b 109 16.00	62-24 Higher The Fewer 114¹ Flashy Pass 114⁶GreenIndian120½ Outrun 9
29Jan76- 3SA fst 6f :22 1:12	⑤Md Sp Wt	5 4 41½ 32½ 31½ 2nk Martini V⁵	b 112 15.90	77-21 Uh Oh 112½ Our Trudy 117¾ Frosty Halo 117½ Driving 12
6Dec75- 2Lrl fst 6f :22½ :47 1:12½ ⑤Md Sp Wt	9 10 1115¹¹117 920 711 Martini V⁵	112 15.90	73-15 Miss Berta 119¾ Woodlark 119¾ Chairperson 119²½ Outrun 11
LATEST WORKOUTS	Feb 16 Crc 3f sly :37¾ b	Jan 30 Crc 6f fst 1:14½ h	Jan 26 Crc 3f fst :38 bg	Jan 20 Crc 6f fst 1:19 b

Fast Freedom had rallied from twelfth to fifth place in her most recent start, at six furlongs, earning a creditable figure. Now she was entered at a mile and one-sixteenth, and her record indicated that her best performances had been at a route. Even though these credentials were not exactly dazzling, Fast Freedom looked clearly superior to her rivals in this mediocre field.

I was only mildly worried about Linda M. P., who had earned a good figure three races back, and Uh Oh, who had shown promise in her first start of the year. My major concern was Fast Freedom's trainer: Jim Bracken was the man the stewards didn't like. I knew that another outrageous disqualification would put me on the brink of suicide, so I visited Bracken in the paddock before the race and suggested that he tell his jockey to avoid even breathing heavily on the other horses. Then I went to the windows and bet $400 on Fast Freedom at 4 to 1.

Satan's Hen took the early lead along the rail, and Fast Freedom moved alongside to challenge her on the stretch turn. But I was not feeling optimistic, because the favorite Sweet Lizanne was stalking the leaders and looked as if she could blow past them any time her jockey wanted.

Suddenly, Satan's Hen stumbled badly and threw her jockey, setting off a chain reaction of calamities behind her. Sweet Lizanne's jockey had to check so sharply that his feet slipped out of the irons; he finished the race holding on for dear life. Uh Oh's rider pulled her up to avoid disaster, too. Fast Freedom managed to stay clear of the trouble and crossed the finish line a length in front.

Immediately the stewards posted the INQUIRY sign and, feeling as if I had been through all this before, I raced upstairs to the press box to watch the films. And I saw that I could have no quarrel with either the stewards or fate this time. Fast Freedom did not deserve to win; Sweet Lizanne would have beaten her by five lengths in a cleanly run race. Moreover, Fast Freedom deserved to be disqualified. She had angled in toward Satan's Hen, causing her to fall. I knew that the stewards were not going to give Bracken's horse the benefit of any doubts, so I resigned myself to the inevitable. Then I saw the word OFFICIAL light up on the tote board and the payoff $10.60 appear next to Fast Freedom's number.

EIGHTH RACE Gulfstream FEBRUARY 17, 1977

1 1/16 MILES. (1.40⅕) ALLOWANCE. Purse $7,000. Fillies and Mares, 4-year-olds and upward which have not won two races. Weight, 122 lbs. Non-winners of $6,300 allowed 3 lbs. $5,400, 5 lbs. Maidens, 8 lbs. (Winners preferred)

Value of race $7,000, value to winner $4,442, second $1,400, third $700, fourth $350, balance of starters $36 each. Mutuel pool $117,887.

Last Raced	Horse	Eqt.	A.	Wt	PP	St	¼	½	¾	Str	Fin	Jockey	Odds $1
19Jan77 ^{7}GP^5	Fast Freedom	b	4	117	2	7	$3^{1/2}$	$2^{1/2}$	1^{hd}	2^3	1^1	Fieselman J	4.30
8Feb77 ^{6}GP^3	Dungaree Doll		4	117	5	3	$4^{1\frac{1}{2}}$	$4^{1\frac{1}{2}}$	$3^{1/2}$	$1^{1/2}$	2^1	Brumfield D	6.50
8Feb77 ^{6}GP^2	Sweet Lizanne	b	4	119	3	6	5^3	5^1	4^1	$3^{1\frac{1}{2}}$	$3^{3/4}$	Rivera M A	1.00
5Feb77 ^{3}GP^8	Singing Monarch		4	110	6	4	7	7	7	4^2	4^2	Diaz J R^7	49.60
27Jan77 ^{7}GP^5	Linda M. P.		4	112	4	1	2^1	$3^{1/2}$	$6^{1\frac{1}{2}}$	5	5	Harbacek D^5	3.50
8Feb77 ^{6}GP^4	Uh Oh		4	117	7	5	$6^{1\frac{1}{2}}$	6^2	5^2	—	—	Saumell L	7.40
8Feb77 ^{6}GP^7	Satan's Hen		4	117	1	2	1^1	$1^{1\frac{1}{2}}$	$2^{1/2}$	—	—	Manganello M	23.50

Uh Oh, Eased; Satan's Hen, Lost rider.

OFF AT 4:44, EST. Start good, Won driving. Time, :24, :48⅗, 1:14, 1:40⅕, 1:46⅘ Track fast.

$2 Mutuel Prices:			
2-FAST FREEDOM	10.60	5.80	3.20
5-DUNGAREE DOLL		6.40	3.20
3-SWEET LIZANNE			2.60

Ch. f, by Vertex—Freedom At Last, by Needles. Trainer Bracken James. Bred by Meadowbrook Farm Inc (Fla).

FAST FREEDOM raced forwardly gained command approaching head of stretch was bumped by SATAN'S HEN responded when displaced by DUNGAREE DOLL in midstretch regained the advantage in late stages and was clear at the finish. DUNGAREE DOLL well placed rallied along the outside to gain command in midstretch but was outfinished by winner. SWEET LIZANNE well placed along the inside and racing in hand moved out approaching head of stretch was bumped hard by SATAN'S HEN at head of stretch causing rider to lose irons. SWEET LIZANNE raced through stretch on own courage with riders feet out of irons. SINGING MONARCH was forced wide at head of stretch. LINDA M. P. was outrun. UH OH racing behind SATAN'S HEN was taken up sharply coming to head of stretch to avoid fallen rider and was not perservered with through stretch run. SATAN'S HEN set the pace to head of stretch bore out when FAST FREEDOM was abreast to bump that one causing her rider to lose position and then went out into SWEET LIZANNE causing the rider of that one to lose irons.

Owners— 1, Lacroix J W; 2, Hooper F W; 3, Galbreath D M; 4, Shefry Farms; 5, Irish Acres Farm; 6, Bate N; 7, Crimson King Farm.

Trainers— 1, Bracken James; 2, Metcalf Raymond F; 3, Rondinello Thomas L; 4, Moerman Gerald C; 5, Hickey P Noel; 6, Viera Christine; 7, Salmen Peter W Jr.

The gods had begun to even the score for What A Lucky Star's disqualification, and they weren't yet finished for the afternoon. In the ninth race I cashed a $9.40 payoff when the favorite picked an opportune time to go lame. Then in the tenth race I took a flyer on a longshot, Tudor Chief, without knowing that I was betting against a very hot horse. Shortly before post time, Charlie bumped into a New Yorker named Bill, who confided that he had acquired some very reliable information, had just bet $2000 on Rapid Barb, and was going back to the windows for more.

"Didn't you hear that there was a jockey change?" Charlie asked him.

Bill shrugged, "With this horse it doesn't matter. Just as long as it's not Tommy Wallis or Hugo Dittfach."

Charlie clasped his friend's shoulder sympathetically. "Well," he said, "it ain't Dittfach."

Wallis had Rapid Barb eight horses wide on the first turn, rushed to the lead on the backstretch, and practically took a detour into the parking lot as he rounded the final turn. Rapid Barb inevitably weakened after losing so much ground, and Tudor Chief came bounding down the stretch to pay $35.40. I had won nearly $3000 for the day.

In a ten-day period, I had suffered a loss which I didn't deserve, and now had scored a triumph which I didn't deserve. It was like a microcosm of every gambler's life: the good luck and the bad luck offset each other in the long run. Even when we suffer a horrible betting calamity, we should accept it stoically with the knowledge that somewhere, some time—even though it may be years later—we will have a counterbalancing stroke of good fortune. I wished I could have been more philosophical in the immediate aftermath of What A Lucky Star's disqualification, but now I saw that race in perspective, and I felt purged of all my ire and frustration. I was ready to start betting the horses rationally again, and I felt that I was going to start winning again.

I was right. Even though there was still a dearth of solid betting situations at Gulfstream, I was making some inspired moves. One day I left the track early, gave Charlie $100, and asked him to bet a parlay on the favorites in the last three races. I opened the newspaper that night to learn I had hit for $1300. Then on February 21 I made my biggest single score of the meeting on a race which I ordinarily would have passed. It was a classic example of the way a relaxed, self-confident state of mind can pay off at the racetrack.

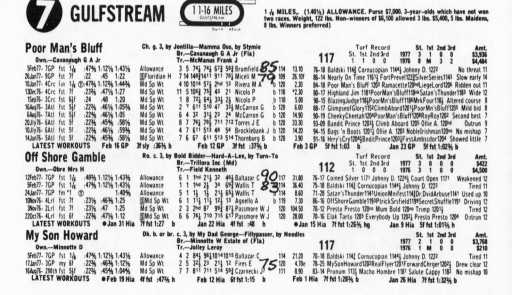

```
Model Sailor          Dk. b. or br. c. 3, by Crewman—I'm Poised, by Ambiopoise                 Turf Record       St. 1st 2nd 3rd     Amt.
                           Br.—Whitacre W J (Ky)                                        117  St. 1st 2nd 3rd  1977  3  0   0   0   $1,274
  Own.—Whitacre W J        Tr.—Picou Clarence E                                               2   0   0   0   1976 11  1   4   1   $9,200
   Entered 19Feb77- 7 GP
 5Feb77- 9GP  fm 1    Ⓣ:47⅖ 1:12⅘ 1:39⅖  Gldn Grass H  9 3 41  41¾121212 15 Breen R  b 114  33.70  58-24 Caviar Kid 1132 Nashua's Song 115¾ Sonny Collins 114¾  Tired 15
28Jan77- 7GP  fm *1 1/16 Ⓣ        1:46  Allowance     4 1 12  12  1hd 47 Breen R     b 117  26.20  70-22 ⒹBig Bearing 117no Sonny Collins 1173½BlazingJudge1173½  Tired 10
19Jan77- 9GP  fst 6f   :22⅕  :46⅕ 1:12⅗  Preview       4 7 41¼ 53¼ 54¼ 57 Breen R     b 112  29.70  69-30 SmshingNtive114nkCheekyCheeth1133½CribePirt111nk  No mishap 7
28Dec76- 9Crc fst 1    :48  1:13⅘ 1:41⅕  Allowance     2 1 11½ 12  13  2½ Cruguet J   b 114   5.00  82-20 Fame International117½ModelSailor114¾Exploratory1041½  Gamely 8
18Dec76- 3Crc fst 6f   :23   :46⅖ 1:12⅘  Allowance     6 1 1hd 2hd 2hd 2hd Barrow T   b 120   8.20  89-14 DeeDee'sRuler120hdModelSilor1201RocketPunch1201  Just missed 8
 9Dec76- 9Crc fst 6f   :22⅖  :45⅗ 1:12⅗  Allowance     5 8 32  42½ 33½ 25 Barrow T    b 120 338.30  85-14 Herecomesthebride1175ModlSilor1202Stn'sPoppy120nk  Game try 12
23Nov76- 7CD  fst 6f   :22   :45⅘ 1:12⅖  Allowance     2 6 1hd 33½ 34  912 Sayler B   b 117  16.60  72-29 Kodiack 1224½ Weque 1171 Satan's Poppy 122no  Tired 11
18Nov76- 7CD  fst 6f   :22   :46  1:12⅖  Allowance     5 5 21½ 21½ 44½ 611 Sayler B   b 115  24.90  73-25 Stonehead 1222½ Tony's Game 1172¾ Marve 1221¼  Tired 10
 2Nov76- 7CD  fst 6f   :22   :45⅘ 1:12⅗  Allowance    10 2 22½ 2hd 54½ 610 Sayler B   b 114   9.70  73-22 Prince Of Mystery 122hd FerDeKing117½CertainGolden1176  Tired 10
13Oct76- 4Kee fst 6f   :22⅕  :44⅘ 1:09⅕  Allowance     4 3 22½ 711 615 622 Sayler B   b 114  33.40  74-11 Stonehead 1145 Bob's Dusty 1154½ Polemicist 1122  No factor 7
   LATEST WORKOUTS   Feb 3 Hia  4f fst :48⅗ b    Jan 13 Hia  5f fst :59⅖ h    Dec 23 Hia  5f fst 1:02⅖ b

Dr. David Arbuse      Dk. b. or br. c. 3, by Finance Minister—Top Brat, by Mamboreta           Turf Record       St. 1st 2nd 3rd     Amt.
                           Br.—Arbuse Mrs (Fla)                                         117  St. 1st 2nd 3rd  1977  4  0   2   1   $3,545
  Own.—Meadow Ridge Stable Tr.—Paley Herb                                                     1   0   0   1   1976 10  1   0   4   $6,170
 5Feb77- 7GP  fst 1 1/16 :47⅘ 1:12⅕ 1:43⅕  Allowance   6 6 52¾ 52¾ 44¼ 47¼ Saumell L    114  12.70  78-18 Baldski 114¾ Cornucopian 1144½ Johnny D. 1222  No mishap 11
24Jan77- 7GP  fm *1   Ⓣ          1:40⅘  Allowance     9 9 85¾ 75½ 52½ 31¾ Saumell L    114   6.30  75-28 Satan'sThunder1141UnionManifest114¾Dr.DvidArbuse1141  Rallied 10
12Jan77- 9Crc fst 6½f  :23   :47⅕ 1:20⅖  Allowance     2 6 54  32  4¾  2½ Saumell L     116   *.60  88-18 CaribePirate120½Dr.DavidArbuse116noNashua'sSong1201½  Gamely 7
 1Jan77- 8Crc fst 6f   :23   :46⅘ 1:12⅗  Allowance     3 7 74½ 63½ 52  2hd Saumell L    116  26.50  90-18 Ruthie'sNtive122hdDr.DvidArbuse116hdTimeForFun1221  Sharp try 8
10Dec76- 8Crc fst 170  :48⅖ 1:13⅖ 1:45⅕  Allowance     7 6 74¾ 77½ 912 99½ Solomone M   117   5.30  79-14 DremingOfMoe114¾WineTresure1172BigBering1093  Showed little 10
25Nov76- 8Crc fst 6½f  :22⅘  :46⅕ 1:20   Allowance     7 3 66½ 55  42½ 31 Rivera M A    116  19.10  90-13 Pete's Hubby 1201 ColonyRuler116hdDr.DavidArbuse116hd  Rallied 9
 6Nov76- 8Mth fst 170  :46⅘ 1:11⅗ 1:41⅕  Middletown   10 10 1112 1113 1114 1117 Gomez M A 114 53.70  75-20 Shady Shay 1181¼ Corre Pronto 1148 Telly Hill 118no  Bore in 11
30Oct76- 5Mth fst 6f   :21⅘  :45⅘ 1:12⅕  Clm 18000     5 2 77¾ 86¼ 26  13½ Solomone M   117 *1.60eⒹ 79-20 ⒹDr.DvidArbuse1173½Sonny'sSupreme1203HiddenJt1171½  Bore in 8
   30Oct76-Disqualified and placed third
16Oct76- 6Mth fst 170  :46⅘ 1:11⅘ 1:42⅗  Allowance     1 3 1hd 47  514 417 Nemeti W     117   9.60  68-20 Corre Pronto 117¾ Plantaris 11711 Don Sebastian 1175  Tired 8
21Sep76- 1Mth fst 6f   :22⅖  :46⅕ 1:11⅗  Md 17000      4 7 64½ 54¾ 42¾ 1½ Solomone M    115   7.90  82-20 Dr. David Arbuse115½DonSebastian118nkChiefAssagai1183  Driving 11
   LATEST WORKOUTS   Feb 17 GP  5f gd 1:01 h    Feb 12 GP  4f fst :49 b    Feb 1 GP  4f fst :48 h    Jan 10 GP  4f fst :49 b

Stutsmanville         B. g. 3, by Grand Central—Forelass, by Miss Guide                        Turf Record       St. 1st 2nd 3rd     Amt.
                           Br.—Polk A F (Ohio)                                          117  St. 1st 2nd 3rd  1977  3  1   1   0   $4,884
  Own.—Polk A F            Tr.—Gomez Frank                                                    1   0   0   0   1976  0  M   0   0
 2Feb77- 4GP  fst 1 1/16 :48⅕ 1:13⅘ 1:45⅕  Md 30000    9 4 43½ 21  13  13½ Vasquez J  b 120  *1.30  75-14 Stutsmnville1203½Tieyellowribbon1172NevrGuilty1176  Ridden out 11
27Jan77- 3GP  fm *1 1/16 Ⓣ       1:47⅖  Md Sp Wt      6 4 45½ 43  55½ 57½ Brumfield D   120   3.60  62-24 That's A Nice 1153½ Silver Greek 1201½ OvertheBridge120no  Tired 10
14Jan77- 3Crc fst 6½f  :23⅘  :47⅖ 1:19⅗  Md Sp Wt     1 10 95¾ 88¼ 53  21½ Brumfield D  120 *2.40e  91-13 Time Call 1201½ Stutsmanville 1203 Gun Blast 1202  Best others 10
   LATEST WORKOUTS   Feb 18 Crc  5f fst 1:07⅖ b    Jan 31 Crc  3f fst :39⅖ bg    Jan 20 Crc  4f fst :52 b    Jan 10 Crc  4f fst :50⅘ bg

Full of Royalty       Dk. b. or br. c. 3, by Native Royalty—Beanery, by Cavan                                    St. 1st 2nd 3rd     Amt.
                           Br.—Carolaine Farm & Thomas (Ky)                             117               1977  1  1   0   0   $4,103
  Own.—Guthrie Thomas A    Tr.—Conway James P                                                             1976  5  M   0   0
 1Feb77- 6GP  fst 1 1/16 :47⅘ 1:12⅘ 1:44⅗  Md Sp Wt    3 2 2½  1½  12  12 MacBeth D     120  46.60  78-21 Full of Royalty 1202 Silver Greek 1208½ Wellspoken 120nk  Driving 11
11Dec76- 4Aqu fst 6f  ⊡:23⅖  :47⅖ 1:12⅕  Md Sp Wt      4 1 2½  34½ 59  510 Martens G    122  22.80   —.— Coffee 1222¼ Johnny D. 1224¾ Portraiture 1221¼  Weakened 7
27Nov76- 3Aqu fst 7f   :23   :46⅕ 1:23⅘  Md Sp Wt      7 3 52¼ 42¼ 68¾ 610 Castaneda M  122  38.80  72-14 Hasty Spring 122¾ Caribert 1221 Pumpkin Moonshine 122½  Tired 8
23Nov76- 5Aqu fst 6f   :22⅘  :47⅕ 1:11⅘  Md Sp Wt      1 7 79½ 712 611 613 Turcotte R   122  16.20  71-21 ⒹForecst122nkDelWithStrength1225¾BoldPltt1221¾  Swerved start 9
15Jly76- 4Aqu fst 5½f  :22⅘  :47⅕ 1:05⅘  Md Sp Wt     11 7 32  42  810 913 Turcotte R   122  30.70  71-22 Turn of Coin 122nk Red Rolfe 117hd Highland Light 1224½  Tired 12
30Jun76- 4Aqu fst 5½f  :22⅕  :45⅖ 1:03⅗  Md Sp Wt      8 6 42  79  718 820 Turcotte R   122   7.80  75-10 IronConstitution122¾BroadwayForli1225¾HighlndLight1222¼  Tired 8
   LATEST WORKOUTS   Feb 16 GP  4f sly :49 b    Feb 10 GP  5f fst 1:02 b

Rocket Punch          B. c. 3, by Reflected Glory—Stew Zoo, by Sunrise Flight                  Turf Record       St. 1st 2nd 3rd     Amt.
                           Br.—Clark & Jones (Ky)                                       117  St. 1st 2nd 3rd  1977  3  0   0   1   $722
  Own.—Reineman R L Stable Inc Tr.—Bollero Joseph M                                           1   0   0   0   1976  6  1   2   3   $8,940
10Feb77- 6GP  fst 6f   :22⅖  :45⅗ 1:10⅖  Allowance     4 3 3nk 3nk 2hd 32¼ Rivera M A   117  15.10  85-21 BlndDistinctiv117¾Brch'sHlrous1171½RocktPunch117nk  Weakened 9
28Jan77- 7GP  fm *1 1/16 Ⓣ        1:46  Allowance     9 5 55  53  74¼ 59½ Wallis T     117  22.00  67-22 ⒹBig Bearing 117noSonnyCollins1173½BlazingJudge1173½  No rally 10
21Jan77- 8GP  fst 6f   :22⅖  :46  1:11⅗  Allowance     3 6 42½ 54½ 54½ 55 Fires E      114● *2.10e  76-29 IronConstitution1141Brch'sHilrious1152BeGllnt1141  Lacked rally 9
   21Jan77-Dead heat
18Dec76- 3Crc fst 6f   :23   :46⅖ 1:12⅘  Allowance     1 8 34  33  31½ 31 Anderson J R  120   3.10  88-14 Dee Dee's Ruler 120hd Model Sailor1201RocketPunch1201  Rallied 8
28Oct76- 5Kee fst 6f   :22⅕  :45⅖ 1:11   Allowance     3 9 53½ 63¾ 21½ 31 Brumfield D   118 *1.50e  86-21 Marve 113hd Governor's Pardon 1121 Rocket Punch 1181  Hung 9
16Oct76- 5Kee fst 6f   :21⅘  :44⅘ 1:10⅕  Allowance     6 4 53½ 31½ 32  36½ Gavidia W    118   3.50  84-13 SwoonSwept1126Governor'sPardon112½RocketPunch1182  Rallied 7
16Sep76- 4AP  fst 6f   :22⅗  :46⅗ 1:12⅕  Md Sp Wt      3 6 3½  3nk 1hd 1½ Fires E       120   2.20  82-18 Rocket Punch 120½ Barely Safe 1202½ Solo Singer 120½  Driving 9
 8Sep76- 1AP  fst 6f   :22⅕  :45⅗ 1:12   Md Sp Wt     10 3 53  32  32½ 21¼ Patterson G  120  *1.00  82-12 Lightning Barb 1201¼ Rocket Punch 120hd Dravir 120¾  Gamely 10
19Aug76- 1AP  fst 6f   :21⅘  :45  1:10⅖  Md 25000      8 6 53¾ 34  35  22 Snyder L      119  10.70  89-13 Brach's Honey 1192 Rocket Punch1194SocietyScion119hd  Gamely 10
   LATEST WORKOUTS   Feb 18 GP  5f fst 1:03⅗ b    Feb 9 GP  3f gd :36 b    Feb 5 GP  4f fst :49⅖ b    Jan 27 GP  3f fst :36⅖ b

True Statement        Ch. c. 3, by Nodouble—Specious, by Prince John                                             St. 1st 2nd 3rd     Amt.
                           Br.—Elmendorf Farm (Ky)                                      117               1977  1  1   0   0   $4,074
  Own.—Elmendorf           Tr.—Weipert John J                                                             1976  0  M   0   0
 8Feb77- 3GP  fst 1 1/16 :47⅕ 1:12⅖ 1:43⅗  Md Sp Wt    5 8 712 45½ 2½  13½ Rivera M A   120   3.70  83-19 True Statement 1203½ Silver Greek 1205 Xmas Box 1206  Handily 10
   LATEST WORKOUTS   Feb 18 GP  3f fst :36 b    Feb 14 GP  3f fst :36 b    Feb 7 GP  3f fst :36 b    Jan 26 GP  4f fst :49 b
```

True Statement was a standout according to the figures, but I thought his 2-to-5 odds were unrealistically low. By now, of course, I was skeptical of just about any animal Jack Weipert put on the track. And I thought the track might hinder this one's chances. For most of the season, Gulfstream had a slight bias in favor of speed horses. On February 21 the bias seemed especially strong; horses had to get a position near the lead and near the rail in order to win. True Statement would have to break from the outside post and try to rally from far behind.

Usually I would abstain from playing such a race; I couldn't bet on or against True Statement. But with my self-confidence and my profits at a high level, I was feeling loose and aggressive enough to take a shot for a big payoff. I saw three horses who figured to show early speed and get a good position. Rocket Punch looked like the quickest of them all. He had battled good sprinters head-and-head in his most recent start, running the first half-mile in a swift 45⅗ seconds. Off Shore Gamble and Model Sailor were breaking from favorable post positions—two and four—and they always showed good early speed. I eliminated Full of Royalty, even though his figure was competitive, because he seemed not to have as much early speed as the others. I took a $20 box on Off Shore Gamble, Model Sailor, and Rocket Punch, investing a total of $120 in the race. I knew this was a stab I would never take if I were feeling prudent, but I also knew that I would probably have longshots running one-two-three when the field turned into the stretch. On a speed-favoring track, that was a pleasant prospect.

SEVENTH RACE
Gulfstream
FEBRUARY 21, 1977

1 1/16 MILES. (1.40⅕) ALLOWANCE. Purse $7,000. 3–year–olds which have not won two races. Weight. 122 lbs. Non–winners of $6,100 allowed 3 lbs. $5,400, 5 lbs. Maidens, 8 lbs. Winners preferred)

Value of race $7,000, value to winner $4,370, second $1,400, third $700, fourth $350, balance of starters $36 each. Mutuel pool $113,624. Perfecta Pool $146,515.

Last Raced	Horse	Eqt.	A.	Wt	PP	St	¼	½	¾	Str	Fin	Jockey	Odds $1
12Feb77 ^{7}GP^4	Off Shore Gamble		3	117	2	1	$5^{1\frac{1}{2}}$	5^2	$4^{\frac{1}{2}}$	2^{hd}	1^3	Cruguet J	13.90
10Feb77 ^{6}GP^3	Rocket Punch		3	117	8	6	3^3	3^6	2^3	3^3	2^{hd}	Saumell L	22.40
5Feb77 ^{9}GP^{12}	Model Sailor	b	3	117	4	4	$1^{1\frac{1}{2}}$	$1^{1\frac{1}{2}}$	$1^{1\frac{1}{2}}$	$1^{\frac{1}{2}}$	3^1	Brumfield D	20.80
5Feb77 ^{7}GP^5	Poor Man's Bluff	b	3	117	1	2	$8^{1\frac{1}{2}}$	6^{hd}	6^{hd}	5^1	$4^{3\frac{1}{2}}$	Miceli M	19.90
5Feb77 ^{7}GP^{10}	My Son Howard		3	117	3	3	4^{hd}	4^{hd}	5^2	6^2	5^1	Fires E	42.80
2Feb77 ^{4}GP^1	Stutsmanville	b	3	117	6	7	$7^{\frac{1}{2}}$	$7^{\frac{1}{2}}$	7^2	$4^{\frac{1}{2}}$	$6^{2\frac{1}{2}}$	Vasquez J	12.50
8Feb77 ^{3}GP^1	True Statement		3	117	9	8	6^{hd}	$8^{1\frac{1}{2}}$	8^3	7^4	7^5	Rivera M A	.40
5Feb77 ^{7}GP^4	Dr. David Arbuse		3	117	5	5	$2^{1\frac{1}{2}}$	2^1	3^1	8^3	$8^{\frac{3}{4}}$	Solomone M	7.30
1Feb77 ^{6}GP^1	Full of Royalty	b	3	117	7	9	9	9	9	9	9	MacBeth D	7.60

OFF AT 4:13 EST. Start good, Won ridden out. Time, :23⅘, :47, 1:11⅖, 1:37⅖, 1:44 Track fast.

$2 Mutuel Prices:			
2–OFF SHORE GAMBLE	29.80	20.40	9.00
8–ROCKET PUNCH		21.00	11.80
4–MODEL SAILOR			11.40

$2 PERFECTA 2–8 PAID $382.80.

Ro. c, by Bold Bidder—Hard–A–Lee, by Turn–To. Trainer Field Kenneth. Bred by Trillora Inc (Md).

OFF SHORE GAMBLE raced forwardly, rallied along the inside in the drive, gained command inside the final ighth and drew out. ROCKET PUNCH well-placed, reached the attending position on the second turn, could ot run with the winner in the final sixteenth, but outfinished the others. MODEL SAILOR set the pace to inside he final eighth and continued on well when displaced. POOR MAN'S BLUFF was improving position at the inish. TRUE STATEMENT in hand early, failed to respond to pressure. DR. DAVID ARBUSE steadily fell back fter a half. FULL OF ROYALTY showed little.

Owners— 1, Obre Mrs H; 2, Reineman R L Stable Inc; 3, Whitacre W J; 4, Cavanaugh G A Jr; 5, Minnotte 6, Polk A F; 7, Elmendorf; 8, Meadow Ridge Stable; 9, Guthrie Thomas A.

Trainers— 1, Field Kenneth; 2, Bollero Joseph M; 3, Picou Clarence E; 4, McManus Frank J; 5, Jolley eroy; 6, Gomez Frank; 7, Weipert John J; 8, Paley Herb; 9, Conway James P.

Corrected weight: Off Shore Gamble 117 pounds.

Scratched—Capitanus (4Feb77 ^{3}GP^4); Gordon Pasha (3Feb77 ^{6}GP^2); America Behave (5Feb77 ^{7}GP^7).

When Off Shore Gamble won and Rocket Punch ran second, I collected $3828 and saw my profits for the meeting climb into five figures. But as good as this guesswork had been, it was only a prelude to February 25.

Every gambler experiences a few days when a benevolent higher power seems to be controlling his destiny: he makes an incredible string of passes at the craps table; he catches inside straights whenever he needs them to win a poker hand; he picks all the right horses and wins all the photo finishes. I had no forewarning that February 25 was going to be one of those days.

I went to Gulfstream with a strong conviction about only one horse, Royal Graustark in the eighth race, and a few marginal opinions. In fact, the horse I liked in the second race was so marginal that when I told Charlie about him, I had to preface my analysis by saying, "I know this is ridiculous, but . . ."

Big Coach — B. g. 3, by Mr Leader—Mick B Quick, by Hasty Road
Own.—Blum Peter E — **$6,000** — Br.—Headley Mrs G (Ky) — Tr.—Jerkens Steven T — **112**

	St.	1st	2nd	3rd	Amt.
1977	1	M	0	0	$36
1976	2	M	0	0	

27Jan77- 1GP	fst	7f	:22	:45⅕	1:24	Clm 5000	7	10	12^10	12^16	9^12	8^13	Gustines H	52	b	116	11.70	71-15	Certainty 116^10 Storm Lake Man 116^2 HastaLarista116½	No factor 12
9Oct76- 4Bel	sly	6½f	:23	:48	1:21⅗	Md 18000	7	13	13^22	13^26	13^26	—	Gustines H		b	122	33.60	— —	Ray's Trouble 118¾ Wendy's Andy 122^3 Chairman Ox 122¾	Eased 13
22Sep76- 5Bel	fst	6½f	:23⅕	:46⅗	1:18⅘	Md 25000	9	9	7^10	8^15	7^17	7^17	Gustines H		b	122	16.80	65-17	Picture Show 122¾ Delta Mike 115^1¼ KennyKnows122^1¼	No factor 9

LATEST WORKOUTS Feb 24 Hia 3f fst :36 b — Feb 14 Hia 3f fst :37 b — Jan 26 Hia 3f fst :36⅗ hg — Jan 22 Hia 4f fst :50⅖ b

Big Coach had a dismal set of past performances, but his thirteen-length defeat in his only recent race was not as bad as it looked. The winner had scored by ten lengths in very fast time; Big Coach had finished only three lengths behind the runnerup. And he had earned a semirespectable figure of 52, which was only 8 points (or about five lengths) behind the top horse in today's field.

Speed handicappers hold varying views about figures a horse earns while he is being outrun. Some maintain they are utterly meaningless. This is indisputably true in harness racing: a pacer who could never go a mile in 2:04 on his own can do it while trailing a champ who runs in 1:59. But I have always had a personal weakness for thoroughbreds like Big Coach. I had to assume that his jockey was not pressuring him when he was hopelessly beaten, and that he would probably run better if he ever found himself in contention. Furthermore, I thought that since he had rallied from twelfth to eighth place in his last start, he might prefer today's longer distance of a mile and one-sixteenth.

Charlie politely restrained himself from laughing while he listened to my discourse on this absurd animal. But a few minutes later, he made an observation which had escaped me. He had looked at the probable daily-double payoffs and he said, "You know, that horse of yours is alive." Big Coach should have been paying astronomical prices in the double, but he was not. Somebody was betting him. And this was the kind of situation in which betting action can be very meaningful. Had I stumbled onto a good thing?

I invested $100 in the daily double, combining Big Coach with three horses in the first race. Baybaytim, a 3-to-1 shot who had my top figure, led until midstretch, was passed by two horses, and miraculously came on again in the final yards to win a tight three-way photo finish. Now I was alive with a $40 bet on a daily-double combination worth $164.60.

Big Coach went off at the remarkably short price of 11 to 1. He stalked the leaders, Pride King and Feather's First, all the way around the track, and challenged them as he turned into the stretch. The leaders shook him off, drawing away from him by more than a length, and I gave up hope, because cheap horses almost never make two separate moves in a race. But jockey Heliodoro Gustines wasn't giving up. He was riding as if he were aboard Forego in the Jockey Club Gold Cup, or at least as if he had bet his bankroll at 11 to 1. Under Gustines's frantic urging, Big Coach surged back at the leaders and they hit the finish line almost simultaneously. Could I possibly win another three-horse photo finish? On this day I could. Big Coach's nose brought me a return of $3292.

In the third race I bet $300 on Minnie Ripperton, a standout on the figures. She won by six lengths and paid $4.60. In the fourth race I lacked a strong opinion and so used the shotgun approach, boxing my top four figures in the exacta. I hit for a few hundred more dollars. I lost a token $50 bet on the fifth race and passed the sixth.

A filly named Casual Acquaintance was a standout in the seventh race, a $1\frac{1}{16}$-mile event on the grass, and she was justifiably favored at 4 to 5. I wanted to take a shot at the exacta, but the rest of the horses looked inscrutable until I remembered something about one of them.

Uh Oh — B. f. 4, by T V Commercial—True, by Bold Bidder
Own.—Bate N — Br.—Bate N P (Md) — Tr.—Viera Christine — **117**

	St.	1st	2nd	3rd	Amt.
1977	2	0	0	0	$386
1976	6	1	0	0	$4,135

17Feb77- 8GP	fst	$1\frac{1}{16}$	:48⅗	1:14	1:46⅘	ⒻAllowance	7	6	6^{5}	5^{2}	—	—	Saumell L		117	7.40	— —	Fast Freedom 117^{1} Dungaree Doll 117^{1} Sweet Lizanne $119^{\frac{3}{4}}$	Eased 7
8Feb77- 6GP	fst	$1\frac{1}{16}$	:48⅗	1:13⅗	1:44	ⒻAllowance	7	1	1^{hd}	3^{nk}	3^{5}	4^{12}	Lopez R D		114	10.30	69–19	Klassy Reason 114^{8} Sweet Lizanne $119^{1\frac{1}{2}}$ DungareeDoll114^{2}	Tired 9
20Jly76- 9AP	fst	6f	:22⅕	:45⅘	1:11⅗	ⒻClm 16500	3	10	10^{11}	$10^{7\frac{1}{4}}$	6^{6}	$6^{1\frac{3}{4}}$	Viera H		114	9.90	83–16	Shelly's Star 112^{nk} Zippy Dream 114^{nk}PagoFlyer117^{nk}	Stride late 10
4Jun76- 2Hol	fst	$6\frac{1}{2}$f	:22	:45	1:17⅕	ⒻClm 16000	8	12	$11^{8\frac{1}{4}}$	$10^{5\frac{1}{4}}$	5^{3}	$4^{3\frac{1}{2}}$	Pierce D		116	37.70	80–12	MyLittleMargie116^{3}CactusValleyRose120^{no}BylineGirl$116^{\frac{1}{2}}$	Rallied 12
21May76- 1Hol	fst	6f	:22	:45⅕	1:11⅖	ⒻClm 20000	1	11	11^{14}	11^{13}	10^{10}	$10^{7\frac{3}{4}}$	Martini V^{5}	b	111	36.50	74–17	Never Promised 111^{2} Sing Back116^{1}ThirteenthHope116^{hd}	Outrun 11
26Mar76- 2SA	fst	$1\frac{1}{16}$	:47⅖	1:11⅗	1:44⅘	ⒻClm 25000	5	9	$8^{5\frac{3}{4}}$	$8^{9\frac{1}{4}}$	$7^{7\frac{1}{2}}$	$8^{9\frac{1}{4}}$	Martini V^{5}	b	111	21.00	69–18	Silver Slip 116^{6} Gaelic Envoy 116^{1} Rafaga 115^{1}	No factor 9
3Mar76- 7SA	sl	1	:47⅕	1:11⅘	1:38	ⒻAllowance	4	8	$9^{6\frac{1}{2}}$	9^{13}	9^{12}	8^{17}	Martini V^{5}	b	109	16.00	62–24	Higher The Fewer 114^{1} Flashy Pass 114^{8}GreenIndian$120^{\frac{1}{2}}$	Outrun 9
29Jan76- 3SA	fst	6f	:22⅕	:46	1:12⅖	ⒻMd 20000	3	12	12^{20}	11^{12}	$5^{5\frac{1}{2}}$	$1^{\frac{1}{2}}$	Martini V^{5}	b	112	36.70	77–21	Uh Oh $112^{\frac{1}{2}}$ Our Trudy $117^{\frac{1}{2}}$ Frosty Halo $117^{\frac{1}{2}}$	Driving 12
6Dec75- 2Lrl	fst	6f	:22⅗	:47	1:12⅗	ⒻMd Sp Wt	9	10	11^{15}	11^{17}	9^{20}	7^{11}	Martini V^{7}		112	15.90	73–15	Miss Berta $119^{\frac{1}{2}}$ Woodlark 119^{3} Chairperson $119^{3\frac{1}{2}}$	Outrun 11

LATEST WORKOUTS — Feb 16 Crc 3f sly :37⅘ b — Jan 30 Crc 6f fst 1:14⅗ h — Jan 26 Crc 3f fst :38 bg — Jan 20 Crc 6f fst 1:19 b

Uh Oh's past performances demonstrate the importance of watching races or at least maintaining a set of result charts. The filly had run creditably on February 8, her first race after an eight-month layoff. She figured to improve in her next start, which happened to be the race in which I undeservingly cashed a bet on Fast Freedom. Uh Oh had been lying within striking distance until her jockey had to pull her up to avoid a disaster. But the past-performance line offered no hint of the trouble which had prevented Uh Oh from finishing the race; it merely said, "Eased." As a result, she was ignored at 16 to 1. I could not be positive that she was the second-best filly in the race, but she was certainly the best value, and so I bet a $60 exacta on Casual Acquaintance and Uh Oh. They ran one-two, beating the rest of the field by six lengths and returning an exacta of $56.60. I was winning more than $5000, and my favorite horse of the day was yet to come.

Fast Invader — Ch. f. 3, by Night Invader—Red Jess, by Red Hannigan
Br.—Farnsworth Farm (Fla)
Own.—Korhumel N F — Tr.—Viera Christine — **117**

	St.	1st	2nd	3rd	Amt.
1976	6	1	1	0	$6,320

13Sep76- 5AP fst 6f :22⅕ :45⅕ 1:10⅗ ⒻAllowance 3 5 3½ 31 44½ 78¼ Rubbicco P b 117 10.90 82-12 Whats Good 1202¼ Casaro Doll 120nk Proper Princess 107nk Tired 9
13Aug76- 7AP fst 6f :22⅗ :46⅖ 1:11⅘ ⒻAllowance 4 4 2hd 1hd 2½ 43 Viera H b 120 5.40 81-19 FadedLdy1202LeFormidble115¾Mkejoyfulnoise117nk Speed, tired 7
6Aug76- 7AP gd 6f :23⅕ :47⅖ 1:12⅗ ⒻAllowance 1 4 21½ 2hd 1hd 54 Viera H 120 3.10 76-19 My BoldBeauty1153FreeDate112¾TemperedTuff120nk Speed, tired 8
24Jly76- 3AP fst 5½f :22 :46 1:05⅗ ⒻMd Sp Wt 7 3 22 13 12½ 1nk Viera H 118 *1.00 87-13 Fast Invader 118nk Appetizer 118no Luna Moon 1183½ Lasted 8
2Jly76- 8AP fst 5½f :22 :45⅗ 1:04⅖ ⒻLa Petite 2 4 41 54½ 48 713 Viera H 114 23.10 80-13 Miss Cigarette 1225FancyGambler115nkDon'tCryBarbi1172¼ Tired 11
26Jun76- 1AP fst 5½f :22 :45⅘ 1:05⅕ ⒻMd Sp Wt 8 5 21½ 1½ 1hd 22 Viera H 118 7.70 87-10 Southern Date 1182FastInvader1182FadedLady1131¾ Second best 9
LATEST WORKOUTS Feb 23 Crc 3f fst :39 bg Feb 18 Crc 5f fst 1:06 b Feb 12 Crc 5f fst 1:07 b Feb 4 Crc 4f fst :51 b

Bold Dell — Ch. f. 3, by Bold Reason—Seadell, by Sea-Bird
Br.—Schiff J M (Fla)
Own.—Schiff J M — Tr.—Kelly Thomas J — **119**

	St.	1st	2nd	3rd	Amt.
1977	1	0	0	0	$375
1976	3	1	0	1	$6,600

14Feb77- 8GP sly 7f :22⅘ :45⅘ 1:23 ⒻAllowance 3 6 22 32 46 411 Solomone M 76 115 4.60 78-16 Grand Luxe 1144½ Nice and Warm 1143 Swanky Lady 1143 Tired 7
28Aug76- 6Sar gd 6f :21⅘ :45⅕ 1:11⅕ ⒻAllowance 6 6 65¼ 67½ 65¼ 55¼ Maple E 66 114 4.40 79-12 Little Happiness 119nk Resolver 114no Allow Princess1145 Outrun 6
10Aug76- 6Sar sly 6f :21⅘ :45⅘ 1:12⅕ ⒻAllowance 1 6 35 34½ 33½ 32¾ Maple E 77 116 3.50 76-22 Trim The Sail 1131¼ Autumn Weather1131½BoldDell1161¼ No rally 7
14Jly76- 4Aqu fst 5½f :22⅘ :47⅕ 1:06⅘ ⒻMd Sp Wt 7 7 68 69½ 44½ 1½ Maple E 119 8.80 79-22 Bold Dell 119½ Spy Flag 119¾ Disturber 119½ Driving 8
LATEST WORKOUTS Feb 20 Hia 5f fst 1:01 h Feb 7 Hia 3f fst :36⅗ bg ●Feb 2 Hia 5f fst 1:00 h Jan 23 Hia 6f fst 1:14⅖ h

Lady Lt. — B. f. 3, by Lt Stevens—Belthazar, by War Admiral
Br.—Madden Preston (Ky)
Own.—Madden Preston — Tr.—Stevens Thomas H Sr — **117**

	St.	1st	2nd	3rd	Amt.
1976	5	1	0	1	$4,825

26Nov76- 8CD sly 7f :24⅕ :47⅗ 1:27 ⒻPocahontas 8 4 63½ 66½ 714 711 McKnight J b 115 19.10 61-39 Ciao 121nk Shady Lou 1213¼ Every Move 1122 No factor 9
17Nov76- 8CD fst 7f :23⅕ :46⅘ 1:26⅖ ⒻAllowance 7 8 79½ 65 66 66¼ McKnight J b 113 9.30 69-30 Chatta 1081½ Flying Cindy 1192¾ Blowfish 1191¾ No factor 10
6Nov76- 5CD fst 6f :21⅘ :46⅖ 1:13⅘ ⒻMd Sp Wt 6 5 35½ 33½ 2½ 12¼ McKnight J b 119 2.60 77-25 Lady Lt. 1192¼ Two Dusty 119¾ Spontaneous 1191¾ Driving 11
22Oct76- 5Kee fst 7f :23⅖ :47⅕ 1:26⅘ ⒻMd Sp Wt 5 3 42 52¼ 44½ 31½ McKnight J 119 4.80 70-20 Rock Fever 119hd Dream O' Loot 1191½ Lady Lt. 1191 Rallied 12
9Oct76- 3Kee sly 7f :23⅖ :46⅗ 1:26⅘ ⒻMd Sp Wt 6 8 912 917 813 77 McKnight J 120 4.20 65-19 SparklingDust1201½LuckyThirtyThree1203RitaMenke117hd Outrun 11
LATEST WORKOUTS Feb 23 Hia 4f fst :48⅖ h Feb 21 Hia 3f fst :37 bg Feb 10 Hia 6f fst 1:14⅗ h Feb 7 Hia 3f fst :36⅗ bg

Royal Graustark — Ch. f. 3, by Graustark—Princess Roycraft, by Royal Note
Br.—Franklyn Stable (Fla)
Own.—Franlyn Stable — Tr.—Trotsek Harry — **117**

	St.	1st	2nd	3rd	Amt.
1977	1	1	0	0	$3,732
1976	1	M	0	0	

16Feb77- 5GP my 6f :22⅘ :46⅖ 1:11⅖ ⒻMd Sp Wt 6 6 31 21½ 2hd 11 Arroyo H 98 119 4.80 82-24 RoyalGraustark1191CumLaudeLaurie1193½Banrullah1192½ Driving 12
20Nov76- 4CD fst 6f :22⅘ :46⅗ 1:13⅗ ⒻMd Sp Wt 8 8 51½ 77 68 67½ Arroyo H 119 2.50 70-24 RitMenke1193Sysomethingcindy119nkWltzMeSue1191¾ No factor 12
LATEST WORKOUTS Feb 23 GP 3f fst :38⅗ b Feb 13 GP 5f fst 1:03⅖ b Feb 9 GP 3f gd :37 b Feb 3 GP 6f fst 1:18⅗ b

Royal Graustark had won her only start at Gulfstream, running six furlongs in 1:11⅖. Her time might not look impressive, but it was in fact sensational, because she had been competing on one of the slowest tracks of the season. On the same afternoon, a filly named Bronze Point scored her fourth consecutive stakes victory while covering the distance in 1:11⅘. In an allowance race that day, the stakes-class filly Free Journey ran in 1:12⅗. Royal Graustark's time looked almost too good to be true.

I wondered if her fast time might have been due to some freaky track conditions. I have seen rainy days at Belmont Park when the track becomes extraordinarily fast for one or two races, and a group of horses who ought to run in 1:11 record a clocking of 1:10 instead. They beguile the speed handicappers, but when they make their next starts they all run in the 1:11 range again. If Royal Graustark had won by ten lengths, I could easily believe that she had run an extraordinary race. But she had scored by only a length, and it seemed implausible that there would be more than one stakes-class filly in the same maiden race.

When I went to the track, I was not entirely convinced that Royal Graustark's big figure was true. But I had the opportunity to get some important evidence before she ran. The filly who had finished fourth behind Royal Graustark, beaten seven lengths, was Minnie Ripperton. She was entered in the third race, and if the time of her previous performance was really as good as it looked, she figured to demolish her opposition. When she won by six lengths, I knew that Royal Graustark was indeed an exceptional animal.

I had one other reservation. Royal Graustark had earned her figure in the mud, and some horses only run their best on a wet track. She could have been a female Cinteelo. But I thought there was evidence to the contrary. Royal Graustark had gone off at 5-to-2 odds in her racing debut at Churchill Downs, and had been 9 to 2 in her first appearance at Gulfstream, prices which were undoubtedly the result of stable betting. Obviously, her trainer had seen signs of ability in the filly long before she ever competed on a muddy track.

Royal Graustark's closest competition was Banrullah, whom she had already beaten by 4½ lengths. She had an edge of 22 points (nine lengths) over Bold Dell and 32 points (thirteen lengths) over Royal Dux. Yet the crowd at Gulfstream did not recognize her vast superiority, and was letting her go to the post as a tepid 2-to-1 favorite. She deserved my biggest wager of the meeting, and I was delighted to be in a financial position that permitted me to make it. I bet $1200 to win.

EIGHTH RACE
Gulfstream
FEBRUARY 25, 1977

6 FURLONGS. (1.07⅘) ALLOWANCE. Purse $7,000. Fillies, 3-year-olds which have not won two races. Weight, 122 lbs. Non-winners of $6,300 allowed 3 lbs. $5,400, 5 lbs. Maidens, 8 lbs. (Winners preferred)

Value of race $7,000, value to winner $4,370, second $1,400, third $700, fourth $350, balance of starters $36 each. Mutuel pool $138,062.

Last Raced	Horse	Eqt.	A.	Wt	PP	St	¼	½	Str	Fin	Jockey	Odds $1
16Feb77 ^{5}GP^{1}	Royal Graustark		3	117	9	1	2^{2}	2^{4}	$1^{\frac{1}{2}}$	1^{3}	Arroyo H	2.10
18Feb77 ^{8}GP^{3}	Royal Dux		3	117	4	5	1^{hd}	1^{1}	2^{3}	$2^{1\frac{1}{2}}$	Vasquez J	2.40
18Feb77 ^{8}GP^{5}	Luna Moon	b	3	117	1	8	6^{hd}	4^{3}	$3^{1\frac{1}{2}}$	$3^{\frac{3}{4}}$	Gavidia W	13.60
18Feb77 ^{8}GP^{4}	Wanton Woman		3	117	5	3	3^{2}	3^{hd}	4^{4}	4^{5}	Brumfield D	7.50
16Feb77 ^{5}GP^{3}	Banrullah		3	114	3	6	$7^{\frac{1}{2}}$	$5^{\frac{1}{2}}$	5^{hd}	5^{hd}	Fell J	a-12.30
26Nov76 ^{8}CD^{7}	Lady Lt.	b	3	117	8	7	$4^{\frac{1}{2}}$	6^{2}	$6^{1\frac{1}{2}}$	6^{3}	Fires E	23.10
14Feb77 ^{8}GP^{4}	Bold Dell		3	119	7	2	8^{3}	8^{2}	8^{2}	$7^{1\frac{1}{2}}$	Solomone M	2.70
13Sep76 ^{5}AP^{7}	Fast Invader		3	117	6	4	5^{hd}	$7^{\frac{1}{2}}$	7^{2}	$8^{1\frac{1}{2}}$	Lopez R D	27.00
31Jan77 ^{9}GP^{10}	Affectionate One	b	3	114	2	9	9	9	9	9	Thornburg B	a-12.30

a-Coupled: Banrullah and Affectionate One.

OFF AT 4:28 EST Start good, Won ridden out. Time, :22⅖, :45⅖, 1:10⅖ Track fast.

$2 Mutuel Prices:				
	9-ROYAL GRAUSTARK	6.20	3.80	2.80
	3-ROYAL DUX		4.20	3.20
	2-LUNA MOON			4.80

Ch. f, by Graustark—Princess Roycraft, by Royal Note. Trainer Trotsek Harry. Bred by Franklyn Stable (Fla).

ROYAL GRAUSTARK vied for command along the backstretch was unhurried when outrun on turn gained advantage in midstretch and steadily increased margin. ROYAL DUX set pace to midstretch then could not run with winners in final sixteenth. LUNA MOON outfinished others. WANTON WOMAN lacked a stretch response. BOLD DELL was outrun.

Owners— 1, Franlyn Stable; 2, Briardale Farm; 3, Benjamin C; 4, Green Mrs Robert; 5, Mangurian H T Jr; 6, Madden Preston; 7, Schiff J M; 8, Korhumel N F; 9, Mangurian H T Jr.

Trainers— 1, Trotsek Harry; 2, Armstrong Kenneth D; 3, Kelley Thomas W; 4, Poole George T III; 5, Root Thomas F Sr; 6, Stevens Thomas H Sr; 7, Kelly Thomas J; 8, Viera Christine; 9, Root Thomas F Sr.

Royal Graustark won with authority, and even though I lost the next two races, I finished the afternoon with a profit of $7300. But instead of feeling invincible, I suspected that I had reached my high-water mark for the Florida season. An 0-for-10 performance the next day strengthened that impression. If I believed that I had mastered handicapping at Gulfstream, or if I were cashing one or two bets a week on solid horses like Royal Graustark, I would have extended my stay in Miami indefinitely. But I was winning with helter-skelter stabbing, and that is a rather fragile basis for consistent success at the track. I hit winners like Big Coach and Off Shore Gamble only when I am extraordinarily sharp (and lucky), and I doubted that I could stay sharp much longer. After six weeks of intensive, nonstop gambling, I was weary; handicapping can be physically as well as mentally exhausting. I was ready to return to Washington and rest before my assault on Pimlico.

I was leaving Gulfstream with a profit of $16,186 and a renewed respect for the speed figures which had been responsible for most of the winnings. This had been a meeting during which I had many opportunities to go awry. I had been frustrated by the lack of solid betting situations and had been traumatized by adversity. With my equanimity disturbed, I was ready to sink into a losing streak, but the figures wouldn't let me. Because they are unambiguous, they frequently dictate the horses I must bet. Even in the aftermath of that outrageous disqualification which wrecked my mental state and my handicapping judgment, I couldn't overlook figure horses like Fast Freedom, Royal Graustark, and the others. And they transformed a potential disaster into the most lucrative two weeks of my life.

3

Pimlico:
There's No Place
Like Home

After I left Miami and came back home to Washington, I found myself as seriously disenfranchised as the man without a country. I was a horseplayer without a racetrack. The mutuel clerks at the Maryland tracks had been working without a contract since the start of the year, and during the final week of the Bowie season they called a strike. Even then their negotiations with management went nowhere. So on March 21, the scheduled opening day of Pimlico Race Course, the track was dark and surrounded by a picket line.

Racing and government officials were wringing their hands and citing statistics about how much the strike was costing the state, the horsemen, the employees, and the track owners. I was desolate because I knew that the strike was costing me money, too. I won at Pimlico almost every spring, and my success there was no coincidence or accident. I understood the track, and I understood its place in the context of Maryland racing.

Maryland is unique. An unsuspecting horseplayer who visited the state's tracks for the first time would be mystified by the race results until he learned one great lesson. Here trainers are the key factor in handicapping; they are even more important than the past performances of their horses.

Three men dominate racing in the state. Dick Dutrow, King Leatherbury, and Buddy Delp all ranked among the top six race-winning trainers in America during 1976 and 1977. The sheer size of their stables gives them an insuperable advantage over their rivals, but the

Big Three may possess other edges as well. My press-box colleague Clem Florio is a keen judge of horses' appearance, and he can see incredible week-to-week changes in the animals from the major Maryland stables. He concludes that the performance of these horses is determined by the drugs they are being given. Once a Dutrow horse came onto the Pimlico track so lame that the jockey dismounted and refused to ride, necessitating a late scratch. A week later Dutrow entered the horse again. This time the jockey could hardly control the animal in the post parade. "If he had approached a wall," Clem said, "he wouldn't have stopped in his tracks or gone around it. He would have run right through it." Dutrow's horse won by seven lengths.

Maryland's racing fans saw how the game was being played, and they learned to bet blindly on horses trained by the Big Three. The crowd might make Dutrow 8 to 5, Leatherbury 2 to 1 and Delp 5 to 2 in the same race. Because of the depressed odds, it became generally unprofitable to wager on the leading trainers' horses. But it was usually fatal to bet against them. As a result, I grew increasingly disenchanted with racing in the state, and I did not spend much time at Bowie and Laurel.

At Pimlico, however, the game is different. The track bias principally determines the outcome of races and negates the impact of the leading trainers. A stretch-runner breaking from post position twelve won't win at Pimlico even if he is touched by Dutrow's magic.

Pimlico is a mile in circumference, like many major racetracks, but it has an unusually long stretch and unusually sharp turns. Horses who stay close to the rail on these turns have a great advantage, because their rivals who try to accelerate on the outside lose ground and lose momentum. The contour of the track is especially important in races at a mile and one-sixteenth. These events start so close to the first turn that horses in outside posts never have a chance to work their way to the rail.

This built-in bias is often compounded by the condition of the racing surface itself. The inside part of the track can become much harder and faster than the outside. When I handicap a race under such conditions, I picture in my mind a track for human runners whose inside lane is made of asphalt and whose other lanes consist of sand. The runner who takes the lead on the inside will be almost unbeatable, because his opponents have to slog their way through the sand in order to pass him.

As I reviewed previous Pimlico meetings, I saw that these extreme conditions usually prevailed during the first two weeks of a season. After that the track would tend to become more normal. In the first two weeks of the 1975 meeting, for example, these were the results of the six-furlong races according to post position:

Post	Winners	Starters	Percentage
1	19	65	29
2	10	65	15
3	8	65	12
4	5	65	8
5	9	65	14
6	8	64	13
7	2	60	3
8	2	43	5
9	0	34	0
10	0	25	0
11	2	21	10
12	0	14	0

Even when the bias was so pronounced, with post position one winning 29 percent of the time, many horseplayers were slow to recognize its existence. They bet on Dutrow, Leatherbury, and Delp just as they always had, and helped create generous odds on horses who were standouts because of the bias. I knew I would win big at Pimlico—if I got the chance to bet at all.

As the stalemate between the mutuel clerks and the track owners continued, I became more frustrated and restless. I had $16,186 burning a hole in my pocket, and I was hungry for action. I found myself doing things like betting the Detroit Pistons against the San Antonio Spurs, buying Xerox October 60 options on the basis of a hot tip, or flying to New York for an afternoon at Aqueduct (despite the $100-a-day overhead for planes and taxis). On the night of the Academy Awards, I was drinking in a bar heavily populated by other idled horseplayers, and jotted my odds for all the Oscar races onto a placemat. Then I invited my friends to put their money down on their choices for Best Adapted Screenplay or Best Color Cinematography. I made $54 for the night.

I had to content myself with such diversions for five weeks, until the track owners finally made their first realistic contract offer and the strikers voted to accept it. Pimlico rescheduled its opening for April 16, and I went there that day as joyously as a pilgrim visiting a shrine.

Pimlico's physical plant, designed to accommodate immense crowds on the day of the Preakness Stakes, is sprawling, cavernous, and, in some corners, dingy. But I love the place anyway. It sits in the midst of a heavily populated, bustling Baltimore neighborhood, and it always seems surrounded by an aura of vitality. I feel a rush of excitement whenever I get near the track.

On this opening day, my excitement was almost uncontrollable. Even though the first race was a nondescript, indecipherable $3000 claiming event for fillies, I couldn't resist playing it. I put a token wager on Lady Green, who was breaking from post position four and seemed to have enough early speed to lead all the way. I was proved wrong, but I have rarely been so happy to lose a bet.

Favored Child, a filly in post position one who had never displayed early speed in her career, broke on top and hugged the rail. Lady Green challenged her briefly from the outside, couldn't pass her, and so dropped to the rail and followed the leader around the track. Nobody else got into contention. Dutrow's entrant, Foxie Dealer, was one of the favorites and showed brief speed from the ten post, but stayed wide and collapsed after half a mile. The order of finish, by post positions, was 1–4–3–2–5. The track bias had not only reappeared; it seemed stronger than ever.

I cashed modest bets on speed horses in the second and third races, and then in the fourth ventured $250 on a front-runner named Father's Angel. He took the early lead and went to the rail, as I had expected, but on the last turn he was challenged by a Dutrow horse, Blue Barbizon. I knew the race was over. Blue Barbizon was a confirmed stretch-runner, and Father's Angel had lost ground in the stretch in each of his last nine races. But Father's Angel kept bounding along the rock-hard rail and wrested the lead back from Blue Barbizon, who was faltering in the deeper footing on the outside. Father's Angel won by a head, paying $8.40 and proving that this bias was even strong enough to imbue fainthearted animals with courage for the first time in their lives.

The fifth race was similarly incredible. Bobed possessed blazing early speed, and he had run well earlier in the season, but he had finished next-to-last in his two most recent races. Now he had drawn the inside post position at a mile and one-sixteenth. Not many handicapping books recommend betting horses who have lost their last two starts by a combined total of 37 lengths, but I steeled my nerve and put $150 on an exacta combination coupling Bobed with the logical favorite. The race was never in doubt. Bobed sprinted to a four-length lead, hugged the rail, and won comfortably, with the favorite following him around the track. The Pimlico meeting was five races old, and I was already $2400 ahead.

In the past I would have been confounded by these conditions. I adhered to my handicapping principles so dogmatically that I could never abandon them. If a horse possessed superior figures and was running against a strong bias, I felt intellectually obligated to bet him anyway. I was the dutiful captain who went down with the ship. But by 1977 I had learned that on a track like Pimlico's, the bias means everything. A horse's figures, his class, his recent form, his trainer, his physical condition are all secondary.

So in the sixth race at Pimlico I did not hesitate to eliminate the 1-to-5 favorite, Royal Ski, who had been voted the second-best two-year-old in America during 1976, but was a stretch-runner breaking from the number-five position. I handicapped the race to find the horse who was going to get the lead on the rail, bet my choice in the exacta, and collected another $1400 when Royal Ski struggled home fourth. As I studied the seventh race, I asked myself the same question: Who is going to get the lead on the rail?

PIMLICO

6 FURLONGS
PIMLICO

6 FURLONGS. (1.08½) ALLOWANCE. Purse $11,000. 4-year-olds and upward, which have not won $4,825 twice other than maiden, claiming, starter or bonus payment since November 15. Weight, 122 lbs. Non-winners of $4,800 twice in 1977 allowed 3 lbs. Once, 5 lbs. $4,500 twice since October 22, 7 lbs. Once, 10 lbs. (Maiden, claiming and starter races not considered in estimating allowances.)

Hamoud
Own.—Worthington R W

B. c. 4, by Big Brave—Hamper, by Canadian Champ
Br.—Worthington Mrs R W (Md)
Tr.—Ravich Hyman

Turf Record — St. 1st 2nd 3rd — Amt.
115 — 1977 1 0 0 0 — $4,600
1976 13 5 2 3 — $44,512

Irish Snip
Own.—Davis Susan F

Dk. b. or br. g. 5, by Jersey Legend—Miss Milt, by Mr Milt
Br.—Mulligan S (Md)
Tr.—Johnson Norman A

St. 1st 2nd 3rd — Amt.
122 — 1977 7 2 1 1 — $12,450
1976 9 1 1 2 — $8,360

Odd Man
Own.—Sharp Bayard

B. g. 6, by Round Table—Even Out, by Swaps
Br.—Brandywine Stable (Ky)
Tr.—Peoples Charles

Turf Record — St. 1st 2nd 3rd — Amt.
112 — 1976 15 2 2 0 — $34,010
1975 16 4 2 0 — $17,690

Kimani *
Own.—Magrogan R F

Dk. b. or br. g. 7, by Beechpark—Yes You Gal, by Yes You Will
Br.—Magrogan R F (Md)
Tr.—Stewart Charles

Turf Record — St. 1st 2nd 3rd — Amt.
112 — 1977 6 0 1 1 — $4,630
1976 20 2 1 3 — $16,900

Nighcut * Blk. g. 6, by Bold Monarch—Shiralee, by Piano Jim
Br.—Christmas Jr & Thompson (Md)
Own.—Christmas D Jr Tr.—Green Eugene E **112**
St. 1st 2nd 3rd Amt.
1977 3 0 0 0 $540
1975 3 1 0 0 $9,120
4Apr77- 7GS fst 6f :22⅘ :46⅗ 1:12 Clm 25000 2 3 2hd 4¾ 21½ 98½ Barrera C b 116 *1.60 74-27 Danny Boy 1121 Webelo 1163 Forward Dancer 1201½ Speed, tired 10
10Mar77- 7Bow fst 1 1/16 :48 1:13⅖ 1:45⅗ Clm 30000 2 1 16 13½ 32 612 Jenkins L Jr7 107 5.90 68-23 Famous Jim 1141½ Polar Light 1141½ Terricle 1192½ Bumped 6
2Mar77- 8Bow fst 6f :22⅕ :45⅖ 1:10⅕ Allowance 7 1 12½ 11½ 21 45½ Jenkins L Jr7 106 20.10 83-22 SportingPowdr1191½Ptrck'sShmrock1153½HuntrF.115¾ Weakened 8
1Feb75- 6Bow gd 1 1/16 :47⅖ 1:13⅖ 1:48 Allowance 2 2 1hd 45¼ 714 723 Brodsky D5 b 114 11.40 45-28 Gala Double 119no Spirit Rock 116¾ Jolly Johu 1192¾ Bore out 7
25Jan75- 7Bow sly 7f :23⅘ :48 1:27 Allowance 6 3 11½ 1½ 11½ 43¼ Brodsky D5 b 114 4.70 67-34 Mo Bay 1171¼ Port Conway Lane 1121¼FlightToGlory112¾ Outrun 6
13Jan75- 8Bow sly 6f :23⅕ :46⅕ 1:13 Ⓢ Allowance 4 4 11½ 15 15 1¾ Brodsky D5 b 110 1.80 78-29 Nighcut 110¾ Splitting Headache 1197 Remembered 1153 Driving 5
18Sep74- 7Bow fst 7f :22⅘ :46⅕ 1:25 3+ Allowance 1 2 11 12 15 14¾ McCarron C J5 b 108 *.80 80-30 Nighcut1084¾Mr.Dougl1131½MisterYouEssy1191½ Merely breezing 11
2Sep74- 8Tim fst 1 :46⅗ 1:12⅕ 1:36⅗ Ⓢ Handicap 3 3 2½ 31 35½ 38½ Wright D R 115 4.60 85-09 Eager Native 1244½ Cool SpringPark1164Nighcut115nk Weakened 7
17Aug74- 8Tim fst 1 :47 1:12⅖ 1:37⅖ 3+ Ⓢ Handicap 3 2 22½ 2hd 1hd 21 Gino L 109 2.10e 89-15 Eager Native 1161 Nighcut 1097 Noor Side 1172 Gamely 8
20Jly74- 8Tim fst 7f :23⅖ :45⅗ 1:25⅖ Ⓢ Allowance 2 5 67 33 33½ 21¼ Gino L 122 4.10 97-08 Song Of Praise 1221¼ Nighcut 1222½ OutaDeQuestion1125 Gamely 7
LATEST WORKOUTS ● Mar 26 Bow 5f fst :59⅗ h Mar 8 Bow 4f fst :49⅗ b

Ben S. B. h. 5, by Hasty Road—White Mist, by Misty Flight
Br.—Mars F E (Va)
Own.—Scherr N Tr.—Hine Hubert **112**
Turf Record: St. 1st 2nd 3rd — 1 0 0 0
St. 1st 2nd 3rd Amt.
1977 2 0 0 1 $2,400
1976 12 3 3 2 $23,870
26Jan77- 6SA fst 6f :21⅗ :44⅖ 1:09⅖ Allowance 6 4 52½ 52½ 66 77½ Castaneda M 114 5.50 84-11 Featherfoot 116nk Ascetic 117¾ Udonegood 1151½ Dull try 7
7Jan77- 7SA my 6f :22⅕ :45⅖ 1:10⅘ Allowance 1 2 2hd 21 23 32 Castaneda M 115 28.10 83-25 Guerrintado 115no Tiltin Milton 1212 Ben S. 115½ Weakened 6
28Dec76- 8SA fst 6f :21⅘ :44⅕ 1:08⅗ P. Verdes H. 3 7 52½ 109¼ 1217 1218 Castaneda M 112 37.50f 78-12 Maheras 119½ Sure Fire 1163 Ancient Title 1263½ Done early 13
9Oct76- 7Key sly 6f :22⅘ :46 1:12 3+ Allowance 6 6 69½ 66¼ 65¾ 63¼ Black A S 119 *2.60 79-26 Webelo 122nk Silver Doctor 1191 Gentleman J. G.114nk Stumbled 6
13Sep76- 5Bow fst 6f :22⅖ :45⅗ 1:10⅗ 3+ Allowance 4 1 32 3nk 1½ 11¾ Agnello A 122 2.80 87-21 Ben S. 1221¾ Yallissos 1122¼ Outcoat 1161 Drew clear 6
31Jly76- 5Key fst 6f :22 :45 1:10⅘ 3+ Allowance 5 3 33 45 49½ 47¼ Cusimano G 119 *1.20 81-15 Come On Jay 119¾ Midnight Joker 116½ Banian 1176 Tired 5
10Jly76- 8Pim fst 6f :23 :46⅕ 1:11⅕ Allowance 6 1 31 1hd 1hd 22½ Agnello A 122 1.50 87-15 Moving Cloud 1192½ Ben S. 122nk Island Count 115¾ Weakened 7
29Jun76- 6Pim fst 6f :23 :45⅘ 1:10⅘ Allowance 1 2 11½ 11½ 13 12½ Agnello A 112 *1.30 92-19 Ben S. 1122½ Stomp and Go 1193 Siren's Gent 113nk Mild drive 5
4Jun76- 7Pim fst 6f :22⅘ :45⅖ 1:10⅗ Allowance 1 2 21½ 22 2½ 11¾ Agnello A 112 *.70 93-17 Ben S. 1121¾ Beau Sock 1152½ Green Beret 119hd Driving 7
24May76- 8Pim fm 5f Ⓣ:22⅗ :45⅘ :57⅘ Allowance 2 3 1hd 3nk 63¾ 43 Agnello A 112 *1.80 95-10 Oxford Flight 1122 IronInTheFire114½LeaderoftheBand114½ Tired 8
LATEST WORKOUTS Apr 13 Pim 5f fst 1:01 h Apr 6 Pim 5f my 1:02 b ● Mar 28 Pim 5f fst 1:00⅖ h Mar 13 SA 4f fst :49⅕ h

Fleetwood's Lady * B. f. 4, by Big Brave—Ribon, by Sir Ribot
Br.—Newcomer & Watson (W.Va.)
Own.—Newcomer & Watson Tr.—Newcomer Thomas W **107**
St. 1st 2nd 3rd Amt.
1977 1 1 0 0 $1,860
1976 8 2 1 2 $7,859
4Apr77- 8CT sly 4½f :21⅘ :46 :52⅕ Allowance 1 4 13 13 13½ Witte N b 109 3.30 97-09 Fleetwood's Lady 1093½ Frigid Gidgit1171½Sailplane1142½ Driving 8
2Nov76- 5Lrl fst 6f :22⅖ :46⅗ 1:11⅖ 3+ Ⓕ Allowance 7 4 11½ 2½ 88½ 810 Espinosa V 117 27.50 80-12 Satin Dancer 1141½ Across the Bar 1141½ Scheming 114nk Tried 9
20Oct76- 7Key sly 6f :22 :45⅖ 1:11⅗ 3+ Ⓕ Allowance 1 4 11½ 2½ 2hd 1nk Black A S b 117 1.40 84-21 Fleetwood'sLdy117nkTyphoonDottie1101SpringDremr1175 Driving 6
6Oct76- 8Key fst 6f :22⅗ :46⅕ 1:12⅖ 3+ Allowance 7 2 53 43¼ 54½ 21¼ Kimball R b 114 23.90 79-25 PrinceleeAir1221¼Fltwood'sLdy1141½MurdrInc.117¾ Lacked room 9
27Sep76- 7Bow gd 6f :22⅘ :46 1:12 3+ Ⓕ Allowance 3 3 41¾ 59½ 56½ 64 Witte N5 b 107 51.60 76-22 Native Buff 1193 Paige Price 115nkBrightWork116no Brief factor 10
7Sep76- 7Tim fst *6½f :22⅘ :46⅕ 1:17⅘ 3+ Allowance 6 5 44½ 512 512 612 Greco T b 112 6.00 83-16 Plum Passion 118nk Fairly Rough 1152 Hunter F. 1193 Tired 6
25Aug76- 7Tim fst 4f :22⅗ :46⅗ Ⓕ Allowance 3 6 42½ 43 3½ Witte N5 b 112 10.70 93-06 BoldPerky117nkOmrBunny122nkFleetwood'sLdy112¾ Found room 8
5Jly76- 6Pen fst 6f :21⅘ :45⅕ 1:10⅗ Allowance 4 3 21½ 22 33½ 310 Espinosa V 116 5.90 83-16 The Good Monk 1148Tickets1122Fleetwood'sLady1161 Weakened 9
26May76- 6Pen sly 6f :22⅕ :46⅕ 1:13⅖ Allowance 9 1 11½ 12 12 11½ Greco T b 110 26.80 79-20 Fleetwood'sLady1101½CramertonsJoy1151GhostTown1211 Driving 12
LATEST WORKOUTS Mar 30 CT 3f gd :37⅗ h ● Mar 19 CT 3f fst :36 hg

Royal Jete Ch. g. 4, by Nijinsky II—Bid High, by Bold Bidder
Br.—Gilman Paper Co (Ky)
Own.—Wright Mrs W C Tr.—Gill Rodger M **115**
Turf Record: St. 1st 2nd 3rd — 3 0 0 1
St. 1st 2nd 3rd Amt.
1977 2 0 0 1 $2,250
1976 14 4 3 2 $23,290
4Apr77- 8GS fst 6f :22⅗ :46⅗ 1:12⅖ Allowance 5 4 43¼ 1hd 4nk 41¾ McCarron G 115 4.70 79-27 Princely Song 113¾ Ⓓ Kohoutek 115½ Old Mystery 113½ Brushed 8
4Apr77-Placed third through disqualification
26Feb77- 8Bow fst 6f :22⅘ :46 1:10⅘ Allowance 5 7 75 97¾ 75¼ 42¼ Lee T 115 31.40 84-20 Moving Cloud 1191¼ Hamoud 108nk Bidding Fool 119¾ Stride late 9
27Nov76- 7Lrl fst 1 :45⅘ 1:11⅕ 1:37⅘ 3+ Allowance 5 4 33½ 2½ 2½ 1no McCarron G 113 3.10 84-16 Royal Jete 113no Juvenile Jr. 1161¼ Hempt's Lark 113½ Driving 7
19Nov76- 8Lrl fst 7f :22⅗ :45⅘ 1:24⅕ 3+ Allowance 4 7 76¾ 66½ 1½ 2nk Agnello A 114 5.40 90-17 Godolphin 120nk Royal Jete 1144 Bumpy Landing 1222 Gamely 9
6Nov76- 7Lrl fst 1 :45⅗ 1:10⅘ 1:36⅘ 3+ Allowance 2 4 43 4¾ 41¾ 45 Moyers L 112 5.70 84-13 Ravidus 1123½JuvenileJr.1161VisibleDifference120½ Bid, weakened 8
26Oct76- 7Lrl gd 6f :22⅗ :46⅗ 1:12⅕ 3+ Allowance 4 3 45½ 43¼ 23 1no Agnello A 113 8.80 86-25 Royal Jete 113no Sporting Powder 1138 Crossbones119no Driving 7
13Oct76- 9Bow fst 7f :22⅗ :45⅘ 1:23 3+ Allowance 4 1 65 43½ 25 28 Agnello A 116 *1.90 82-19 Visible Difference 1198 Royal Jete 1161 Swift's Copy1166 Gamely 11
6Oct76- 7Bow fst 1 1/16 :47 1:12 1:45⅖ 3+ Allowance 7 5 56½ 11 12 21¼ Agnello A 115 3.00 80-24 Kabori 1151¼ Royal Jete 1154 Father's Angel 1113½ Gamely 8
24Sep76- 8Bow fst 7f :22⅗ :46 1:24⅗ 3+ Allowance 3 7 68 57 54 3½ Canessa J 118 14.70 81-22 Pocotaligo 112nk Crossbones 118nk Royal Jete 118hd Rallied 8
16Sep76- 7Bow sly 1 1/16 :49⅖ 1:14⅖ 1:45⅘ 3+ Allowance 5 5 43 43 46 46¼ Canessa J 116 5.40 73-25 Hempt's Lark 1161½ Solid Delivery 119¾ Haf Pro 1144 No factor 6
LATEST WORKOUTS Apr 13 Pim 4f fst :48 h Apr 3 Pim 3f my :38⅗ b Mar 29 Pim 6f fst 1:18 b Mar 24 Pim 6f fst 1:16⅕ b

Finding the horse with the best early speed in a field usually does not require much subtlety. I do not bother with sophisticated analyses of fractional times. I simply look for a horse who frequently takes the lead in races at today's distance or shorter. (Getting the lead in prior route races does not mean much if today's race is a sprint, because the pace is so much slower in longer events.) I also look at the horse's previous opposition to see if he has been able to outrun other known speedballs.

Nighcut seemed likely to be the front-runner in the seventh race. On March 2, his first start in two years, he had outrun the stakes-class Sporting Powder for a quarter of a mile. I looked up Sporting Powder's record and saw that he had taken the early lead in each of his ten previous races. Nighcut had battled for the lead in his most recent performance at Garden State, running in fast fractions over a dull track.

No other horse in this field possessed comparable speed. Hamoud had never taken the early lead in a sprint. Irish Snip and Fleetwood's Lady had done it, but only against much cheaper allowance company. Ben S. had run well in the past against high-quality sprinters, but he was breaking from a post position outside Nighcut and did not appear quick enough to get past him cleanly and cut over to the rail. If he merely showed speed equal to Nighcut's, he would have to race on the outside all the way.

I assumed that Nighcut would come flying out of the gate and take the lead along the rail. Then what? Hamoud was starting from the inside post, and he figured to stay on the rail behind the leader. But I did not see how any of the other horses would be able to get to the rail. Ben S., Kimani, and Royal Jete would have been contenders on a normal track, but they seemed certain to lose ground once Nighcut and Hamoud had commandeered the choice positions along the inside.

The race was between Nighcut and Hamoud. Nighcut had tired badly in all of his races during 1977. He was not going to collapse on this biased track, but he might not be able to hold off Hamoud, who was in razor-sharp condition and was going to be saving ground through most of the race. So I decided to bet a pair of $50 exactas, with Hamoud on top of Nighcut and vice versa. This was no cinch, by any means, but my perception of the track bias gave me an edge in the race and I wanted to try to profit from it.

SEVENTH RACE
Pimlico
APRIL 16, 1977

6 FURLONGS. (1.09⅘) ALLOWANCE. Purse $11,000. 4-year-olds and upward, whih have not won $4,825 twice other than maiden, claiming, starter or bonus payment since November 15. Weight, 122 lbs. Non-winners of $4,800 twice in 1977 allowed 3 lbs. Once, 5 lbs. $4,500 twice since October 22, 7 lbs. Once, 10 lbs. (Maiden, claiming and starter races not considered in estimating allowances.)

Value of race $11,000, value to winner $6,600, second $2,420, third $1,320, fourth $660. Mutuel pool $93,750. Exacta Pool $100,999.

Last Raced	Horse	Eqt.A.Wt	PP	St	¼	½	Str	Fin	Jockey	Odds $1
4Apr77 ^{7}GS^{9}	Nighcut	b 6 112	5	2	1^{2}	1^{2}	$1^{2\frac{1}{2}}$	$1^{4\frac{3}{4}}$	Wright D R	13.10
10Apr77 ^{7}Pen^{2}	Hamoud	4 115	1	5	$4^{\frac{1}{2}}$	2^{hd}	$2^{2\frac{1}{2}}$	2^{nk}	Bracciale V Jr	1.30
10Apr77 ^{7}Pen^{3}	Irish Snip	b 5 122	2	6	5^{hd}	6^{4}	6^{5}	3no	Cusimano G	9.20
4Apr77 ^{8}GS^{3}	Royal Jete	4 115	8	4	6^{4}	5^{3}	4^{1}	$4^{\frac{3}{4}}$	McCarron G	3.80
26Jan77 ^{6}SA^{7}	Ben S.	5 112	6	1	2^{2}	3^{2}	$3^{\frac{1}{2}}$	5no	Pineda R	3.30
4Apr77 ^{8}CT^{1}	Fleetwood's Lady	b 4 109	7	3	3^{2}	$4^{1\frac{1}{2}}$	$5^{1\frac{1}{2}}$	6^{6}	Witte N	34.30
5Mar77 ^{8}Bow^{4}	Kimani	b 7 112	4	7	7^{5}	7^{5}	7^{4}	7^{4}	Lee T	13.60
15Aug76 ^{8}Del^{13}	Odd Man	6 113	3	8	8	8	8	8	Black A S	25.00

OFF AT 4:07, EST. Start good, Won driving. Time, :23, :46⅕, 1:11⅖ Track fast.

$2 Mutuel Prices:			
5-NIGHCUT	**28.20**	**9.60**	**5.60**
1-HAMOUD		**3.00**	**2.80**
2-IRISH SNIP			**4.00**

$2 EXACTA 5-1 PAID $108.20.

Blk. g, by Bold Monarch—Shiralee, by Piano Jim. Trainer Green Ernest E. Bred by Christmas Jr & Thompson (Md).

NIGHCUT quickly sprinted clear and held sway under steady pressure. HAMOUD advanced inside rivals, swung out to reach closest pursuit then was taken in hand the final seventy yards when unable to menace the top one. IRISH SNIP and ROYAL JETE bested tired rivals. BEN S. and FLEETWOOD LADY were hard used early.

Owners— 1, Christmas D Jr; 2, Worthington R W; 3, Davis Susan F; 4, Wright Mrs W C; 5, Scherr N; 6 Newcomer & Watson; 7, Magrogan R F; 8, Sharp Bayard.

Trainers— 1, Green Ernest E; 2, Ravich Hyman; 3, Johnson Norman A; 4, Gill Rodger M; 5, Hine Hubert; 6, Newcomer Thomas W; 7, Stewart Charles; 8, Peoples Charles.

Overweight: Fleetwood's Lady 2 pounds; Odd Man 1.

Scratched—Ramaru (26Feb77 ^{7}Bow^{7}).

The race followed my script perfectly. Nighcut sprinted to the lead, stayed on the rail, and won by nearly five lengths. Hamoud sneaked along the inside and finished second. The exacta paid $108.20. I hit the eighth race, too, completing a sweep of all seven exactas on the card, and then lost the ninth-race triple. I drove back home with a $5800 profit and a feeling of omniscience.

In the following days, I maintained a steady rhythm in my betting. I handicapped every race by identifying the horses who were likely to show early speed and get a position near the rail. I could usually narrow a field to two or three contenders, and I would play these horses in the exacta. I was betting nine races a day. I did not want to make the mistake of waiting for a few ironclad opportunities—and risk seeing the bias disappear before they materialized.

On April 22 I made a routine wager on the ninth race and collected my first payoff of the year over $5000. A Leatherbury filly, Dixie Spears, was the even-money favorite in the maiden-claiming event. She had displayed high speed and had been narrowly beaten in all three of her previous starts. Now she was breaking from post position four and figured to get the lead on the rail. Of the other horses in decent post positions, only Nos. 2, 5, and 6 had ever flashed speed or finished creditably. So I invested $300 in the triple, taking Dixie Spears on top with all the combinations of 2, 5, and 6 for second and third place. My pulse didn't quicken before the race, but it did afterward, when 4–2–6 paid $334 and I held twenty winning tickets. With the Pimlico meeting one week old, I was $11,000 ahead.

As my winning streak gathered momentum, I learned a valuable lesson about the psychology of gambling. One night I was celebrating my success at Pimlico in a number of Georgetown bars and informed my cronies that I loved a horse at Aqueduct the next afternoon. I would jot the animal's name on a napkin and proclaim that he was a sure thing, the degree of sureness increasing in proportion to my liquor consumption. The next day I woke up late, made an unsuccessful attempt to contact a bookie, and rushed to Pimlico. I forgot about my New York horse until that evening, when friends started telephoning me to offer their thanks for the $18.20 winner.

There was a time when such a missed opportunity would have impelled me to drive my fist through the nearest wall. I would have been frustrated by the realization that I should have won thousands of dollars, stung by the injustice that other people had collected on my horse while I hadn't. My handicapping might have been adversely affected for days or weeks. But this time I could shrug off the whole experience, because I knew for certain that I was going to win at Pimlico the next day, or the day after. There was no reason to get upset over one missed opportunity when so many more lay ahead.

Suddenly I understood what enabled professionals like Charlie always to remain so cool, so rational, so unflappable—even in the face of extreme adversity. Charlie did not have some superhuman psychological makeup; he simply had complete confidence in the inevitability of his own success. Any loss was only a temporary setback; it wasn't worth worrying about. For the first time in my life, I was developing this sort of self-confidence. I knew that as long as the bias existed at Pimlico, I was going to win. Losing my composure would be pointless and counterproductive.

Unfortunately, I was going to have to interrupt my steady accumulation of profits at Pimlico for ten days. I have the freedom to write my newspaper column from any track I choose, but in the spring I am obligated to cover the Kentucky Derby as well as the pre-race hoopla.

When I started my career as a turf writer, going to Kentucky hardly felt like an obligation. It was a thrill, for the Derby fever in Louisville is highly contagious. I find it oddly moving to walk into a sleazy bar whose little combo strikes up "My Old Kentucky Home," and to see everybody rise and sing along solemnly, with even the hookers looking misty-eyed. The excitement of the Derby is further heightened by the sense of historical importance which envelops even mediocre races. It is easy to forget who won last year's Super Bowl, but every Derby winner has his name etched in history. Even Louisville schoolboys know who won in 1948, who lost in 1953.

Although I never lost my appreciation for the Derby spectacle, I quickly developed a strong distaste for Kentucky racing. Not only did I lose money every year, but I lost for reasons that made me feel as if I were as much a sucker as the tourists who get their pockets picked on Derby Day.

Racetrack betting is a constant battle of wits between outsiders and insiders—between handicappers with superior analytical skills and horsemen with access to private information. I could win the battle in Florida and Maryland, but Kentucky had rigged the game against me. The sport seemed to be conducted principally for the pleasure and profit of the racing and breeding establishment. Stewards, racing commissioners, and track owners would not dream of denying horsemen their inalienable right to cash a bet at the public's expense.

A filly named Al's New Gal, trained by Kaye Bell, epitomized the nature of the game. I encountered her in a two-year-old maiden race on my first day in Kentucky, the day of the Blue Grass Stakes at Keeneland. Half of the field consisted of first-time starters with no workouts. While some states require unraced horses to have published workouts so bettors can have some basis for evaluating them, Kentucky does not. Its maiden races are benefits for owners, trainers, and breeders. The public can only guess at the ability of the entrants. In this case the public guessed wrong, making Al's New Gal the 2-to-1 favorite. She finished fourteen lengths behind one of the first-time starters with no workouts.

Al's New Gal was entered again on the day before the Derby, a time when betting coups are as much a part of Churchill Downs tradition as mint juleps. The presumed perpetrator of the most brazen coups is Dr. Alex Harthill, a veterinarian who cannot get a license to practice in many states, but who has been called "the godfather of the backstretch" in Kentucky. Harthill is thought to use the horses of Kaye Bell as the instruments of his handiwork.

In the last few minutes before post time, such a flood of money poured onto Al's New Gal that half of Kentucky must have known what was happening. Even though the filly had been trounced in the only start of her career, she went off the 9-to-5 favorite. The price was a bargain. Al's New Gal exploded out of the gate, opened a five-length lead in the first eighth of a mile, and coasted to a ridiculously easy victory. At almost any other track, fans would have booed and yelled, suspecting strongly that they had been robbed. But at Churchill Downs, where horseplayers think that the game is supposed to be played this way, there was not a peep of protest. And I doubt that the stewards ever asked Bell or Harthill for an explanation of the form reversal.

I can cope with an occasional bit of racetrack larceny; I even managed to cash a small bet on Al's New Gal. But I cannot function well when the frequency of the larceny renders me constantly paranoid, when I never knew whether to handicap a race or listen for hot tips on it. There may be some way to win at Churchill Downs, but for the eighth consecutive year I failed to discover it. I suffered a $2500 loss, as well as some embarrassment after telling my readers that Seattle Slew was an overrated, improperly trained mediocrity who was not going to win the Derby. I was very happy to leave Kentucky and return to the familiar, pleasant environs of Pimlico.

I was even happier to discover that the track bias was as strong as ever. On May 10, my first day back at Pimlico, the winning post positions were 3, 3, 4, 3, 1, 1, 1, 4, 1. And on the next day I found the ironclad betting opportunity which I had been waiting for ever since the meeting began. I found a horse who had superior figures, who looked certain to get the lead on the rail, and who was an absolute cinch—even though he had lost his last start by thirty-seven lengths.

1 PIMLICO (6 FURLONGS — PIMLICO — Finish)

6 FURLONGS. (1.09⅕) MAIDEN CLAIMING. Purse $5,500. 3- and 4-year-olds. Weights: 3-year-olds, 114 lbs., 4-year-olds, 124 lbs. Claiming Price $18,500; for each $1,000 to $16,500 1 lb.

Say Darling — Ch. f. 3, by North Flight—Calm Dream, by To Market
Own.—Obre Mrs H — $18,500 — Br.—Trillora Inc (Ky) — Tr.—Field Kenneth — 109
St. 1st 2nd 3rd Amt. — 1977 2 M 0 0 — 1976 0 M 0 0
4May77- 3Pim gd 6f :23⅘ :46⅖ 1:12⅕ 3↑Md 30000 4 6 68 615 517 515 Agnello A 50 114 13.70 70–16 My Iron Lass 112hd Colonel Shula 1141½ Bitina 11413 No mishap 7
16Apr77- 2Pim fst 6f :23⅘ :47 1:12⅖ 3↑Ⓕ Md Sp Wt 1 11 1111111181020 917 McCarron G 114 16.00 67–16 Rani Baba 114nk Majestic Julie 1248 Family First 1141 No factor 12
LATEST WORKOUTS May 2 Pim 3f fst :37 b — Apr 23 Pim 4f fst :49 b — Apr 13 Pim 4f fst :50⅖ bg — Apr 8 Pim 5f fst 1:03 b

English Favorite — Ch. g. 3, by Bold Favorite—Trackabu, by My Babu
Own.—Lockwood W M — $18,500 — Br.—Lockwood W M (Md) — Tr.—Dearstyn Alan T — 114
St. 1st 2nd 3rd Amt. — 1977 7 M 1 1 $2,458 — 1976 0 M 0 0
5May77- 5Pim fst 1 1/16 :46⅘ 1:12⅖ 1:45⅕ 3↑Md Sp Wt 11 3 1hd 62¾11321137 Sim M C b 112 9.10 42–18 Celluloid 1142¾ Sea Skimmer 114¾ Retrace 112hd Tired 12
19Apr77- 9Pim fst 6f :23⅕ :46⅗ 1:12⅗ 3↑Md 18500 2 5 3½ 2hd 2hd 21½ Brown H5 81 b 109 8.20 81–19 Ticket Taylor 1121½ English Favorite 1092¼ Retrace 112nk Gamely 12
24Mar77- 3GS fst 6f :23⅕ :48 1:14⅕ 3↑Md Sp Wt 10 1 1½ 31 67½ 712 Adams J K b 112 27.40 60–31 Parnis 1141½ Mike Delucia 108¾ Eastern Monarch 114no Tired 12
2Mar77- 6Bow fst 6f :22⅘ :46 1:11⅗ Ⓢ Md Sp Wt 11 2 22½ 22 33½ 32¾ Adams J K 77 b 120 82.20 78–22 Unruly Sire 120¾ Crunch Bird 1202 English Favorite 120no Evenly 12
18Feb77- 5Bow fst 6f :23⅘ :47⅕ 1:12⅘ Md 25000 2 5 52¼ 54¾ 78 89¼ Adams J K b 120 25.60 67–28 Swaps Ego 1201¼ Great White 118hd Stammer 1201¾ Outrun 8
30Jan77- 3Pen fst 6f :23⅘ :48 1:15⅗ Md Sp Wt 8 1 1½ 2½ 512 45½ Baxis J 118 6.60 63–28 Shimmering Jen 1132½ Tim Ed D. 1102 SlimNative1151 Weakened 9
22Jan77- 3Pen fst 6f :23⅘ :48⅖ 1:14⅗ Md Sp Wt 7 2 12 23 53¾ 69 Gress D 118 2.20 64–27 Wall Town 1183 Ataboy Abner 1151 Slim Native1151 Speed; tired 7
LATEST WORKOUTS Apr 16 Pim 4f fst :47⅘ h — Apr 7 Pim 5f gd 1:07 b — Mar 19 Bow 3f gd :38 b — Mar 15 Bow 5f fst 1:03 b

Hayes Prince — B. g. 3, by Call Me Prince—Haljeanne, by Commodore M.
Own.—Herring R L — $16,500 — Br.—Hayes T W (Ky) — Tr.—Ferris Richard D — 112
St. 1st 2nd 3rd Amt. — 1977 0 M 0 0 — 1976 0 M 0 0
LATEST WORKOUTS May 7 Pim 6f my 1:17⅗ b — Apr 28 Pim 6f fst 1:16⅗ bg — Apr 23 Pim 5f fst 1:02⅕ b — Apr 16 Pim 3f fst :38⅘ b

Hiawatha — B. c. 3, by Chieftain—Hesione, by Hyperion
Own.—Powhatan — $18,500 — Br.—Guest R R (Va) — Tr.—Graham R — 114
St. 1st 2nd 3rd Amt. — 1977 1 M 0 0 — 1976 1 M 0 0
2May77- 4Pim fst 6f :23 :46⅘ 1:13⅕ 3↑Md 25000 6 8 912 914 714 711 McCarron G 44 114 10.70 69–18 Stammer 114½ Tall Ships 1142 Be An Asset 1144½ Outrun 10
23Dec76- 4Lrl fst 6f :22⅖ :46 1:12 Md Sp Wt 10 2 77¾ 914 917 916 Sim M C 120 13.00 71–15 Knightly Marvin 120¾ Mum Bold 1202 Im Laze 1203 No factor 11

Viteange — Dk. b. or br. c. 3, by Son Ange—Swiftybyrd, by Crozier
Own.—Swift G H — $18,500 — Br.—Swift G H Jr (Ky) — Tr.—Williams David E — 114
St. 1st 2nd 3rd Amt. — 1977 6 M 1 1 $1,420 — 1976 0 M 0 0
6Apr77- 1Pen fst 6f :22 :45⅗ 1:11⅘ Md Sp Wt 3 4 32½ 21 2hd 21¾ Lloyd J S b 118 *2.50 85–16 CornishVerdict1181¾Viteange1182FlowerO'Hr1134 Bid, weakened 11
1Mar77- 3Bow fst 6f :23 :46⅕ 1:11⅘ Md 25000 5 3 33½ 44 54½ 55¼ Moyers L 74 120 9.70 78–25 Nickleby 1201½ Stammer 1201¼ Great White 1182 Faltered 7
18Feb77- 5Bow fst 6f :23⅘ :47⅕ 1:12⅘ Md 25000 8 4 42 42¾ 42½ 54½ Hinojosa H 74 120 6.60 71–28 Swaps Ego 1201¼ Great White 118hd Stammer 1201¾ Wide 8
7Feb77- 3Bow fst 7f :23⅕ :46⅗ 1:27⅘ Md 25000 2 5 1hd 21½ 1hd 53 Gilbert R B 120 7.00 63–32 Flo'sFirst120hdJvelinThrow120¾BerkleyMlendrino1202 Used early 7
26Jan77- 4Bow fst 6f :23⅘ :47⅕ 1:14 Md Sp Wt 7 5 41½ 43 56 57½ Wright D R 120 8.40 62–33 Mum Bold 120no Quadremper 1202 Im Laze 1202 Tired 7
14Jan77- 9Bow fst 5½f :22⅘ :46⅖ 1:06⅗ Md 25000 7 8 64¾ 33½ 25 35¾ Wright D R 120 11.30 80–21 Elusive Glory 1205 Como No 118¾ Viteange 120nk No mishap 11

Gala Gusto — Ch. g. 3, by Spring Double—Wind Song, by Mr. Music
Own.—Moshe-Asher Stable — $18,500 — Br.—Glade Valley Farms Inc (Md) — Tr.—Dutrow Richard E — 114
St. 1st 2nd 3rd Amt. — 1977 0 M 0 0 — 1976 0 M 0 0
LATEST WORKOUTS May 7 Pim 6f my 1:14⅘ h — May 2 Pim 5f fst 1:02⅖ bg — Apr 27 Pim 5f fst 1:01 hg — Apr 20 Lrl 4f fst :51⅗ bg

Darcy Spice — Ch. c. 4, by Jim J—Craftyette, by Crafty Admiral
Own.—Clark Mrs R V — $18,500 — Br.—Clark Mrs R V (Va) — Tr.—Watters Margaret G — 124
St. 1st 2nd 3rd Amt. — 1977 1 M 0 0 — 1976 0 M 0 0
22Feb77- 5Bow fst 6f :23 :46⅗ 1:12⅗ Md Sp Wt 1 11 1120112311241116 Sasser B 120 36.60 61–24 SleepytimGl115noFrnk'sAc120hdAnybody'sSpry1201¼ Awkward St. 11

Platoon — Dk. b. or br. g. 3, by Go Marching—Bunched, by Invigorator
Own.—Bird C S Jr Mrs — $16,500 — Br.—Bird Mrs C S Jr (Pa) — Tr.—Secor John B — 112
St. 1st 2nd 3rd Amt. — 1977 0 M 0 0 — 1976 0 M 0 0
LATEST WORKOUTS May 6 Lrl 4f fst :49⅘ bg — ●May 1 Lrl 6f fst 1:14⅗ h — Apr 27 Lrl 5f fst 1:04 bg — Apr 9 Lrl 4f fst :50 b

Able Count — Ch. c. 3, by Count Brook—Elba, by Free France
Own.—Vogelman R E Jr — $18,500 — Br.—Vogelman R E Jr (Md) — Tr.—Vogelman Raymond Jr — 104 10
St. 1st 2nd 3rd Amt. — 1977 6 M 1 2 $2,938 — 1976 8 M 0 1 $624
11Mar77- 4Bow fst 6f :23⅕ :47 1:11⅗ Md 20000 6 6 95¾ 87¾ 916 916 Wright D R 118 19.60e 66–25 Battle Ally 1201½ Blue Streaker 120½ Stammer 1201 No factor 9
28Feb77- 3Bow fst 7f :23⅕ :46⅕ 1:26⅕ Md 14500 2 3 1½ 2½ 34½ 39½ Bradford B 49 120 2.40 64–22 Archie Ben 1181½ Swing North 1208 Able Count 1202 Speed, tired 5
17Feb77- 3Bow fst 6f :23⅕ :47⅖ 1:13⅗ Md 13500 1 5 1½ 1hd 2hd 22 Bradford B 67 118 10.40 69–30 Witchfire 1202 Able Count 118no Near Pete 120¾ Held gamely 7
4Feb77- 4Bow fst 6f :23 :47 1:13⅕ Md 14500 8 6 85¾ 78 69½ 78¾ Bradford B 120 3.50 65–30 Dynaright 120½ Swaps Ego 1205 Sweet Admiral 120¾ No factor 10
27Jan77- 4Bow fst 7f :24 :48 1:27⅖ Ⓢ Md Sp Wt 8 3 2½ 2½ 35 49¼ Bradford B 120 12.80e 59–35 Potted Pear 1202½ Native Search 1206 Misty Dell 120¾ Weakened 8
12Jan77- 4Bow fst 5½f :22⅕ :46 1:05⅖ Ⓢ Md 16500 10 7 89 88½ 45½ 35 Bradford B 118 38.50e 87–14 Hello Smartee 1204½ Turn Around 120½ Able Count 118½ Rallied 10
17Dec76- 1Lrl fst 6f :22⅖ :46⅕ 1:11⅗ Md 10000 4 8 86½ 914 819 719 Wright D R 120 11.80 70–19 Clarbo 1205 Montana Eagle 1203½ Selfish Way 1204 No factor 10
13Dec76- 4Lrl sl 6f :23 :48⅕ 1:15⅕ Clm 8500 2 5 56 59½ 57 34¾ Wright D R 116 43.20 66–26 Gallant Dewan 1184 Bold Grader 119¾ Able Count 116nk Rallied 9
20Nov76- 2Lrl fst 6f :23⅘ :46⅗ 1:12⅗ Ⓢ Md Sp Wt 1 6 64½ 711 812 814 Wright D R 120 69.90 70–13 Everybody Up 1202 Blue WizKid1201½ScoreForOrr1202 No factor 11
10Nov76- 4Lrl fst 7f :23⅕ :46⅗ 1:25 Ⓢ Md Sp Wt 11 4 32 46½ 9221028 Wright D R 119 132.20 58–16 OffShoreGamble1193PatrickSarsfield1199SecretShuffle1191 Tired 12
LATEST WORKOUTS May 3 Pim 3f fst :39 b — Apr 10 Pim 5f fst 1:04 b — Apr 4 Pim 5f sl 1:05⅖ b

Cover The Spread — Dk. b. or br. c. 3, by Mitey Prince—Tiptopmost, by Tim Tam
Own.—Brittingham B C — $17,500 — Br.—Brittingham B C (Md) — Tr.—Leatherbury King T — 113
St. 1st 2nd 3rd Amt. — 1977 2 M 0 1 $660 — 1976 0 M 0 0
28Apr77- 5Pim fst 6f :23⅘ :47⅕ 1:12⅗ 3↑Md 14500 10 1 1½ 1hd 32 33 McCarron C J 70 b 114 3.70 81–18 ConvoyAhead1142½TripleReef114½CoverTheSpred1143 Weakened 12
19Apr77- 9Pim fst 6f :23⅕ :46⅗ 1:12⅗ 3↑Md 18500 7 3 42 55 66½ 910 Cusimano 61 b 114 5.50 73–19 Ticket Taylor 1121½ English Favorite 1092¼ Retrace 112nk Tired 12
LATEST WORKOUTS Apr 2 Pim 5f fst 1:02 hg — Mar 25 CT 5f fst 1:05 hg

I almost never make a serious bet on a horse whose most recent race was bad. And I think most handicappers need to curb their willingness to excuse a poor performance—even when the excuse seems perfectly valid. If an animal has been running consistently well over fast tracks and then loses by 20 lengths in the mud, the track condition may account for his defeat. But it may not. It is very

possible that the horse's form was deteriorating and that he would have run poorly under any circumstances. There is no way to know for certain. A horse's last race is the single most important piece of evidence about his current condition, and I don't want that evidence to be equivocal when I am risking a large sum of money.

English Favorite had displayed speed in all his races and had earned respectable figures before his 37-length rout on May 5. Yet despite the margin of the defeat, his performance was a positive one. English Favorite was running a mile and one-sixteenth for the first time, and his previous tendency to tire at six furlongs suggested he was incapable of going that far. To make matters worse, he had drawn the number-eleven post position. He would have to lose ground all the way around the first turn, plowing through the deep going while some of his rivals hugged the rail. It seemed unlikely that he would ever get into contention.

But English Favorite managed to lead the race for a half mile, even while running against the bias. His time of 46⅘ seconds for that portion of the race was very impressive. On the same afternoon, an allowance-class speedball covered the first four furlongs of a route race in 47⅕. After such an effort, it was not surprising that English Favorite would tire badly. But he had left no doubt that he was in razor-sharp condition.

Now he was entered at the proper distance, six furlongs, and I assumed he was at least ready to duplicate his last performance in a sprint. English Favorite's figure in that April 19 race, an 81, was good enough to beat this field. But he had another edge as well. He had drawn the favorable number-two post position and was certain to get the rail from the plodder inside him. None of the horses outside him appeared quick enough to dislodge him from the rail.

English Favorite looked unbeatable, and I went to the track expecting to get substantial odds and make my biggest score of the year. I was disappointed. The bettors at Pimlico were getting smarter every day, and they made the horse a 2-to-1 favorite. Even at that price, I thought English Favorite was worth a $1000 bet.

FIRST RACE
Pimlico
MAY 11, 1977

6 FURLONGS. ($1.09\frac{3}{5}$) MAIDEN CLAIMING. Purse $5,500. 3- and 4-year-olds. Weights: 3-year-olds, 114 lbs., 4-year-olds, 124 lbs. Claiming Price $18,500; for each $1,000 to $16,500 1 lb.

Value of race $5,500, value to winner $3,300, second $1,210, third $660, fourth $330. Mutuel pool $38,110.

Last Raced	Horse	Eqt.A.Wt	PP	St	¼	½	Str	Fin	Jockey	Cl'g Pr	Odds $1
5May77 ^{5}Pim^{11}	English Favorite	b 3 114	2	4	1^{1}	1^{4}	1^{4}	$1^{3\frac{1}{2}}$	Adams J K	18500	2.20
28Apr77 ^{5}Pim^{3}	Cover The Spread	b 3 113	10	1	4^{6}	4^{6}	4^{4}	2^{1}	McCarron C J	17500	4.60
6Apr77 ^{1}Pen^{2}	Viteange	b 3 114	5	3	$3^{\frac{1}{2}}$	3^{2}	2^{hd}	3^{1}	Sim M C	18500	5.10
	Hayes Prince	3 112	3	6	5^{1}	5^{2}	5^{2}	$4^{3\frac{1}{2}}$	McCarron G	16500	14.00
	Gala Gusto	3 114	6	5	$2^{1\frac{1}{2}}$	2^{hd}	$3^{1\frac{1}{2}}$	5no	Bracciale V Jr	18500	5.10
11Mar77 ^{4}Bow^{9}	Able Count	3 106	9	7	6^{3}	$6^{1\frac{1}{2}}$	6^{3}	6^{1}	Eseman E^{10}	18500	28.60
4May77 ^{3}Pim^{5}	Say Darling	3 109	1	8	9^{3}	8^{3}	7^{3}	7^{4}	Agnello A	18500	6.50
	Platoon	3 113	8	9	7^{1}	9^{4}	$8^{\frac{1}{2}}$	8^{2}	Canessa J	16500	13.00
2May77 ^{4}Pim^{7}	Hiawatha	b 3 114	4	10	8^{2}	7^{2}	9^{4}	$9^{\frac{1}{2}}$	Lee T	18500	20.00
22Feb77 ^{5}Bow^{11}	Darcy Spice	4 124	7	2	10	10	10	10	Cusimano G	18500	52.90

OFF AT 1:00 EDT. Start good, Won ridden out. Time, :$22\frac{4}{5}$, :46, 1:$12\frac{2}{5}$ Track fast.

Official Program Numbers↘

$2 Mutuel Prices:			
2-ENGLISH FAVORITE	6.40	3.80	2.80
10-COVER THE SPREAD		5.40	3.20
5-VITEANGE			3.20

Ch. g, by Bold Favorite—Trackabu, by My Babu. Trainer Dearstyn Alan T. Bred by Lockwood W M (Md).

ENGLISH FAVORITE sprinted to the lead on the backstretch, opened a long lead on the turn and remained clear under intermittent urging. COVER THE SPREAD, never far back while wide, could not match the winner but finished second best. VITEANGE, well placed, lacked a response when set down for the drive. HAYES PRINCE lacked a rally. GALA PARTY had speed to the stretch and weakened. ABLE COUNT showed little. HIAWATHA was outrun.

Owners— 1, Lockwood W M; 2, Brittingham B C; 3, Swift G H; 4, Herring R L; 5, Moshe-Asher Stable; 6, Vogelman R E Jr; 7, Obre Mrs H; 8, Bird C S Jr Mrs; 9, Powhatan; 10, Clark Mrs R V.

Trainers— 1, Dearstyn Alan T; 2, Leatherbury King T; 3, Williams David E; 4, Ferris Richard D; 5, Dutrow Richard E; 6, Vogelman Raymond Jr; 7, Field Kenneth; 8, Secor John B; 9, Graham R; 10, Watters Margaret G.

Overweight: Able Count 2 pounds; Platoon 1.

When English Favorite sprinted to the lead and won by 3½ lengths, I was back in stride at Pimlico. Two days later I bet $100 on an exacta coupling two horses with early speed and inside posts and collected a $46.40 payoff. The next day I bet $800 on a speed-on-the-rail cinch who returned $5.80. While I was rolling up my profits, I was chagrined that the Kid was not capitalizing on the track bias as much as he should. He was still waiting for standouts with unshakable credentials and substantial odds and was passing up many decent betting opportunities. I argued that while patience is usually a virtue at the track, Pimlico demanded a more aggressive style of betting. I urged him to be more flexible in his approach to the game. But the Kid rejected my suggestion and continued to show restraint—until May 19, when he informed me, "There's a horse today who figures by ten lengths."

I had already studied the card thoroughly, and I had seen no such standout. "In the fifth race," the Kid said, "give Carolina Horn a figure of 78." Unlike me, the Kid had a set of speed figures for Charles Town Race Track in West Virginia. After our preparation for Gulfstream, when we had learned how to make our figures for Florida and New York interchangeable, the Kid had used the same process so he could compare horses from West Virginia and Maryland. His work had now produced the most esoteric, exciting bet of the Pimlico meeting.

Restless Dave — Dk. b. or br. g. 3, by Ishkoodah—Eleanor Dale, by Restless Cloud
Own.—Samvan Stable — $5,000 — Br.—Snow J (WVa) — Tr.—Delp Grover G — 112

	St.	1st	2nd	3rd	Amt.
1977	5	1	0	2	$3,204
1976	12	1	3	3	$6,512

22Apr77- 3Pim	fst	1 1/16	:47⅗	1:12⅗	1:47⅘	Clm c-4000	1	2	2^{5}	2^{8}	2^{10}	3^{12}	Bracciale	41	b	119	*.50	54-20	Cavadurli 114^{12} Rainbow King 114no RestlessDave119^{5}	No excuse	8
1Mar77- 2Bow	fst	1 1/16	:50⅘	1:16	1:49⅕	Clm c-3000	3	2	$3^{2\frac{1}{2}}$	$2^{1\frac{1}{2}}$	$2^{\frac{1}{2}}$	$1^{1\frac{1}{4}}$	McCarron	58		113	*.90	62-25	Restless Dave$113^{1\frac{1}{4}}$CuisineMinceur$112^{2\frac{3}{4}}$OnlyFishing115^{no}	Driving	7
23Feb77- 3Bow	fst	1 1/16	:50	1:15⅘	1:49	Clm 4000	3	2	$2^{\frac{1}{2}}$	$3^{3\frac{1}{2}}$	$3^{2\frac{1}{2}}$	3^{4}	McCarron	54		114	*2.10	59-21	Mitey Balmy $114^{\frac{1}{2}}$ Dancers Descent $114^{3\frac{1}{2}}$ RestlessDave114^{5}	Hung	7
15Feb77- 4Bow	fst	1 1/16	:49⅘	1:15	1:49⅕	Clm 6500	7	7	$6^{7\frac{1}{4}}$	6^{11}	$6^{9\frac{1}{2}}$	5^{11}	McCarron C J			114	*2.20	51-31	U. R. Great $112^{\frac{1}{2}}$ Sassy Pic 114^{6} Podic Creek 106^{4}	Dull try	8
9Feb77- 3Bow	fst	1 1/16	:50	1:16	1:49⅗	Clm 7500	5	5	$6^{2\frac{1}{2}}$	$4^{2\frac{1}{4}}$	$4^{5\frac{1}{2}}$	$5^{7\frac{3}{4}}$	McCarron C J			113	3.00	52-25	Trinity Row 115^{1} Exchange Time $113^{\frac{1}{2}}$ Our Nadja 107^{6}	Weakened	8
13Dec76- 4Lrl	sl	6f	:23	:48⅕	1:15⅕	Clm 8500	4	6	$7^{9\frac{1}{2}}$	7^{15}	7^{12}	$7^{7\frac{3}{4}}$	McCarron C J			118	4.00	63-26	Gallant Dewan 118^{4} Bold Grader $119^{\frac{3}{4}}$ Able Count 116^{nk}	Outrun	9
25Nov76- 5Lrl	fst	6f	:22⅗	:47	1:13	Clm 8500	10	6	$8^{6\frac{1}{4}}$	$6^{5\frac{1}{2}}$	$7^{9\frac{1}{4}}$	8^{11}	Lee T			118	7.40	71-19	CustersLastStand$118^{3\frac{3}{4}}$ShawBy118^{no}PlesntHighwy$116^{\frac{3}{4}}$	No factor	12
5Nov76- 4Lrl	fst	6f	:22⅖	:47⅕	1:13⅕	Clm 11500	6	4	$6^{4\frac{3}{4}}$	$5^{2\frac{3}{4}}$	6^{4}	$6^{4\frac{1}{2}}$	Duncan R R^{5}			111	9.00	76-19	Fighting Johnny 118no Yokum $120^{2\frac{1}{2}}$ GallantDewan$118^{\frac{1}{2}}$	No factor	10
25Oct76- 5Lrl	sly	6f	:23	:47⅘	1:14⅕	Clm c-8500	5	6	$5^{4\frac{1}{2}}$	$5^{4\frac{3}{4}}$	3^{3}	2^{1}	Bracciale V Jr			116	3.60	75-20	Willow Whip 115^{1} Restless Dave $116^{\frac{3}{4}}$ Rash King $112^{1\frac{3}{4}}$	Gamely	8
20Oct76- 3Bow	sly	6f	:22⅘	:46⅘	1:13⅖	Clm 8500	6	3	$3^{2\frac{1}{2}}$	$4^{4\frac{1}{2}}$	5^{8}	$4^{7\frac{1}{2}}$	Bracciale V Jr			117	2.00	65-24	Imperial Jumbo 117^{nk} Prince Hill 112^{4} Shaw Bay $117^{3\frac{1}{4}}$	Cut leg	7

LATEST WORKOUTS May 17 Pim 3f fst :37⅗ b — May 11 Pim 3f fst :37 b — May 5 Pim 3f gd :37 b — Apr 30 Pim 3f fst :38 b

O'Bie's Tim — Ch. g. 3, by Well Liked—Oak Wood Lady, by Correspondent
Own.—O'Brien Betty J — $5,000 — Br.—O'Brien Betty J (Md) — Tr.—Johnson James A — 112

	St.	1st	2nd	3rd	Amt.
1977	8	2	1	3	$4,648
1976	3	M	0	1	$365

13May77- 2CT	fst	6½f	:23⅕	:47	1:22⅕	Clm 5000	6	9	8^{12}	$5^{8\frac{1}{2}}$	$4^{7\frac{1}{2}}$	3^{5}	Grove P	49	b	120	3.00	69-22	Get Noble 120^{5} Fast Wolf 120no O'Bie's Tim 120^{3}	Rallied	9
3May77- 1Pim	fst	6f	:23⅗	:47⅘	1:13⅘	Clm 4000	5	8	8^{12}	8^{12}	$7^{7\frac{1}{4}}$	3^{4}	Cape E	52	b	119	22.00	73-20	Proper Fool 114no Foreglow 122^{4} O'Bie's Tim 119^{nk}	Rallied	9
20Apr77- 6Pen	fst	6f	:22⅘	:46⅗	1:11⅘	Clm 5000	8	2	$7^{4\frac{1}{4}}$	$7^{7\frac{1}{4}}$	7^{12}	7^{17}	Brocklebank J		b	118	7.00	70-19	Charlie Gay 112^{4} Sir Dark $105^{\frac{1}{2}}$ Dashing Archie 113^{7}	No factor	8
24Mar77- 8CT	fst	6½f	:24⅖	:49⅕	1:25	Clm 5000	1	5	$5^{2\frac{3}{4}}$	2^{1}	1^{hd}	1^{nk}	Grove P		b	117	3.10	60-39	O'Bie's Tim 117^{nk} Mighty Levy $120^{\frac{1}{2}}$ Salicylate 115^{1}	Driving	7
10Mar77- 5CT	fst	6½f	:24	:48⅘	1:24⅗	Clm 5000	3	5	6^{7}	$6^{7\frac{1}{2}}$	5^{3}	$3^{3\frac{1}{4}}$	Freshman W		b	120	*3.30	59-41	Mighty Levy 120^{nk} Solongtolove 120^{3} O'Bie's Tim 120no	Rallied	10
28Feb77- 6Pen	gd	5f	:23⅖	:48	1:00⅘	Clm 4000	3	3	$4^{2\frac{1}{2}}$	$4^{2\frac{1}{2}}$	4^{4}	2^{nk}	Freshman W		b	118	8.20	82-21	Trace O'Surge 118^{nk} O'Bie'sTim118^{no}Typewriter118^{3}	Just missed	7
15Feb77- 8CT	fst	6½f	:24⅗	:49⅕	1:26⅕	Clm 5000	1	8	$7^{8\frac{1}{4}}$	$7^{8\frac{3}{4}}$	6^{8}	6^{6}	Freshman W		b	120	4.70e	48-49	Day Drill 114no Hojo Joh $120^{1\frac{1}{2}}$ Sadat $120^{1\frac{1}{2}}$	Outrun	8
28Jan77- 1CT	fst	6½f	:25⅗	:49⅖	1:24⅖	Md 5000	8	8	$5^{6\frac{1}{2}}$	2^{3}	$2^{\frac{1}{2}}$	$1^{1\frac{1}{2}}$	Freshman W			120	4.30	63-27	O'Bie's Tim $120^{1\frac{1}{2}}$ Space Smash 115^{1} Blank Page 120^{4}	Driving	9
22Dec76- 2Lrl	fst	6f	:22⅗	:46⅘	1:12⅖	Md 6000	2	10	11^{13}	11^{18}	10^{16}	11^{11}	Shuk N			116	39.40	74-16	Peck 120^{5} Rose Spectre $111^{\frac{1}{2}}$ Looms Boy 120^{1}	No factor	11
24Nov76- 1CT	fst	4½f	:23⅕	:48⅗	:55⅖	Md 5000	3	7		$3^{1\frac{1}{2}}$	3^{2}	$3^{3\frac{1}{2}}$	Cape E			120	3.00	77-16	Satan'sShadow$120^{2\frac{1}{2}}$SabeCommnd120^{1}O'Bie'sTim120^{2}	No mishap	9

I had confidence in the Kid's ability as a speed handicapper, but I nevertheless thought it implausible that Carolina Horn could have run such a big figure while losing his last race by ten lengths. The winner of the race, Alamance Road, would have to be a truly phenomenal $5000 claimer, and horses in West Virginia usually aren't that good. So I looked back at the Charles Town results and saw that Alamance Road had run a full three seconds faster than a field of solid $2500 claimers did on the same evening. I learned that three of the also-rans behind Alamance Road, who all had lost by more than twenty lengths, had come back to run first or second in their subsequent starts. I concluded that Carolina Horn's figure was legitimate, and it was good enough to destroy this field. Carolina Horn's next-to-last number, a 70, was also sufficient to win.

Although he did not need any extra advantages, Carolina Horn would be breaking from the inside post position at a mile and one-sixteenth. The speed he had shown against Alamance Road would probably get him to the lead in this field of plodders.

But the bettors at Pimlico could not recognize how superior this horse was. They always shun invaders from minor-league tracks like Charles Town. And so Carolina Horn was 6 to 1 a few minutes before post time, when we went to the windows. After I had invested $1000 in win wagers and various exacta combinations, and a number of my friends had bet, too, the horse was 7 to 2.

FIFTH RACE
Pimlico
MAY 19, 1977

1 $\frac{1}{16}$ MILES. (1.41) CLAIMING. Purse $4,800. 3-year-olds. Weight, 120 lbs. Non-winners of two races since April 14, allowed 3 lbs. A race, 5 lbs. A race since April 7, 8 lbs. Claiming price $5,000. (Races where entered for $4,000 or less not considered.)

Value of race $4,800, value to winner $2,880, second $1,056, third $576, fourth $288. Mutuel pool $49,598. Exacta Pool $57,662.

Last Raced	Horse	Eqt.A.Wt	PP	St	¼	½	¾	Str	Fin	Jockey	Cl'g Pr	Odds $1
23Apr77 ^{6}CT^{2}	Carolina Horn	b 3 113	1	1	$1^{1\frac{1}{2}}$	1^{hd}	1^{3}	1^{4}	1^{6}	Chastine B	5000	3.50
6May77 ^{1}Pen^{1}	Noble Clown	b 3 117	3	4	5^{3}	$4^{\frac{1}{2}}$	$3^{1\frac{1}{2}}$	2^{3}	2^{3}	Culberson R	5000	10.70
2May77 ^{3}Pim^{3}	Peck	b 3 113	5	7	$6^{\frac{1}{2}}$	6^{1}	$5^{\frac{1}{2}}$	4^{2}	3no	Pineda R	5000	2.70
9May77 ^{8}CT^{3}	Proper Fool	b 3 112	2	5	3^{hd}	2^{2}	2^{1}	$3^{\frac{1}{2}}$	$4^{\frac{1}{2}}$	Ho G	5000	3.20
12May77 ^{1}Pim^{6}	Rainbow King	b 3 112	4	6	7^{3}	7^{4}	6^{2}	6^{5}	5^{1}	Graham S	5000	22.70
22Apr77 ^{3}Pim^{3}	Restless Dave	b 3 112	7	2	2^{hd}	3^{hd}	4^{1}	$5^{\frac{1}{2}}$	6^{5}	Sasser B	5000	4.80
27Apr77 ^{1}Pim^{2}	Cupie Cakes	b 3 108	6	8	8	8	8	7^{2}	7^{4}	Sim M C	5000	21.50
13May77 ^{2}CT^{3}	O'Bie's Tim	b 3 112	8	3	4^{2}	5^{2}	7^{1}	8	8	Grove P	5000	7.50

OFF AT 2:52, EDT. Start good, Won handily. Time, :24, :48⅕, 1:13⅖, 1:39, 1:45⅖ Track fast.

$2 Mutuel Prices:			
1–CAROLINA HORN	**9.00**	**8.60**	**4.80**
3–NOBLE CLOWN		**11.40**	**6.80**
5–PECK			**3.00**

$2 EXACTA 1–3 PAID $90.00.

B. g, by Spouting Horn—Carolina Fly, by Carolina Joy. Trainer Brown Larry R. Bred by Poe A O (Va).

CAROLINA HORN set the early pace, responded gamely to draw clear on the second turn and was not threatened in the drive. NOBLE CLOWN, reserved early, finished willingly to be second best. PECK passed tiring horses. PROPER FOOL, well placed, weakened after six furlongs. RAINBOW KING lacked a rally. RESTLESS DAVE was through early. CUPIE CAKES was outrun. O'BIE'S TIM had brief speed.

Owners— 1, Wheeler G L; 2, Colee F; 3, DiNatale J M; 4, Roberts G; 5, Goldenleaf Stable; 6, Samvan Stable; 7, Brothers Jr & Emory; 8, O'Brien Betty J.

Trainers— 1, Brown Larry R; 2, Colee Frank; 3, Dinatale John F; 4, Williams Alfred W; 5, Tapscott Radcliff C; 6, Delp Grover G; 7, Brothers Granville C; 8, Johnson James A.

Overweight: Carolina Horn 1 pound; Peck 1; Cupie Cakes 1.

Carolina Horn was claimed by Heard D; trainer, Leatherbury King T; Noble Clown was claimed by R X Stable; trainer, Gross Mel W; Proper Fool was claimed by McManus W L Jr; trainer, Campbell Michael J.

Bettors who saw Carolina Horn's odds plummet just before he breezed to a six-length victory must have suspected that larceny was afoot, that shrewd insiders had orchestrated an audacious betting coup. They could not have imagined that this was all triggered by a scholarly twenty-three-year-old with a good set of speed figures.

I felt like a proud father after the race. Seeing my protégé make such a brilliant selection gave me more satisfaction than if I had done it myself. And the Kid's work had given me tangible as well as psychic rewards. I hit one of my prime exacta combinations and won more than $6000, boosting my profits for the Pimlico season near the $20,000 level.

The bias at Pimlico was beginning to look like a permanent condition, which I found delightful but also a little surprising. In previous years it had lasted for two or three weeks at the most and then disappeared. So I visited Clark Robinson, the track superintendent, and asked him if he could explain why almost every race was being won by a horse on the rail.

Robinson looked at me blankly. "Just the other day," he said, "a horse in the nine post came from behind and won in the middle of the track."

I cited some more meaningful facts, such as a string of twenty consecutive races won by horses breaking from posts one, two, three, or four. Robinson shrugged. "The track's in the best shape it's ever been," he said. "The cushion is uniform. I wouldn't say that the rail is any faster than the rest of the track."

If the people in Pimlico's management did not even recognize the existence of an abnormality in their racing strip, they were not going to change it. And the bias, which until now had only affected local horses and local horseplayers, was going to make an impact on the national racing scene.

Seattle Slew was coming to Pimlico to run in the Preakness and continue his pursuit of the Triple Crown. The racing fans who were hailing him as a superhorse might have thought that the outcome of the Preakness was a foregone conclusion, but I did not. My figures said that Seattle Slew was no faster than his chief rival, Cormorant. Their head-to-head duel was likely to be determined by the draw for post positions—and the track bias.

Cormorant ✻ — B. c. 3, by His Majesty—Song Sparrow, by Tudor Minstrel — **126**
Own.—Berry C T Jr — Br.—Roach Ben (Ky) — Tr.—Simpson James P

	St.	1st	2nd	3rd	Amt.
1977	4	3	1	0	$94,686
1976	5	4	0	0	$30,258

14May77- 8Aqu	fst	1	:45⅘	1:10⅘	1:37	Withers	4	1	1hd	1hd	1½	2no	Wright D R	115	126	*.30	81–22	Iron Constitution 126no Cormorant 1265 Affiliate 126¾	Just failed	8
9Apr77- 8Aqu	fst	1 1/16 ⊡	:47	1:11⅘	1:43⅗	Gotham	2	1	11½	1hd	11½	12¼	Wright D R	114	123	*1.10	100–09	Cormorant 1232¼ Fratello Ed 121½ Papelote 1142¾	Driving	9
26Mar77- 8Aqu	fst	6f ⊡	:22⅗	:46⅕	1:10⅘	Bay Shore	6	1	32	31½	2½	11¼	Wright D R	113	121	*.70	95–13	Cormorant 1211¼ Medieval Man 1195¾ Hey Hey J. P. 1141	Driving	6
5Mar77- 8GS	my	6f	:22⅕	:45⅕	1:10⅗	Iroquois H	9	3	42½	33	2hd	15	Wright D R		120	*1.00	90–26	Cormorant 1205 Iron Derby 119nk Do The Bump 1232½	Handily	9
16Oct76- 8Bow	fst	7f	:22⅘	:45⅗	1:22⅗	Marl Nursery	4	2	1½	1hd	1hd	1nk	Wright D R	111	113	2.80	92–19	Cormorant 113nk Do TheBump1163RoyalSki1227	Long, hard drive	8
1Oct76- 7Bow	sly	7f	:23⅕	:46⅕	1:24	Allowance	3	3	3½	1½	13	15	Wright D R		117	*1.70	85–27	Cormorant 1175 John U To Berry 1177 Artic Son1171	Ridden out	6
14Sep76- 6Bow	fst	6f	:23⅕	:46⅗	1:11⅖	Allowance	9	1	3nk	1hd	12½	15	Wright D R		120	*.70	83–20	Cormorant 1205 John U To Berry 1135 Zikali 112nk	Driving	11
1Sep76- 2Del	fst	6f	:22⅕	:45⅘	1:10⅘	Md Sp Wt	10	2	1hd	1hd	11½	15½	Wright D R		120	*1.40	91–15	Cormorant 1205½ Madoc 120nk Bird Jay 1201¼	Handily	12
22Jun76- 9Pim	sly	5f	:22⅘	:47	:59⅗	Md Sp Wt	8	1	31½	825	815	714	Wright D R		b 120	4.50	73–12	Royal Ski 1202 Angler I. 1201½ French Admiral 1203	Bolted turn	8

LATEST WORKOUTS ●May 11 Lrl 5f fst :57⅗ h ●May 4 Lrl 1 fst 1:37 h ●Apr 26 Lrl 5f fst :58 h Mar 24 Aqu ⊡ 4f fst :52 b

Cormorant had run a spectacular figure of 111 as a two-year-old at Bowie, and horses who display such precocity often develop into top-class runners. I thought Cormorant had the potential to win the Kentucky Derby, but I doubted the ability of trainer Jim Simpson, who had never operated in the upper echelon of racing and was handling this gifted thoroughbred as if he were one of the run-of-the-mill allowance horses to which he was more accustomed. I expressed this opinion in a newspaper column, cutting off future communications with the Cormorant camp. My only 1977 telephone interview with the trainer went: "Mr. Simpson, this is Andrew Beyer." "I have nothing to say to you." Click.

Somehow, Simpson managed to train Cormorant as a three-year-old without my help. The colt reeled off figures of 113 and 114, but was knocked out of training by a minor injury and was forced to miss the Kentucky Derby. He returned to competition in the Withers Stakes and ran a 115 while losing by a nose. Despite the consistent excellence of his performances, Cormorant never received any acclaim. He had, in fact, been winning by modest margins over horses with modest reputations, and he had been displaying no great élan in the process. But figures do not lie, and they said Cormorant had the ability to be a champion.

Seattle Slew Dk. b. or br. c. 3, by Bold Reasoning—My Charmer, by Poker
Own.—Taylor Karen L Br.—Castleman B S (Ky) Tr.—Turner William H Jr **126**

	St.	1st	2nd	3rd	Amt.
1977	4	4	0	0	$375,690
1976	3	3	0	0	$94,350

7May77- 8CD	fst	1¼	:45⅘	1:36	2:02⅕	Ky Derby	4	2	2hd	1hd	13	11¾	Cruguet J	112	126	*.50	86-12	Seattle Slew 126 1¾ RunDustyRun126nk Sanhedrin126 3¼ Ridden out 15
23Apr77- 8Aqu	fst	1⅛	:47⅘	1:12⅕	1:49⅗	Wood Mem	6	1	1hd	11½	16	13¼	Cruguet J	114	126	*.10	87-13	Seattle Slew 126 3¼ Sanhedrin 126 4½ Catalan 126hd Handily 7
26Mar77- 9Hia	fst	1⅛	:45⅕	1:09	1:47⅖	Flamingo	4	1	11½	16	16	14	Cruguet J		122	*.20	95-15	Seattle Slew 122 4 Giboulee122nk FortPrevel122 4½ Speed in reserve 13
9Mar77- 9Hia	fst	7f	:22⅕	:44	1:20⅗	Allowance	2	6	1hd	12	14	19	Cruguet J		117	*.10	102-10	Seattle Slew 117 9 WhiteRammer122 3½ SmashingNative119 2½ Easily 8
16Oct76- 8Bel	fst	1	:46	1:10	1:34⅖	Champagne	3	1	12	12	13	19¾	Cruguet J	115	122	*1.30	96-13	SeattleSlew122 9¾ FortheMoment122 1¼ SailToRome122 3 Easy score 10
5Oct76- 7Bel	fst	7f	:22⅗	:45⅘	1:22	Allowance	1	8	11½	11	13	13½	Cruguet J	106	122	*.40	92-13	Seattle Slew 122 3½ Cruise On In 119 6 Lancer'sPride117 2¼ Handily 8
20Sep76- 5Bel	fst	6f	:22⅖	:45⅖	1:10⅕	Md Sp Wt	8	10	1½	12	15	15	Cruguet J		122	*2.60	91-12	Seattle Slew 122 5 Proud Arion 122½ Prince Andrew 122 2 Easily 12

LATEST WORKOUTS May 20 Pim 3f fst :36 b ●May 15 Bel 7f fst 1:22⅘ h ●May 6 CD 3f fst :34⅖ h May 1 CD 1 fst 1:41⅘ b

Seattle Slew had won all seven of his races with ease, prompting his legion of admirers to believe that he had not yet displayed more than a fraction of his enormous potential. But I thought I knew just how good Seattle Slew was. He was, give or take a point or two, a 114. I estimated his Kentucky Derby figure to be 112. I would not accept the universal belief that he could have run much faster if his jockey had urged him, or if other horses had pressed him. I consider this notion a fallacy. In my handicapping of ordinary races, I know that a horse who won his last race easily will rarely improve upon his figure when he is forced to run all-out. In fact, he will usually run worse. In 1976, the same arguments which were being used for Seattle Slew had been applied to Honest Pleasure. He was billed as a superhorse because he was winning easily, even though his times were mediocre. But when Bold Forbes tested him in the Derby, he proved that Honest Pleasure didn't have limitless potential after all.

At first I viewed Seattle Slew with tempered enthusiasm, but I grew to detest him. I bristled every time he was compared with Secretariat, who routinely ran figures of 129 and would have blown Seattle Slew off the track on any day of their lives. And I found myself heaped with abuse whenever I tried to point out Seattle Slew's limitations. A stream of letters to the editor of the *Star* denounced me for failing to give the horse proper credit. Worse, my one-time handicapping mentor Steve Davidowitz started talking to me as if I were a dunderhead, telling me I lacked the sophistication and the visual skills to appreciate Seattle Slew's greatness.

I do not often let emotions affect my handicapping judgment, but I passionately wanted to cash a big bet against Seattle Slew and thumb my nose at the world. I knew I could do it in the Preakness, if Cormorant had the track bias in his favor. When the post positions were drawn, I could barely contain my enthusiasm. Cormorant would be breaking from post position number one, Seattle Slew from number eight. I decided that I was going to make the first $2000 bet of my life.

Suddenly Pimlico's track bias became a *cause célèbre*. Reporters covering the Preakness studied the previous results at the meeting and learned how important the rail was. They asked Seattle Slew's trainer, Billy Turner, whether he thought his horse would be affected by his post position. Publicly Turner said no, but privately he discussed the condition of the track with Pimlico's general manager Chick Lang.

Pimlico was still recovering from an embarrassment in the 1973 Triple Crown series. The electric timer at the track had been malfunctioning for years; it had credited a mediocre allowance-class filly with the six-furlong track record of 1:09⅕, when stopwatches showed that her time was 1:12. But Lang stubbornly maintained that nothing was wrong with the timer. He did, that is, until it misfired in the Preakness, depriving Secretariat of a track record and triggering months of controversy over how fast he actually ran. The next year Pimlico had a timer that worked.

On the day before Seattle Slew's Preakness, Lang remained true to form and asserted that his racetrack was uniform and fair. But he evidently had told his superintendent to do something about the rail, because the track changed overnight. I could hardly believe my eyes when I watched the third race on Preakness day and saw a horse break from the number-seven post position, circle the field, and win going away. In the seventh race a sprinter trailed for half a mile, swung to the middle of the track, and rallied to win. The bias was gone.

I knew that Cormorant no longer possessed a significant edge over Seattle Slew, but I still felt committed to him. I cut my planned wager in half, bet $1000 on Cormorant at 9 to 2, and watched an epic duel. Jockey Danny Wright, who understood the Pimlico track better than any rider in Maryland, broke Cormorant out of the gate sharply, took the lead, and made sure that he kept Seattle Slew outside him. The two colts battled head-and-head through a half-mile in a blazing 45⅗ seconds, and three-quarters of a mile in 1:09⅘. If this had been the old Pimlico track, Seattle Slew would have been finished after plowing through the deeper going on the outside. But now it was Cormorant who started to give way. Seattle Slew inched ahead as he approached the final turn, opened a clear lead as he entered the stretch, and went on to an impressive victory, as Cormorant struggled home fourth.

Steve Davidowitz gloated. Letters to the editor of the *Star* pointed out that the paper's racing columnist was an ignoramus. The whole world hailed Seattle Slew as an invincible champion. But I will always believe that he would have lost the Preakness if the condition of the track had not been rearranged for his benefit.

Two days later the bias reappeared, as strong as ever, and I resumed my usual pattern of betting. Almost. I was no longer merely putting my money through the mutuel windows at Pimlico. As a result of a casual conversation outside a Baltimore delicatessen, I found myself involved with the shadowy world of bookmaking.

I had not had a good relationship with a bookmaker since I was fifteen, when my bookie canceled a $6 debt and gave me a toy pinball machine as a Christmas present. But during the Pimlico meeting I developed a friendship with a bookmaker named Jerry, who had recently been divorced and was now patronizing some of the same Washington bars that I did. When he told me how his marriage had broken up over a Michigan-Oklahoma football game, I felt that we were kindred spirits with the same kind of sheer enthusiasm for gambling.

Jerry had met Pam four years earlier, and they had become involved in such a wonderful, exciting romance that she hardly bothered to ask him how he earned his living. She knew that he gambled, but she never quite comprehended that he was a professional whose livelihood came principally from betting on sports events, and sometimes from making book on them. The young lovers married, bought an old house, and spent much of their time refurbishing it, with Jerry's winnings providing an endless supply of money for the project. The couple still never discussed the source of their income.

Sometimes it was difficult for Jerry to bottle up his passion for gambling when he was with his wife. Once they were having Thanksgiving dinner with Pam's parents when Jerry excused himself from the table, called his bookmaker, and whispered a $10,000 bet on Mississippi. He fidgeted through the meal until he could get to the television set, and when he learned that Mississippi had beaten the point spread he still had to suppress his excitement. His only outlet was to go outside and run down the street with his dog, telling him, "Ten big ones! Don't worry, boy! You'll be in Puppy Chow for life!"

Even though their marriage wasn't exactly founded on honest communication, Jerry and Pam were happy as long as the money kept rolling in. But after two years of successful betting, Jerry's luck finally turned sour. Pam perceived the change in her husband, and finally asked him what was wrong.

"I've been losing," Jerry said.

"How much?" Pam asked.

Jerry told her the figure, and he knew from the look of utter disbelief on her face that the marriage was almost over. He needed to recoup, quickly. A few days later he called his bookie and bet everything he had, $16,500, on Michigan plus 6½ points against Oklahoma. He sat transfixed in front of the television set as Oklahoma opened a 14–0 lead; Michigan came back to score in the last minute to make it 14–6, attempted a two-point conversion—and missed by inches. Jerry screamed. Then he kicked in the television set. With sparks flying through the living room, his wife ran in and confronted him. "You bet on that game," she deduced.

"Right," Jerry shouted. "I just lost sixteen thousand five hundred dollars on a football game."

"You're crazy," she said.

Jerry held his hands inches apart. "I was this far from the goal line," he said, but before the sentence was finished he was speaking to an empty room. That was his last stab at conventional respectability. Jerry immersed himself fully in the gambling life, betting on all sports and driving regularly to Pimlico with the Kid and me.

One day he made a slight detour from our usual route to the track, explaining that he had to conduct a transaction with a business associate named Sneaky Pete. He parked in front of a delicatessen, directly behind a large Cadillac, got out of his car, conversed with the driver, and then returned to the Kid and me. "Pete wants to know if we can give him a little parlay today," Jerry said.

"Sure," I told him. "Majestic Julie in the sixth and Splitting Headache in the seventh."

Both horses won easily, and the next day Pete called Jerry to tell him he had hit the parlay for $1000. "Tell your boys," he said, "that if they ever need to get a bet down, I'll get it down for them."

I had always thought that having a reliable bookie could be very useful. I was betting so heavily now that I was sometimes hurting my own odds by wagering at the track, as in the case of Carolina Horn. And I followed the national racing scene closely enough that I often wanted to place bets at inaccessible tracks. But I had never found a trustworthy bookie who would handle the action. I thought most members of the profession shunned horses nowadays in favor of football and basketball.

That was not the case, Jerry informed me. Plenty of bookmakers still deal with horses, but they are wary of handling very large bets because of the possibility that they will be stung by inside information. You can't call a bookie and bet $5000 on a horse as you could on a professional football game. But you can call twenty-five bookies and bet $200 with each of them—if you happen to know the phone numbers of twenty-five bookies.

Sneaky Pete knew them. His network of contacts in the gambling world was enormous. Pete was a small-scale bookie himself, Jerry told me, but mostly he was a middleman and a trafficker in information. One day he might take a wager from A and place it with B. The next day he might take a bet from B and place it with C. While he was conducting these transactions, he was evaluating the information and the sources and was placing bets for himself accordingly. So when he volunteered to place horse bets for Jerry, his motives were not purely altruistic.

I was happy to oblige him, and I responded to the chance to bet out-of-town races as if I were a kid with a new toy. In the span of a few days I had Jerry place six small bets through Sneaky Pete. Remarkably, five of the horses won and one ran second. I was doing this primarily for entertainment, but on May 26 I needed Pete's services for a serious transaction.

The Kid and I liked a horse at Pimlico, and loved one at Monmouth Park the same afternoon. We wanted to make a healthy bet on the New Jersey race, but I was apprehensive about entrusting a large sum of money to people I had never met. Jerry suggested that it might be a good idea if Pete developed a proper amount of respect for the unseen horse bettors he was now dealing with. So he telephoned Pete and said, "This is seven winners out of eight that my boys have given you."

"I know it, baby," Pete said. "Never seen anything like it in my life."

"You know, Pete, nobody can handicap horses like that."

"You don't have to tell me that, baby. Never seen anything like it. Where are these horses coming from, anyway?"

"They're coming from . . . up north," Jerry said, evasively.

"You mean the mob?"

"Pete, please."

"Sorry, baby. I don't want to know who they're coming from or where they're coming from or how they're winning. Just tell me what you want to bet."

"All right," Jerry said. "Get us fifteen hundred to win on Just John in the eighth at Monmouth."

"I'll get right on it," Pete said.

(8) MONMOUTH — 1 1-16 MILES — MONMOUTH PARK

1 1/16 MILES. (1.41) ALLOWANCE. Purse $8,500. 3-year-olds and Upward which have not won three races other than Maiden, Claiming or Starter. Weight 113 lbs., Older 124 lbs. Non-winners of $7,200 in 1977 allowed 3 lbs. $4,800 twice 5 lbs. $4,800 in 1977, 7 lbs. (Maiden and Claiming and Starter races not considered.)

Brave Scout

Dk. b. or br. c. 4, by Hail to Reason—Silver Bright, by Barbizon
Br.—Whitney C V (Ky)
Tr.—Poole George T III
Own.—Whitney C V

117

Turf Record — St. 1st 2nd 3rd — Amt.
St. 1st 2nd 3rd — 1977 6 0 0 1 — $1,178
6 1 1 1 — 1976 13 3 3 2 — $20,465

LATEST WORKOUTS May 24 Mth 4f fst :49½ b ● May 20 Mth 5f fst 1:00 h ● May 17 Mth 3f fst :35½ h May 2 CD 4f fst :51 b

Best Bee

B. c. 4, by Better Bee—Goldflower, by Greek Song
Br.—Fisher Marty V (Ky)
Tr.—Werstler Charles R
Own.—Dixiana

121

St. 1st 2nd 3rd — Amt.
1977 4 0 0 2 — $2,061
1976 10 2 0 1 — $13,690

LATEST WORKOUTS May 25 Mth 3f fst :35½ b May 21 Mth 6f fst 1:16 h Apr 23 Hia 5f fst 1:01 h Apr 9 Hia 5f fst 1:01 h

Get The Axe

Dk. b. or br. c. 3, by The Axe II—Bwamazon Lady, by Hail to Reason
Br.—Bell M H
Tr.—Bwamazon Farm
Own.—Bwamazon Farm

110

St. 1st 2nd 3rd — Amt.
1977 4 0 1 0 — $14,967
1976 13 3 4 3 — $52,062

LATEST WORKOUTS May 22 Mth 4f fst :50 b May 4 CD 4f my :48½ b Apr 25 Kee 5f my 1:00 h Apr 20 Kee 1 fst 1:42 b

Verna's Pride

Ch. g. 5, by Florida State—Early Bird, by Barbizon
Br.—Early Bird Stud (Fla)
Tr.—Fallon Martin L
Own.—Fallon M L

117

Turf Record — St. 1st 2nd 3rd — Amt.
St. 1st 2nd 3rd — 1977 3 0 1 0 — $2,540
5 0 1 2 — 1976 23 5 1 3 — $39,537

14Sep76-Awarded Second Purse Money

LATEST WORKOUTS May 24 Mth 4f fst :48 h May 20 Mth 3f fst 1:15½ b May 15 Mth 4f fst :49 b May 9 GS 6f gd 1:17½ b

Nodouble Trouble

Ch. g. 4, by Nodouble—Vita Mia, by Ribot
Br.—Brady W T (Ky)
Tr.—Zatesio George
Own.—Epstein S

119

Turf Record — St. 1st 2nd 3rd — Amt.
St. 1st 2nd 3rd — 1977 7 1 0 0 — $6,074
6 1 0 0 — 1976 17 2 3 4 — $17,605

LATEST WORKOUTS May 25 Mth 3f fst :39 b Apr 11 GP 3f sly :35½ h

Just John

Ch. g. 6, by Stage Door Johnny—Born To Reason, by Hail to Reason
Br.—Combs L II & Kernan F (Ky)
Tr.—Bardaro Anthony J
Own.—Bright View Farm

117

Turf Record — St. 1st 2nd 3rd — Amt.
St. 1st 2nd 3rd — 1977 2 0 1 0 — $1,500
5 0 0 0 — 1976 17 1 2 0 — $10,090

LATEST WORKOUTS May 21 Mth 6f fst 1:16½ b May 4 Atl 5f fst 1:01½ b Apr 17 GS 4f fst :51 b Apr 9 GS 6f fst 1:16½ b

Lord Harry L. uk. b. or br. g. 5, by Sir Ivor—Theme Song, by Nearctic
Own.—Landry H L Br.—Taylor E P (Md) Tr.—Perlsweig Daniel
117

Turf Record	St.	1st	2nd	3rd		St.	1st	2nd	3rd	Amt.
	3	0	1	1	1977	6	1	2	1	$6,435
					1976	14	0	4	1	$8,825

13Mar77- 7Pen	sly	5½f	:22	:45⅕	1:04⅕		Allowance	2	8	64¾	55½	43½	33½	Torre M J5	114	8.30	94-15	Velvet Flight 1132½ Jiva Coolit 1221 Lord Harry L. 114½	Rallied	10
27Feb77- 7Pen	fst	6f	:22⅕	:45	1:10		Allowance	5	4	77	57½	47½	45	Lloyd J S	122	4.30	91-11	Jiva Coolit 1151 All Ambition 1221 Real Guy 1153	Mild gain	8
13Feb77- 7Pen	gd	6f	:22⅗	:46⅖	1:12⅖		Allowance	6	5	53¼	45½	34½	22	Lloyd J S	122	3.00	82-22	All Ambition 1132 Lord Harry L. 122½ [D]VenetianJam111½	Gamely	8
30Jan77-11Pen	fst	5½f	:22⅘	:47	1:06		Allowance	4	9	99¼	65¾	52½	1no	Heim K	114	11.00	89-28	Lord Harry L. 114no All Ambition 113hd Jiva Coolit 114hd	Driving	9
16Jan77- 7Pen	gd	6f	:23⅕	:46⅘	1:11⅘		Allowance	4	7	54½	44	32½	22½	Lloyd J S	113	6.40	84-22	Official Record 1142½ Lord Harry L. 1132 Premediate113½	Gamely	8
4Jan77- 7Bow	fst	1 1/16	:47⅕	1:12	1:44⅗		Allowance	3	4	49	58½	34½	611	Lloyd J S	112	8.80	74-23	Jamison 1195 Father's Angel 1133¼ Battle Hawk 1172	Tired	7
18Dec76- 5Aqu	fst	1 1/16 [•]	:48⅕	1:13⅗	1:45⅗	3↑	Allowance	1	2	21½	43½	59½	69½	Lloyd J S	117	11.10	— —	To The Tune 122hd Freedom Calling112nkIrishEra1193	No excuse	6
9Dec76- 6Aqu	fst	6f [•]	:23	:46⅗	1:11⅖	3↑	Allowance	3	5	32½	34	36	45½	Lloyd J S	117	19.00	— —	Bright Discovery 1153½ MasterJorge1101¼NorthofTown115¾	Tired	5
27Nov76- 5Key	fst	6f	:23	:46⅘	1:11⅘	3↑	Allowance	4	5	66½	44½	46½	24	Lloyd J S	113	3.10	79-25	Bradley's Alibi 1084 Lord Harry L. 113nkIberianIngot105½	Gamely	6
13Nov76- 6Lrl	fst	6f	:22⅖	:45⅘	1:11⅕	3↑	[S]Allowance	3	8	24½	37	26	24¼	Lloyd J S	116	38.10	87-17	Born Noble 1174¼ Lord Harry L. 1163 Chennault 1173	2nd best	9

LATEST WORKOUTS May 20 Mth Ⓣ 1fm 1:42 h May 14 GS 6f fst 1:16 b May 10 GS 4f fst :51 b

Although I did not make figures for the New Jersey tracks, I suspected at once that Just John's last race at Atlantic City had been exceptional. He had lost by a half length to Talc, a tough stakes horse who I knew had gone to New York a week later and earned a figure of 112. When I studied the results of the other races on the day Just John and Talc had run, I confirmed my initial impression. They had covered seven furlongs in 1:23⅗. Half an hour later, a stakes-winning filly named Exerene, who I remembered had been running figures in the high 90s at Gulfstream, went the same distance in 1:25. I estimated that Just John's figure had been about a 112, and I thought he might even improve upon that at Monmouth. He had raced only twice in 1977, and he might be rounding into form. And now he was entered at a mile and one-sixteenth, a distance at which he had run his best races the year before.

As strong as Just John's credentials were, the crowd at Monmouth was likely to prefer Get The Axe on the basis of his fourth-place finish in the Kentucky Derby. This was my chance to capitalize at last on my understanding of Seattle Slew's limitations. I knew that Slew himself had run only about a 112 figure in the Derby, and so Get The Axe's five-length loss to him was not a noteworthy achievement.

While my thoughts and prayers were with Just John on the afternoon of May 26, I was at Pimlico to bet a filly named Bee Nun. In much the same way that I had improvised a figure for Just John's Atlantic City performance, I had estimated figures for Bee Nun's races at Penn National. She looked clearly superior to her Maryland competition, and she was a front-runner breaking from post position two in a route race. When she led all the way to pay $14.40, I collected more than $4000. But I could not savor that windfall as Jerry drove me back to Washington. I was staring at my watch, counting the minutes until post time in New Jersey. Finally, as we approached Washington, I told Jerry to stop the car. I dashed to a phone booth, called my sports department, and asked for the results of the eighth race at Monmouth. Waiting for the answer was more nerve-racking than watching the race. Then it came: "Just John. Fourteen-sixty." I bounded out of the phone booth, embraced Jerry, and yelled, "We did it!" I had just experienced the first $10,000 day in my life as a gambler.

EIGHTH RACE			1 1/16 MILES. (1.41) ALLOWANCE. Purse $8,500. 3-year-olds and Upward which have not

Monmouth

won three races other than Maiden, Claiming or Starter. Weight 113 lbs., Older 124 lbs. Non-winners of $7,200 in 1977 allowed 3 lbs. $4,800 twice 5 lbs. $4,800 in 1977, 7 lbs.

MAY 26, 1977

(Maiden and Claiming and Starter races not considered.)

Value of race $8,500, value to winner $5,100, second $1,700, third $935, fourth $519, fifth $255. Mutuel pool $89,060.

Last Raced	Horse	Eqt.A.Wt	PP	St	1/4	1/2	3/4	Str	Fin	Jockey	Odds $1
7May77 7Atl2	Just John	b 6 117	6	4	31½	31	1hd	11	12	Nied J Jr	6.30
2May77 9Hia3	Best Bee	b 4 121	2	5	4hd	41	42½	22½	23	Miceli M	10.90
7May77 8CD4	Get The Axe	3 110	3	3	51	66	51	41	33¾	Barrera C	.50
13Mar77 7Pen3	Lord Harry L.	5 117	7	7	62½	5½	65	64	41	Black A S	30.80
21Apr77 7Pim4	Verna's Pride	b 5 117	4	2	12½	12½	2hd	3hd	52	Thomas D B	4.20
14Apr77 9Hia5	Nodouble Trouble	b 4 119	5	6	7	7	7	7	6½	Gomez M A	14.50
4May77 7CD9	Brave Scout	4 117	1	1	21	2hd	32	52	7	Perret C	16.20

OFF AT 5:26, EDT. Start good, Won driving. Time, :23⅖, :47, 1:11, 1:36⅘, 1:43⅖ Track fast.

$2 Mutuel Prices:	6–JUST JOHN	14.60	5.40	4.00
	2–BEST BEE		8.20	3.80
	3–GET THE AXE			2.80

Ch. g, by Stage Door Johnny—Born To Reason, by Hail to Reason. Trainer Bardaro Anthony J. Bred by Combs L II & Kernan F (Ky).

JUST JOHN, reserved within easy striking distance of the early pace, moved to the lead outside rivals on the far turn and maintained a safe margin in the final furlong. BEST BEE, never far back, rallied between horses in the stretch but could not finish with the winner. GET THE AXE, never far back, stayed a bit wide to rally through the final quarter and failed to seriously threaten. LORD HARRY L. had no excuse. VERNA'S PRIDE tired in the final quarter, as did BRAVE SCOUT.

Owners— 1, Bright View Farm; 2, Dixiana; 3, Bwamazon Farm; 4, Landry H L; 5, Fallon M L; 6, Epstein 7, Whitney C V.

Trainers— 1, Bardaro Anthony J; 2, Werstler Charles R; 3, Bell M H; 4, Perlsweig Daniel; 5, Fallon Martin 6, Zateslo George; 7, Poole George T III.

Scratched—Repaupo (9Apr77 8GS9).

After hitting a spectacular pair of winners like Bee Nun and Just John in the same afternoon, I ordinarily would have celebrated and rested on my laurels for a few days. But I was so excited that I couldn't relax; I felt so obsessed that I couldn't divert my thoughts from gambling for even a short time. When I came back home from the track, I would immediately begin to work on my figures, study the next day's races, and think about them all evening. At night I slept fitfully, and when I did I dreamed about horses instead of Candice Bergen. I thought I had outgrown this sort of feverishness in my youth, but I had never experienced such a winning streak before. It was hard to keep my feet on the ground while I was living out a fantasy and averaging nearly $2000 every time I passed through the turnstiles at Pimlico. In my rare moments of lucidity I apologized to my non-gambling friends for my antisocial preoccupation with the horses, and explained that I had to capitalize on this streak as long as it lasted. When it was over I could become a civilized human being again.

The night after Just John's victory, I could hardly sleep at all, because I kept running the next day's feature race over and over in my mind. And I kept seeing the same outcome.

8 PIMLICO

1 1-16 MILES
PIMLICO
▲Start ▲Finish

1 1/16 MILES. (1.41) THE CITY OF BALTIMORE HANDICAP 12th Running. $25,000 Added. A handicap for 3-year-olds and upward. By subscription of $50 each, which should accompany the nomination, $200 additional to start, with $25,000 added, of which 65% of all monies to the winner, 20% to second, 10% to third and 5% to fourth. weighhs five days before the race. Staters to be named through the entry box by the usual time of closing. Trophy to the owner of the winner. Closed Friday, April 22, 1977 with 39 nominations.

Talc
B. h. 5, by Rock Talk—Heat Rash, by Rash Prince
Br.—Erlanger M C (Md)
Tr.—Harraway Thomas P
Own.—Tinton Falls Stable
118 Turf Record St. 1st 2nd 3rd: 5 1 2 1 | St. 1st 2nd 3rd Amt. | 1977 2 1 1 0 $10,000 | 1976 19 6 1 5 $93,699

19May77- 8Aqu sly 1 :45⅖ 1:10 1:35⅕ Handicap 3 3 32 1½ 11½ 2¾ Vasquez J b 122 *1.80 89-12 Co Host 113¾ Talc 1227 Cliff Chesney 1122 Gamely 6
7May77- 7Atl fst 7f :22 :45⅗ 1:23⅖ Allowance 4 5 46 31 1½ 1½ Nemeti W b 122 *.40 85-22 Talc 122½ Just John 112no Our Hermis 1173½ Driving 8
4Dec76- 8Lrl fst 6f :22⅕ :46 1:10 3↑W Haight H 2 3 35½ 32½ 21½ 1¾ Bracciale b 118 1.60 97-14 Talc 118¾ Sporting Powder 1123 In a Trance118 Brushed, driving 3
25Nov76- 8Key fst 1 1/16 :47⅘ 1:12 1:44⅕ 3↑Quaker H 2 4 44½ 43 35 37¼ Broussard R b 123 *.70 75-24 Pistol White 1165½ Terriobu 1132 Talc 1231¼ Bid, weakened 8
13Nov76- 8Mth fst 1 1/16 :45⅗ 1:10⅕ 1:43 3↑Brookdale H 8 6 45 3½ 11½ 13¾ Perret C b 119 *1.40 90-19 Talc 1193¾ Get Permission 1144 Wishing Stone 122½ Driving 14
3Nov76- 7Mth fst 170 :45⅘ 1:09⅘ 1:41 3↑Allowance 6 2 21 1½ 12 15 Perret C b 116 *.60 93-18 Talc 1165 Dan Horn 1131 Just A Dandy 1165 Mild drive 6
15Oct76- 8Mth fst 170 :45⅗ 1:10⅖ 1:41 3↑Allowance 3 6 56 43½ 2hd 11 Perret C b 122 *.80 93-16 Talc 1221 Verna's Pride 1175 Mongongo 1134 Driving 7
6Oct76- 7Mth my 6f :22⅖ :45⅗ 1:09⅘ 3↑Allowance 3 6 31 12½ 12 13 Perret C b 122 *1.20 91-22 Talc 1223 Can You Beat That 1177 Boy Emperor 1123 Easily 8
18Sep76- 8Bow fst 1 1/16 :46⅘ 1:11⅕ 1:43⅘ 3↑Ⓢ ChesapeakeH 7 4 45½ 22 3nk 31 Bracciale V Jr b 114 2.30 88-20 Resound 113no American Trader 1151 Talc 1144 Weakened 8
11Sep76- 8Bow fst 6f :22⅕ :44⅗ 1:09⅗ 3↑Patuxent H 7 6 67¾ 48 45 31 Moyers L b 114 14.50 91-20 See The U. S. A. 117hd North Call 1171 Talc 114no Rallied 8
LATEST WORKOUTS Apr 27 Mth 4f my :48 h

Festive Mood *
B. g. 8, by Johns Joy—Penny Hearts, by Double Jay
Br.—Ocala Stud Farms Inc (Fla)
Tr.—Small Richard W
Own.—Gibson Sally M
119 Turf Record St. 1st 2nd 3rd: 12 0 1 1 | St. 1st 2nd 3rd Amt. | 1977 5 2 1 0 $43,455 | 1976 17 5 0 4 $189,598

7May77- 7Pim gd 1 1/16 :46⅖ 1:10⅘ 1:43⅕ Allowance 1 1 1hd 2hd 1hd 1no Wright D R b 122 *1.10 89-14 Festive Mood 122no BossuetII1123TakeThePledge122½ Hard drive 6
16Apr77- 8Aqu fst 1⅛ ⊡:47⅘ 1:12⅘ 1:51 3↑Excelsior H 3 2 2hd 2hd 11 21¼ Hinojosa H b 115 4.10 96-14 Turn andCount1231¼FestiveMood1153GabeBenzur112½ Weakened 6
4Apr77- 8Aqu fst 1 1/16 ⊡:47⅘ 1:12⅘ 1:45⅗ Allowance 6 3 31½ 44 66 53¾ Vasquez J b 122 *1.90 86-14 Gabe Benzur 117½ DivineRoyalty115hdSilverBadge1151¼ Gave way 6
19Mar77- 6Aqu gd 1 1/16 ⊡:46⅘ 1:11⅖ 1:43 Handicap 6 2 22 21½ 21 1no Cordero A Jr b 116 4.70 103-04 FestiveMood116noTurnandCount125noRzzleDzzleRey1071½ Driving 6
5Mar77- 9Bow fst 1 1/16 :47⅕ 1:12 1:44⅕ 3↑Nat Dancer H 3 3 36 43 75¾ 73½ Adams J K b 118 4.90 83-18 Jolly Johu 112no Ripon 112¾ Go Go Roger 120no Tired 8
1Dec76- 8Aqu fst 1⅛ :47⅕ 1:11⅕ 1:49 3↑Stuyvesant H 2 1 1½ 3nk 42½ 43½ Cordero A Jr b 118 2.50 87-16 Distant Land 111hd Blue Times 1142½ It'sFreezing115¾ Weakened 9
6Nov76- 8SA fst 1¼ :45⅘ 1:35 2:00 3↑Champions H 10 2 32 42¼ 22 31¾ Hinojosa H b 115 74.60 96-09 King Pellinore 126no L'Heureux 1181¾ FestiveMood1154 Good try 10
16Oct76- 8Key fst 1⅛ :48⅕ 1:12⅘ 1:50⅖ 3↑Hessian H 5 2 22 2½ 11½ 13¼ Hinojosa H b 119 2.80 83-24 FestiveMood1193¼OnTheSly1141¼Queen'sChrger1104½ Ridden out 6
9Oct76- 8Bow sly 1⅛ :48 1:12⅗ 1:51⅘ 3↑Explorer H 3 5 44 43 48 55 Hinojosa H b 118 *1.20 81-23 Delay 1123½ On The Sly 1131 Peppy Addy 114½ No response 10
25Sep76- 7Bow fst 1 1/16 :47⅗ 1:12 1:43⅖ 3↑Allowance 4 2 32 3½ 11 17 Hinojosa H b 119 *.90 91-15 Festive Mood 1197SurelyRoyal119noTakeThePledge119hd Handily 7
LATEST WORKOUTS May 23 Pim 7f fst 1:25⅕ h Apr 12 Pim 6f fst 1:14⅘ b Mar 31 Pim 6f fst 1:15 b

Jolly Johu *
Gr. h. 6, by Restless Native—Avie, by Gallant Man
Br.—Nichols T S (Md)
Tr.—Adams Robert L
Own.—Rolling Ridge Farm
113 Turf Record St. 1st 2nd 3rd: 5 0 0 0 | St. 1st 2nd 3rd Amt. | 1977 8 1 1 3 $55,999 | 1976 17 3 4 5 $59,998

16May77- 8Pim fst 1⅛ :46⅗ 1:11⅖ 1:49⅖ 3↑Ⓢ Jennings H 1 1 1hd 1hd 1hd 2no Turcotte R b 114 *1.80 97-13 Resound 112no Jolly Johu 1143½ Gala Harry 111no Gamely 8
16May77-Run in Two Divisions 7th & 8th Races.
7May77- 7Pim gd 1 1/16 :46⅖ 1:10⅘ 1:43⅕ Allowance 3 4 33 42¼ 43¼ 54 Moyers L b 122 3.50 85-14 Festive Mood 122no Bossuet II 1123 Take The Pledge 122½ Tired 6
9Apr77- 8GS fst 1⅛ :48⅕ 1:13⅕ 1:51 3↑Whirlaway H 7 1 2½ 2½ 1hd 32 Moyers L b 114 6.20 80-25 On The Sly 1172 Resound 113no Jolly Johu 1141 Weakened late 4
30Mar77- 8GS fst 1 1/16 :48⅗ 1:13 1:45⅘ Allowance 2 2 2½ 3½ 32 31 Moyers L b 122 4.80 75-29 Take The Pledge 1151 Hat Full 113hd Jolly Johu 122nk No rally 10
5Mar77- 9Bow fst 1 1/16 :47⅕ 1:12 1:44⅕ 3↑Nat Dancer H 1 2 23 32 23½ 1no Moyers L b 112 12.00 87-18 Jolly Johu 112no Ripon 112¾ Go Go Roger 120no Just up 8
26Feb77- 5Bow fst 1 1/16 :49⅕ 1:13 1:44⅗ Allowance 4 1 11 23 33½ 3½ Moyers L b 112 6.50 84-20 Chati 112½ Eastern Pageant 112hd Jolly Johu 112¾ Came again 6
5Feb77- 9Bow fst 1 1/16 :48⅖ 1:14⅕ 1:48⅖ 3↑Ⓢ Stryker H 2 2 32 41½ 2hd 52¼ Hinojosa H b 114 4.30 64-30 King of Fools 1121½ Gala Harry 114hd Pistol White 120½ Tired 8
15Jan77- 8Bow sly 1 1/16 :48⅗ 1:14⅕ 1:48⅖ 3↑Bowie H 3 2 36½ 46 46 414 Wright D R b 115 3.60 52-45 Piped Aboard 1134½ Bold Play 1137 Dancer 1122¾ Tired 6
31Dec76- 8Lrl fst 1⅛ :47 1:11⅗ 1:50⅖ 3↑Ⓢ Handicap 2 2 2½ 2hd 2hd 1no Hinojosa H b 114 2.20 95-17 Jolly Johu 114no Piped Aboard 113½ Gala Harry 1139 Driving 6
18Dec76- 8Lrl fst 1⅛ :45⅕ 1:10⅖ 1:49⅖ 3↑Congres'l H 4 2 2hd 2hd 2½ 31¼ Hinojosa H b 113 7.50 99-15 Piped Aboard 1091 Go Go Roger 117nk Jolly Johu1136 Weakened 9
LATEST WORKOUTS Apr 30 Pim 7f fst 1:25⅗ h Apr 23 Pim 3f fst :37⅖ b

Resound
Dk. b. or br. h. 5, by Gun Shot—Sound Sweep, by Besomer
Br.—Schneider H G (Md)
Tr.—Field Thomas E
Own.—Schneider H G
113 Turf Record St. 1st 2nd 3rd: 3 0 1 1 | St. 1st 2nd 3rd Amt. | 1977 10 1 2 1 $49,459 | 1976 20 5 4 3 $92,581

16May77- 8Pim fst 1⅛ :46⅗ 1:11⅖ 1:49⅖ 3↑Ⓢ Jennings H 8 7 67 3½ 2hd 1no Adams J K b 112 6.50 97-13 Resound 112no Jolly Johu 1143½ Gala Harry 111no Driving 8
16May77-Run in Two Divisions 7th & 8th Races.
7May77- 7Pim gd 1 1/16 :46⅖ 1:10⅘ 1:43⅕ Allowance 6 3 43¼ 32 33 43½ McCarron G b 117 2.50 85-14 Festive Mood 122no Bossuet II 1123 Take The Pledge 122½ Tired 6
30Apr77- 3Pim fst 1 1/16 :46⅖ 1:10⅖ 1:41⅖ Allowance 6 3 32 22 26 210 Hinojosa H b 115 *.50 88-13 Royal Jete 11510 Resound 1155 Gala Harry 1191¼ No match 6
9Apr77- 8GS fst 1⅛ :48⅕ 1:13⅕ 1:51 3↑Whirlaway H 2 3 1½ 1½ 2hd 22 Hinojosa H b 113 16.40 80-25 On The Sly 1172 Resound 113no Jolly Johu 1141 Gamely 9
30Mar77- 8GS fst 1 1/16 :48⅗ 1:13 1:45⅘ Allowance 1 1 1½ 1½ 1½ 41¼ Hinojosa H b 115 2.70 75-29 Take The Pledge 1151 Hat Full 113hd Jolly Johu 122nk Faltered 10
5Mar77- 9Bow fst 1 1/16 :47⅕ 1:12 1:44⅕ 3↑Nat Dancer H 4 4 46 1½ 13½ 51 Hinojosa H b 113 19.70 86-18 Jolly Johu 112no Ripon 112¾ Go Go Roger 120no Faltered 8
6Feb77- 9FG fst 140 :47 1:12⅕ 1:39⅗ 3↑Handicap 7 6 64½ 66¾ 77 58¼ Suire L P b 116 4.60 86-14 Cylinder 1142 Minnie Buss 1102 Almost Grown 1151 No factor 8
23Jan77- 9FG fst 1⅛ :47⅘ 1:12⅖ 1:51⅘ 3↑Letellier H 5 7 76¾ 41½ 41 31¾ Suire L P 116 14.70 83-24 Inca Roca 114nkSoyNumeroUno1281½Resound116½ Altered course 9
16Jan77- 9FG fst 6f :22 :45 1:10⅕ 3↑Handicap 5 9 914 915 912 54¼ Delahoussaye E b 118 20.40 90-16 TudorTmbourn1152RpThCndy115nkSkyCommndr115hd Slow early 9
2Jan77- 9FG sly 1 1/16 :47⅖ 1:12⅘ 1:47⅖ 3↑Handicap 6 8 917 917 919 911 Hinojosa H b 121 2.90 67-23 Soy Numero Uno 1261¾ Inca Roca 112nk Cylinder 112½ Outrun 9
LATEST WORKOUTS May 24 Pim 5f fst 1:02⅖ b May 14 Pim 4f fst :49 b Apr 26 Pim 1 my 1:36⅖ h Apr 21 Pim 4f fst :48 b

Go Go Roger *
B. h. 7, by Pago Pago—Roger Ann, by Hasty Road
Br.—Wilson R W Estate of (Ky)
Tr.—Leatherbury King T
Own.—Quality Hill Stables
118 Turf Record St. 1st 2nd 3rd: 6 2 0 2 | St. 1st 2nd 3rd Amt. | 1977 6 3 0 2 $56,944 | 1976 7 3 4 0 $30,956

30Apr77- 8Pim fm 1 1/16 Ⓣ:47⅕ 1:12 1:43⅗ 3↑Riggs H 4 8 913 75¾ 32½ 33¾ Bracciale V Jr b 119 2.80 89-11 Chati 1183¾ Piped Aboard 112hd Go Go Roger 1192 Lacked room 10
30Apr77-Run in Two Divisions, 7th & 8th Races.
5Mar77- 9Bow fst 1 1/16 :47⅕ 1:12 1:44⅕ 3↑Nat Dancer H 7 5 58½ 65½ 44½ 3¾ Passmore W J b 120 3.60 86-18 Jolly Johu 112no Ripon 112¾ Go Go Roger 120no Rallied 8
19Feb77- 8GS fst 1 1/16 :47⅗ 1:12⅗ 1:46⅕ 3↑Rancocas H 2 7 65 21½ 1hd 11 Guadalupe J b 118 *1.10e 74-30 Go Go Roger 1181 Proud Kenn1102½WesteringHome1095½ Driving 7
12Feb77- 9Bow fst 1 1/16 :48⅕ 1:13 1:45 Allowance 4 4 57 41½ 3½ 1½ Passmore W J b 119 3.50 83-21 Go Go Roger 119½ Chati 115¾ Eastern Pageant 115nk Driving 7
15Jan77- 8Bow sly 1 1/16 :48⅗ 1:14⅕ 1:48⅖ 3↑Bowie H 5 6 69 56½ 58 516 McCarron C J b 118 *1.40 50-45 Piped Aboard 1134½ Bold Play 1137 Dancer 1122¾ Dull try 6
1Jan77- 8Key fst 1 1/16 :46⅖ 1:11 1:42⅘ Germantown H 5 8 68½ 64 41¾ 1¾ Guadalupe J b 116 3.20 90-21 Go Go Roger 116¾ Ⓓ Judging Man 112no Bold Play 1144 Hard ride 8
18Dec76- 8Lrl fst 1⅛ :45⅕ 1:10⅖ 1:49⅖ 3↑Congres'l H 6 5 58 4¾ 3½ 21 Passmore W J b 117 3.20 99-15 Piped Aboard 1091 Go Go Roger 117nk Jolly Johu 1136 Gamely 9
4Dec76- 7Lrl fst 1 :46⅕ 1:11⅘ 1:37 3↑Allowance 7 6 66½ 53½ 2½ 11¼ McCarron C J b 115 *1.50 88-14 Go Go Roger 1151¼ Delay 1223 Jolly Johu 115¾ Drew clear 7
20Nov76- 7Lrl fst 1 :46 1:11⅗ 1:36⅖ 3↑Allowance 1 4 42½ 41 21½ 1nk McCarron C J b 117 *1.30 91-13 Go Go Roger 117nk Dancer 1227 Lexington Park 1173 Driving 7
27Oct76- 8Key fst 1 1/16 :47⅘ 1:12 1:44⅘ 3↑Allowance 3 2 2½ 2½ 22 23½ Anaya A5 b 117 *.70 76-23 LastTriumph1153½GoGoRoger1173½BoldWennie115hd Second best 6
LATEST WORKOUTS Apr 27 Pim 5f fst 1:02 b ●Apr 16 Pim 3f fst :34⅘ h Apr 6 Pim 3f my :37 b

***Bossuet II** — B. h. 5, by Bonin—Lisistrata, by Jardiniere
Br.—Haras El Pelado (Arg)
Own.—Wright Mrs W C — Tr.—Gill Rodger M

108

Turf Record	St.	1st	2nd	3rd			St.	1st	2nd	3rd	Amt.
	1	0	0	0		1977	4	1	1	0	$10,060
						1976	4	1	0	0	$5,400

14May77- 4Pim	fst	$1\frac{1}{16}$	:46⅕	1:10⅗	1:41⅘	Allowance	1	1	$1^{1\frac{1}{2}}$	1^{2}	1^{6}	1^{15}	Agnello A 118	112	*1.20	96–16	Bossuet II 112^{15} Con Man 112^{8} Pistol White 122^{1}	Ridden out	6
7May77- 7Pim	gd	$1\frac{1}{16}$	:46⅖	1:10⅘	1:43⅕	Allowance	4	2	2^{hd}	1^{hd}	2^{hd}	2no	Agnello A 103	112	19.90	89–14	Festive Mood 122no Bossuet II112^{3}TakeThePledge$122^{\frac{1}{2}}$	Sharp try	6
30Apr77- 7Pim	fm	$1\frac{1}{16}$ Ⓣ	:47⅘	1:12	1:44	3↑Riggs H	1	1	1^{hd}	1^{hd}	$3^{2\frac{1}{2}}$	$5^{4\frac{1}{2}}$	Agnello A	107	18.70	86–11	Ripon $112^{\frac{3}{4}}$ All The More 110^{1} Quick Decision $112^{\frac{1}{2}}$	Weakened	7
30Apr77-Run in Two Divisions 7th & 8th Races.																			
2Mar77- 8Bow	fst	6f	:22⅕	:45⅖	1:10⅕	Allowance	1	4	$5^{4\frac{1}{4}}$	$6^{8\frac{1}{2}}$	$6^{6\frac{1}{2}}$	$5^{6\frac{1}{4}}$	Lee T	112	23.10	83–22	SportingPowder$119^{1\frac{1}{4}}$Patrick'sShmrock$115^{3\frac{1}{2}}$HunterF.$115^{\frac{3}{4}}$	Evenly	8
22Dec76- 8Lrl	fst	6f	:22⅗	:46	1:10⅗	3↑Allowance	4	4	$6^{4\frac{1}{4}}$	$7^{9\frac{1}{2}}$	7^{10}	$5^{9\frac{1}{2}}$	Canessa J	113	15.40	84–16	Bold Man 120^{nk} Rest The Quadrant 115^{2} Kimani 117^{7}	No factor	7
6Dec76- 8Lrl	fst	6f	:22⅖	:46⅕	1:11⅕	3↑Allowance	5	4	$6^{5\frac{1}{4}}$	6^{12}	7^{15}	7^{15}	Canessa J	113	*1.70e	76–17	Avalon Beach $113^{1\frac{1}{2}}$ Dancer $122^{\frac{3}{4}}$RedheadedCatfish113^{1}	No factor	8
5Jun76- 6Del	fst	170	:47	1:13⅕	1:44	Allowance	1	1	$1^{1\frac{1}{2}}$	1^{2}	$1^{2\frac{1}{2}}$	$1^{1\frac{1}{2}}$	Canessa J	112	3.80	77–23	BossuetII$112^{1\frac{1}{2}}$Dancer'sProfile112^{1}BlueMountinBoy$112^{3\frac{1}{2}}$	Driving	7
22May76- 8Pim	fst	$1\frac{1}{16}$	:45⅘	1:10	1:41⅘	3↑Baltimore H	5	5	$5^{7\frac{1}{2}}$	6^{13}	6^{15}	6^{22}	McCarron G	107	27.40	74–13	Dancing Champ 119^{6} Resound $114^{\frac{1}{2}}$ Festive Mood 121^{1}	Outrun	6
22May76-Run in Two Divisions, 7th and 8th Races.																			
9Nov75♦6Palermo(Arg)	fst	*1⅞			3:07⅖	Gr.Pr.Carlos Pellegrini						9^{14}	Dominguez O	117	13.75	— —	Meyi 117^{1} ElAndaluz 132^{3} Ezequiel $117^{\frac{1}{2}}$	Well placed, tired	18
5Oct75♦6Palermo(Arg)	fst	*$1\frac{9}{16}$			2:35⅗	Gran Premio Nacional						$4^{3\frac{1}{4}}$	Cosenza O	126	2.80	— —	Kalabana $119^{\frac{3}{4}}$ Yakarto 126^{2} Meyi $126^{\frac{1}{2}}$	With pace to midst	21

LATEST WORKOUTS May 21 Pim 1 fst 1:39 h May 5 Pim 4f gd :52⅘ b ●Apr 26 Pim 6f my 1:14 h Apr 23 Pim 4f fst :50 b

The City of Baltimore Handicap was like a final examination. It involved all the lessons I had learned about handicapping on Pimlico's biased racetrack. All six horses in the field had good records, and all of them demanded scrutiny.

Talc was obviously a top-notch racehorse in sharp condition. He had beaten Just John in the sprint at Atlantic City for which I had estimated a figure of 112. Then he had gone to Aqueduct and run another excellent race. And now he had the advantageous inside post position at a mile and one-sixteenth.

Festive Mood had captured his only start at Pimlico, but he had done so by breaking from the number-one post position and hugging the rail all the way. Even with the track bias in his favor, he had not earned an exceptional figure. In this race he was not going to take the rail away from Talc.

Jolly Johu had raced along the inside part of the track in the Jennings Handicap and had not been able to hold on. Now he would have both Talc and Festive Mood between him and the rail.

Resound had made three starts at Pimlico and had the incredible misfortune to draw the outside post position for all of them. Even so, he had managed to overcome the bias and catch Jolly Johu in the Jennings Handicap. The *Racing Form*'s footnotes for that race suggested how impressive his performance had been: "Resound broke out at the start, was wide on the first turn and forced to steady while running up horses' heels, moved wide on the second turn to challenge for the lead and responded to strong urging in a prolonged drive to narrowly edge Jolly Johu." Resound was obviously a much better animal than his naked figure of 102 suggested.

Go Go Roger had run a 100 and had been beaten by Jolly Johu in his last start on the main track at Bowie. Breaking from the number-five post at Pimlico, he did not figure to be a contender.

Bossuet II had performed spectacularly in his last start, winning by fifteen lengths and earning a figure of 118. But that was the first time in his life that the five-year-old had ever run such a race; only a week earlier, he had lost to Festive Mood. What happened? Had

Bossuet II suddenly been transformed into a superhorse? Or had he run so well because he had been on the rail?

So many horses at Pimlico had improved so dramatically when they broke from the number-one post position that I suspected Bossuet II's extraordinary wakeup was due principally to the track bias. And that bias was going to be working against him now. I envisioned Talc, Festive Mood, Jolly Johu, and Bossuet II all showing speed, leaving Bossuet II parked four-wide around the first turn. At Pimlico that would be fatal.

If I could assume that Bossuet II was not going to run well, Talc was clearly the best horse in the field. And Resound was clearly second-best. He had earned a figure as good as Festive Mood or Jolly Johu while he had been running against the bias and they had been running with it.

Furthermore, I thought the bias would favor both Talc and Resound in this race. Talc would have the rail all the way around the track. If Festive Mood, Jolly Johu, and Bossuet II all tried to challenge him from the outside, as seemed likely, Resound might be able to lay off the pace and drop over to the inside. I saw the City of Baltimore Handicap as a cold Talc-Resound exacta. I went to the track intending to bet $400 on the combination.

The Kid shared my thinking on the race, but he didn't like the early part of the Pimlico card. So instead of accompanying me to the track, he waited until midafternoon when he and a friend, Ray, set out for Baltimore. The Kid was driving an ancient Pontiac which was a relic of his undergraduate days and which had gone to the track one time too many. On the Baltimore Beltway, the car started to run as feebly as a $1500 claimer at Charles Town, and finally stopped altogether. The Kid and Ray walked a half-mile to summon a wrecker, which hauled the car to a service station. The attendant diagnosed the ailment as a clogged gas filter and started puttering under the hood.

"Let's just take a cab to the track," Ray suggested, "and pick up the car on the way back."

"No, we've got plenty of time," the Kid said, looking at the gas station clock, which he did not know was ten minutes slow. They waited. And waited. When the Kid had paid $5.50 for the new filter, they sped toward the track.

The outcome of this trip was foreordained, because there is an immutable law governing such circumstances. If you are running late on a trip to the track, but get there in the nick of time, your horse will lose. If you are shut out of a chance to bet, your horse will win. Jerry and I had once been rushing to Charles Town to bet an exacta in the second race when we passed through a speed trap in Harper's Ferry and were stopped by the police. By the time we got to the track, our exacta had already won and paid $30. On another occasion I was traveling to Bowie aboard a Gray Line bus that sputtered and died. I loved a horse in the first race, and post time was drawing near, so I scurried off the bus and waved my *Racing Form* at passing motorists. I got a ride in a black Cadillac whose driver knew all the shortcuts to the track, and got to Bowie just in time to bet my horse. He finished eleventh. It never fails.

So the Kid and Ray were speeding to the track with a cloud of doom hanging over their heads. They parked their car, sprinted from a remote corner of the parking lot, and dashed breathlessly into the track, just in time to hear the announcer say, "They're off!" By the time they got to a television monitor, they were seeing Talc open a five-length lead and Resound move decisively into second place.

EIGHTH RACE

Pimlico

MAY 28, 1977

1 $\frac{1}{16}$ MILES. (1.41) THE CITY OF BALTIMORE HANDICAP 12th Running. $25,000 Added. A handicap for 3-year-olds and upward. By subscription of $50 each, which should accompany the nomination, $200 additional to start, with $25,000 added, of which 65% of all monies to the winner, 20% to second, 10% to third and 5% to fourth. weighhs five days before the race. Staters to be named through the entry box by the usual time of closing.

Trophy to the owner of the winner. Closed Friday, April 22, 1977 with 39 nominations.

Value of race $28,150, value to winner $18,298, second $5,630, third $2,815, fourth $1,407. Mutuel pool $96,105. Exacta Pool $93,312.

Last Raced	Horse	Eqt.A.Wt PP St	¼	½	¾	Str	Fin	Jockey	Odds $1
19May77 8Aqu2	Talc	b 5 118 1 1	1¹	11½	1⁴	1⁵	1⁵	Bracciale V Jr	2.20
16May77 8Pim1	Resound	b 5 113 4 5	5hd	5½	3½	2²	2⁴	Adams J K	10.30
7May77 7Pim1	Festive Mood	b 8 119 2 2	42½	3½	5⁵	31½	31½	Wright D R	3.30
14May77 4Pim1	Bossuet II	5 108 6 4	3²	2²	2¹	4hd	4¹	Agnello A	2.10
30Apr77 8Pim3	Go Go Roger	b 7 118 5 6	6	6	4½	5⁷	5⁹	Lee T	5.20
16May77 8Pim2	Jolly Johu	b 6 113 3 3	2hd	4²	6	6	6	Pineda R	12.40

OFF AT 4:34 EDT. Start good, Won ridden out. Time, :23, :45⅗, 1:09⅗, 1:34⅘, 1:41⅖ Track fast.

$2 Mutuel Prices:

1–TALC	6.40	3.60	2.60
6–RESOUND		7.00	4.00
4–FESTIVE MOOD			3.00

$2 EXACTA 1–6 PAID $43.20.

B. h, by Rock Talk—Heat Rash, by Rash Prince. Trainer Harraway Thomas P. Bred by Erlanger M C (Md).

TALC broke alertly to gain a slight lead going to the first turn, made the pace under moderate restraint, drew off on the second turn then was not seriously threatened through the stretch while under intermittent pressure and brisk hand urging. RESOUND came outside rivals while advancing after five furlongs and was clearly second best. FESTIVE MOOD, hustled along to prompt the early pace while saving ground, failed to respond when called upon after six furlongs. BOSSUET II raced closest to the pace for three quarters and gave way. JOLLY JOHU raced closest to the winner while outside that one early, bobbled suddenly at the five eighths pole then gradually weakened.

Owners— 1, Tinton Falls Stable; 2, Schneider H G; 3, Gibson Sally M; 4, Wright Mrs W C; 5, Quality Hill Stables; 6, Rolling Ridge Farm.

Trainers— 1, Harraway Thomas P; 2, Field Thomas E; 3, Small Richard W; 4, Gill Rodger M; 5, Leatherbury King T; 6, Adams Robert L.

Scratched—Splitting Headache (16May77 7Pim1); On The Sly (30Apr77 7Pim4); King of Fools (16May77 7Pim2); Piped Aboard (16May77 8Pim4); Walk Tall (16May77 7Pim5); Pistol White (14May77 4Pim3).

The Kid waited to see that the exacta paid $43.20, and estimated that he would have won more than $3000 if he had arrived at the track one minute sooner. He belted down a shot of scotch and headed back home. I collected $8640 on my $400 exacta bet—the largest one-race score of my life—but I felt as emotionally drained as the Kid.

Instead of celebrating that night, I went straight home, collapsed into bed, and slept for fourteen hours.

Two days later the Pimlico season was over. During the course of it I had made sixteen trips to the track, won on thirteen of them, amassed a net profit of $34,073, and driven myself to a state of mental and physical exhaustion. I wanted to quit gambling for a while, but I couldn't. I was still at the crest of a great winning streak; my handicapping was as sharp as it had ever been; I knew all the Pimlico horses, and now they were moving to Bowie. I believed that I could cash many bets on horses who had been hindered by the bias at Pimlico and now were running on a relatively normal track.

I went to Bowie on opening day because I loved a mare named Double Skip, who had earned a superior figure while running wide in a route race at Pimlico. I bet $1200 and watched her finish a distant and inexplicable fourth. By the end of the afternoon I had lost $2500, and I was not finished yet. From Bowie I drove to Rosecroft Raceway, the local harness track, where I utilized my total ignorance of pacers and trotters to bring my losses past the $3000 mark and establish May 31 as the most expensive day of my life.

I have no basic self-destructive instincts, but on this day I believe I was subconsciously trying to lose. I could not stop gambling while I was in the midst of a torrid winning streak. But on the night of May 31, I could proclaim that the streak was over. The next day I didn't even look at the *Racing Form*. I lingered over a long lunch at Le Bagatelle, lingered over a long dinner at Duke Zeibert's, romanced a leggy blonde that night, and felt as if I had just rejoined the human race.

I planned to wait until Saratoga opened to make my next major assault on a racetrack, but I did have one unfinished piece of business from Pimlico to which I had to attend. In the last race of the season, a filly named Spot Two won a maiden-special-weight event in the published time of 1:13⅗ for six furlongs. When I calculated my figures for the day, the time of the race seemed to make no sense at all. Two weeks earlier, on a very dull track, Spot Two had covered the distance in 1:12⅕. I could not understand the disparity between her two performances, and I expressed my puzzlement to Clem Florio, who agreed that something was wrong. So late one afternoon, after the press box had emptied, he arranged to have Spot Two's victory rerun over the closed-circuit television monitor and timed her with his stopwatch. It said 1:11⅗. He had the race replayed again; 1:11⅗ again. Clem reported his discovery to me but cautioned, "Don't wake up anybody. This is money."

Spot Two was entered in an allowance race at Bowie on June 21. As I studied the past performances the night before, I saw that I might have a tremendous betting opportunity—if the price was right.

8 BOWIE

6 FURLONGS — BOWIE (START / FINISH)

6 FURLONGS. (1.08) ALLOWANCE. Purse $6,500. Fillies, 3-year-old which have never won two races, weights, 120 lbs. Non-winners of a race other than claiming, since May 16, allowed 3 lbs. Such a race since April 15, 5 lbs. Such a race since March 15, 8 lbs. (Winners Preferred).

Coupled—Sea Tale and Bitina.

My Iron Lass

Dk. b. or br. f. 3, by Iron Peg—My O Me, by Reneged
Br.—Kincheloe J G (Md)
Tr.—Mobberley John C
Own.—Kincheloe J G
112

	St.	1st	2nd	3rd	Amt.
1977	4	1	0	1	$4,080
1976	3	M	0	0	$1,055

6Jun77- 5Bow gd 6f	:22⅘ :46⅘ 1:11⅗	ⒻAllowance	1 5 57½ 54 54½ 33	Lee T	112	18.70	79-19	Sene Rene 1121½ Power 1201½ My Iron Lass 1121¼	Lacked rally 6
20May77- 4Pim fst 6f	:22⅗ :45⅖ 1:11	ⒻⓈAllowance	4 5 57 57¾ 55½ 54	Lee T	112	68.50	87-13	Nationette 1201½ TieARibbon107hdSoloValentine120no	No mishap 5
14May77- 6Pim fst 6f	:22⅘ :46 1:11⅖ 3↑	ⒻAllowance	6 2 87 69½ 612 613	Lee T	112	11.60	76-16	Plenty Calm 1123½ Dixie Spears 1121¾ Sene Rene 1123	Outrun 9
4May77- 3Pim gd 6f	:23⅖ :46⅖ 1:12⅕ 3↑	Md 25000	2 5 33½ 38 35 1hd	Lee T	112	5.80	85-16	My Iron Lass 112hd Colonel Shula 1141¼ Bitina 11413	Just up 7
8Nov76- 9Lrl fst 6f	:22⅕ :46⅗ 1:13	ⒻⓈMd Sp Wt	11 7 1112 913 57½ 42¾	Lee T	119	8.20	79-15	Witch 119no A Las Vientos 1191 Silklady 1191¾	Rallied 12
25Oct76- 1Lrl sly 6f	:22⅖ :46⅘ 1:13⅖	ⒻⓈMd Sp Wt	10 1 711 512 513 46½	Lee T	119	48.00	73-20	CornishSong1192¼Candy'sCharm1192¾GalaAnn1191½	Belated rally 12
3Sep76- 4Tim fst 4f	:23⅘ :48⅕	Md 11500	2 3 21 44½ 46	Lee T	117	37.10	80-15	Linc Ford 1203½ Boredom 1201½ Tommy R. 1161	Tired 7

LATEST WORKOUTS Jun 18 Bow 3f my :39 b — Apr 30 Pim 5f fst 1:02 b — Apr 23 Pim 6f fst 1:15 h

Spot Two

Ch. f. 3, by Hagley—One Spot, by Cavan
Br.—Helsing E A (Md)
Tr.—Bradley Donald C
Own.—Witching Hour Farm
120

	St.	1st	2nd	3rd	Amt.
1977	3	1	1	0	$4,620
1976	0	M	0	0	

30May77- 9Pim fst 6f	:22⅘ :46 1:13⅗ 3↑	ⒻMd Sp Wt	1 6 44 22 12½ 15	Hinojosa H	b 114	*1.10	78-15	Spot Two 1145 Pulsar 114no Airy Imp 1141½	Handily 9
13May77- 2Pim fst 6f	:23 :46⅖ 1:11 3↑	ⒻMd Sp Wt	10 2 44½ 44 24 26	McCarron G	b 114	*3.80Ⓓ	85-16	Nationette 1146 ⒹSpot Two 114½ Power 1143½	Bore in 12
13May77-Disqualified and placed eleventh									
2May77- 2Pim fst 6f	:22⅘ :45⅗ 1:11 3↑	ⒻMd Sp Wt	5 4 2½ 24 25 24	McCarron G	b 114	6.10	87-18	Dark Cherry 1144 Spot Two 1143½ Misty Oaks 1143½	Second best 11

LATEST WORKOUTS May 26 Pim 5f gd 1:01 h — May 10 Pim 4f fst :49⅗ b

Power

Ch. f. 3, by Jim J—Will's Gray, by Native Dancer
Br.—Faulconer P H (Va)
Tr.—Bond Bernard P
Own.—O'Keefe W
120

	St.	1st	2nd	3rd	Amt.
1977	4	1	2	0	$6,050
1976	0	M	0	0	

13Jun77- 7Bow fst 6f	:22⅗ :46 1:11 3↑	ⒻAllowance	6 5 32 32 42½ 51¾	Cusimano G	b 114	*1.00	83-19	Island Search 1091 Ernest Ruler 114½ High Rulerae 119nk	Tired 9
6Jun77- 5Bow gd 6f	:22⅘ :46⅘ 1:11⅗	ⒻAllowance	6 1 1hd 1hd 21½ 21½	Cusimano G	b 120	*1.60	80-19	Sene Rene 1121½ Power 1201½ My Iron Lass 1121¼	Gamely 6
20May77- 6Pim fst 6f	:23 :46⅕ 1:11 3↑	ⒻMd Sp Wt	4 3 11 12 11 1nk	Cusimano G	b 114	*1.00	91-13	Power 114nk Wanda's Tear 1148 Song Stealer 114½	Driving 12
13May77- 2Pim fst 6f	:23 :46⅖ 1:11 3↑	ⒻMd Sp Wt	11 3 32½ 22 34½ 36½	Cusimano G	114	11.70	84-16	Nationette 1146 ⒹSpot Two 114½ Power 1143½	Weakened 12
13May77-Placed second through disqualification									

LATEST WORKOUTS Jun 5 Bow 3f fst :36 h — May 28 Pim 5f fst :58 h — May 19 Pim 3f fst :37 bg — May 9 Pim 5f fst 1:01⅖ hg

Foster's Fuzzy

Dk. b. or br. f. 3, by John William—Hill Behaving, by Ambehaving
Br.—Rosoff A (Fla)
Tr.—Dutrow Richard E
Own.—Sniadowski A J
112

	St.	1st	2nd	3rd	Amt.
1976	5	1	1	1	$3,925

7Aug76- 5Del fst 5½f	:22⅕ :46⅘ 1:07⅖	ⒻAllowance	2 4 46½ 46 35½ 33	Adams J K	112	3.10	78-19	ChrgeAndSnd1151½DrmingAgin1121¾Fostr'sFuzzy112no	No threat 4
24Jly76- 4Del fst 5½f	:22⅗ :47⅖ 1:06⅗	Clm 12500	6 4 33½ 34 34½ 2nk	Gilbert R B5	108	*1.70	85-14	Mysto Hill 116nk Foster's Fuzzy 1082½Foreglow1112½	Just missed 6
27Jun76- 1Del fst 5f	:23⅕ :48⅗ 1:01⅗	ⒻMd c-8000	7 8 77 56 44½ 1no	Martens G5	116	*1.60	78-18	Foster's Fuzzy116noRomanVillage1142¼MarketTrader1173	Driving 11
21Jun76- 4Bel fst 5½f	:22⅘ :46⅗ 1:05⅘	ⒻMd 22500	6 7 76 812 513 510	Richards C H	117	24.60	76-15	HppyHuntington1196¾RunBckyRun1191¾ForCrtin119nk	No factor 10
14Jun76- 1Bel fst 5½f	:23⅖ :47⅗ 1:07⅖	ⒻMd 20000	8 8 76½ 66¾ 68½ 79¼	Richards C H	119	11.20	69-21	Wincoma Lass 1171¾ At Timberline 1173½ For Certain1173	Outrun 9

LATEST WORKOUTS Jun 12 Lrl 4f fst :51 b — Jun 7 Lrl 3f fst :37 b — Jun 2 Lrl 5f fst 1:03⅗ b — ●May 27 Lrl 5f gd 1:03 b

Sea Tale

B. f. 3, by Rock Talk—Paulines Neptune, by Neptune
Br.—Helmore Farm (Md)
Tr.—Adams Robert L
Own.—Helmore Farm
112

	St.	1st	2nd	3rd	Amt.
1977	4	0	1	1	$3,290
1976	3	1	0	0	$2,700

26Feb77- 6Bow fst 6f	:22⅘ :46⅖ 1:11⅘	ⒻAllowance	2 9 910 811 78¼ 613	Gilbert R B	b 112	5.80	70-20	Barley Mill 1125 Noble Heights 1203¾ Creek 117¾	Broke poorly 9
10Feb77- 8Bow fst 6f	:22⅘ :46⅖ 1:11⅘	ⒻⓈAllowance	2 9 99¾ 710 44½ 34	Passmore W J	b 113	25.20	77-24	Enthused 1131 Silklady 1203 Sea Tale 1133	Poor start 9
1Feb77- 3Bow fst 7f	:23⅖ :46⅗ 1:27⅗	ⒻⓈAllowance	3 5 65¼ 64¾ 43 22	Gilbert R B	b 112	10.60	65-32	Silklady 1172 Sea Tale 112hd Tiz She 1201½	Gaining 6
25Jan77- 8Bow fst 7f	:23⅕ :47 1:27⅕	ⒻAllowance	6 8 86½ 810 79½ 513	Gilbert R B	b 112	8.10	56-43	Biljonette 1172½ Barley Mill 1127 Well Hit 1123	No factor 8
30Dec76- 3Lrl fst 6f	:23 :46⅘ 1:12	ⒻMd 16000	3 8 73 53¼ 12 16	Gilbert R B	b 119	*3.20	87-18	Sea Tale 1196 Camotop 1153 We Have A Date 1122	Ridden out 12
24Nov76- 2Lrl fst 7f	:23 :46⅗ 1:24⅕	ⒻMd Sp Wt	5 7 53½ 34 512 515	Adams J K	119	91.10	75-17	Stamina 1199 Sugar Talk 119¾ Gala Ann 1193½	Tired 10
8Nov76- 9Lrl fst 6f	:22⅕ :46⅗ 1:13	ⒻⓈMd Sp Wt	1 12 88 1014 1015 1012	Lindberg G	119	8.90	70-15	Witch 119no A Las Vientos 1191 Silklady 1191¾	Outrun 12

LATEST WORKOUTS ●Jun 15 Pim 6f fst 1:15 h — Jun 11 Pim 4f fst :49⅕ hg — Jun 4 Pim 5f fst 1:01⅕ h — May 31 Pim 3f fst :37⅕ h

Sword Play

B. f. 3, by Damascus—Alyce Clover, by Needles
Br.—Linder B N (Ky)
Tr.—Hadry Charles H
Own.—Locust Hill Farm
112

	St.	1st	2nd	3rd	Amt.
1977	2	0	0	0	$390
1976	7	1	3	1	$8,320

6Jun77- 5Bow gd 6f	:22⅘ :46⅘ 1:11⅗	ⒻAllowance	2 4 68 43½ 44 44½	Adams J K	112	7.40	78-19	Sene Rene 1121½ Power 1201½ My Iron Lass 1121¼	Lacked rally 6
14May77- 6Pim fst 6f	:22⅘ :46 1:11⅖ 3↑	ⒻAllowance	8 9 912 913 918 922	McCarron C J	112	5.20	67-16	Plenty Calm 1123½ Dixie Spears 1121¾ Sene Rene 1123	Outrun 9
11Dec76- 2Lrl fst 6f	:23 :48 1:14⅕	ⒻMd Sp Wt	6 9 97½ 65 34½ 1½	McCarron C J	119	*1.00	76-22	Sword Play 119½ⒹMarkedCourse1192½NobleHeights119nk	Driving 11
2Dec76- 2Lrl gd 6f	:22⅘ :47⅖ 1:13⅕	ⒻMd Sp Wt	10 7 73¼ 53½ 23 21½	Moseley J W	119	2.70	79-22	Harry's T. 1191½ Sword Play 1194 Creek 119½	Checked 10
9Nov76- 4Lrl fst 7f	:23 :46⅖ 1:23⅘	ⒻMd Sp Wt	5 3 64¼ 21½ 24 210	Moseley J W	119	3.60	82-16	Sweet Alliance 11910 SwordPlay1195Propagator1191	Swerved out 11
1Nov76- 4Lrl fst 6f	:22⅘ :47⅕ 1:12⅗	ⒻMd Sp Wt	10 9 106¼ 915 513 34¾	Moseley J W	119	*1.70	79-15	Count To Ten 1191 Colonel Shula 1193¾ Sword Play 1192	Rallied 12
2Oct76- 3Bel sly 6f	:23 :46⅕ 1:11⅖	ⒻMd Sp Wt	5 6 63½ 41¾ 22 48¼	Vasquez J	119	*.60	76-11	Your Place or Mine 1096½ Sabar 119¾ Bagiorix 1191¼	Weakened 8
18Sep76- 4Bel fst 6f	:22⅕ :45⅗ 1:10⅗	ⒻMd Sp Wt	7 5 67 43 24 23¾	Shoemaker W	119	5.30	85-10	Penny Catcher 1193¾ Sword Play 119½ Fia 1192	Game try 12
4Sep76- 1Bel fst 6f	:23 :46⅘ 1:11⅗	ⒻMd Sp Wt	11 12 96 74½ 69½ 613	Santiago A	119	6.30	71-15	Pearl Handle 119¾ Flying Buttress 1199 TooLucky119½	Off slowly 12

LATEST WORKOUTS ●Jun 16 Lrl 4f fst :49⅕ b — Jun 12 Lrl 4f fst :49⅘ b — Jun 5 Lrl 3f fst :37 b — Jun 1 Lrl 4f fst :49 b

Ernest Ruler

Dk. b. or br. f. 3, by Spring Double—Delta Ruler, by Delta Judge
Br.—Reinhart E A (Md)
Tr.—Rockey Gerald W
Own.—Petrullo C
120

	St.	1st	2nd	3rd	Amt.
1977	2	1	1	0	$4,130
1976	0	M	0	0	

13Jun77- 7Bow fst 6f	:22⅗ :46 1:11 3↑	ⒻAllowance	1 1 12 1½ 2½ 21	Adams J K	b 114	2.30e	84-19	Island Search 1091 Ernest Ruler 114½ High Rulerae 119nk	Hung 9
1Jun77- 9Bow fst 6f	:22⅗ :46 1:12 3↑	Md Sp Wt	11 1 1½ 14 11½ 1no	Adams J K	b 109	19.30	80-22	Ernest Ruler 109no Prince Bery 114no Black Choice 1145	Lasted 11

LATEST WORKOUTS Jun 19 Bow 3f fst :37 b — Jun 11 Bow 3f fst :36⅖ b — May 28 Bow 4f fst :49⅗ bg — May 21 Bow 5f fst 1:03 b

Bitina

Ro. f. 3, by Tinajero—Bilzown Native, by Restless Native
Br.—Rauck W H (Md)
Tr.—Adams Robert L
Own.—Rauck W H
113 7

	St.	1st	2nd	3rd	Amt.
1977	6	1	1	2	$5,230
1976	6	M	0	1	$1,170

8Jun77- 2Bow fst 6f	:22⅗ :46⅖ 1:11⅗ 3↑	ⒻMd Sp Wt	9 5 3½ 2hd 11½ 1¾	Bracciale V Jr	b 114	3.80	82-18	Bitina 114¾ Pro Supper 1142 Family First 114nk	Driving 11
4May77- 3Pim gd 6f	:23⅖ :46⅖ 1:12⅕ 3↑	Md 25000	7 1 21½ 24 23 31¼	Bracciale V Jr	114	5.40	84-16	My Iron Lass 112hd Colonel Shula 1141¼ Bitina 11413	Weakened 7
23Apr77- 9Pim fst 6f	:23 :46⅖ 1:12⅕ 3↑	ⒻMd Sp Wt	10 5 55½ 57½ 714 816	Gilbert R B	b 114	48.60	69-13	Solo Valentine 114¾ Ringaround 1142½ Majestic Julie 1248	Tired 11
16Feb77- 3Bow fst 6f	:23⅕ :47⅕ 1:12⅘	ⒻMd 25000	5 1 54¼ 44½ 46 27	Gilbert R B	b 120	4.90	69-24	Council House 1187Bitina1201½HistoricMinutes1201¾	Second best 6
3Feb77- 3Bow fst 6f	:23⅖ :47⅘ 1:13⅖	ⒻMd 25000	4 1 2hd 31 32 34½	Gilbert R B	b 120	4.80	68-31	Uncomplicated 1203 Historic Minutes 1201½Bitina120¾	Weakened 7
3Jan77- 2Bow fst 6f	:22⅖ :46 1:11	ⒻⓈMd Sp Wt	1 11 1112 119½ 109½ 99	Gilbert R B	b 119	5.30	76-10	Over The Stile 119¾ Solo Valentine 1191 Tiz She 119¾	Poor start 12
11Dec76- 2Lrl fst 6f	:23 :48 1:14⅕	ⒻMd Sp Wt	3 2 3nk 31 44½ 43½	Moseley J W	b 119	12.30	73-22	SwordPly119½ⒹMrkdCours1192½NoblHghts119nk	Forced to check 11
3Dec76- 4Lrl fst 7f	:23⅗ :47⅗ 1:26⅗	ⒻⓈMd Sp Wt	7 4 74½ 53½ 55 52¼	Bracciale V Jr	b 119	7.20	76-20	Biljonette 119no Gala Ann 119nk Colonel Shula 119hd	No mishap 7
19Nov76- 2Lrl fst 6f	:22⅕ :46⅕ 1:12⅖	ⒻMd 20000	4 3 64¾ 711 715 48	Cusimano G	119	2.80	77-17	Savage Call 1152 Biljonette 1152 Helivibreeze 1154	Best others 11
8Nov76- 9Lrl fst 6f	:22⅕ :46⅗ 1:13	ⒻⓈMd Sp Wt	4 3 43 44½ 44½ 53¼	McCarron G	119	6.30	79-15	Witch 119no A Las Vientos 1191 Silklady 1191¾	Tired 12

LATEST WORKOUTS Jun 18 Pim 3f my :36⅖ h — Jun 4 Pim 4f fst :48 h — May 21 Pim 4f fst :53 b

Spot Two was obviously superior. She had only to duplicate any performance of her career in order to win this race. If the crowd at Bowie knew how fast she had run in her last start, she would probably be an odds-on favorite. But with that 1:13⅗ besmirching her record, she might go to the post at a bettable price.

I have a regrettable tendency to hurt the odds on my winners by talking about them too much in advance. Hot tips travel fast along the Georgetown bar circuit. Once I liked a longshot at Laurel and mentioned his name to a single bartender the night before the race. By the next morning people were giving me tips on my own horse, and that afternoon he went off at 2 to 1. I watched the race on a closed-circuit television in the dining room where my friends usually congregate, and when my horse crossed the wire in front, the place erupted as Kennedy Stadium does when the Redskins have scored against the Cowboys. I turned and saw at least twenty acquaintances clutching tickets on the winner. Some of them had won more money on the race than I did. While a rare toutee might occasionally show his gratitude —my neighborhood Chinese restaurateur gives me free carry-out orders of Gon Boo Gai Ding—too many bettors fail even to say thank you for a winner. By the end of the Pimlico meeting, I was feeling exploited by many of my acquaintances. Now I needed to reciprocate. Spot Two was running on a Tuesday, when the betting pools would be small, so I had to protect the price I would be getting. Or even boost it a bit.

On the night before the race I visited a Georgetown drinking establishment and ordered a beer. "Like anything tomorrow?" the bartender inquired. I motioned him aside, took a paper napkin, and scribbled on it, "SWORD PLAY—8TH BOWIE." "Don't let it out," I whispered. "But this horse can't miss."

I made my way down M Street that night, ordering beers and whispering the name of Sword Play in the eighth. The next day at the track I saw a sea of familiar faces at the track, most of whom had received the hot tip second- or third-hand. About an hour before the race, Jerry excused himself, left the track, drove to a nearby phone booth, and telephoned Sneaky Pete, who was waiting for his call. Meanwhile I stayed at the track and watched the tote board with fascination. Sword Play, who was a justifiable 12 to 1 in the morning line, got surprising support and dropped to 5 to 1. Spot Two was holding at a steady 5 to 2.

EIGHTH RACE

Bowie

JUNE 21, 1977

6 FURLONGS. (1.08) ALLOWANCE. Purse $6,500. Fillies, 3–year–old which have never won two races, weights, 120 lbs. Non–winners of a race other than claiming, since May 16, allowed 3 lbs. Such a race since April 15, 5 lbs. Such a race since March 15, 8 lbs. (Winners Preferred).

Value of race $6,500, value to winner $3,900, second $1,430, third $780, fourth $390. Mutuel pool $40,754. Exacta Pool $47,390.

Last Raced	Horse	Eqt.A.Wt	PP	St	¼	½	Str	Fin	Jockey	Odds $1
30May77 9Pim1	Spot Two	b 3 120	2	4	12½	11½	12½	12½	Hinojosa H	2.80
13Jun77 7Bow5	Power	3 120	3	3	22½	22½	21½	2¾	Cusimano G	3.30
13Jun77 7Bow2	Ernest Ruler	b 3 120	7	2	31½	32	32	32	Adams J K	2.20
6Jun77 5Bow3	My Iron Lass	3 112	1	6	72½	64	52½	4½	Lee T	15.50
8Jun77 2Bow1	Bitina	b 3 113	8	1	43	42	4½	53½	Eseman E E7	a-6.40
6Jun77 5Bow4	Sword Play	3 112	6	5	5hd	5hd	64	63	McCarron C J	5.60
26Feb77 6Bow6	Sea Tale	b 3 113	5	8	8	8	7½	71½	Passmore W J	a-6.40
7Aug76 5Del3	Foster's Fuzzy	3 114	4	7	6hd	7hd	8	8	Edwards J W	29.90

a–Coupled: Bitina and Sea Tale.

OFF AT 4:10 EDT. Start good, Won handily. Time, :22⅕, :45⅕, :57⅗, 1:10⅕ Track fast.

$2 Mutuel Prices:

3–SPOT TWO	7.60	3.80	2.80
4–POWER		4.00	3.00
7–ERNEST RULER			2.60

$2 EXACTA 3–4 PAID $30.80.

Ch. f, by Hagley—One Spot, by Cavan. Trainer Bradley Donald C. Bred by Helsing E A (Md).

SPOT TWO broke alertly to duel for the early advantage while saving ground, was confidently rated on the lead and held a safe margin without need of strong urging. SPOT TWO worked an additional furlong following the finish. POWER, closest to the pace from the outset, could not reach the winner and outfinished ERNEST RULER. The latter lodged a mild late bid outside POWER. MY IRON LASS was not a serious threat.

Owners— 1, Witching Hour Farm; 2, O'Keefe W; 3, Petrullo C; 4, Kincheloe J G; 5, Rauck W H; 6, Locust Hill Farm; 7, Helmore Farm; 8, Sniadowski A J.

Trainers— 1, Bradley Donald C; 2, Bond Bernard P; 3, Rockey Gerald W; 4, Mobberley John C; 5, Adams Robert L; 6, Hadry Charles H; 7, Adams Robert L; 8, Dutrow Richard E.

Overweight: Sea Tale 1 pound; Foster's Fuzzy 2.

Scratched—Sea Wren (14Jun77 5Bow1); Dead End (21May77 4Pim7); Dixie Spears (6Jun77 5Bow5); Camotop (1Jun77 5Bow3).

I tried to maintain a look of disgust as Spot Two sprinted to the lead and went on to win by 2½ lengths, while Sword Play failed to reach contention. Nor did I permit myself a smile when Spot Two paid $7.60 and I calculated that I would collect $3800 on my $1000 bet with Sneaky Pete.

I did not feel terribly guilt-ridden about the deception. Most people have to behave like SOBs their whole lives in order to get rich. I had to do it only occasionally. And I was getting rich. My profit for the first six months of 1977 was nearly $60,000. I was going to take a few weeks' rest now, but by the end of the Saratoga season, this was going to be a $100,000 year.

Saratoga: Graveyard of Champions

In the years before 1977, when my gambling was not so remunerative, I often suffered doubts and anxieties about the life I had chosen for myself. My obsession was one which society—as well as many of my friends—viewed with disapproval or contempt. It obliged me to spend much of my time in unattractive, vulgar environments. After enduring a winter afternoon in the dismal confines of Bowie Race Course and losing my money on cheap, broken-down animals, I sometimes questioned my sanity for doing it.

But these self-doubts would be instantly dispelled as soon as August arrived. When the racing season began at Saratoga and I walked into the track for the first time after a year's absence, I was reminded of all the wonderful virtues of the racing game. I could not possibly want a better life.

Saratoga is the last survivor of an era when racing was a genteel sport rather than an industry which exists principally to crank out tax revenue for state treasuries. There is an intimacy about the place that makes it unique among America's racetracks. Horses are saddled under the elm trees in a large outdoor paddock, where spectators can stand within an arm's length of them. Jockeys must walk through the crowd to get to the saddling area, so children can besiege them for autographs and disgruntled bettors can offer critiques of their riding ability. Trainers, owners, and jockey agents traditionally congregate by the porch of an administration building near the paddock, and a horseplayer who passes through the area can hear more gossip and hot tips per square foot here than anywhere else in the racing world.

But Saratoga owes its special character less to the charm of the track than to the community of which it is a part. Saratoga Springs, New York, is a town steeped in legend and tradition. It has been a mecca for the social elite for more than one hundred years, enjoying its heyday at the turn of the century, when legendary high-rollers like Diamond Jim Brady and Bet-a-Million Gates gambled till dawn at the Canfield Casino.

Saratoga is still the August home of the Whitneys, the Vanderbilts, and the rest of horsey society. And it is still the scene of some of the most dazzling high-stakes gambling in America. With the casino now converted into a museum, the action has moved to the pavilion of the Saratoga Yearling Sales, where the annual auctions of one-year-old thoroughbreds offer a subtle but engrossing spectacle. When a man gestures imperceptibly to acquire an untested yearling for $100,000, accepts the handshakes of his peers and a kiss from his blonde companion, and then signs the sales slip with a world-weary air, he is gambling on a scale that few of us could ever dream of.

But even for those of us who bet on a more modest level, Saratoga is special. It is a place where a horseplayer can spend four weeks doing nothing but betting horses, thinking about horses, and talking about horses. There are few distractions, and no killjoys to suggest that such monomania is abnormal. My fondest memories of Saratoga are the nocturnal vigils in front of Joe Deuel's newsstand, where as many as a hundred horseplayers would wait for the *Racing Form* to be delivered from downstate. They would be clustered in little groups, reviewing the afternoon's races or anticipating the next day's card, until the car bearing the *Forms* arrived and a charge of excitement shot through the crowd. Impatient to get their hands on the paper sixteen hours before post time, the horseplayers would jostle and elbow each other as they stormed the newsstand. And then they would quickly disperse, with everyone going home to plunge into study.

There is much to study in the past performances for each day's races at Saratoga. In contrast to the cloying diet of six-furlong claiming events at most tracks, Saratoga offers a gourmet banquet of racing. A handicapper has to deal with stakes races, grass races, steeplechase races, two-year-old maiden races. He has to evaluate top horses coming from different sections of the country. He has to reckon with as many as thirty skilled trainers.

At other tracks I could win with just a few insights; at Pimlico I needed little more than an understanding of the bias. But Saratoga demands such a wide range of knowledge and skills that it poses a supreme test for a handicapper. Over the years, I gauged my development as a horseplayer according to my annual performance at Saratoga.

I went to Saratoga for the first time in 1970, optimistically renting an apartment for the whole month. By the second week of the meeting I was wiring my newspaper for money, and in the third week I returned home, defeated and bewildered.

On the opening day of the 1971 season, I met Steve Davidowitz, and our casual conversation in the paddock started a long-standing friendship. For the first time in my life, I got to watch a real professional operate, and I saw that it was indeed possible to master the art of handicapping. But I still did not survive past the third week of the season.

The next year Steve and I attacked Saratoga together, and I learned to combine my speed figures with the flexible, comprehensive approach to the game that he advocated. I beat Saratoga for the first time, and I felt that I had come of age as a horseplayer.

I suffered no further doubts about my ability until 1975, when I found myself mired in a terrible losing streak and went to Saratoga with the hope of curing it. Instead I bet forty-nine consecutive losers and sneaked out of town aboard an Adirondack Trailways bus, too embarrassed even to say good-bye to my friends.

That was my last serious defeat. In 1976 I returned to Saratoga with my confidence restored, joined forces with the Kid for the first time, and enjoyed a profitable meeting. During the course of it I realized that Saratoga had become an easy track to beat.

The odds at the track were once mainly determined by knowledgeable insiders and handicappers who were spending the season in Saratoga. In order to win, a horseplayer had to be even smarter than the "smart money." But when the New York City Off-Track Betting Corporation was created in 1971, money bet downstate was added to the wagering pools at the track. By 1976, more than half of the money bet on Saratoga races came from OTB customers who were mostly unsophisticated handicappers and who could not know about horses' appearance, changes in track condition, late betting action, or other important information to which people at the track have access. Once a sudden, unexpected rainstorm forced the shift of a scheduled grass race to the main track. Of the six entrants, only one had ever shown any ability in the mud. But because OTB customers had already bet on the assumption that this was a turf race, the lone mud-runner paid 6 to 1. Every day the regulars at the track found themselves staring in disbelief at similar bargain prices on the tote board and feeling grateful for the largesse of the OTB bettors.

As I prepared to leave Washington for the 1977 Saratoga meeting, I did not feel any of the apprehension which had characterized so many of my previous trips there. The Kid was not worried, either. "You know," he said, "if I don't make money this summer, I'll give up the game." I delivered a brief lecture on the dangers of overconfidence, telling him that nobody can ever beat this game so steadily and automatically that he can take success for granted. But my admonition was a perfunctory one. I agreed with the Kid. We couldn't lose in Saratoga.

After getting settled in our Saratoga house, the Kid and I immersed ourselves in study of the opening-day program. The featured Schuylerville Stakes was a typical Saratoga race: a tough, competitive field, populated by well-bred young horses from good stables. None of the horses leaped off the page of the *Racing Form*, as speed-on-the-rail standouts did at Pimlico, but after analyzing the race for more than an hour the Kid and I found a possible bet.

8 **SARATOGA**

6 FURLONGS. (1.08) 60th Running THE SCHUYLERVILLE. $35,000 added. Fillies, 2-year-olds, weights, 119 lbs. By subscription of $50 each, which shall accompany the nominationg; $125 to start, with $35,000 added. The added money and all fees to be divided 60% to the winner, 22% to secind, 12% to third an 6% to fourth. Winners of a sweepstakes since June 15, an additional 2 lbs. Non-winners of a sweepstakes allowed 3 lbs. Of a race other than maiden or claiming, 5 lbs. Maidens, 7 lbs. Starters to be named at the closing time of entries. A trophy will be presented to the owner of the winner. (Closed Monday, July 18, 1977, with 25 nominations.)

L'Alezane — Ch. f. 2, by Dr Fager—Northern Willow, by Northern Dancer — Br.—Taylor E P (Can) — Own.—Levesque J L — Tr.—Starr J — **121** — St. 1st 2nd 3rd Amt. 1977 3 3 0 0 $24,790
9Jly77- 7WO fst 6f :22⅖ :46⅘ 1:12⅕ ⒻⓈShady Well 7 3 22 21½ 2hd 15 Souter J P 114 *.60e 82-18 L'Alezane 1145 La Sorciere 1131¼ Gay Apparel 1192 Mild drive 11
1Jly77- 5WO fst 5½f :22⅘ :45⅘ 1:05⅕ ⒻAllowance 1 3 1½ 1hd 11½ 13½ Souter J P5 109 3.75 91-15 L'Alezane 1093½ Hattabs Spirit 1073DancersLimit1121 Ridden out 7
4Jun77- 3WO fst 5f :22⅘ :46⅘ :59⅗ ⒻMd Sp Wt 6 6 63¾ 4¾ 12 1hd Souter J P5 107 *.95 89-13 L'Alezane 107hd Time Slips Away 1172½Kelly'sInvader1122 Lasted 8

My First Word — Dk. b. or br. f. 2, by Verbatim—First Chapter, by Disciplinarian — Br.—Reineman R L (Ky) — Own.—Reineman R L — Tr.—Stephens Woodford C — **114** — St. 1st 2nd 3rd Amt. 1977 1 1 0 0 $6,000
7Jly77- 3Bel fst 5½f :22⅗ :46⅖ 1:04⅖ ⒻMd Sp Wt 7 7 34 32½ 2hd 14 Wallis T 83 119 5.70 93-12 My First Word 1194 Caption 1191¼ Wellesly 1191½ Ridden out 10
LATEST WORKOUTS Jly 27 Bel 5f fst 1:00 h Jly 23 Bel 4f fst :47⅗ h Jly 18 Bel 4f fst :47⅗ h Jly 14 Bel 4f fst :49 b

Irish Rising — B. f. 2, by Explodent—Easter Card, by Errard — Br.—Thorough Breeding Corp (Ky) — Own.—Kaplowitz J — Tr.—Hirsch Jerome — **114** — St. 1st 2nd 3rd Amt. 1977 5 1 1 2 $8,345
22Jly77- 6Mth fst 5½f :22⅖ :46⅕ 1:04⅘ ⒻAllowance 5 1 34 34 36½ 39¼ Klidzia S7 110 3.00 84-19 Duffy Ducket 1173¼ Bimbo Sue 1176 Irish Rising11012 Weakened 6
8Jly77- 3Bel fst 5½f :22⅘ :46⅕ 1:05 ⒻMd 25000 4 2 32 2½ 15 16¾ Cotto E7 78 112 *2.20 90-12 IrishRising1126¾ProudCatherine1152PlyBehving1191¾ Ridden out 10
30Jun77- 4Bel fst 5½f :23 :47 1:06⅕ ⒻMd 25000 4 1 2hd 12 2½ 24 Cotto E7 62 112 3.40 80-19 Lakeville Miss 1194 Irish Rising 1126¾ Hypsipyle 119¾ 2nd best 9
22Jun77- 4Bel fst 5½f :23⅕ :47⅖ 1:06⅗ ⒻMd 35000 4 2 11 2hd 21½ 32½ Montoya D 119 5.60 79-15 CavyCakes1152½BrownsvilleBabe115hdIrishRising1191¾ Weakened 10
17Jun77- 4Bel fst 5½f :23⅕ :47⅘ 1:07⅖ ⒻMd 45000 3 2 2hd 2hd 45½ 613 Montoya D 119 3.80 65-22 Comet Aflair 1198 Itsamaza 115½ Wha Doin Amy 115hd Gave way 10
LATEST WORKOUTS Jly 30 Bel 3f fst :35⅕ h Jly 19 Bel tr.t 4f fst :48 h Jly 7 Bel tr.t 3f fst :38 b Jun 9 Bel tr.t 5f fst 1:00⅕ h

Lakeville Miss — Dk. b. or br. f. 2, by Rainy Lake—Hew, by Blue Prince — Br.—Weinsier R (Ky) — Own.—Weinsier R — Tr.—Martin Jose — **114** — St. 1st 2nd 3rd Amt. 1977 1 1 0 0 $4,800
30Jun77- 4Bel fst 5½f :23 :47 1:06⅕ ⒻMd 25000 5 7 33 22 1½ 14 Hernandez R 73 119 2.40 84-19 Lakeville Miss 1194 Irish Rising 1126¾ Hypsipyle 119¾ Easily 9
LATEST WORKOUTS Jly 30 Sar 3f fst :36⅖ bg Jly 23 Bel tr.t 5f fst 1:01⅘ h Jly 17 Bel tr.t 5f fst 1:01⅖ h Jly 10 Bel tr.t 4f fst :48⅘ h

Crab Apple Lane — B. f. 2, by Graustark—Candalita, by Olympia — Br.—Galbreath J W (Ky) — Own.—Darby Dan Farm — Tr.—Rondinello Thomas L — **114** — St. 1st 2nd 3rd Amt. 1977 1 1 0 0 $6,000
14Jly77- 4Bel fst 5½f :22⅖ :46 1:05 ⒻMd Sp Wt 1 2 1½ 11 11½ 12¾ Velasquez J 82 119 3.70 90-12 CrabAppleLane1192¾MistyNtive119noAllForAmy1192¼ Ridden out 10
LATEST WORKOUTS Jly 30 Sar 4f fst :47 h Jly 25 Bel 6f fst 1:14 h Jly 20 Bel 4f fst :48⅘ b Jly 13 Bel 3f sly :36 b

Big Rhapsody — Dk. b. or br. f. 2, by Big Burn—King's Rhapsody, by King Hairan — Br.—Massey H (Fla) — Own.—Grandview Stable — Tr.—Nash Joseph S — **121** — St. 1st 2nd 3rd Amt. 1977 4 2 0 0 $21,954
11Jly77- 8Bel fst 5½f :22⅖ :46 1:05⅕ ⒻAstoria 5 1 2hd 2hd 3½ 55½ Graell A 67 119 4.60 83-15 Akita 114nk Sweeping View 114nk Stub 1145 Speed; gave way 6
2Jly77- 8Key fst 5½f :22 :46⅕ 1:05 ⒻSignature 2 6 1½ 1½ 12 12½ Graell A 115 4.40 95-20 Big Rhapsody 1152½ Surprise Trip 115hd Sahsie 1154½ Driving 9
20Jun77- 8Bel fst 5½f :22⅖ :46⅘ 1:06 ⒻFashion 3 2 76¼ 89¾ 66¼ 44¾ Graell A 72 116 50.60 80-18 Sunny Bay 116nk Stub 1162½SweepingView1162 Passed tired ones 8
10Mar77- 3Hia sly 3f :22 :33⅗ ⒻMd Sp Wt 6 3 1hd 1nk Cruguet J 119 6.80 94-06 BgRhpsody119nkVrsAndChors1192FnnySnst1191½ Brushed, lasted 10
LATEST WORKOUTS Jly 19 Bel tr.t 5f fst 1:00 h ●Jun 26 Bel tr.t 5f gd :59⅗ h Jun 16 Bel 5f fst 1:01⅕ h Jun 13 Bel 4f fst :48 h

Akita — Dk. b. or br. f. 2, by Restless Native—La Froide, by Nearctic — Br.—Moore Marie A (Ky) — Own.—Moore Marie A — Tr.—Freeman Willard C — **121** — St. 1st 2nd 3rd Amt. 1977 3 2 0 0 $27,870
11Jly77- 8Bel fst 5½f :22⅖ :46 1:05⅕ ⒻAstoria 2 6 55 53¾ 42 1nk Velasquez J 81 114 9.80 89-15 Akita 114nk Sweeping View 114nk Stub 1145 Strong handling 6
20Jun77- 8Bel fst 5½f :22⅖ :46⅘ 1:06 ⒻFashion 6 7 41¾ 42¼ 33 76½ Velasquez J 67 116 8.80 78-18 Sunny Bay 116nk Stub 1162½ Sweeping View 1162 Tired in drive 8
30May77- 4Bel fst 5½f :23 :47⅕ 1:06⅗ ⒻMd Sp Wt 3 6 62 42½ 2½ 12½ Campanelli T 72 119 16.30 82-14 Akita 1192½ Randye La Fabuleux 119nk MistyNative1191¾ Handily 9
LATEST WORKOUTS Jly 25 Aqu 6f fst 1:15⅖ b ●Jly 21 Aqu 4f fst :46⅘ h ●Jly 10 Aqu 3f fst :34⅖ h ●Jly 5 Aqu 5f fst :59 h

Tempermental Pet — Dk. b. or br. f. 2, by Gallant Man—Queen's Mark, by Rash Prince — Br.—Elmendorf Farm (Ky) — Own.—Elmendorf — Tr.—Campo John P — **112** — St. 1st 2nd 3rd Amt. 1977 2 M 2 0 $4,400
22Jly77- 4Bel fst 5½f :22⅘ :46⅗ 1:05⅖ ⒻMd Sp Wt 2 2 1hd 1hd 2hd 2nk Amy J 77 b 119 *1.80 88-17 Caption 119nk Tempermental Pet1191½MistyNative1193 Stumbled 10
29Jun77- 4Bel fst 5½f :23 :47 1:05⅗ ⒻMd Sp Wt 8 6 33 21½ 22 22¾ Amy J 78 119 *1.70e 84-21 Laura D. 1192¾ Tempermental Pet1191¾Dr.FeelGreat119hd Gamely 10
LATEST WORKOUTS Jly 19 Bel tr.t 5f fst 1:02⅖ h Jly 15 Bel tr.t 4f fst :49 b Jly 6 Bel tr.t 4f fst :50 b Jun 25 Bel tr.t 4f fst :48⅖ h

The two-year-old fillies in New York seemed to be a poor crop. Akita had won the Astoria Stakes at Belmont with a figure of 81, which would not be good enough to win a stakes race in a normal year. The top-figure entrant in the Schuylerville, My First Word, was not much faster, having earned an 83 for her maiden victory.

Now a Canadian filly, L'Alezane, had come into the midst of the New Yorkers. Her last performance, a six-furlong race in 1:12⅕, did not look particularly impressive, either. But I checked a back issue of the *Racing Form* for the results on the day she had run at Woodbine, and saw that the filly Polder Pie had won an earlier allowance race in 1:11⅗. In another allowance event on the same afternoon, Green Ribbon had defeated Point of Balance in 1:11⅘. I had only a vague notion of who these animals were, until the Kid burrowed through subsequent issues of the *Form* and found this small news item:

> WOODBINE, Ont., July 18—Monte Clark's Polder Pie, one of the top older fillies and mares on the local circuit, won the six and a half furlong $22,175 Hendrie Handicap on Sunday. . . . She set her own fractions and completed the distance in 1:17, a stakes record. . . . Royal Mount Stable's 7-year-old mare, Point of Balance, finished second.

L'Alezane's 1:12⅕ performance, only slightly slower than the times of stakes-quality elders, had been a good effort. I estimated that she had the top figure in the Schuylerville field, and I liked other things about her, too. She had done everything right in her three-race career, even while being ridden by apprentice jockey J. P. Souter, whom I had seen in Florida and knew was not the next Arcaro. Now L'Alezane was getting the services of the veteran Ron Turcotte. And she had drawn the number-one post position on a track that often favors inside speed.

There was still another positive factor about L'Alezane, one which involves the special peculiarities of handicapping at Saratoga. At the time when I had viewed the track as utterly unfathomable, Steve Davidowitz had attempted to offer a clarification. "Saratoga," he told me, "is in a way one of the most predictable tracks in the country. Every year they run a four-week meet, every year they offer the same type of racing and the same stakes. And every year it's the same big stables, and the same trainers, who win the races."

When the Kid and I undertook a serious study of trainers before our 1976 trip to Saratoga, we saw how right Steve was. Trainers tended to perform with the same degree of effectiveness at various Saratoga meetings, regardless of what they did during the intervening eleven months. George Poole, for example, merited little respect at Aqueduct and Belmont, but he usually fared well at Saratoga, perhaps because his employer C. V. Whitney insisted on winning races while he was fraternizing with his peers during August.

Jack Starr, the trainer of L'Alezane, was another one of those names which recurred in the Saratoga results. Starr was based in Canada but he occasionally invaded upstate New York with high-class young horses. He won the prestigious Alabama Stakes with Fanfreluche in 1970. His filly La Prevoyante captured the Adirondack and Spinaway Stakes in 1972. When he brought horses from Canada to the big races at Saratoga, Starr was not guessing that they had quality. He already knew.

I went to Saratoga on opening day feeling confident of L'Alezane's chances but doubtful that her odds would be decent. On the first flash of the tote board, however, with $129,000 from OTB patrons already in the pool, L'Alezane opened at an incredible 7 to 1. That bargain price started a virtual stampede to the betting windows, and I joined it, wagering $700 to win and $300 to place. By post time L'Alezane was 3 to 1.

EIGHTH RACE		6 FURLONGS. (1.08) 60th Running THE SCHUYLERVILLE. $35,000 added. Fillies, 2-year-olds, weights, 119 lbs. By subscription of $50 each, which shall accompany the nominationg; $125 to start, with $35,000 added. The added money and all fees to be divided 60% to the winner, 22% to secind, 12% to third an 6% to fourth. Winners of a sweepstakes since June 15, an additional 2 lbs. Non-winners of a sweepstakes allowed
Saratoga		
AUGUST 1, 1977		

3 lbs. Of a race other than maiden or claiming, 5 lbs. Maidens, 7 lbs. Starters to be named at the closing time of entries. A trophy will be presented to the owner of the winner. (Closed Monday, July 18, 1977, with 25 nominations.)
Value of race $37,250, value to winner $22,350, second $8,195, third $4,470, fourth $2,235. Mutuel pool $172,105, OTB pool $129,989.

Last Raced	Horse	Eqt.A.Wt PP St	¼	½	Str	Fin	Jockey	Odds $1
9Jly77 7WO1	L'Alezane	2 121 1 1	1½	1½	11½	1no	Turcotte R	3.20
11Jly77 8Bel1	Akita	2 121 7 4	41	21½	22	2nk	Velasquez J	4.50
30Jun77 4Bel1	Lakeville Miss	2 114 4 7	71½	61½	41½	33½	Hernandez R	18.80
11Jly77 8Bel5	Big Rhapsody	2 121 6 3	5½	41	3hd	4¾	Graell A	19.20
14Jly77 4Bel1	Crab Apple Lane	2 114 5 8	6½	7½	5½	51	Cordero A Jr	3.30
22Jly77 4Bel2	Tempermental Pet	b 2 112 8 5	8	8	62	65½	Cruguet J	9.40
7Jly77 3Bel1	My First Word	2 114 2 6	2½	3hd	74	73½	Wallis T	2.00
22Jly77 6Mth3	Irish Rising	2 114 3 2	3½	5hd	8	8	Cotto E	24.00

OFF AT 5:17 1/2, EDT. Start good, Won driving. Time, :22⅗, :46⅕, 1:11⅘ Track fast.

$2 Mutuel Prices:				
	1-(A)-L'ALEZANE	8.40	5.60	4.00
	7-(G)-AKITA		5.40	4.20
	4-(D)-LAKEVILLE MISS			5.20

Ch. f, by Dr Fager—Northern Willow, by Northern Dancer. Trainer Starr J. Bred by Taylor E P (Can).

L'ALEZANE saved ground while making the pace, settled into the stretch with a clear advantage and lasted over AKITA. The latter, away in good order, made a run from the outside approaching the stretch and finished gamely, just missing. LAKEVILLE MISS, wide into the stretch, finished strongly. BIG RHAPSODY rallied leaving the turn but lacked the needed late response. CRAB APPLE LANE, off slowly, raced very wide into the stretch and failed to seriously menace. TEMPERMENTAL PET was without speed. MY FIRST WORD, rushed into contention between horses soon after the start, remained a factor to the stretch and gave way. IRISH RISING tired badly.

Owners— 1, Levesque J L; 2, Moore Marie A; 3, Weinsier R; 4, Grandview Stables; 5, Darby Dan Farm; 6, Elmendorf; 7, Reineman R L; 8, Kaplowitz J.

Trainers— 1, Starr J; 2, Freeman Willard C; 3, Martin Jose; 4, Nash Joseph S; 5, Rondinello Thomas L; 6, Campo John P; 7, Stephens Woodford C; 8, Hirsch Jerome.

While L'Alezane took the lead and hugged the rail, bad things were happening to all her opponents. My First Word, the favorite, broke tardily. Lakeville Miss had to swing extremely wide on the turn, losing valuable ground. Crab Apple Lane was forced even wider. With all these advantages, L'Alezane still had to struggle to eke out the decision in a tight, three-horse photo finish. The result was not exactly a great vindication of my handicapping, but it put me $2500 ahead with the Saratoga meeting one day old.

That proved to be my only triumph during the first week of the season. It happened to be a week when the handicapping methods I favor were not working; I made three serious plunges on standout-figure horses and they all lost badly. I had no doubts about the accuracy of my New York figures. Instead, I realized that the racetrack results go through phases when certain methods succeed and certain methods fail. Toney Betts described the cyclical nature of the game nicely in his book *Across the Board:* "One day the speed charters come up with the winners; the next day the classifiers come up with the winners; and some days nobody comes up with the winners, except a sweet old lady in the grandstand holding a ticket on a $1384 daily double."

During the first week at Saratoga, it was neither the speed handicappers nor the class handicappers nor the little old ladies who came up with the profitable winners. It was the members of a school of handicapping which didn't even exist a few years ago. They call themselves chartists, and instead of studying the *Racing Form,* they stand with clipboards in hand, studying the television monitors that flash probable payoffs for exactas and daily doubles.

Horseplayers have been watching the fluctuation of odds, looking for evidence of "smart money," for as long as the sport has existed. Even fledgling handicappers know that when they see a horse's price drop from 15 to 1 to 10 to 1 on the last flash of the tote board, they had better run to the windows. In the last few years, though, watching odds has become a sophisticated art. With exacta betting permitted on so many races, sharp insiders can wager through this medium and make a killing without affecting the price on the tote board.

In New York, some of the money in the exacta pools is bet at OTB, while the rest is bet at the track. This fact underlies the whole handicapping approach of Manny Inquiry, a chartist who gets his name because he takes side bets on the outcomes of foul claims and stewards' inquiries at the New York tracks. "You've got to assume that a smart trainer is not going to bet at OTB because of the five percent surtax," Manny said. "He's going to bet at the track." Manny declined to elaborate upon his methodology, but I can guess how he operates. Suppose the average exacta price with a particular horse is $100 when the betting opens; this is all uninformed OTB money. As the track money comes in, the price drops to $80. Then, midway through the wagering period, a new batch of OTB money is added to the exacta pool. The price rises to $100 again. Now more track money knocks the payoff down to $60. Manny would conclude that this is a very hot horse, one being bet powerfully by insiders at the track. But the vast majority of horseplayers will never know it, because the betting action is not being reflected on the tote board. As with every form of handicapping, a person who uses this approach has to supplement it with good judgment and creative thinking. "Lots of guys are doing charting nowadays," Manny said, "but you've got to be good at it to win. You've got to know the trainers: who bets early, who bets late, who bets big, who bets small. And you've got to work hard at it."

The third race at Saratoga on August 4 was made to order for the chartists. It was a $45,000 claiming race for maiden two-year-old fillies, with five first-time starters in the field.

3 SARATOGA 6 FURLONGS SARATOGA (Start / Finish)

6 FURLONGS. (1.08) MAIDEN CLAIMING. Purse $8,500. Fillies, 2-year-olds. Weight, 119 lbs. Claiming price $45,000; for each $2,500 to $40,000 allowed 2 lbs.

Freedom First — B. f. 2, by Pronto—Conversation Piece, by Bold Ruler — $45,000 — Br.—Chenery C T est of (Va) — Tr.—DiMauro Stephen — Own.—Meadow Stable — **119** — St. 1st 2nd 3rd Amt. — 1977 1 M 0 0
29Jun77- 4Bel fst 5½f :23 :47 1:05⅗ ⒻMd Sp Wt 7 10 912 9151018 1019 Graell A 119 42.50 68-21 LaurD.119²¾TempermentlPet119¹¾Dr.FeelGret119hd Broke slowly 10
LATEST WORKOUTS Aug 1 Sar 4f fst :49⅘ bg Jly 27 Bel tr.t 3f fst :37⅗ b Jly 9 Bel tr.t 5f fst 1:03 b Jly 4 Bel 4f fst :47⅖ hg

Marston's Mill — Dk. b. or br. f. 2, by In Reality—Millicent, by Cornish Prince — $45,000 — Br.—Mellon P (Va) — Tr.—Miller Mack — Own.—Rokeby Stables — **114^5** — St. 1st 2nd 3rd Amt. — 1977 0 M 0 0
LATEST WORKOUTS Jly 31 Sar 4f fst :48⅖ h Jly 26 Bel 4f sly :47⅗ h Jly 20 Bel 6f fst 1:15⅗ b Jly 15 Bel 4f fst :48 h

Irish Noel — Dk. b. or br. f. 2, by Irish Ruler—Noel's Baby, by Hilarious — $45,000 — Br.—Equi F (Fla) — Tr.—Luro Horatio A — Own.—Davis True Jr — **119** — St. 1st 2nd 3rd Amt. — 1977 1 M 0 1 $1,020
20Jly77- 4Bel fst 5½f :23 :46⅗ 1:05 ⒻMd 45000 4 5 73¾ 58½ 48 38¾ Vasquez J 65 115 2.30 81-19 Itsamaza 115⁸ Stevlove 115¾ Irish Noel 115hd Bore in 9
LATEST WORKOUTS Aug 1 Sar 4f fst :49 b Jly 27 Bel 5f fst 1:03⅗ b Jly 16 Bel 4f fst :48⅗ b Jly 9 Bel 4f fst :46⅖ hg

Miller Miss — Dk. b. or br. f. 2, by Poker—Wendy S, by Persian Road II — $40,000 — Br.—Farnsworth Farms & Sainer (Fla) — Tr.—Cotter Mary M — Own.—Miller L I — **115** — St. 1st 2nd 3rd Amt. — 1977 0 M 0 0
LATEST WORKOUTS Aug 2 Sar 3f fst :35⅖ hg Jly 27 Bel 5f fst 1:02⅖ b Jly 20 Bel 5f fst 1:04 b Jly 15 Bel 3f fst :37⅘ bg

Princess Polly — B. f. 2, by Crozier—Polly N., by Quiby — $45,000 — Br.—Hooper F W (Fla) — Tr.—Tinsley Joe E Jr — Own.—Hooper F W — **119** — St. 1st 2nd 3rd Amt. — 1977 2 M 0 0 $1,500
24Jly77- 6Hol fst 5½f :22⅘ :45⅘ 1:05 ⒻMd Sp Wt 10 4 75 712 612 47½ Pierce D 115 3.60e 78-16 Circle The Day 115²½ Glory Stride 110⁵ Thin Set 115hd Rallied 10
15Jun77- 4Hol fst 5½f :22⅘ :45⅘ 1:04⅖ ⒻMd Sp Wt 7 1 66½ 76¾ 68½ 49½ McHargue D G 115 9.40e 79-19 Beautification115¹½LdyKennedy115²SunshineKmp117⁶ No threat 7
LATEST WORKOUTS Jly 31 Sar 6f fst 1:14⅘ h

Lehua — B. f. 2, by Big Brave—Flower Mart, by To Market — $45,000 — Br.—Cohn S (Md) — Tr.—Hunt Leonard H — Own.—Hallman Paula C — **119** — St. 1st 2nd 3rd Amt. — 1977 0 M 0 0
LATEST WORKOUTS Aug 1 Sar 3f fst :35⅕ hg Jly 27 Bel 5f fst 1:02 hg Jly 23 Bel 5f fst 1:03⅗ b Jly 19 Bel 3f fst :36 hg

Misty Native — B. f. 2. by Native Charger—Miss Cor, by Correlation — $45,000 — Br.—Hellman N (Fla) — Tr.—LaBoccetta Frank — Own.—Hellman N — **119** — St. 1st 2nd 3rd Amt. — 1977 3 M 1 2 $4,600
22Jly77- 4Bel fst 5½f :22⅘ :46⅗ 1:05⅖ ⒻMd Sp Wt 9 6 41¾ 3½ 31 31¾ Maple E 72 119 3.60 66-17 Caption 119nk Tempermental Pet119¹½MistyNative119³ Stumbled 10
14Jly77- 4Bel fst 5½f :22⅘ :46 1:05 ⒻMd Sp Wt 5 1 2½ 31 21½ 22¾ Cordero A Jr 75 119 4.20 87-12 Crab AppleLane119²¾MistyNative119noAllForAmy119²¼ No match 10
30May77- 4Bel fst 5½f :23 :47⅕ 1:06⅗ ⒻMd Sp Wt 4 7 75 74½ 53 32¾ Maple E 65 119 6.50 79-14 Akita 119²½ Randye La Fabuleux 119nk Misty Native119¹¾ Bore in 9
LATEST WORKOUTS Jly 31 Sar 4f fst :48⅕ h Jly 11 Aqu 4f fst :49 h ● Jly 7 Aqu 5f fst 1:01⅕ h Jly 2 Aqu 4f fst :49 h

Estelle's Lyric — Dk. b. or br. f. 2, by Highbinder—Sugar Cone, by Royal Note — $42,500 — Br.—Rosoff A (Fla) — Tr.—Zito Nicholas P — Own.—Rosoff A — **110^7** — St. 1st 2nd 3rd Amt. — 1977 0 M 0 0
LATEST WORKOUTS Aug 2 Sar tr.t 3f fst :37 b Jly 30 Sar 5f fst 1:01 hg Jly 20 Bel tr.t 4f fst :49⅘ b Jly 16 Bel tr.t 5f fst 1:01⅗ h

Lavishly — Ch. f. 2, by Stevward—Roof Raiser, by Raise A Native — $45,000 — Br.—Harbor View Farm (Fla) — Tr.—Barrera Lazaro S — Own.—Harbor View Farm — **119** — St. 1st 2nd 3rd Amt. — 1977 0 M 0 0
LATEST WORKOUTS Jly 30 Sar 5f fst 1:00⅗ hg Jly 22 Bel tr.t 4f fst :48⅕ h Jly 14 Bel tr.t 4f gd :51 b Jly 12 Bel tr.t 4f fst :49 b

Our Delilah — B. f. 2, by Sham—Treachery, by Promised Land — $40,000 — Br.—Mangurian H T Jr (Ky) — Tr.—DeStasio Richard T — Own.—Flying Zee Stables — **115** — St. 1st 2nd 3rd Amt. — 1977 1 M 0 0
20Jly77- 4Bel fst 5½f :23 :46⅗ 1:05 ⒻMd 45000 6 8 913 915 716 615 Imparato J 48 115 15.50 75-19 Itsamaza 115⁸ Stevlove 115¾ Irish Noel 115hd Outrun 9
LATEST WORKOUTS Jly 25 Bel 5f fst 1:02 b Jly 5 Bel tr.t 4f fst :50⅕ b Jun 23 Bel 4f fst :49 b Jun 18 Bel 4f fst :50⅕ b

Eavesdrop — Dk. b. or br. f. 2, by Rock Talk—East Branch, by Delta Judge — $40,000 — Br.—Walker Mrs J Jr (Pa) — Tr.—Maloney James W — Own.—Walker J Jr Mrs — **115** — St. 1st 2nd 3rd Amt. — 1977 1 M 0 0
29Jly77- 4Bel fst 5½f :22⅘ :46⅖ 1:05⅖ ⒻMd Sp Wt 4 2 42 53 55 56 Vasquez J 61 119 16.90 82-15 Envisioned 119³¾ Satan Sez 119hd Restless Lover 119² No mishap 10
LATEST WORKOUTS Jly 25 Bel 4f fst :48⅕ h Jly 20 Bel 3f fst :35⅗ h Jly 15 Bel 4f fst :47⅗ hg Jly 11 Bel 4f fst :48⅕ h

Sue Me Not — Dk. b. or br. f. 2, by Verbatim—Trotta Sue, by Promised Land — $45,000 — Br.—Runnymede Farm Inc & Smith A B (Ky) — Tr.—Dunham Bob G — Own.—Gartrell Mrs C — **119** — St. 1st 2nd 3rd Amt. — 1977 1 M 0 0
14Jly77- 4Bel fst 5½f :22⅘ :46 1:05 ⒻMd Sp Wt 6 8 813 78½ 77½ 55¾ Velez R I 68 119 60.20 84-12 Crab AppleLane119²¾MistyNative119noAllForAmy119²¼ No factor 10
LATEST WORKOUTS Jly 23 Aqu 5f fst 1:03 b Jly 11 Aqu 5f fst 1:04 b Jly 6 Aqu 5f fst 1:00⅗ h Jly 1 Aqu 5f fst 1:03 b

When I handicapped this race, I held fairly strong convictions about it. Misty Native was a bit too obvious for my tastes, but she had solid credentials. She had lost her debut to Akita, who went on to win a stakes race. Then she had been beaten by Crab Apple Lane, who ran creditably despite bad luck in the Schuylerville Stakes on opening day. In her most recent start Misty Native had stumbled but finished a close third. Now she was entered for the first time in a claiming race, where she was much less likely to encounter any budding stakes horses. If one of the first-time starters was that good, she would probably receive heavy betting action and I would be forewarned.

Of the first-time starters, Lavishly went off at a tepid 7 to 1 (despite the presence of popular Steve Cauthen in the saddle); Estelle's Lyric was 9 to 1; and all the rest were 30 to 1 or more. There did not seem to be any prodigies in the field. So I invested $200, coupling Misty Native with Sue Me Not, the second-best figure; and also with Lavishly, because trainer Laz Barrera usually does well with young horses at Saratoga.

While I thought the betting action on the race appeared rather tame, Manny saw that the exacta boards were being practically short-circuited. The Barrera camp was betting with gusto on Lavishly. And Alan Rosoff, the high-roller who owned Estelle's Lyric, was evidently betting his filly as if there were no tomorrow. Presumably, neither of the stables knew that it was running into another sharp first-time starter. Only the chartists realized that there were two hot horses in this field, and that knowledge sent them scurrying to the windows as post time approached.

THIRD RACE

Saratoga

AUGUST 4, 1977

6 FURLONGS. (1.08) MAIDEN CLAIMING. Purse $8,500. Fillies, 2-year-olds. Weig 119 lbs. Claiming price $45,000; for each $2,500 to $40,000 allowed 2 lbs.

Value of race $8,500, value to winner $5,100, second $1,870, third $1,020, fourth $510. Mutuel pool $82,131, OTB pool $69,090. Track Exacta Pool $103,509. OTB Exacta Pool $149,299.

Last Raced	Horse	Eqt.A.Wt PP St	¼	½	Str	Fin	Jockey	Cl'g Pr	Odds $1
	Lavishly	b 2 119 9 6	5½	3¹	3²	1no	Cauthen S	45000	7.80
	Estelle's Lyric	2 110 8 4	3½	1hd	2²	2nk	Cotto E⁷	42500	9.50
22Jly77 4Bel³	Misty Native	2 119 7 2	1¹	2²	1¹	3²¼	Velasquez J	45000	1.30
14Jly77 4Bel⁵	Sue Me Not	2 119 11 3	7¹	7¹	4½	4³	Velez R I	45000	7.10
	Marston's Mill	2 114 2 12	6hd	6½	6¹½	5hd	Velez H Jr⁵	45000	31.00
20Jly77 4Bel³	Irish Noel	2 119 3 7	8²	8⁴	5hd	6¹¾	Vasquez J	45000	5.30
24Jly77 6Hol⁴	Princess Polly	2 119 5 8	12	11hd	10³	7hd	Cruguet J	45000	12.80
29Jly77 4Bel⁵	Eavesdrop	2 115 12 1	2½	4½	8¹	8hd	Maple E	40000	10.00
20Jly77 4Bel⁶	Our Deliiah	2 115 10 10	11½	10¹½	9½	9¹½	Imparato J	40000	64.90
	Lehua	2 119 6 5	4¹	5²	7½	10²¼	Amy J	45000	46.00
	Miller Miss	2 115 4 11	10⁵	12	11¹½	11¹²¼	Venezia M	40000	33.40
29Jun77 4Bel¹⁰	Freedom First	b 2 119 1 9	9½	9½	12	12	Santiago A	45000	30.70

OFF AT 2:34 1/2, EDT. Start good, Won driving. Time, :22⅗, :46⅕, 1:11⅖ Track fast.

$2 Mutuel Prices:

9-(K)-LAVISHLY	17.60	9.40	4.00
8-(J)-ESTELLE'S LYRIC		8.40	4.80
7-(I)-MISTY NATIVE			2.80

$2 EXACTA 9-8 PAID $347.80.

Ch. f, by Stevward—Roof Raiser, by Raise A Native. Trainer Barrera Lazaro S. Bred by Harbor View Farm (Fla).

LAVISHLY, never far back, raced wide into the stretch and finished strongly to be up in the final stride. ESTELLE'S LYRIC raced forwardly into the stretch and continued on gamely, just missing. MISTY NATIVE alternated for the lead while remaining well out from the rail, edged away from ESTELLE'S LYRIC nearing midstretch but weakened slightly. SUE ME NOT finished with good energy while racing wide. MARSTON'S MILL broke slowly, rushed up along the inside approaching the end of the backstretch but lacked a late response. IRISH NOEL failed to seriously menace. EAVESDROP gave way leaving the turn and lugged in while tiring. LEHUA tired.

Owners— 1, Harbor View Farm; 2, Rosoff A; 3, Hellman N; 4, Gartrell Mrs C; 5, Rokeby Stables; 6, Davis True Jr; 7, Hooper F W; 8, Walker J Jr Mrs; 9, Flying Zee Stables; 10, Hallman Paula C; 11, Miller L I; 12, Meadow Stable.

Trainers— 1, Barrera Lazaro S; 2, Zito Nicholas P; 3, LaBoccetta Frank; 4, Dunham Bob G; 5, Miller Mack; 6, Luro Horatio A; 7, Tinsley Joe E Jr; 8, Maloney James W; 9, DeStasio Richard T; 10, Hunt Leonard H; 11, Cotter Mary M; 12, DiMauro Stephen.

Scratched—Angel L. (30Jly77 4Bel⁴); Funny Nun (28Jly77 4Bel⁵); Cindy Gayle (28Jly77 4Bel²); Dancing Flower (12Jly77 3Bel⁸); Call Vera; Hospital Ship (20Jly77 4Bel⁴).

In a thrilling stretch duel, Lavishly beat Estelle's Lyric by a nose, with Misty Native another neck behind. The exacta returned $347.80. When the probable exacta prices had been flashed initially on the television monitors, reflecting OTB wagering, the combination had been worth more than $1000. The supporters of each of the first-time starters had accounted for some of the drop in the price, but the chartists were responsible for the rest. There were many smiling faces behind the clipboards for the remainder of the season.

Another segment of the horseplaying population was also enjoying a banner Saratoga season. They were not a lunatic fringe—as I still considered the chartists—but a serious intellectual camp which was causing a revolution in the art of handicapping. The new wave did not even have a proper name yet, but its adherents sometimes made me feel as if I were handicapping with tools from the Dark Ages— as I did after the first race on August 9.

1 SARATOGA

7 FURLONGS (SARATOGA) — Start / Finish

7 FURLONGS. (1.21) CLAIMING. Purse $13,000. 3-year-olds, weights, 122 lbs. Non-winners of a race since July 15 allowed 3 lbs. Of a race since july 1, 5 lbs. Claiming price $45,000; for each $2,500 to $40,000, 2 lbs. (Races when enered to be claimed for $35,000 or less not considered).

Don Alfonso

Ch. c. 3, by High Echelon—Dawn Sky, by Imbros
Own.—Escudero R — $40,000 — Br.—Asbury C A & T H (Ky) — Tr.—Barrera Lazaro S — 113
Turf Record: St. 1st 2nd 3rd — 1 0 0 0
1977: 12 0 4 2 $20,870
1976: 6 3 1 1 $8,300
(Formerly named Sky High)

```
1Aug77- 4Sar fst 7f   :22⅘ :46   1:23⅘    Clm 35000      6 2 65½ 65½ 33½ 21¾ Cauthen S    b 117  *2.40  84-20 Red Sam 1131¾ Don Alfonso 117nk Rapid Barb 115½           Gamely 9
18Jly77- 4Bel fst 7f   :23   :46⅕ 1:23     Clm 42500      5 2 41½ 31 2hd 23½ Cordero A Jr  b 115   4.60  83-11 Watching N Wait 1133½ Don Alfonso 115¾ Hive 117½          Gamely 7
22Jun77- 6Bel fst 7f   :22⅗ :45⅗ 1:22⅘ 3+Allowance    8 8 95½107¾ 711 711 Cordero A Jr b 113  6.90  77-15 Blue Spark 1193½ Private Practice114nkFiveontheside1192 Outrun 10
3Jun77- 6Bel fst 7f   :23   :46   1:23⅖ 3+Allowance    5 3 75 89¾ 86½ 65¾ Cordero A Jr  b 113  *1.90  79-20 Aeronaut 1191½ [D]Introienne 1191 Debtor's Haven119no No factor 8
24May77- 6Bel fst 6f   :23   :46⅘ 1:11⅘ 3+Allowance    6 4 56½ 45 32½ 2nk Cordero A Jr  b 113   7.00  83-21 To The Quick109nkDonAlfonso1132½VeryDistinguished1091½ Wide 7
14May77- 6Aqu fm 1⅛ Ⓣ:47  1:11⅗ 1:41⅘ 3+Allowance    8 3 32 53 612 716 Cordero A Jr   b 112  14.20  81-03 Babas Fables 114½ Valiant Tribute 1194HarborSprings119hd Tired 8
6May77- 8Aqu my 1⅛ ⊡:49   1:14   1:44⅘ 3+Allowance    5 1 1hd 2hd 1hd 2no Cordero A Jr    112   2.70  94-09 Federation 119noDonAlfonso112¾Debtor'sHaven11411 Just missed 6
21Apr77- 8Aqu fst 1⅛ ⊡:48⅗ 1:13⅖ 1:44⅖ 3+Allowance   5 5 42½ 41½ 34 36½ Cordero A Jr   b 112  12.30  90-11 Silver Greek 112¾FreedomCalling1195½DonAlfonso1121½ Bid,tired 6
9Apr77- 6SA fst 1⅛  :46⅘ 1:10⅗ 1:41     Allowance      6 5 58 512 511 417 Mercado V V5  b 109  21.10  80-14 [DH]Highland Light 12012[DH]Affiliate12012Crorosean1205 No threat 6
3Apr77- 6SA fst 1    :10⅗       1:36     Allowance      7 7 46 56½ 58 59¾ Mercado V V5   b 109   7.00  79-15 Crorosean 115hd Code Three 116¾ Antoine 1143          No factor 7
LATEST WORKOUTS   Jly 25 Bel tr.t 4f fst :51⅗ b   Jly 10 Bel tr.t 4f fst :50 b   Jly 2 Bel tr.t 4f fst :50⅗ b   Jun 19 Bel tr.t 4f fst :50⅖ b
```

Very Distinguished

B. c. 3, by Steward—Meadow Queen, by Raise A Native
Own.—Sommer S — $40,000 — Br.—Harbor View Farm (Fla) — Tr.—Martin Frank — 113
1977: 16 5 2 2 $55,948
1976: 11 2 1 1 $15,070

```
20Jly77- 5Bel fst 1    :46⅗ 1:11⅘ 1:37⅗    Clm 23000      4 1 13 12 12½ 1¾ Cauthen S     b 117   *.90  80-19 Very Distinguished117¾Marlago1154½SeaneyBear1153½ Ridden out 8
22Jun77- 6Bel fst 7f   :22⅗ :45⅗ 1:22⅘ 3+Allowance    5 3 31½ 65 913 914 Venezia M     b 111  9.40e  74-15 Blue Spark 1193½ Private Practice 114nk Fiveontheside1192 Tired 10
11Jun77- 8Key fst 1⅛  :46   1:11   1:44⅖    Keystone H     6 4 34½ 34 42 45¾ Rodriguez J A b 113   4.00  76-24 Pruneplum 1131½SparklingFellow1153HeyHeyJ.P.1201½ Weakened 6
24May77- 6Bel fst 6f   :23   :46⅘ 1:11⅘ 3+Allowance    4 3 21½ 21 21½ 32¾ Venezia M     b 109  *1.50e  80-21 ToTheQuick109nkDonAlfonso1132½VeryDistinguished1091½ Evenly 7
5May77- 8Aqu gd 7f   :22⅘ :44⅗ 1:22     Allowance      2 6 43½ 45½ 57¾ 48¾ Cauthen S5    b 117   6.80  82-10 Vencedor 119½ Cruise On In 1195 Hey Hey J. P. 1173½    Evenly 6
13Apr77- 8Aqu fst 1⅛ ⊡:47⅗ 1:12⅘ 1:51⅗ 3+Allowance   7 2 23 21¾ 48½ 411 Cauthen S5   b 107   *.70e  83-13 Lightning Bob 1195 Freedom Calling 119nk Famed1196 Weakened 8
29Mar77- 7Aqu fst 170 ⊡:47  1:12⅕ 1:42⅗ 3+Allowance    1 3 35½ 1hd 11 12¾ Cauthen S5    b 107   *1.40  92-11 VeryDistinguished1072¾Pndmus113nkButtonwoodLn119hd Driving 6
17Mar77- 8Aqu fst 1⅛ ⊡:47⅕ 1:12  1:43     Allowance      3 1 1½ 1hd 1hd 1¾ Cauthen S5    b 110   2.80  103-08 VeryDistinguished110¾HonorableGuest1155½GallntWy1152 Driving 6
9Mar77- 7Aqu fst 1⅛ ⊡:49   1:13⅘ 1:45⅕    Allowance      7 3 3½ 3½ 31½ 43 Maple E        b 115   *1.10  89-13 Pandamus 122hd Bay Laurel 1172¾ Drums and Fife 115nk    Evenly 7
1Mar77- 7Aqu fst 170 ⊡:47⅘ 1:13⅗ 1:43     Allowance      4 2 2² 21 2hd 2½ Maple E        b 115   3.50  90-13 WesternWind115½VeryDistinguished1156DrumsndFif1155 Gamely 7
LATEST WORKOUTS   Aug 1 Sar 4f fst :47⅕ h   ●Jly 18 Bel tr.t 4f fst :47⅖ h   Jly 12 Bel tr.t 4f fst :47⅗ h   ●Jly 4 Bel tr.t 5f fst :59⅗ h
```

Double Gemini

Ch. c. 3, by Macarthur Park—Vi's Flower, by Moondust II
Own.—Ken-Mort Stable — $40,000 — Br.—Sabinske R J (Cal) — Tr.—Marcus Alan B — 113
1977: 16 4 2 3 $53,405
1976: 0 M 0 0

```
28Jly77- 6Bel fst 1⅛  :46⅗ 1:11  1:41⅘ 3+Allowance    6 5 31 2hd 32½ 44¾ Velasquez J   b 112   2.60  88-15 Bold N Bizarre 119¾RareJoel1193¾TripleTheScore113nk Weakened 7
13Jly77- 6Bel my 1⅛  :46⅘ 1:11⅖ 1:42⅖    Clm 25000      6 3 2½ 1hd 13 19½ Velasquez J   b 117   *.80  90-17 Double Gemini 1179½ Human Error117½Marlago1132½ Ridden out 7
4Jly77- 5Bel fst 1⅛  :46⅗ 1:11⅖ 1:42⅘    Allowance      1 3 1hd 11½ 31½ 27 Velasquez J   b 115   4.20  81-16 Tacitus 1157 Double Gemini 115no Stab 1154               Gamely 8
28Jun77- 3Bel fst 1⅛  :46⅕ 1:11⅗ 1:43⅘    Clm c-18000    2 5 56½ 41½ 13 17 Cauthen S      b 119   1.70  83-18 DoubleGmini1197DlWithStrngth112nkAllNinYrds1173½ Drew clear 7
14Jun77- 4Bel fst 1⅛  :47   1:12⅘ 1:44⅗    Clm 20000      3 4 43½ 3½ 3nk 33¼ Vasquez J     b 119   4.70  75-21 Jet To Pago 1173½ TaxiCabDriver112nkDoubleGemini119no Rallied 7
2Jun77- 2Bel fst 1⅛  :47⅗ 1:13  1:45     Clm 17500      3 5 51¾ 41 1½ 1hd Vasquez J      b 117   *.80  77-20 Double Gemini117hdAllNineYards1172½HonorLocker1226¾ Driving 6
23May77- 9Bel fst 1⅛  :47⅗ 1:12⅘ 1:44⅘    Clm 20000      5 4 41½ 11 11½ 21½ Vasquez J     b 117   6.80  77-17 Albie'sTruckStop1171½DoubleGmini1176½HonorLockr1173 Gamely 10
13May77- 3Aqu fst 7f   :23⅗ :48⅘ 1:26   3+Md 30000     1 5 41½ 31 11 12 Vasquez J       b 113   5.30  71-26 Double Gemini 1132 Revaluation 107hd Butchcee 1127½     Driving 8
28Apr77- 5Aqu my 1⅛ ⊡:47⅘ 1:13  1:44⅖ 3+Md Sp Wt    5 8 76 43½ 37 38 Vasquez J        b 112  16.00  88-11 TripleTheScore107nkPatriotStnd1127¾DoubleGemini1123¾ Fair try 9
15Apr77- 5Aqu fst 1⅛ ⊡:47⅘ 1:13  1:53⅗ 3+Md Sp Wt    4 2 12 12 46½ 612 Vasquez J       b 112   8.10  73-14 Fleet Beam 112½ Xmas Box 1122 New Castle Chief 1122½   Tired 9
LATEST WORKOUTS   Aug 8 Sar 3f my :36⅗ h   Jly 27 Bel tr.t 3f fst :36 h   Jun 23 Bel 6f fst 1:14⅘ h
```

Roy Roy

Ch. g. 3, by Roi Dagobert—Well In Hand, by Bold Ruler
Own.—Flying Zee Stable — $40,000 — Br.—Maple Lawn Farm Inc (Ky) — Tr.—DeStasio Richard T — 108[5]
1977: 8 1 2 4 $20,160
1976: 15 1 1 2 $7,746

```
26Jly77- 7Bel fst 6f   :23   :46⅗ 1:10⅘    Clm 25000      2 5 32½ 21½ 31½ 33 Imparato J    b 117  18.00  87-14 Time To 117hd Rapid Barb 1173 Roy Roy 1172               Weakened 8
9Mar77- 7Aqu fst 1⅛ ⊡:49   1:13⅕ 1:45⅕    Allowance      6 5 41½ 53½ 68 611 Imparato J    b 115   5.60  81-13 Pandamus 122hd Bay Laurel 1172¾ Drums and Fife 115nk    Tired 7
5Mar77- 6Aqu sly 170 ⊡:47⅗ 1:13  1:44⅕ 3+Allowance    5 3 1hd 11½ 2hd 32½ Imparato J    b 112   4.80  82-13 Pepysian 1191 Bakor 1191½ Roy Roy 112nk                Weakened 8
21Feb77- 6Aqu fst 1⅛ ⊡:47⅕ 1:12  1:46     Allowance      4 5 3½ 34 37 39¾ Imparato J    b 115   2.10  78-12 BoldPalette1191½VeryDistinguished1158½RoyRoy1153½ No mishap 6
11Feb77- 6Aqu fst 170 ⊡:48⅕ 1:12⅘ 1:42     Allowance      6 4 31½ 2½ 24 29 Imparato J    b 115   3.70  87-10 Metaphor 1109 Roy Roy 1153½ Hive 1157½                Second best 6
1Feb77- 7Aqu fst 170 ⊡:48⅕ 1:13⅗ 1:44⅗    Allowance      2 2 11½ 2½ 2hd 22 Imparato J   b 115   4.60  81-18 Cross Rip 1152 Roy Roy 1156¾ Aspiring 1151½            Gamely 6
24Jan77- 6Aqu fst 170 ⊡:47⅖ 1:13  1:44⅗    Allowance      2 3 2hd 2hd 21 33½ Imparato J   b 115   3.20  80-13 Kerinag 110nk Gallant Way 1153 Roy Roy 115hd           Weakened 6
10Jan77- 4Aqu sly 1⅛ ⊡:47⅗ 1:12⅘ 1:46⅕    Clm c-20000    4 2 2hd 11 15 110 Santiago A     b 117   3.60  87-14 Roy Roy 11710 Sea Stopper 112hd Low Lead 1157          Handily 7
22Dec76- 1Aqu fst 6f ⊡:22⅘ :45⅘ 1:12⅕    Clm 25000      3 10 98½ 76¾ 46 42¾ Santiago A   b 117  19.70  — — ComedyKing119hdVryDistinguishd117¾Sonny'sSuprm1122 Rallied 12
13Dec76- 7Aqu fst 6f ⊡:23   :47⅗ 1:13⅗    Clm 30000      2 10 101010 13 911 811 Cauthen S5  b 112   6.50  — — Prize Native 1172 Spanish Eagle 117¾ Jolly Quill 117¾  Poor start 10
LATEST WORKOUTS   Jly 23 Bel tr.t 4f fst :50⅘ b   Jly 7 Bel 5f fst 1:00 hg   Jly 2 Bel 4f fst :47⅕ h   Jun 28 Bel tr.t 4f fst :50⅘ b
```

Best Hour

Ch. c. 3, by Bold Hour—Best Go, by Mongo
Own.—Allen Herbert — $45,000 — Br.—Smiser-West Mr-Mrs R (Ky) — Tr.—Jacobs Eugene — 117
Turf Record: St. 1st 2nd 3rd — 7 0 1 2
1977: 12 1 1 2 $12,390
1976: 4 M 0 0 $1,170

```
27Jly77- 5Bel gd 1⅛ Ⓣ:48   1:12   1:43⅕ 3+Clm 50000    2 5 53 31½ 66¾ 66½ Vasquez J     b 112  17.20  — — Lad Of Vision 115nk Desert Flag 122¾ UppercutII1132½ Weakened 8
18Jly77- 7Bel fm 1¼ Ⓣ:47⅘ 1:37  2:01⅗ 3+Allowance    1 6 65 66 68¾ 45 Day P            b 112  10.20  87-08 Desert Flag 1222½ Bold Giant 1192½ Chance To Go 107½  Rallied 7
9Jly77- 7Bel fm 1⅛ Ⓣ:46   1:10   1:41⅗ 3+Allowance    3 6 73½ 85½ 59 36¾ Vasquez J     b 112  10.80  86-07 True Colors 115¾ Bold Giant 1196 Best Hour 112nk        Rallied 10
30Jun77- 6Bel fm 1¼ Ⓣ:48   1:38  2:02   3+Allowance    9 1 1hd 1hd 31½ 33¾ Vasquez J    b 112  19.70  86-10 Nijisty 1142½ Rare Pleasure 1111½ Best Hour 112½      Weakened 10
21Jun77- 7Bel fm 1⅛ Ⓣ:47⅕ 1:11⅗ 1:43  3+Allowance    2 3 41 73¾ 78 58 Vasquez J       b 112   6.70  77-15 KanawhRiver111hdForwrdChrger114nkRrePlesure1116½ No mishap 9
14Jun77- 7Bel fm 1⅛ Ⓣ:48⅕ 1:11⅗ 1:43⅕ 3+Allowance    3 3 33½ 36½ 25 21 Vasquez J     b 113  19.80  — — Ad Alley 1141 Best Hour 113¾ Stir The Embers 1142¾    Gamely 8
7Jun77- 5Bel fst 1⅛  :46⅘ 1:11⅗ 1:44   3+Allowance    6 1 1½ 3½ 3nk 41½ Vasquez J      b 112   8.70  81-14 Handsome Tod 114hd Cyano 111hd Hacer Furor 1191       Weakened 6
31May77- 7Bel hd 1⅛ Ⓣ:45   1:09⅕ 1:41⅘ 3+Allowance   11 3 69½ 8151117 1113 Graell A      b 109  37.60  78-09 Arachnoid 119nk Blue Baron 1134 Sensitive Sam 109¾     Tired 12
19May77- 6Aqu sly 1    :46⅕ 1:10⅗ 1:36⅖    Allowance      4 6 63½ 89½ 813 58½ Vasquez J    b 115  42.40  76-12 Leading Scorer 1102½ Lynn Davis 122hd Johnny D. 1155½   Outrun 8
5May77- 4Aqu my 6f    :22⅘ :46⅕ 1:11⅘ 3+Md 35000     2 2 2½ 32½ 32 11¾ Gonzalez B5   b 107   2.30  87-14 Best Hour 1071¾ [DH]All Arranged107[DH]Butchcee1082½ Drew clear 4
LATEST WORKOUTS   Aug 4 Sar 4f fst :50 b   Jly 26 Bel tr.t 3f gd :36⅖ h   Jly 16 Bel tr.t 3f fst :37⅖ b   Jly 6 Bel tr.t 4f fst :49⅕ b
```

Glorious Sheik

Ch. c. 3, by Sheik of Bagdad—Summer Point, by Summer Tan
Own.—Brazil Stables — $40,000 — Br.—Noonan H B (Ky) — Tr.—Schmitt William F — 113
1977: 6 0 1 2 $9,440
1976: 2 2 0 0 $7,140

```
18Jly77- 4Bel fst 7f   :23   :46⅕ 1:23     Clm 45000      2 7 63½ 63½ 63¾ 58¼ Turcotte R    117⁴  6.60  78-11 Watching N Wait 1133½ Don Alfonso 115¾ Hive 117½         Outrun 7
       18Jly77-Dead heat
24Jun77- 7Bel fst 1⅛  :45⅗ 1:09⅘ 1:43  3+Allowance    3 4 47 59 511 49½ Venezia M      111  20.40  78-20 Mr. International 119¾[D]WarmFront1118Johnsquillo112½ Impeded 7
       24Jun77-Placed third through disqualification
11Jun77- 8Key fst 1⅛  :46   1:11   1:44⅗    Keystone H     1 3 45 44½ 53½ 56½ Rosado O      b 113  17.10  76-24 Pruneplum 1131½ Sparkling Fellow 1153 Hey Hey J. P.1201½ Tired 6
1Jun77- 8Bel fst 1⅛  :47⅕ 1:12  1:49⅕    Peter Pan      9 3 61¾ 51½ 712 715 Hernandez R  b 114  56.80  66-27 Spirit Level 114hd Sanhedrin 1142 Lynn Davis 1141½      Tired 9
19May77- 7Aqu my 1⅛ ⊡:47   1:12⅕ 1:43⅗ 3+Allowance    3 5 55 43½ 37 29 Turcotte R     b 112   *1.30  91-12 Bakor 1199 Glorious Sheik 1122½ Alias Smith 1192        Gamely 6
9May77- 8Crc sly 1    :47⅗ 1:12⅘ 1:38⅖    J Cole H       3 3 34 32 23 32 Astorga C         112   4.10  95-10 Wininreno 1132PoorMan'sBluff114hdGloriousSheik112hd Good try 9
       9May77-Run in Two Divisions, 8th & 9th Races.
30Oct76- 5Crc fst 1    :48⅗ 1:14⅗ 1:41⅗    Allowance      5 5 45½ 32 1½ 11 Astorga C         114  22.90  81-17 Glorious Sheik 1141 Sonny Collins 1202 Fast Warrior1141 Driving 9
22Oct76- 2Crc fst 7f   :23⅗ :47⅘ 1:27⅗    Md 15000       5 8 72¾ 63½ 2hd 14 Astorga C         118  11.40  78-19 Glorious Sheik 1184 Social Del 118½ Twin Double1152 Ridden out 11
```

Hive — Ch. g. 3, by Dr Fager—Quilting, by Princequillo — **$45,000** — Br.—Tartan Farms (Fla) — Tr.—Nerud Jan H — **117**
Own.—Tartan Stable

Turf Record St.	1st	2nd	3rd		St.	1st	2nd	3rd	Amt.
1	0	0	0	1977	13	1	2	4	$19,720
				1976	0	M	0	0	

18Jly77- 4Bel	fst	7f	:23	:46 1/5	1:23	Clm 45000	4	3	5^2 1/2	5^3	5^2 3/4	3^4 1/4	Venezia M	87	117	4.50	83-11 Watching N Wait 113^3 1/2 Don Alfonso 115^3/4 Hive 117^1/2	Rallied	7
9Jly77- 7Bel	fm	1 1/16	Ⓣ:46	1:10	1:41 2/5	3↑Allowance	4	3	5^2	7^4 1/4	6^9	4^7	Montoya D		112	14.70	86-07 True Colors 115^3/4 Bold Giant 119^6 Best Hour 112^nk	Rallied	10
28Jun77- 6Bel	fst	7f	:22 3/5	:45 3/5	1:22 4/5	3↑Allowance	1	2	3^1 1/2	2^1	2^4	3^6 1/4	Montoya D	93	111	16.10	82-18 Nice Catch 112^4 Pumpkin Moonshine 114^2 1/4 Hive 111^1 1/4	Weakened	6
20Jun77- 6Bel	fst	6f	:22 4/5	:46 2/5	1:10 1/5	3↑Allowance	11	3	6^5 1/2	6^7	5^8	4^7 1/4	Montoya D		111	*1.10e	84-18 Doctor'sOrdrs114^no Dr.Ptchs111^2 1/2 PumpkinMoonshin114^4 3/4	Evenly	11
11Jun77- 9Bel	my	7f	:22 3/5	:46	1:22 4/5	3↑Allowance	3	2	3^2	3^3 1/2	5^7	7^9 1/4	Venezia M		111	22.80	79-17 Johnsquillo 114^nk Golden Reserve 112^3/4 Nice Catch 111^2 1/2	Tired	11
25Mar77- 7Aqu	fst	6f	⊡:23	:47 3/5	1:12 2/5	Allowance	5	4	5^2 1/2	5^3 1/4	5^6 1/2	6^7 3/4	Woodhouse R		115	8.20	79-19 Instant Profit 122no Solly 110^1 3/4 Winter Wind 110^1 3/4	Tired	8
14Mar77- 7Aqu	sly	6f	⊡:22 3/5	:46	1:10 2/5	Allowance	7	2	5^4	5^6	6^8 1/4	6^15	Woodhouse R		b 119	2.90	82-08 Society Hill 117^3 3/4 Red Rolfe 117^6 One Review 110^1 3/4	Tired	8
8Mar77- 6Aqu	fst	6f	⊡:22 2/5	:45 4/5	1:11 3/5	3↑Allowance	3	5	4^3	3^3	2^1	2^hd	Woodhouse R		b 109	3.60	91-13 Finger Paints 119^hd Hive 109^1/2 Elena's Boy 119^1 3/4	Lost whip	6
28Feb77- 7Aqu	fst	6f	⊡:22 3/5	:46 3/5	1:12 2/5	3↑Allowance	3	8	9^10	9^10	5^7 1/2	3^3 1/2	Woodhouse R		b 112	4.50	83-17 Denign 119^1 3/4 Amber Spy 114^1 3/4 Hive 112^hd	Rallied	9
19Feb77- 6Aqu	fst	6f	⊡:22 3/5	:45 4/5	1:11 2/5	3↑Allowance	1	5	6^3 3/4	6^6 1/2	5^5	4^2	Woodhouse R		b 112	4.10	90-10 Quill Prince 109^hd Silk Heriz 114^1 1/4 Zayer Shane 119^3/4	Wide	8

LATEST WORKOUTS Aug 3 Sar 3f fst :38 b   Jly 4 Bel tr.t 4f fst :52 1/5 b

Double Gemini embodied my idea of handicapping perfection. He was a reliable animal with figures consistently superior to his opposition. His last four figures had been 96, 97, 91, 90. None of his rivals had run better than an 89 in the last month.

I went to the track confident that Double Gemini was going to resuscitate my declining fortunes, and mentioned to Charlie that I thought this might be the best bet of the meeting. "Well," he said, "Glorious Sheik might be more dangerous than you think." He did not elaborate. I glanced at my *Racing Form,* saw that Glorious Sheik had never run a race which could threaten Double Gemini, dismissed Charlie's opinion, and headed to the windows to bet $600. At about the same time, in another part of the track, some of the Kid's friends were looking for him so they could tell him to bet on Glorious Sheik. But the Kid was busy betting Double Gemini, too.

FIRST RACE
Saratoga
AUGUST 9, 1977

7 FURLONGS. (1.21) CLAIMING. Purse $13,000. 3-year-olds, weights, 122 lbs. Non-winners of a race since July 15 allowed 3 lbs. Of a race since july 1, 5 lbs. Claiming price $45,000; for each $2,500 to $40,000, 2 lbs. (Races when enered to be claimed for $35,000 or less not considered).

Value of race $13,000, value to winner $7,800, second $2,860, third $1,560, fourth $780. Mutuel pool $65,989, OTB pool $119,476.

Last Raced	Horse	Eqt.	A.	Wt	PP	St	1/4	1/2	Str	Fin	Jockey	Cl'g Pr	Odds $1
18Jly77 ⁴Bel⁵	Glorious Sheik		3	114	6	2	6^1/2	6^4	1^2	1^4 1/4	Turcotte R	40000	12.10
1Aug77 ⁴Sar²	Don Alfonso	b	3	113	1	7	2^1	2^hd	2^hd	2^1/2	Cordero A Jr	40000	2.30
28Jly77 ⁶Bel⁴	Double Gemini	b	3	113	3	5	3^1/2	3^2	4^1	3^1/2	Velasquez J	40000	2.30
20Jly77 ⁵Bel¹	Very Distinguished	b	3	113	2	3	1^hd	1^hd	3^1	4^1 3/4	Cauthen S	40000	4.30
27Jly77 ⁵Bel⁶	Best Hour	b	3	117	5	4	5^4	5^hd	5^8	5^9 1/2	Vasquez J	45000	9.50
18Jly77 ⁴Bel³	Hive		3	117	7	1	4^1/2	4^1/2	6^1	6^nk	Venezia M	45000	5.20
26Jly77 ⁷Bel³	Roy Roy	b	3	108	4	6	7	7	7	7	Samyn J L⁵	40000	10.10

OFF AT 1:30 EDT. Start good, Won driving. Time, :23, :46, 1:10 4/5, 1:23 3/5 Track fast.

Official Program Numbers↘

$2 Mutuel Prices:			
6–(G)–GLORIOUS SHEIK	26.20	12.00	5.40
1–(A)–DON ALFONSO		4.40	2.60
3–(D)–DOUBLE GEMINI			2.60

Ch. c, by Sheik of Bagdad—Summer Point, by Summer Tan. Trainer Schmitt William F. Bred by Noonan H B (Ky).

GLORIOUS SHEIK moved through inside the leaders leaving the turn and drew off under brisk urging. DON ALFONZO rushed up along the inside early, showed speed to the stretch while remaining well out from the rail and was no match for the winner. DOUBLE GEMINI moved to the leaders from the outside on the turn but weakened under pressure. VERY DISTINGUISHED was used up vying for the lead. BEST HOUR saved ground to no avail. HIVE was finished leaving the turn.

Owners— 1, Brazil Stables; 2, Escudero R; 3, Ken-Mort Stable; 4, Sommer S; 5, Allen Herbert; 6, Tartan Stable; 7, Flying Zee Stable.

Trainers— 1, Schmitt William F; 2, Barrera Lazaro S; 3, Marcus Alan B; 4, Martin Frank; 5, Jacobs Eugene; 6, Nerud Jan H; 7, DeStasio Richard T.

Overweight: Glorious Sheik 1 pound.

Scratched—Big Broker (4Aug77 ⁶Sar⁷).

When Glorious Sheik ran away with the race by 4¼ lengths, I did not understand. I knew only that Charlie and the other bettors who liked the horse had been impressed by the manner in which he had run his last two races. They had seen, among other things, that the jockey had not persevered with Glorious Sheik in the stretch run of his last race. To me, such observations seemed a rather imprecise basis for a serious wager, but horseplayers like Charlie believe in their own visual perceptions as strongly as I do in my figures.

They hold to the philosophy that winners and losers are determined not so much by their inherent speed or class, but by the way a race develops, by the fact that certain horses are forced to run wide on the turns and lose ground, while others stay on the rail and enjoy a perfect trip. The majority of successful professional bettors in New York now are practitioners of what might be called "trip handicapping."

All bettors recognize the importance of watching races to spot horses who are blocked or bumped or encounter some form of bad luck. But the trip handicappers look for things much more subtle, and they have had to invent a private language to describe what they are doing. One day I was discussing a race with John Pricci, the handicapper for the Long Island paper *Newsday*, and he said he liked a horse who impressed me as having no merit whatsoever. When I asked John for his reasons, he leafed through his notes and said, "Hard held early, five on the turn, nine entering, no push late." This meant that the animal was under restraint early, was forced to run five horses wide rounding the turn, and was nine-wide when the field fanned out into the stretch. Once he was obviously beaten, his jockey did not punish him.

By watching races so carefully, the trip handicappers can evaluate horses in a completely new way. A class handicapper might say, "This horse has been meeting better opposition." A speed handicapper might say, "He gets my top figure." But a trip handicapper could say, as Charlie did to me one day at Saratoga, "This horse isn't as good as he looks on paper. In both of his last two races, he had a perfect trip sitting on the rail behind the early speed, and he inherited the lead when the horses in front of him fell apart. Today he's got two other speed horses inside of him, and he's got to have a much tougher trip."

Horseplayers never talked in such terms five years ago. But this approach to the game has evolved because of some subtle but important changes in the sport itself. One such change is the growing popularity of grass racing. Because of their sharp turns and congested fields, turf events are almost always won by horses who save ground and enjoy good racing luck. Most trip handicappers have their greatest successes on the grass. Because I do not possess the necessary visual skills, I have never done well in turf races and rarely bet them anymore.

Nowadays tracks card many races that are a virtual rematch of an entire field that ran a week earlier. If five horses who finished a length apart are meeting each other again, a bettor won't be able to decipher the race with conventional methods. But a trip handicapper can know that one of the horses is a standout.

While the trip handicappers and the chartists seemed to be operating confidently and effectively with their own methodologies, I was foundering. I could not seem to establish the kind of steady, winning rhythm I had at Pimlico. I found no strong track bias on which I could base my wagers. And my figures were still not producing. Unable to hit winners with consistency, I found myself trying to beat Saratoga with one spectacular knockout punch; with horses like Cut the Talk.

Cut the Talk — **Ro. g. 6, by The Axe II—Hot Gossip, by Correspondent**
Own.—Vendome Stables — **$5,000** — **Br.—Polk A F Jr (Ky)** — **Tr.—Vonskopczynski R** — **117**

Turf Record: St. 1st 2nd 3rd — 5 0 1 0

	St.	1st	2nd	3rd	Amt.
1977	3	0	0	2	$1,008
1976	4	0	0	0	$90

30Jly77- 2WO	my	7f	:23⅗	:46⅘	1:25⅗	3↑ Clm 10000	5	5	3½	4^{3¼}	6^{12}	7^{17}	Parsons W	b 117	3.30	64–19	Alynkyle 114^{4} Fleet Mood 116^{6} Near the High Sea 116^{2}	Tired	7
14Jly77- 5WO	fst	6f	:22⅕	:46⅖	1:11	3↑ Clm 10000	1	7	4^{5}	4^{3½}	4^{2}	3½	Parsons W	b 117	22.10	87–16	Minnedoso 112^{hd} Pancho Villa 120½ Cut the Talk 117½	Rallied	8
1Jly77- 7FE	fst	6½f	:24	:48⅖	1:20⅘	3↑ Allowance	5	2	1^{hd}	1½	2½	3^{3¾}	Brown F	b 121	7.95	71–24	Dervish Banditti 114^{2½} Likes O'Lori 110^{1¼} Cut the Talk 121^{2½}		5
3Apr76- 5Aqu	fst	7f	:23	:46⅖	1:24⅖	Clm 25000	11	4	6^{6}	11^{13}	11^{19}	11^{23}	Gustines H	b 117	12.20	56–19	Judge Power 117^{2¼} Gs Silver A 113^{nk} ChangeofVenue 107^{hd}	Outrun	11
16Mar76- 7Aqu	sly	1	:47	1:13⅕	1:38⅘	Clm 35000	6	4	4^{3}	4^{5}	6^{8¼}	8^{15}	Maple E	b 117	6.10	57–24	Ligur 117^{3¾} Fairways Image 117^{1} Green As Grass 115^{1}	Tired	8
14Jan76- 9Crc	fst	1⅛	:48⅖	1:13	1:52⅖	3↑ Silberman H	8	6	6^{5¼}	6^{5}	7^{7½}	7^{12}	St Leon G	b 117	14.40	87–18	Emperor Rex 120^{1} Hasty Flyer 122^{hd} Manchon 117^{2}	No threat	9
2Jan76- 9Crc	fm	1 1/16 Ⓣ	:47⅗	1:11⅕	1:42⅕	Allowance	3	4	6^{4½}	7^{3¼}	7^{6¼}	7^{6½}	Castaneda M	b 122	19.20	90–05	Zografos 116^{1} Specialite 116^{1¼} Return To Reality 116no	Tired	11
11Dec75- 8Aqu	fst	1	:46	1:10⅕	1:34⅗	3↑ Allowance	3	3	3^{nk}	5^{7}	5^{8½}	6^{14}	Cordero A Jr	115	26.00	79–15	Right Mind 115^{7½} Famous Leader 107^{1¾} Big Band 119½	Tired	6
4Dec75- 6Aqu	fst	1	:47⅕	1:12⅕	1:37	3↑ Clm 40000	3	5	5^{2}	3½	1^{1½}	1^{nk}	Hole M	117	4.90	81–21	Cut the Talk 117^{nk} HandsomeNative 117no Expropriate 117^{3½}	All out	6
26Nov75- 4Aqu	fst	1⅛	:47⅘	1:12⅕	1:49	3↑ Clm 40000	1	3	3^{1½}	2^{hd}	2^{1}	3^{3½}	Hole M	114	4.10	86–15	Roger's Dandy 119^{2¾} Our Reward 117¾ Cut the Talk 114^{2½}	Tired	7

Cut the Talk had run creditably in a $10,000 claiming race at Woodbine, and then had been routed by seventeen lengths in the same company. Now he had been shipped to Saratoga and was entered for $5000. Usually I spurn horses dropping sharply in class, because their lower price tag almost always indicates that they have serious physical problems and the stable is trying to get rid of them. But if Cut the Talk were indeed on his last legs, why had trainer R. Vonskopczynski bothered to bring him to Saratoga? He could have entered the animal for $5000 back home in Canada. It did not make sense. I could only conclude that Cut the Talk was here for a betting coup, and that his dismal last race was a phony, designed to throw bettors off the scent. I bet $600 to win on Cut the Talk at 6-to-1 odds, and saw my suspicions confirmed. After breaking poorly, the gelding rushed into contention on the backstretch, raced wide all the way around the turn, closed gamely through the stretch—and lost by less than a length. The moral, perhaps, is that when you bet strictly on the basis of a trainer's intentions, you should be certain that the trainer is sharp enough to get the job done. R. Vonskopczynski evidently was not.

A few days later, on August 19, I found an even more interesting situation involving a trainer's intentions. It arose, oddly enough, in a maiden steeplechase race, but the more I looked at the past performances, the more I believed that I had found an exciting opportunity.

4 SARATOGA

STEEPLECHASE
2 1-16 MILES
SARATOGA
Start Finish

2 1/16 MILES. (STEEPLECHASE). (3.40⅕) MAIDEN CLAIMING. Purse $7,500. 3-year-old and upward. Weights, 3-year-olds, 139 lbs. 4-year-olds, 149 lbs. Older, 156 lbs. Claiming price $10,000; for each $500 to $8,500, 3 lbs.

Tell Me

Own.—Randolph Theodora A — **$10,000** — **B. f. 4, by Sky Wonder—Happy News, by Black Gang** — **Br.—Randolph Mrs T A (Va)** — **Tr.—Watters Eric**

144

Turf Record St.	1st	2nd	3rd		St.	1st	2nd	3rd	Amt.
1	0	0	0	1977	4	M	0	0	$510
				1976	0	M	0	0	

10Aug77- 4Sar fm 2 1/16 S'chase 3:50⅗ 3↑Md 10000 6 5 75 811 612 419 Stack T B 144 11.10 — — DonMiguelII14717CommissionerJim1391¼Gnrl'sChoic144¾ Rallied 9
3Aug77- 4Sar fm 1⅞ S'chase 3:30 3↑Md Sp Wt 5 7 614 611 644 653 Cushman J 147 9.40 — — Pinino 1532¼ Yes Sir Buddy 1587½ Cultivating 1525¼ Unruly post 8
19Jly77- 3Del fm 2 S'chase 3:49⅗ 3↑Md Sp Wt 6 7 76 78¼ 410 519 Cushman J 143 23.70 — — Durbish 1385 Feroz II 1582½ Pesky 1537 No real threat 12
30May77- 5Fai hd *1 5/16 Ⓣ 2:15 3↑Md Sp Wt 4 8 810 73 4¾ 44¼ Cushman J 150 23.60 — — Say Darling 137¾ Misty Picture 139no Bijou Beach 1523½ Late bid 11

Pamphlet

Own.—Hershey H — **$8,500** — **Dk. b. or br. g. 4, by Tobin Bronze—Day Line, by Day Court** — **Br.—Elmendorf Farm (Ky)** — **Tr.—Fenwick H Bruce**

133^7

Turf Record St.	1st	2nd	3rd		St.	1st	2nd	3rd	Amt.
2	0	0	0	1977	7	1	2	1	$5,565
				1976	25	1	1	4	$7,973

20Jly77- 9Del fm 1 1/16 Ⓣ:48 1:12⅘ 1:45⅖ Clm 6000 6 3 36 56 73¼ 89 Adams J K 112 18.40 68-23 Boardwalk Baron 1072½HizirReis1121½FlitAround112½ Speed, tired 9
30Mar77- 5GS fst 1⅛ :48⅘ 1:13⅘ 1:54⅘ Clm c-5000 1 3 33 25 35½ 410 Nied J Jr b 114 9.20 53-29 Inahaystack 1071½ Straight Car 1158 Mambo Mambo 114½ Tired 9
17Mar77- 9GS fst 170 :47⅘ 1:14⅖ 1:47 Clm 3000 1 1 1½ 11 13 1nk Nied J Jr b 117 *2.10 59-24 Pamphlet 117nk Flight of Apollo 1173 Never Gone 110nk Driving 12
8Mar77- 9GS fst 170 :47 1:13 1:44⅗ Clm 6000 1 3 64¼1213122012²² Samyn J L5 b 107 11.00 49-26 SpanishIndian1161½ReasonableTurn1164WithLife116nk Done early 12
19Feb77- 1GS fst 1 1/16 :47⅗ 1:13 1:50⅕ Clm 5000 3 4 312 312 34 32 Samyn J L5 b 108 7.60 52-30 Cool It Babe 1141 Bemask 1091 Pamphlet 1082 Lacked rally 10
8Feb77- 3GS fst 6f :23 :46⅘ 1:12⅖ Clm 4000 1 7 65 57 46½ 24 Samyn J L5 b 111 2.60 77-28 A Good Way 1094 Pamphlet 111nk Disprove 1221½ Gamely 8
3Feb77- 2GS fst 6f :22⅖ :45⅘ 1:11⅘ Clm 3750 3 11 75¾ 55 35 23½ Samyn J L5 b 109 5.90 80-21 SignOfTrouble1163½Pmphlet1091½Softly'sBrother114¾ Closed well 12
23Dec76- 9Key fst 7f :23 :46⅖ 1:25⅘ 3↑Clm 5000 4 12 87¾ 77½ 48 49½ Samyn J L5 b 106 6.30 70-26 High Road 108½ Brave Game 1105 Bold Who 119' Rallied 12
3Dec76- 2Key fst 7f :22⅘ :46 1:24⅕ 3↑Clm 4000 2 9 43 51¾ 3nk 31¾ Wilson R b 114 10.20 86-16 Promo 1161 De Busschre 114¾ Pamphlet 114nk Bumped 12
23Nov76- 2Key fst 6f :23⅘ :49⅘ 1:15⅖ Clm 4000 9 11 127 103¾ 75¾ 46¾ Wilson R b 116 12.20 58-36 My Dad's Cross 1184 De Busschre 1162 Grand Jewel 116¾ Rallied 12

Rock Music

Own.—Heekin C L — **$8,500** — **B. g. 5, by Stage Door Johnny—New Behavior, by Bold Ruler** — **Br.—Lazy F Ranch (Ky)** — **Tr.—Houghton Ronald B**

144

Turf Record St.	1st	2nd	3rd		St.	1st	2nd	3rd	Amt.
3	0	1	0	1977	3	M	1	0	$230
				1976	5	M	0	0	

10Aug77- 4Sar fm 2 1/16 S'chase 3:50⅗ 3↑Md 8500 7 3 31½ 2½ 23 519 Ruhsam J L 147 8.50 — — DonMiguelII14717CommissionerJim1391¼Generl'sChoic144¾ Tired 9
30Apr77- 2SH hd *1⅞ S'chase 3:33 3↑Md Sp Wt 9 1 2½ 25 53 58¾ Ruhsam J L 155 — — Second Call 145¾ The Scribbler 1456 Uncle Baby 1421 Tired 8
23Apr77- 2Clm fm *1 Ⓣ 1:43⅗ 3↑Allowance 1 3 44 41¾ 51½ 25 Ruhsam J L 147 — — Les Halles 1535 Rock Music 147no Misty Emperor 156nk Rallied 9
30Oct76- 1FH gd *2 1/16 S'chase 4:03 3↑Md Sp Wt 1 2 1½ 55¾ 931 836 Ruhsam J L 154 — — Inns Of Court 1548 Mannlicher 1471¼ Down First154hd Done early 11
6Oct76- 1Lig gd *1⅞ S'chase 3:35⅘ 3↑Md Sp Wt 10 6 87¾ 719 713 742 Elser C 153 — — Dearoldcorny 153¾ Inns Of Court 1536 Its GoodForYou1505 Tired 11
25Sep76- 2Fax hd *2⅛ S'chase 4:00⅗ 3↑Md Sp Wt 10 2 12 22½ — — Taylor D10 143 — — Tingaling Cool 1533 Amber Rick 14812LordRullah1462½ Lost rider 11
11Sep76- 1Fai hd *1 5/16 Ⓣ 2:15⅘ 3↑Md Sp Wt 4 — — — — — Taylor D7 145 15.80 — — MagicHeartII1422WinningWays1429BullRunDraft1521¾ Lost rider 9
17Apr76- 3Clm fm *1 Ⓣ 1:43⅗ 3↑Allowance 8 3 42 82¾ 84¾ 813 Aitcheson J Jr 147 — — Mr. Fagan 1501½ Parade To Glory 1341 Culinary Prince140¾ Tired 8
14Jly75- 2Bel sly 6f :22⅗ :46⅖ 1:11⅘ 3↑Md 18000 8 4 64½ 64 66½ 79 Gustines H 118 21.10 75-15 SheetsToTheWind1181DonJack1182½LuckyCaptain118¾ No factor 9
3Jly75- 1Bel fst 6f :22⅗ :45⅗ 1:10⅖ 3↑Md 30000 10 7 1011101411141114 Gustines H 118 36.60 77-07 One'sTooMny120½StrightAnswer1141½ChiefNocoton1142½ Outrun 11

Royal Barb

Own.—Obre Mrs H — **$8,500** — **Dk. b. or br. g. 7, by Royal Orbit—Flutterbudget, by To Market** — **Br.—Lillian A (Md)** — **Tr.—Field Kenneth**

147

Turf Record St.	1st	2nd	3rd		St.	1st	2nd	3rd	Amt.
4	0	2	0	1977	6	M	2	0	$633
				1976	0	M	0	0	

10Aug77- 4Sar fm 2 1/16 S'chase 3:50⅗ 3↑Md 8500 3 — — — — — Morris G 147 12.50 — — DonMiguelII14717CommissionerJim1391¼Generl'sChoice144¾ Fell 9
21Jly77- 3Del fm 2¼ S'chase 4:26 Clm 5000 9 2 22 412 421 436 Pearce R7 146 8.00 — — Amber Rick 15013 Kid Hank 1458 Londun Fog 14715 Weakened 9
4Jun77- 1Fai hd *1 5/16 Ⓣ 2:18⅖ 3↑Allowance 1 5 45½ 55½ 53¾ 69¾ Pearce R s 147 *2.10 — — Yamasaki 147½ Nataba 1441½ Count Armando 1521½ Tired 9
28May77- 2Pro hd *1 Ⓣ 2:09⅖ 3↑Allowance 8 1 11½ 13½ 1½ 22½ Pearce R 158 e — — D'Errico 1632½ Royal Barb 1581 Grinder's Switch 1604 Gamely 13
14May77- 3PW fm 1 Ⓣ 1:39⅖ 3↑Spec'l Wt 1 1 1nk 31 1hd 2hd Pearce R 160 — — Gentle Sport 160hd Royal Barb 1604 Prince Rudi 160½ Just failed 12
7May77- 8War fm *1¼ Ⓣ 2:37⅕ 3↑Allowance 3 4 31 34 41½ 46 Wayne M3 140 — — Rosa 1392 Silent Kingdom 1473 Cornish Boy 1401 Tired 8

Commissioner Jim

Own.—Walsh Mrs M G — **$10,000** — **B. c. 3, by Chompion—Reunion, by Admiral's Voyage** — **Br.—Basehore S (NJ)** — **Tr.—Walsh Michael G**

139

Turf Record St.	1st	2nd	3rd		St.	1st	2nd	3rd	Amt.
3	0	0	0	1977	4	M	1	0	$1,740
				1976	6	M	0	1	$581

10Aug77- 4Sar fm 2 1/16 S'chase 3:50⅗ 3↑Md 10000 9 4 42½ 51½ 33½ 217 Walsh M III 139 6.10 — — DonMigulII14717CommssonrJm1391¼Gnrl'sChoc144¾ Second best 9
28May77- 2Pro hd *1 Ⓣ 2:09⅖ 3↑Allowance 6 5 711 65¾ 52¾ 58½ Walsh M III 144 — — D'Errico 1632½ Royal Barb 1581 Grinder's Switch 1604 No mishap 13
23Apr77- 2Clm fm *1 Ⓣ 1:43⅗ 3↑Allowance 3 1 12½ 11 3¾ 55¾ Walsh M III 143 — — Les Halles 1535 Rock Music 147no Misty Emperor 156nk Tired 9
16Apr77- 2SoP fm *7f Ⓣ 1:30 3↑Md Sp Wt 9 4 54½ 63½ 52 57 Walsh M III 138 e — — Nataba 1341½ Spring Tra La 1304 Charming Evening 146½ Evenly 12
28Oct76- 9Aqu fst 7f :23⅕ :46⅕ 1:27⅖ Md 16000 3 8 1113112111171113 Velez R I 122 23.60 51-21 Cast Adrift 120nk Hansom Chick 118¾ Stunt Pilot 113hd Outrun 12
16Sep76- 9Bel fst 6f :22⅕ :45⅕ 1:11 Md 25000 4 2 68 914 9181013 Wallis T 118 41.60 74-11 Allsub 113nk Dewan And Only 122hd Jungle Mission 122no Tired 12
26Aug76- 4Del fst 6f :22⅖ :46⅕ 1:12⅗ Clm 10000 2 6 614 611 610 511 Baird R L 112 11.20 71-16 Flash's Memory 1095 Prince Hill 108½Charlie'sRebel1163½ Outrun 6
20Aug76- 3Del fst 6f :22⅘ :46⅘ 1:12⅖ Md 10000 5 3 48 411 412 310 Barrow T 120 30.30 73-14 MyAurorBorlis1203FightingJohnny1207CommssonrJm1202 Evenly 8
12Aug76- 3Del fst 6f :22⅕ :46⅕ 1:14 Md Sp Wt 6 3 79¾ 815 917 820 Barrow T 120 94.40 55-17 Pratique 120nk Madoc 1207 Steel Bandit 1204¼ No factor 10
1Aug76- 1Del fst 5½f :22⅕ :47⅖ 1:07⅕ Md Sp Wt 7 2 914 814 919 716 Barrow T 120 54.90 66-17 Peter Pucker 1201LimitlessDawn1152½NativeGrove1204 No threat 10

Jeopardized

Own.—Brandywine Stable — **$8,500** — **Ch. g. 4, by Commanding II—Sprinter Shoes, by The Shoe** — **Br.—Ellsworth R C (Cal)** — **Tr.—Clancy Joseph P**

133^7

	St.	1st	2nd	3rd	Amt.
1977	1	M	0	0	
1976	0	M	0	0	

21Jly77- 3Del fm 2¼ S'chase 4:26 Clm 5500 2 8 79¼ 738 656 — Phillips M A7 s 135 27.30 — — Amber Rick 15013 Kid Hank 1458 Londun Fog 14715 Lost rider 9

Charming Evening

Own.—Oare E M — **$8,500** — **B. g. 5, by Windsor Charm—Evening Pass, by General Staff** — **Br.—Winkelman D W (NC)** — **Tr.—Oare Ernest M**

147

Turf Record St.	1st	2nd	3rd		St.	1st	2nd	3rd	Amt.
4	1	0	1	1977	8	1	0	1	$410
				1974	1	M	0	0	

10Aug77- 4Sar fm 2 1/16 S'chase 3:50⅗ 3↑Md 8500 8 1 21½ 1½ 713 727 Aitcheson J Jr 147 23.60 — — DonMiguelII14717CommissionerJim1391¼Generl'sChoic144¾ Tired 9
24Jun77- 7CT fst 6½f :23⅘ :47⅖ 1:20⅖ Clm 4500 6 3 41½ 54¼ 811 815 Palmer R W b 114 25.70 68-23 Washington'sHelp1142WhittakersMill1141½JimmyFrank1141 Tired 8
4Jun77- 2Fai hd *2 3/16 S'chase 4:16 3↑Md 6500 5 1 — — — — Twyman N 144 40.10 — — Sunsational 13715 Breaking Ground 144½ Mr. Jam 1535¼ Fell 13
25May77- 5Pim sly 1 1/16 :47⅖ 1:12⅘ 1:44⅘ Clm 5000 11 4 811112111331147 Sasser B b 119 15.70 34-18 Prideful 1138 [DH]To Hunt 112 [DH]Grand Diplomat 1134 Brief ft. 11
7May77- 7War fm *1¼ Ⓣ 2:34 3↑Allowance 7 3 1½ 66 66 724 Ruhsam J L 153 — — HappyIntellectual147nkRoylMystic1475SilverGoose14415 Used up 9
30Apr77- 1SH hd *7f Ⓣ 1:32 3↑Allowance 2 1 12½ 12 1½ 11 Ruhsam J L7 141 — — Charming Evening 141¾ Bijou Beach 1386 Amber Hawk 13410 4
16Apr77- 2SoP fm *7f Ⓣ 1:30 3↑Md Sp Wt 10 5 1½ 11 31¼ 35½ Cushman J 146 — — Nataba 1341½ Spring Tra La 1304 Charming Evening 146½ Tired 12
9Apr77- 4Try fm *1 Ⓣ 1:54⅕ 3↑Allowance 7 8 83½ 911 96½ 919 Quanbeck A Jr 147 — — Sunny Ice 1435 Dream and Scheme 1474ArranTide151no Far back 9

Grand Salute

Own.—Steinman Beverly R — **$10,000** — **B. g. 6, by Hail To Reason—Luquillo, by Princequillo** — **Br.—Cragwood Estates Inc (Ky)** — **Tr.—Fout Paul R**

151^5

Turf Record St.	1st	2nd	3rd		St.	1st	2nd	3rd	Amt.
13	2	3	2	1977	4	0	0	0	$510
				1975	11	1	1	1	$12,400

9Aug77- 4Sar fm 2 1/16 S'chase 3:48 3↑Clm 11000 5 5 55 55½ 413 422 Fout D P5 141 17.00 — — Time Saver 14512 Sun Sign 1474 Rose Marie's Baby 1306¼ Evenly 7
3Aug77- 4Sar fm 1⅞ S'chase 3:30 3↑Md Sp Wt 7 6 715 510 528 529 Fout D P5 153 19.00 — — Pinino 1532¼ Yes SirBuddy1587½Cultivating1525¼ Showed nothing 8
30May77- 2Fai hd *2 3/16 S'chase 4:16⅘ 3↑Md Sp Wt 6 8 828 829 — — Fout D P5 150 8.20 — — Earla Mor 15511 Don Miguel II 1552 YesSirBuddy1481½ Lost rider 9
2Apr77- 6Cam fm 1 Ⓣ 1:42 3↑Allowance 2 3 95 105¼105¼1015 Fout D P3 b 143 — — Pinino 146nk Parade To Glory 149nk Ifeelfree 1495 Far back 11
22Oct75- 8Lrl fst 1 :46⅖ 1:11⅖ 1:36⅕ Allowance 8 9 1115122312271222 Passmore W J 116 55.30 70-18 Ground Breaker 1166 Spiked Drink 112¾ Malaga Bay 1165 Outrun 12
6Oct75- 8Bel fst 1⅛ :47⅕ 1:12⅕ 1:51⅖ 3↑Allowance 1 7 711 711 718 620 Ruane J 116 36.10 50-26 NaleesRialto1127½AttheFront1181¾TrumpeterSwan1163 No factor 7
19Sep75- 6Bel sly 1 1/16 :45 1:09⅕ 1:43 3↑Allowance 2 6 511 613 615 511 Ruane J b 116 24.30 76-19 Ben Adhem 112hdFeatherfoot1142HoleinthePants109½ No mishap 7
6Sep75- 6Bel fm 1 1/16 Ⓣ:46⅖ 1:11 1:41⅖ 3↑Allowance 8 4 75 912 923 928 Ruane J b 118 56.80 66-11 Shredder 1125 Candle Stand 116¾ Intrepid Hero1182¼ Early speed 9
13Aug75- 6Sar gd 1⅛ Ⓣ:48⅕ 1:12⅗ 1:49⅕ 3↑Allowance 1 3 32 33 43 63½ Ruane J b 120 10.60 77-24 Boonesborough 116¾ Brian Boru 1151 Telex Number 113¾ Tired 7
6Aug75- 3Sar gd 1 1/16 Ⓣ:48⅘ 1:13 1:44⅗ 3↑Allowance 7 1 11½ 2hd 21 2nk Ruane J b 116 13.70 74-26 [D]GreatAbove101nkGrandSlute116nk[DH]CoHost111 Altered course 7
6Aug75-Placed first through disqualification

Nahma — Dk. b. or br. g. 5, by Stoic—Windswept, by Windy City II
$10,000 — Br.—Jones M Troy (Md)
Own.—Augustin Stables — Tr.—Sheppard Jonathan E
156 — Turf Record: St. 3, 1st 3, 2nd 0, 3rd 0 — 1977: St. 2, 1st 0, 2nd 0, 3rd 0 — 1976: St. 13, 1st 3, 2nd 3, 3rd 0, Amt. $5,872

3Aug77- 4Sar fm 1⅞ S'chase 3:30 3↑Md Sp Wt 6 3 49 711 746 754 Quanbeck A Jr 158 3.70e — — Pinino 153 2¼ Yes Sir Buddy 158 7½ Cultivating 152 5¼ Done early 8
22Jly77- 3Del fm 2 S'chase 3:51⅗ 3↑Allowance 5 2 64 618 — — Phillips M A7 145 6.50 — — SwssBnkAccount155 10 OhFthrs147 1¾ StdyAsYouGo145 3¾ Pulled up 6
30Oct76- 7FH gd *1½ Ⓣ 2:16 3↑Allowance 6 4 2½ 31¼ 11 110 Cushman J 159 e — — Nahma 159 10 Don Miguel II 142½ Eton 159 1 Ridden out 9
9Oct76- 5Lig sf *7f Ⓣ 1:44⅘ 3↑Allowance 2 4 2nk 13 14 Cushman J5 b 152 e — — Nahma 152 4 Don Miguel II 148 4 Ruling Line 151 6 In hand 7
18Sep76- 1Fai fm *1 5/16 Ⓣ 2:12⅕ 3↑Allowance 6 10 1013 41½ 1½ 12 Cushman J3 b 149 22.50 — — Nahma 149 2 Polly Pot 146 1¾ Bull Run Draft 149 nk Driving 13
9Sep76- 4Key fst 6f :22⅘ :46⅗ 1:12 3↑Clm 9500 8 8 74 66 812 813 Castaneda K b 116 2.70 69-20 Stone'sBell114 2¾ RegalProducer112 3½ MushroomPicker112 hd Tired 10
5Sep76- 4Del fst 6f :22⅗ :46⅕ 1:11⅕ 3↑Clm 7000 7 1 1½ 12½ 12 21½ Gilbert R B b 112 22.20 87-16 Mad King 116 1½ Nahma 112 2 Rattle the Rye 116 1 Sharp 7
26Aug76- 6Del fst 6f :22⅖ :45⅘ 1:10⅕ 3↑Clm 8000 1 3 32 56½ 613 616 Doyne T7 b 109 35.40 78-16 Noble Pilot 113 1½ Sting Like a Bee 118 1¾ Magic Love 116 5 Tired 6
11Aug76- 5Del fst 6f :22⅕ :45⅗ 1:11⅕ 3↑Allowance 5 4 42½ 59½ 714 813 Doyne T7 b 108 47.30 76-17 Billy Pitt 110 hd Hempt's Lark 115 2 Euphoric Beau 114 1 Tired 8
22Mar76- 6Pen fst 5½f :22⅖ :46 1:05⅖ Allowance 1 4 1hd 2hd 2½ 23 Seldomridge A b 116 2.80 91-19 Noble Elm 122 3 Nahma 116 4½ Priam Oak 119 1 Gamely 8

LATEST WORKOUTS Aug 13 Del 4f fst :50⅖ b ●Jly 28 Del 1 fst 1:43⅘ b

Buckshot Brave — Dk. b. or br. g. 5, by Shawnee Brave—Iza Doll, by Johnny L
$8,500 — Br.—Latta J Y (Pa)
Own.—Brittle S F — Tr.—Brittle Sally F
147 — Turf Record: St. 7, 1st 0, 2nd 1, 3rd 0 — 1977: St. 2, 1st M, 2nd 0, 3rd 0, Amt. $30 — 1976: St. 6, 1st M, 2nd 0, 3rd 0, Amt. $468

10Aug77- 4Sar fm 2 1/16 S'chase 3:50⅗ 3↑Md 8500 5 6 53 41 58 624 Skiffington T Jr 147 5.50 — — DonMiguelII147 17 CommissionerJim139 1¼ Generl'sChoic144¾ Tired 9
30May77- 5Fai hd *1 5/16 Ⓣ 2:15 3↑Md Sp Wt 10 1 12 1½ 51¾ 58 Brittle C 155 19.80 — — Say Darling 137¾ Misty Picture 139 no Bijou Beach 152 3½ Tired 11
30Oct76- 2FH gd *2 1/16 S'chase 4:00 3↑Md Sp Wt 7 2 42¾ 68 66 620 Cushman J5 149 e — — Royal Mystic 140 3 Tingledu 154 5 House Warming 154 4 Tired 9
23Oct76- 2RB gd *7f Ⓣ 1:36 3↑Allowance 14 4 2½ 21 53¼ Brittle C 147 e — — Royal Mystic 144 no Tall Award 153 1½ Just a Tinch 146 1½ Tired 14
18Sep76- 3Fai fm *1 5/16 Ⓣ 2:13⅖ 3↑Allowance 4 4 57½ 1212 919 923 Brittle C 146 38.40 — — Magic Heart II 145 nk MistyEmperor142 8 RulingLine149 1¼ Far back 12
23Aug76- 4Sar fm 2 1/16 S'chase 3:49⅕ 3↑Md 8500 7 4 62½ 411 418 426 Cushman J5 145 10.80 — — HiEmperor144 1¾ Lashore150 8½ BostonBeauregarde145 16 Weakened 10
16Aug76- 4Sar gd 2 1/16 S'chase 3:56⅕ 3↑Md Sp Wt 1 4 — — — — Hamilton J W7 142 *2.60e — — UpLikeThunder156 11 PlayEveryDy156 no OhFethers146 2½ Lost rider 10
23Jly76- 9Del yl 1 1/16 Ⓣ :48⅕ 1:14⅕ 1:46⅘ 3↑Md Sp Wt 3 7 69 1117 1136 1135 Brodsky D 122 16.60e 35-30 Paginai 115 no Magic Heart II 115 4 Persian Sunrise 110 1 Outrun 11
15Nov75- 3Cam fm 1 Ⓣ 1:45⅗ 3↑Allowance 4 1 11½ 22½ 43 46 Watson B 133 — — Sunny Ice 137 1 Tight Exchange 147 2 My Friend Irma 141 3 Tired 6
1Nov75- 2Mtp fst 1 1:36 3↑Allowance 5 1 1½ 31 42 45¾ Watson R B 135 [D] — — [D]Enchumao 152 1½ Happy Sea 134 nk Bijou Beach 135 4 Tired 10

1Nov75-Placed third through disqualification. Awarded third purse money.

I used to share most horseplayers' disdain for jumping races because of the obvious hazards involved in them. Before the 1974 Saratoga season, however, I undertook a modest study of the sport, and concluded that although I could not handicap the races with conventional methods, I might beat them using trainer angles. I discovered one Delaware-based trainer, J. V. H. Davis, who in each of the previous two seasons had shipped a horse to Saratoga for his debut over the jumps and had won both times at enormous odds. In 1974, Davis's invader happened to be an eight-year-old maiden, but that did not deter me from betting him and touting all my friends. When the maiden won by eight lengths and paid $49.20, I earned an instant reputation as a steeplechase authority. I knew it was undeserved, but it encouraged me to try to ferret out a similarly esoteric steeplechaser at Saratoga every year. And now I had one.

Pamphlet had spent his entire career running without distinction in cheap races, but on March 30 H. Bruce Fenwick claimed him for $5000. Fenwick is primarily a steeplechase trainer, and he evidently saw some indications that Pamphlet had the potential to be a jumper. The horse did have some early foot, and most successful steeplechasers have been speedsters rather than plodders on the main track because jumping races consist essentially of a succession of dashes between each obstacle. Pamphlet was decently bred. And he had been running with such frequency that he was probably sound and durable.

Pamphlet did not race for nearly four months after he was claimed, and I assumed that Fenwick had been schooling him as a jumper during that period. When the trainer entered him in a 1 1/16-mile turf event at Delaware Park on July 20, he almost certainly viewed that race as a tuneup for his real objective. And that objective was the fourth race at Saratoga on August 19.

I did not know how good a jumper Pamphlet might be, but I did know that all his opponents were well-established mediocrities. Only one of them, Commissioner Jim, had ever finished in the money in a jump race, and he had done it while losing by seventeen lengths. None of the horses in the field seemed to possess much early speed, and judging from the ability he had shown in sprints, I thought Pamphlet might be able to open a clear early lead and control the pace.

Pamphlet went to the post at 20 to 1. If I had been winning substantially at the Saratoga meeting, I would have taken a shot for my biggest killing of the year. But since I was losing more than $2000 for the season, I decided that the circumstances demanded prudence and bet $250 to win.

FOURTH RACE
Saratoga
AUGUST 19, 1977

2 $\frac{1}{16}$ MILES.(steeplechase). (3.40⅕) MAIDEN CLAIMING. Purse $7,500. 3-year-old and upward. Weights, 3-year-olds, 139 lbs. 4-year-olds, 149 lbs. Older, 156 lbs. Claiming price $10,000; for each $500 to $8,500, 3 lbs.

Value of race $7,500, value to winner $4,500, second $1,650, third $900, fourth $450. Mutuel pool $123,318, OTB pool $45,081.

Last Raced	Horse	Eqt.A.Wt	PP	3	6	9	11	13	Fin	Jockey	Cl'g Pr	Odds $1
9Aug77 ^{4}Sar^4	Grand Salute	6 151	8	$2\frac{1}{2}$	$3\frac{1}{2}$	$4^{1\frac{1}{2}}$	$5\frac{1}{2}$	3^8	1^{nk}	Fout D P^5	10000	5.40
20Jly77 ^{9}Del^8	Pamphlet	4 147	2	1^5	1^3	1^4	1^1	1^3	$2^{1\frac{3}{4}}$	Quanbeck A Jr†	8500	20.70
10Aug77 ^{4}Sar^6	Buckshot Brave	5 147	10	$8^{1\frac{1}{2}}$	$7^{1\frac{1}{2}}$	$7^{1\frac{1}{2}}$	6^6	$2\frac{1}{2}$	3^{18}	Fishback J	8500	14.20
10Aug77 ^{4}Sar^2	Commissioner Jim	3 139	5	$5\frac{1}{2}$	6^3	5^5	4^2	5^2	$4^{2\frac{1}{4}}$	Walsh M III	10000	1.80
10Aug77 ^{4}Sar	Royal Barb	7 147	4	$3\frac{1}{2}$	5^2	6^2	8	6^3	5^{nk}	Morris G	8500	31.50
10Aug77 ^{4}Sar^7	Charming Evening	5 147	7	4^{hd}	$4\frac{1}{2}$	2^1	3^2	4^2	6^{13}	Clerc G P	8500	30.50
3Aug77 ^{4}Sar^7	Nahma	5 156	9	$9^{1\frac{1}{2}}$	8^8	8^{24}	7^2	7	7	Skiffington TJr	10000	3.40
10Aug77 ^{4}Sar^4	Tell Me	4 144	1	7^4	2^2	3^1	2^3	—	—	Harty J	10000	8.40
21Jly77 ^{3}Del	Jeopardized	4 133	6	10	9	9	—	—	—	Phillips M A^7	8500	48.80
10Aug77 ^{4}Sar^5	Rock Music	5 144	3	$6^{1\frac{1}{2}}$	—	—	—	—	—	Ruhsam J L	8500	4.50

Tell Me, Fell; Jeopardized, Pulled up; Rock Music, Lost rider.

OFF AT 3:11, EDT. Start good from tape for all but NAHMA, Won driving. Time, 3:52⅕ Course firm.

$2 Mutuel Prices:			
9-(I)-GRAND SALUTE	12.80	7.60	5.20
2-(B)-PAMPHLET		16.80	10.40
11-(K)-BUCKSHOT BRAVE			5.80

B. g, by Hail To Reason—Luquillo, by Princequillo. Trainer Fout Paul R. Bred by Cragwood Estates Inc (Ky).

GRAND SALUTE, never far back, rallied approaching the final jump and continued on gamely to wear down PAMPHLET in the final yards. The latter went right to the front, made mistakes at several hedges while making the pace, turned back a bid from TELL ME leaving the final turn but failed to last in a stiff drive. BUCKSHOT BRAVE, outrun to the final turn, made a bid entering the stretch but wasn't good enough. COMMISSIONER JIM moved within striking distance after entering the backstretch the final time but was finished at the far turn. ROYAL BARB was always outrun. CHARMING EVENING, well placed the initial turn of the course, rallied entering the backstretch the final time, bobbled at the tenth fence and was finished at the far turn. NAHMA, rank at the post, reared at the start. TELL ME, never far back, went after PAMPHLET on the backstretch the final time, remained prominent into the stretch but fell at the final jump. JEOPARDIZED dropped far back while jumping poorly and was pulled up after entering the backstretch the final time. ROCK MUSIC was well placed when he landed badly at the sixth fence unseating his rider.

Owners— 1, Steinman Beverly R; 2, Hershey H; 3, Brittle S F; 4, Walsh Mrs M G; 5, Obre Mrs H; 6, Oare E M; 7, Augustin Stables; 8, Randolph Theodora A; 9, Brandywine Stable; 10, Heekin C L.

Trainers— 1, Fout Paul R; 2, Fenwick H Bruce; 3, Brittle Sally F; 4, Walsh Michael G; 5, Field Kenneth; 6, Oare Ernest M; 7, Clancy Joseph P; 8, Watters Eric; 9, Clancy Joseph P; 10, Houghton Ronald B.

† Apprentice allowance waived: Pamphlet 7 pounds. **Corrected weight:** Pamphlet 140 pounds.

Commissioner Jim was claimed by Hershey H; trainer, Fenwick H Bruce.

Scratched—General's Choice (10Aug77 ^{4}Sar^3).

When Pamphlet sprinted to the lead and quickly opened a five-length lead, I tried to restrain my excitement. Too many things can happen in a race that has thirteen hurdles and lasts for nearly four minutes. But when my horse had raced more than a mile and was still holding a four-length advantage and looking strong, I started to yell. As the field reached the final turn and a rival named Tell Me moved up alongside Pamphlet, I screamed my encouragement, knowing that this was the moment of truth. Jockey Al Quanbeck urged Pamphlet a bit, and he disposed of the challenge with ease. Nobody else was making a move, and the last thing Pamphlet had to worry about was the final jump. Only a 52-inch obstacle stood between me and $5000. Pamphlet cleared it awkwardly, but he cleared it, and approached the finish line with a three-length lead. But suddenly he started to act like a punch-drunk fighter, going through his usual motions but doing so slowly and sluggishly. As Pamphlet practically staggered from exhaustion, a horse named Grand Salute started rallying and gaining with every stride. I was too hoarse and emotionally drained to yell any more, but I silently implored Pamphlet to summon up one last ounce of strength. He didn't have it. Grand Salute caught him in the last few yards and beat him by a neck.

I bet out of frustration and anger for the rest of the afternoon, but when I got home that night my losses for the Saratoga season had reached $4000. I felt more despondent than I had on any day since the disqualification of What A Lucky Star at Gulfstream, and I was annoyed to see that the Kid was acting very cheerful. I asked him if he customarily smiled at funerals, too. But he told me he had good reason for his high spirits.

"I was standing out by the paddock today," he said, "and you know who I saw leaning against a tree, eating an ice-cream cone?" He paused for dramatic effect. "The Fat Man."

The Fat Man runs few horses, wins few races, has no reputation, but he happens to be the most skilled, audacious perpetrator of betting coups in America. When the Kid and I got our initial inkling of the way he operated, we had studied him as intensively as Boswell scrutinized Dr. Johnson.

The Kid had burrowed through stacks of ancient *Racing Forms*, analyzing his methods. I had searched for people who knew the Fat Man and relentlessly pumped them for information and stories about him. "He's got ice water in his veins," a trainer told me. "I remember one time out West he bet thousands of dollars with bookmakers on a horse he had been setting up for months. But at the track the horse was 2 to 1 and that wasn't good enough for him. So he told the jockey to stiff the horse, and he ate his losses."

Another racetracker told me, "Sometimes he wears a beard and sometimes he doesn't. Sometimes he drives a Cadillac and sometimes he drives a pickup truck. Sometimes he runs horses in his own name and sometimes he uses a front." The Fat Man was a shadowy, elusive figure, but now he was in our midst. And we knew what the reason had to be.

Earlier in the summer, Jerry had received a tip along the bookmakers' grapevine on a maiden filly named French Melody. His informant told him that she had been strangled by her jockey every time she had run. Jerry relayed this story to the Kid and me, but we did not pay much attention to it, until we saw that French Melody had been claimed—by the Fat Man. Evidently he had ferreted out the larceny and wanted to capitalize on it himself. The perfect place to do this was a New York track, where the large betting pools would allow him to wager heavily without wrecking his own odds. I studied the conditions of the races scheduled for the remainder of the Saratoga meeting and saw that there was an appropriate maiden event for French Melody on the next-to-last day of the season.

Two nights after the Kid had spotted the Fat Man, French Melody was entered in a race at Atlantic City. We knew what he was doing; he was laying the groundwork for the Saratoga race. The wagering pools at Atlantic City are not large enough to accommodate a Fat Man coup, and many bookmakers refuse to take action on night racing. The Fat Man had not sent French Melody there to win. She was there to lose badly, to acquire the dismal line in her past performances that would insure tremendous odds for her at Saratoga. Otherwise the Fat Man would not have been here in the first place.

While French Melody was traveling out of town, the Kid and I sat at home and talked excitedly about how much she would mean to us. This would be the great moment in our lives as horseplayers. I knew that the Fat Man was almost infallible; I knew that French Melody could be 20 to 1; I thought I had a realistic chance to win as much as $50,000.

The next day we rushed to Joe Deuel's newsstand to get a paper with the Atlantic City results and see how badly French Melody had been beaten, how shamelessly the Fat Man had prepared for his betting coup. We stared at the newspaper in disbelief.

French Melody had won and paid $34.60.

The Fat Man was not under his customary elm tree the next day, or the day after. But wherever he had gone, he must have been reveling in the knowledge that he had fooled the world again, and that he was still the undisputed king of the crooked trainers.

When I failed to profit from French Melody, I strongly suspected that I had missed my last opportunity for salvation at Saratoga. Still, on the Sunday before the final week of the season, I reviewed all the previous results to see if I were committing any handicapping or betting errors that I could rectify. I realized that I might have been guilty of overconfidence and complacency after winning so effortlessly at Pimlico; I had not been studying as hard as I usually did at Saratoga. Nevertheless, I could not find a single lucrative winner which I had wrongly overlooked. Saratoga was simply not offering opportunities on which I could capitalize with my particular handicapping skills. As at Gulfstream, the allowance races and high-priced claiming races were drawing small fields which were uncompetitive and unbettable. Unfortunately, I was responding to the lack of good wagering situations by making large bets on horses who did not deserve them. An animal like Cut the Talk, the R. Vonskopczynski dropdown, would barely have merited a $100 flyer at Pimlico. Now I was making him the object of a $600 plunge. If this had been any other racetrack, I would have packed my bags and left. But this was Saratoga, which I love even during the bad times; and besides, I had to stay in town for one of the highlights of the season, the Socolof Gold Cup.

The event had been the offshoot of a casual remark in the press box several years earlier. A disgruntled bettor was tearing up his tickets and muttering, "I could have run faster than that bum," when a press-box habitué named Pete Socolof overheard him, scoffed, and offered the out-of-shape journalist $100 if he could run around the track once without collapsing. Socolof later amended this proposal and announced that he would post a $100 purse for a 1⅛-mile race for members of the fourth estate. The Gold Cup was born.

Its 1976 running was the object of a betting coup. I had given up smoking earlier in the year and had started running a few miles a day as part of a personal physical-fitness campaign. So I confidently signed up for the race. On the morning of the Gold Cup, Frank Tours of the publicity department asked me what kind of shape I was in. "Terrible," I lied. Tours had touted me off a steeplechase winner a few days before and I wanted to repay the favor. Later in the day I bumped into Charlie's friend Angelo, a burly taxicab dispatcher from the Bronx. Angelo gets very upset when he loses—he was almost ruled off the track when he threatened to bend jockey Ron Turcotte into the shape of a pretzel—and he was losing on this day. So I told him about the impending Gold Cup and suggested, "After the races, go up to the press box and bet everything you can on me. I'm a mortal lock."

Angelo located Frank Tours and bet his last $50. When I jogged to victory by an eighth of a mile, Angelo was at the finish line to greet me with a bear hug. Afterward, Charlie told me, "You've made a friend for life. If you ever need anybody roughed up, or just intimidated a little, you know whom to call."

I had my title and honor to defend in 1977. Socolof had opened the Gold Cup to all racetrack and backstretch employees, and I was running six or seven miles a day to get in shape. On the appointed day, a field of twenty runners assembled on the Saratoga track after the final horse race had been run, and the announcer remained in his stand to call the event. I laid off the early pace, moved to the lead on the backstretch, and fought off a groom's challenge at the eighth pole. Running down the storied Saratoga homestretch, where Upset beat Man O'War, where Jim Dandy scored over Gallant Fox at 100 to 1, I heard the people in the stands applauding and the public-address system intoning, "As they come to the wire, it's Andy Beyer by ten lengths!" That was the zenith of my virtually nonexistent career as an athlete. And it was to be one of the few bright spots of my final days in Saratoga.

On Tuesday and Wednesday, I bet twelve races, pushed $3500 through the mutuel windows, and lost everything. There had been some playable winners on these days, but I was thinking that 3-to-1 shots were not going to do me any good now. I recognized in my few dispassionate moments that I was committing the most amateurish of errors—escalating my wagers in an attempt to get even—but I still could not restrain myself from betting wildly on longshots and exactas. I hated the idea of conceding defeat in Saratoga.

On Thursday the twenty-fifth, I saw one last hope. I made a trip to the bank that morning, left a remainder of $16.83 in my local account, and went to the track to take a final do-or-die shot on the seventh-race exacta.

7 **SARATOGA** 6 FURLONGS SARATOGA (Start / Finish)

6 FURLONGS. (1.08) ALLOWANCE. Purse $11,000. 3-year-olds and upward which have never won a race other than maiden, claiming or starter. Weights, 3-year-olds, 117 lbs. Older, 122 lbs. Non-winners of a race other than claiming since August 1, allowed 3 lbs. Of such a race since July 15, 5 lbs

Ess 'n Eff — Dk. b. or br. c. 3, by Iron Ruler—Susie Q Rice, by Traffic Judge
Own.—Singer J B · Br.—Murrell J (Fla) · Tr.—Kelley Walter A · **107⁵**

	St.	1st	2nd	3rd	Amt.
1977	2	1	0	0	$4,800
1976	3	M	0	0	

Date/Race	Cond.	Dist.	Fractions	Class	Running line	Jockey	Wt	Odds	Speed/Var.	Finishers	Comment	Field
5Aug77- 9Sar	fst	6f	:22⅕ :45⅗ 1:10⅗	3↑ Md 35000	5 1 1½ 1½ 12 1¾	Cordero A 85	117	9.80	87-11	Ess 'n Eff 117¾ Coolidge 1152¼ Decision Revoked 117no	Driving	10
14Jly77- 9Bel	fst	6f	:22⅖ :46 1:11⅖	3↑ Md 35000	3 2 32½ 67½ 813 918	Montoya D	115	125.70	67-12	Tiresome 1152 Always Dancing115noDuncanPhyfe113¾	Done early	10
13Oct76- 9Bel	fst	6½f	:23 :46⅗ 1:17⅕	Md 35000	8 4 63¾ 62¾ 56 515	Ruane J	122	38.40	75-16	Metaphor 1224JungleMission122hdDewanAndOnly1226	No mishap	11
6Oct76- 3Bel	fst	6f	:22⅕ :45⅗ 1:10⅖	Md Sp Wt	4 8 1112 1111 913 919	Ruane J	122	48.30	71-08	Winaben 122¾ Pay the Toll 122¾ Caribert 1224½	Outrun	11
6Sep76- 1Bel	fst	6f	:23 :46⅘ 1:11⅕	Md Sp Wt	7 3 41½ 44¼ 66½ 720	Perrotta M	122	39.70	66-14	Upper Nile 1224 Corruptor 1227 Judge Mauck 1221	Tired	9

LATEST WORKOUTS Aug 22 Sar 3f fst :36 h Aug 12 Sar 5f fst 1:01 h Aug 3 Sar 3f fst :36 b Jly 28 Bel 6f fst 1:13⅖ h

Family Fight — Ch. g. 3, by Jim J—Stepmother, by Rough'n Tumble
Own.—Fourth Estate Stable · Br.—Augustus Peggy (Va) · Tr.—DiMauro Stephen · **112**

	St.	1st	2nd	3rd	Amt.
1976	3	1	0	0	$5,940

Date/Race	Cond.	Dist.	Fractions	Class	Running line	Jockey	Wt	Odds	Speed/Var.	Finishers	Comment	Field
28Aug76- 5Sar	gd	6f	:22⅘ :46⅗ 1:11⅖	Md Sp Wt	5 1 2hd 1hd 11 1¾	Velasquez J 76	122	12.70	83-12	Family Fight 122¾ Catalan 122hd Johnsquillo 1221½	Driving	7
21Aug76- 9Sar	fst	6f	:22⅗ :45⅘ 1:11⅕	Md Sp Wt	5 4 75½ 78½ 79 46	Velasquez J 66	122	26.20	78-12	FirstPretense1223½Johnsquillo122hdDrumsandFife1222½	Late gain	9
7Aug76- 5Sar	sly	6f	:22⅗ :46⅖ 1:12⅕	Md Sp Wt	4 7 57 815 918 922	Velez R I	122	15.40	57-17	Winterlock 1223 Drums and Fife 1229 Gun Blast 115hd	Tired	10

LATEST WORKOUTS Aug 24 Sar 3f fst :36⅕ h Aug 22 Sar 3f fst :38 b Aug 19 Sar 4f fst :48⅗ h Aug 14 Sar 5f fst 1:02⅕ h

Lancer's Pride — Dk. b. or br. c. 3, by Protanto—Dorian League, by Greek Ship
Own.—Whitmore Mrs H P · Br.—Reynolds Monica (Pa) · Tr.—Freeman Willard C · **112**

	St.	1st	2nd	3rd	Amt.
1976	9	1	3	2	$17,974

Date/Race	Cond.	Dist.	Fractions	Class	Running line	Jockey	Wt	Odds	Speed/Var.	Finishers	Comment	Field
23Dec76- 5Aqu	fst	170 ⊡	:46⅘ 1:12 1:43⅘	Allowance	5 6 58 43½ 33 23½	Velasquez J	b 117	5.00	— —	BigJohnTylor1193½Lncer'sPride117noMkeAmends117½	Up for 2nd	9
20Nov76- 9Aqu	fst	1	:47⅕ 1:12⅖ 1:37⅘	Allowance	6 6 62¼ 21 21½ 22	Velasquez J 96	b 115	*1.30	75-17	Michael'sChrge1222Lncer'sPride115nkJungleMission1152	Gamely	9
3Nov76- 8Key	fst	7f	:22⅗ :45⅖ 1:24	Ⓢ Pa. Futurity	1 6 57½ 55½ 44 32¼	Imparato J	b 122	*1.00	87-22	Pay the Toll 122hd Ready Axe 1162¼ Lancer's Pride 1222	Rallied	7
3Nov76-Run in two divisions 6th & 8th races.												
5Oct76- 7Bel	fst	7f	:22⅗ :45⅘ 1:22	Allowance	5 5 75 53½ 37 39½	Velasquez J 87	b 117	7.30	82-13	SeattleSlew1223½CruiseOnIn11s Lancer'sPride1172¼	Lacked rally	8
25Sep76- 6Bel	fst	7f	:23⅖ :46⅗ 1:23⅖	Allowance	7 5 43 32½ 42½ 21¼	Velasquez J	b 117	9.20	84-12	Star Spangled 1171¼ Lancer's Pride 117¾ Catalan 122¾	Gamely	9
16Sep76- 7Bel	fst	6f	:22⅗ :45⅕ 1:09⅖	Allowance	2 7 84¾ 75 67 57¾	Velasquez J	b 115	9.40	87-11	Ruthie'sNtive1153½Albie'sTruckStop1151¾SuprJoy1181¼	No threat	8
3Sep76- 8Bel	fst	6f	:23⅕ :47 1:11⅗	Allowance	4 3 75¼ 64½ 54¼ 41	Velasquez J	b 115	7.50	83-18	Sanhedrin 115½ ⒹRuthie's Native 115nk Chairmanship119nk	Wide	7
25Aug76- 7Sar	fst	6f	:22⅕ :45⅗ 1:11⅕	Allowance	1 6 615 611 610 46	Velasquez J	b 115	13.20	78-17	FortheMoment117hdStarSpngled117noWinterlock1196	Slow early	6
11Jun76- 4Bel	fst	5½f	:23⅘ :48 1:06⅘	Md 45000	2 3 2hd 3nk 2½ 1no	Velasquez J	122	*2.60	81-24	Lncer'sPride122noPrizeNtive118noChooseYourWpon1224¼	Driving	9

LATEST WORKOUTS Aug 22 Sar 5f fst 1:01⅕ hg Aug 17 Sar 6f fst 1:15⅗ b Aug 13 Sar 6f fst 1:14⅖ b Aug 9 Sar 6f fst 1:15⅗ b

Dr. Patches — Ch. g. 3, by Dr Fager—Expectancy, by Intentionally
Own.—Tartan Stable — Br.—Tartan Farms (Fla) — Tr.—Nerud John A — 112
St. 1st 2nd 3rd Amt. — 1977 7 1 3 0 $17,551 — 1976 0 M 0 0

27Jun77- 8Bel fst 1 :45⅘ 1:10⅕ 1:35⅕ Saranac 8 5 31½ 3nk 2hd 42 Vasquez J [104] 114 9.60 90-17 Bailjumper 1141¼ Lynn Davis 114¾ Gift of Kings 114no Weakened 9
20Jun77- 6Bel fst 6f :22⅘ :46⅖ 1:10⅕ 3↑Allowance 8 4 2½ 21 2hd 2no Vasquez J [116] 111 *1.10e 91-18 Doctor'sOrders114noDr.Ptchs1112½PumpkinMoonshin1144¾ Sharp 11
3Jun77- 7Bel fst 6f :22⅘ :46 1:10⅕ 3↑Allowance 7 3 32 32½ 32½ 2nk Vasquez J [108] 112 *1.40 91-20 Intercontinnt114nkDr.Ptchs1122PrfrrdPosition1111¾ Finished well 7
19May77- 6Aqu sly 1 :46⅕ 1:10⅗ 1:36⅖ Allowance 6 2 2½ 25 47½ 48 Venezia M 115 7.50 76-12 Leading Scorer 1102½ Lynn Davis 122hd JohnnyD.1155½ Weakened 8
2May77- 6Aqu fst 6f :22⅗ :45⅘ 1:10⅖ 3↑Allowance 1 5 43 43 52½ 52 Vasquez J 112 *2.00e 89-15 Solly 114hd Bartender's Pride 104¾ Hostile Planet 119hd Tired 7
23Apr77- 4Aqu fst 6f ⊡:22⅖ :45⅘ 1:10⅕ 3↑Md Sp Wt 10 2 33 2hd 1hd 12¾ Vasquez J 112 *.90 98-05 Dr. Patches 1122¾ Leading Scorer 1077¼ Sun Flame 113hd Driving 12
11Apr77- 4Aqu fst 6f ⊡:22⅖ :46 1:11⅕ 3↑Md Sp Wt 8 3 1hd 21½ 22½ 23 Vasquez J 112 5.50 90-13 Spirit Level 1123 Dr. Patches 1121 First Gang 1125 Gamely 11
LATEST WORKOUTS Aug 20 Sar 3f fst :37 b — Aug 14 Sar 4f fst :48⅕ h — Aug 9 Sar 4f fst :50 b — Aug 3 Sar 4f fst :48⅗ b

Peak Top — Dk. b. or br. g. 3, by Bold Hour—Teton Song, by Tudor Minstrel
Own.—Kissam L T — Br.—Harbourton Stud Inc (Ky) — Tr.—Dotter Robert L — 112
Turf Record: St. 1st 2nd 3rd — 3 0 1 0
St. 1st 2nd 3rd Amt. — 1977 6 0 2 0 $4,860 — 1976 9 1 1 3 $10,460

4Aug77- 7Sar fm 1⅟₁₆ Ⓣ:46⅕ 1:10⅖ 1:41⅖ 3↑Allowance 1 1 21½ 21½ 21½ 87¼ Velasquez J 112 4.70 83-10 Owahu 1171¼ Golden Reserve 1122¾ Impressive Blend 105½ Tired 12
27Jly77- 7Bel fm 1⅟₁₆ Ⓣ:47⅖ 1:11⅗ 1:42⅖ 3↑Allowance 6 3 11 2hd 1hd 2nk Velasquez J 113 10.70 88-12 Drums and Fife 112nk Peak Top 113¾ Rhino 115½ Sharp 8
9Jly77- 7Bel fm 1⅟₁₆ Ⓣ:46 1:10 1:41⅖ 3↑Allowance 1 2 2hd 1hd 46 79¾ Velasquez J 113 10.30 83-07 True Colors 115¾ Bold Giant 1196 Best Hour 112nk Tried 10
25Jun77- 7Mth fst 6f :21⅖ :44⅕ 1:10 3↑Allowance 6 1 21 2½ 1hd 2hd Brumfield D b 114 3.70 90-18 Roman Rocket 118hd Peak Top114nkCox'sRidge1134½ Just missed 7
20Jun77- 6Bel fst 6f :22⅘ :46⅖ 1:10⅕ 3↑Allowance 6 7 41½ 42½ 46 67½ Hernandez R [98] 111 4.90 83-18 Doctor'sOrders114noDr.Ptches1112½PumpkinMoonshin1144¾ Tired 11
3Jun77- 7Bel fst 6f :22⅘ :46 1:10⅕ 3↑Allowance 2 4 2hd 2hd 21½ 44 Hernandez R [98] 111 7.20 87-20 Intercontinent 114nkDr.Patches1122PreferredPosition1111¾ Tired 7
3Nov76- 3Aqu fst 6f :22⅕ :45⅕ 1:11⅖ Clm 45000 8 1 3nk 12 13 31 Vasquez J b 117 9.80 85-15 Jungle Mission 122no Metaphor 1151 Peak Top 1172¼ Weakened 9
14Oct76- 6Bel fst 6½f :23⅖ :46⅗ 1:16⅗ Allowance 5 2 1½ 3nk 911 1017 Vargas J L b 117 4.00e 76-15 Proud Arion 122½ Pruneplum 1175 Upper Nile 1191 Stopped 10
10Sep76- 5Bel sly 6f :22⅗ :45⅘ 1:11 Clm c-45000 1 3 21 2½ 21 64¼ Day P b 117 *1.50 83-16 HawaiianWays117hdImpressiveBlend1151¼JollyQuill1181 Gave way 9
28Aug76- 8Sar fst 6½f :22⅖ :45⅖ 1:16⅕ Hopeful 8 2 72½ 72 54¼ 1016 Venezia M 122 56.00 78-12 Banquet Table 1221 Turn of Coin 1226 P. R. Man 122no Tired 13
LATEST WORKOUTS Aug 22 Sar 4f fst :49 h — Aug 18 Sar 4f fst :47⅖ h — Jly 25 Bel 4f fst :47 h — Jly 16 Bel 7f fst 1:27⅗ b

The Prince's Pants — Dk. b. or br. c. 4, by Cornish Prince—Grey Slacks, by Native Dancer
Own.—Hobeau Farm — Br.—Hobeau Farm Inc (Fla) — Tr.—Jerkens H Allen — 122
St. 1st 2nd 3rd Amt. — 1977 1 1 0 0 $6,000 — 1976 3 M 0 1 $1,200

11Aug77- 1Sar sly 6f :22 :44⅘ 1:10 3↑Md Sp Wt 1 8 12½ 13 14 18¼ Smith R C [100] 122 *2.50 90-12 ThePrince'sPnts1228¼ComAwyWithM1171½BowlGm1171½ Handily 8
10Dec76- 5Aqu fst 6f ⊡:22⅕ :45⅘ 1:11⅘ 3↑Md Sp Wt 8 5 21 2hd 2½ 32¼ Smith R C [93] 120 4.90 — — Fresh Native 120nkFranglais1202ThePrince'sPants1201 Weakened 12
1Dec76- 4Aqu fst 6f :22⅖ :45⅖ 1:10⅗ 3↑Md Sp Wt 6 4 2½ 2hd 2hd 52¼ Ruane J [92] 120 3.10e 88-16 Private Practice 120nk Fresh Native 1202 Distant Sail 120no Tired 7
12Aug76- 3Sar fst 6f :22⅖ :45⅖ 1:11⅕ 3↑Md Sp Wt 6 7 32½ 45½ 66 69 Smith R C 117 3.80 75-15 Teton Range1171¼TheseDays117hdLordDictator1176 Broke slowly 7
LATEST WORKOUTS Aug 5 Sar 5f fst 1:01 h — Jly 31 Sar 4f fst :52 b — Jly 28 Bel tr.t 4f fst :48⅗ h — Jly 24 Bel 4f fst :52⅖ b

Jungle Jim — Dk. b. or br. g. 3, by Jim J—Native Tempo, by Restless Native
Own.—Marydel Farm — Br.—Marydel Farm (Md) — Tr.—Odom George P — 114
St. 1st 2nd 3rd Amt. — 1977 5 1 2 0 $11,880 — 1976 0 M 0 0

9Aug77- 6Sar fst 7f :22⅘ :45⅖ 1:22⅘ 3↑Allowance 4 4 3½ 31½ 44½ 46¾ Santiago A [89] 117 3.40 84-17 Cox's Ridge 112nk Bywayofchicago 1176 Winaben 112½ Tired 7
1Aug77- 5Sar fst 6f :22⅗ :46 1:11⅖ 3↑Allowance 5 1 21 21½ 21½ 2nk Santiago A [86] 117 3.70 83-20 May I Rule 112nk Jungle Jim 1172¾ Happy Dorimar 1179¾ Sharp 6
18Jly77- 2Bel fst 6f :22⅖ :46 1:10⅘ Md Sp Wt 10 7 31½ 1hd 15 16 Santiago A [88] 115 *2.30 88-11 Jungle Jim 1156 Sharpstone 1152¾ Rixdal Kenny1152½ Ridden out 10
4Jly77- 9Bel fst 6f :23⅕ :46⅕ 1:10⅖ 3↑Md Sp Wt 3 6 41½ 33 37 46 Santiago A b 115 5.90 84-16 Topsider 1155¾ Iron Table 115nk Medano 115no Lacked rally 12
20Jun77- 3Bel fst 6f :22⅗ :46⅘ 1:11 3↑Md Sp Wt 4 8 99½ 52¾ 35 25½ Maple E b 114 24.70 81-18 Broadway Forli 1145½ Jungle Jim 114no Medano 1143¾ Up for 2nd 12
LATEST WORKOUTS Aug 23 Sar 4f fst :47⅖ h — Aug 19 Sar 5f fst 1:01⅕ h — Aug 16 Sar 4f fst :48⅘ b — Aug 8 Sar 3f my :36 h

Iroquois Tribe — B. c. 4, by Chieftain—Weird, by Tulyar
Own.—Veale T II — Br.—Lin-Drake Farm Inc (Fla) — Tr.—Kennedy Wilma P — 117
Turf Record: St. 1st 2nd 3rd — 1 0 0 0
St. 1st 2nd 3rd Amt. — 1977 6 0 1 0 $3,300 — 1976 9 1 1 2 $10,800

17Aug77- 6Sar fst 7f :22⅕ :44⅘ 1:22⅘ 3↑Allowance 7 7 69 75½ 45½ 48 Martens G [81] 117 8.20 83-15 Bywayofchicago 1142¼ Winaben 1145¼ Cyano 112½ Rallied 7
10Aug77- 6Sar fm 1⅟₁₆ Ⓣ:47⅘ 1:12 1:42⅘ 3↑Allowance 6 6 75 75¼ 68½ 610 Cauthen S 117 3.60 73-10 Winter Walk 1173¼ Sharpstone 1121¾ Hacer Furor 1172 Outrun 7
2Aug77- 6Sar fst 7f :23⅖ :46⅖ 1:24⅕ 3↑Allowance 3 5 53 41½ 23 21½ Vasquez J [87] 117 6.40 82-16 Watching N Wait1121½IroquoisTribe117¾WinterWalk1172 Gamely 6
21Jly77- 4Bel fst 7f :23⅕ :46⅖ 1:22⅗ 3↑Clm 45000 1 6 51¾ 63¾ 67½ 56¾ Martens G 113 38.40 82-15 Littlest Lad 117nk Kool As Ice 1062 Port Authority 1131½ Outrun 6
18May77- 7Aqu fst 1 :45⅘ 1:11 1:36⅕ Clm 50000 2 6 713 712 715 718 Velasquez J 117 25.10 67-22 Jackson Square 1174 ReallyCooking1173½ToTheTune1172¾ Outrun 7
9May77- 7Aqu my 7f :23⅘ :47⅘ 1:25⅗ 3↑Allowance 2 8 85¼ 76½ 65¼ 56¾ Martens G 119 21.20 66-20 Bold Needle 1191¾ Hostile Planet 1191¾ Si SiYou1193¼ Slow start 8
31Aug76- 7Bel fst 6f :23 :46⅗ 1:11⅕ 3↑Allowance 3 9 97 98¾ 912 916 Martens G 118 18.60 70-22 Caspar Milquetoast 1131¾ Bold Needle 113¾ Balancer117¾ Trailed 9
20Aug76- 1Sar fst 6f :22⅖ :45⅘ 1:10⅘ 3↑Md Sp Wt 2 8 57 43 2½ 1no Martens G 117 4.40 86-07 Iroquois Tribe 117no Growler 1175 Lord Dictator 117no Driving 8
3Aug76- 6Sar fst 6f :22⅕ :45⅗ 1:10⅕ 3↑Md Sp Wt 5 7 57½ 46 49 313 Martens G 117 5.00 76-15 Big Z. 1177 Teton Range 1175½ Iroquois Tribe 1173 Wide 8
25Jly76- 5Aqu fst 6f :23⅖ :47⅗ 1:12 3↑Md Sp Wt 2 4 66¼ 44 31½ 2nk Martens G 116 19.80 83-24 Master Jorge 116nk Iroquois Tribe116nkSilentKingdom1221 Sharp 9
LATEST WORKOUTS Jly 17 Bel 6f fst 1:13⅗ h — Jly 15 Bel 3f fst :36⅕ h — Jly 9 Bel 7f fst 1:27 b — Jly 3 Bel 4f fst :47⅗ h

Always Dancing — B. c. 3, by Duck Dance—Always Laughing, by Hilarious
Own.—Whittaker Theodora L — Br.—Hobeau Farm Inc (Fla) — Tr.—Barrera Albert S — 112
St. 1st 2nd 3rd Amt. — 1977 6 2 2 0 $14,340 — 1976 1 M 0 0

11Aug77- 2Sar sly 6f :22⅕ :45⅖ 1:10⅗ Clm c-25000 4 5 2hd 2hd 11½ 13¼ Velasquez J [91] b 119 4.60 87-12 Always Dancing 1193¼ Mini Styls 117½Polemicist1172½ Ridden out 7
29Jly77- 9Bel fst 6f :22⅕ :46 1:11⅗ 3↑Md 25000 9 6 41½ 2hd 1½ 1¾ Vasquez J [82] b 115 *3.20 85-15 AlwaysDancing115¾RoguishManner1152LordCardinl122no Driving 12
14Jly77- 9Bel fst 6f :22⅖ :46 1:11⅖ 3↑Md 35000 7 4 43 22½ 22½ 22 Velez R I [79] 115 9.80 83-12 Tiresome 1152 Always Dancing 115no Duncan Phyfe 113¾ Gamely 10
29Jun77- 2Mth fst 6f :21⅘ :45 1:09⅘ 3↑Md Sp Wt 7 3 23 22½ 25 211 Solomone M b 115 2.20 80-13 Noble Treat11511AlwaysDancing1153¾Stratosphere1153 No match 9
17Jun77- 5Bel fst 6f :22⅗ :46 1:12⅖ 3↑Md 35000 1 1 11½ 15 14 41¾ Turcotte R b 114 19.00 78-22 First Gang 1091¼ Stonecliff 114½ SunFlame114no Jumped Shadow 11
9Jun77- 9Bel sly 6f :22⅖ :46⅗ 1:13⅕ 3↑Md 25000 7 9 811 812 76¼ 65¼ Velez R I 114 12.30 71-23 More Ego 1141¼ Lofting 1132 All For Love 109no No factor 12
13Dec76- 9Aqu fst 6f ⊡:23⅗ :48⅘ 1:15⅗ Md 16000 9 4 51¾ 65¾ 89½ 65¾ Cauthen S 122 8.10 -- — Dr. Joseph 122no Chicago Pro 1222DancingWarrior1152¾ Checked 11
LATEST WORKOUTS Aug 9 Bel tr.t 4f fst :50⅘ h — Jly 28 Bel tr.t 3f fst :37⅖ b — Jly 22 Bel tr.t 5f fst 1:02⅗ b — Jly 11 Bel tr.t 4f fst :49 b

Dr. Patches looked unbeatable. He had run brilliantly in six-furlong races at Belmont Park in June, and then tried to go a mile in the Saranac Stakes, which proved to be a bit beyond his capabilities. Now, after a short rest, he was back at six furlongs against allowance company.

I did not like the horse with the second-best figure in the field. The Prince's Pants had run very fast to win his most recent start by eight lengths. But he had been the only front-runner in a race that was run over a sloppy, speed-favoring strip, and horses often earn unusually large figures when they can take the early lead without a challenge.

The Prince's Pants was going to have a much more difficult chore getting to the front of this tough field.

Peak Top had much better credentials. His two sprints at Belmont in June had been good, as was his subsequent six-furlong race at Monmouth. He had made his last three starts in mile-and-one-sixteenth events on the turf, conditions which he did not seem to favor, but he had shown enough speed to indicate that he was still in form.

I thought the Dr. Patches–Peak Top exacta was a cinch. But I did not know if my thoughts were valid. When I am winning, as I was at Pimlico, my judgment is refined; I can evaluate almost every situation coolly and objectively. But my handicapping becomes distorted when I am losing and start looking desperately for bets that will bail me out. I am like a man in the desert who has seen so many mirages that he cannot be sure of himself when he stumbles onto a real waterhole. I prayed that Dr. Patches and Peak Top were not a mirage. When I saw on the television monitor that the exacta was worth $24, I bet $700 on the combination—enough to make me a winner for the whole Saratoga season.

SEVENTH RACE
Saratoga
AUGUST 25, 1977

6 FURLONGS. (1.08) ALLOWANCE. Purse $11,000. 3-year-olds and upward which have never won a race other than maiden, claiming or starter. Weights, 3-year-olds, 117 lbs. Older, 122 lbs. Non-winners of a race other than claiming since August 1, allowed 3 lbs. Of such a race since July 15, 5 lbs

Value of race $11,000, value to winner $6,600, second $2,420, third $1,320, fourth $660. Mutuel pool $122,640, OTB pool $106,761. Exacta Pool $134,603. OTB Exacta Pool $233,212.

Last Raced	Horse	Eqt.A.Wt PP St	¼	½	Str	Fin	Jockey	Odds $1
4Aug77 7Sar8	Peak Top	3 112 5 2	6⁴	4½	1hd	12¼	Velasquez J	8.60
9Aug77 6Sar4	Jungle Jim	b 3 114 7 6	51½	3²	2¹	24¾	Santiago A	7.70
17Aug77 6Sar4	Iroquois Tribe	4 117 8 9	8¹	71½	6²	3nk	Martens G	25.20
27Jun77 8Bel4	Dr. Patches	3 112 4 3	4½	5¹	51½	41¾	Vasquez J	1.20
11Aug77 1Sar1	The Prince's Pants	4 122 6 4	1hd	21½	3½	51¾	Smith R C	3.00
11Aug77 2Sar1	Always Dancing	b 3 112 9 1	3¹	1hd	4¹	6nk	Cordero A Jr	11.20
23Dec76 5Aqu2	Lancer's Pride	b 3 114 3 8	9	81½	8³	71¾	Turcotte R	15.90
5Aug77 9Sar1	Ess 'n Eff	3 107 1 5	2½	6²	7¹	82¼	Samyn J L5	13.10
28Aug76 5Sar1	Family Fight	3 113 2 7	7hd	9	9	9	Cruguet J	21.40

OFF AT 4:47 1/2, EDT. Start good, Won handily. Time, :22, :45⅕, 1:10⅕ Track fast.

$2 Mutuel Prices:

5-(E)-PEAK TOP	19.20	8.40	6.20
7-(H)-JUNGLE JIM		8.80	5.00
8-(I)-IROQUOIS TRIBE			10.60

$2 EXACTA 5-7 PAID $112.40.

dk b or br. g, by Bold Hour—Teton Song, by Tudor Minstrel. Trainer Dotter Robert L. Bred by Harbourton Stud Inc (Ky).

PEAK TOP, taken up racing into the turn, circled horses entering the stretch, brushed lightly with JUNGLE JIM and drew away under good handling. JUNGLE JIM loomed boldly from the outside leaving the turn, brushed with PEAK TOP near midstretch and was no match for that rival. IROQUOIS TRIBE passed tired horses. DR. PATCHED tired. THE PRINCE'S PANTS and ALWAYS DANCING were used up vying for the lead. ESS 'N NEFF had brief speed.

Owners— 1, Kissam L T; 2, Marydel Farm; 3, Veale T II; 4, Tartan Stable; 5, Hobeau Farm; 6, Whittaker Theodora L; 7, Whitmore Mrs H P; 8, Singer J B; 9, Fourth Estate Stable.

Trainers— 1, Dotter Robert L; 2, Odom George P; 3, Kennedy Wilma P; 4, Nerud John A; 5, Jerkens H Allen; 6, Barrera Albert S; 7, Freeman Willard C; 8, Kelley Walter A; 9, DiMauro Stephen.

Overweight: Lancer's Pride 2 pounds; Family Fight 1.

Scratched—Happy Dorimar (9Aug77 6Sar6); Posture (24Aug77 6Sar5).

Peak Top ran the good race I expected of him, but Dr. Patches did not. He tried to rally up the rail, was blocked briefly, but did not accelerate much when he was clear. What had happened? As I despondently looked over the past performance again, I noticed that Dr. Patches had not had a single good workout since his last start on June 27. His best morning effort was a nondescript half-mile in 48⅕ seconds, suggesting that trainer Johnny Nerud might have viewed this race as a mere prep for his real objective at Belmont in the fall. If I had been razor-sharp, I might have reached this conclusion before the race and bet Peak Top to win. But I was seeing only mirages now.

I was finished. I had just completed the most expensive race meeting of my life, losing $7952 in twenty-two days. But as I had my farewell dinner on Thursday night with Charlie, the Kid, and a few other friends, I did not feel the same sense of shame and embarrassment which had caused me to slip out of town quietly after a previous losing season. I had acquired genuine self-confidence during 1977, and I could view Saratoga as a temporary setback, rather than a disaster which shook the foundations of my existence. I was still a winning horseplayer.

But I was also a horseplayer who had many things to learn. I had to recognize when a race meeting was offering me little promise so that I could bail out early. I had to curb the destructive tendency to escalate my wagers when I was losing badly. And in future years I had to accord Saratoga the proper respect, instead of coming to the track cocky and complacent. After a $7952 loss, that would be easy.

5

Barrington Fair:
Parsley, Sage, Rosemary,
and Crime

Nestled in a valley surrounded by the Berkshire Mountains, the Barrington Fair is one of the most picturesque and quaint racetracks in America. Jockeys sun themselves on a patch of grass by the odds board. The stewards preside from a flower-bedecked open-air tower, so that fans can shout to them suggestions that a winner be disqualified. Horseplayers can watch the action from benches in the infield and then, between races, ride the Tilt-a-Whirl, buy some cotton candy, win a kewpie doll, or visit the Human Pretzel.

But I had not come to Great Barrington, Massachusetts, for either the charm or the autumn foliage. I had come on the advice of Charlie, who had told me over dinner on my last night in Saratoga, "If you want to recoup your losses, go to the Barrington Fair in September. Don't bother to do much handicapping. Just watch the odds board, and when the smart money shows in the last minute before post time, bet along with it. The boys up there don't miss. You'll have to take four to five and three to five a lot, but you can grind out a thousand dollars a day."

I was dubious, because I never believed much in "smart money" and never shared Charlie's conspiratorial view of the sport. But his suggestion appealed to me anyway. I had scrapped my original plan to go from Saratoga to Belmont Park; I had already contributed enough money to the New York State treasury. And after a year of big-league racing, I was feeling a bit nostalgic for the leaky-roof tracks which had provided me with my introduction to the game. So on September 11 I drove through the Berkshires to Stockbridge, Massachusetts, best known as the home of Norman Rockwell and

Alice's Restaurant, checked into the two-hundred-year-old Red Lion Inn, and then consulted with two horseplayers who were veterans of the Massachusetts fairs.

I had met Mark and Chick at Saratoga and had heard them rhapsodize about the delights of the Barrington Fair, the Marshfield Fair, the Northampton Fair, and Berkshire Downs. So I asked them, "Are these tracks really as corrupt as Charlie tells me?"

"You can't believe how much," Mark said. "A couple years ago there was a filly whose record was atrocious and who was 12 to 1 with four minutes to post time. Her odds went: 12–1, 6–1, 7–2, 4–5, 3–5. The place was going crazy. You couldn't get close to the windows. The horse who should have been the favorite took the lead but on the last turn he practically went to the outside fence. You can guess who came up the rail and won it."

"I saw a race even worse than that," Chick interjected. "A few years ago at Berkshire Downs there were two horses in the first race who had run against each other several times before and had always finished necks and noses apart. They were both about 8 to 5 a couple minutes before post time. Then in two flashes of the board, one of them was bet down to 1 to 9. He was on the lead when another horse started getting too close and looked like he might win. The jockey on this other horse stood up in the irons and went to the outside fence, but he was still outrunning the horse who was obviously supposed to win. So about five yards from the finish line, the jockey jumped off. And the 1-to-9 shot won."

Mark and Chick could tell these stories by the hour, and as incredible as they were, they did seem plausible, because the fairs offer opportunities for larceny which don't exist anywhere else. A trainer with a few old, infirm, rock-bottom thoroughbreds cannot find many tracks where he can win races, and the ones that do exist have such small wagering pools that betting coups are infeasible. But Barrington attracts large crowds which wager more than $500,000 a day, giving trainers a rare opportunity to cash a bet. For the jockeys, too, Barrington is special. Most of them are too old, too heavy, or too incompetent to compete successfully anywhere else. A jockey who gets to ride only a few hopeless longshots has few chances to misbehave. But when he comes to Barrington, he may be riding several contenders every afternoon and he will have many chances to make thievery profitable.

After I heard Mark and Chick tell their tales, my appetite was whetted. I spent the rest of the night studying back issues of the *Racing Form*, familiarizing myself with the jockeys and trainers, and learning the handicapping methods that would be relevant at Barrington. Contrary to the opinion of most horseplayers who disdain cheap races and consider them unbettable, I find them both entertaining and predictable. I made the first wager of my life on a $1500 claimer at Randall Park, and I spent my college years betting on similar animals at Lincoln Downs and Narragansett Park. I find such tracks relatively easy to beat, because they demand a mastery of fewer handicapping factors than a complex place like Saratoga. The track bias is always supremely important at a half-mile oval, because the hairpin turns and short straightaways doom stretch-runners and horses in outside post positions.

Class is also a very important factor in cheap races. Ironically, it is more important in the daily double at the Barrington Fair than in a stakes race at Saratoga. Even though a track may offer nothing but $1500 claiming events, there are many different classes running under that pricetag, and they are defined by the conditions of eligibility for the races. The chronically unsuccessful horses at Barrington would run in a $1500 claiming event limited to "nonwinners of a race in 1976–77." Better $1500 horses might be entered against "nonwinners of three races since November 15." A horse moving up from one level to the other would find himself as outclassed as a hobo at a fancy-dress ball.

On the first afternoon of Barrington's ten-day meeting, I was entranced by all the color of the racetrack and the fair, but I was even more entranced by an entrant in the Great Barrington Inaugural Purse, the featured allowance race with a lofty purse of $2200. Sister Rabbit had been running without much success at Rockingham Park, a major-league track. She was trained by P. Noel Hickey, who had been one of the sharpest trainers at Gulfstream Park. Now she was entered against some of the stars of the Massachusetts fair circuit, and appeared to hold a tremendous edge in class over them. Sister Rabbit was 5 to 2 throughout most of the wagering, and I waited by the mutuel windows to see what the smart money was going to do. Two minutes before post time, her odds dropped to 2 to 1. In the next flash she was 8 to 5. I bet $400 as the price dropped another notch to 3 to 2. When Sister Rabbit circled the field and won easily, I regretted that Charlie wasn't at the track so I could thank him for directing me to the source of such easy money.

The next day, to my delight, I saw that Hickey had entered another promising animal.

Ordinarily, I would have dismissed any horse dropping in class so sharply, but this was the Barrington Fair and normal rules did not apply. Von Rincon's dismal performance in his only start of the year was probably designed to prepare him for this coup. So I took my position by the mutuel windows and watched the board. Von Rincon was 2 to 1 until the avalanche began four minutes before post time. He dropped to 9 to 5, then 3 to 2, then even money, then 4 to 5. I fought my way to the $50 window and bet $700, and knew that I would not even need to root.

And I didn't. Von Rincon barely picked up his feet. After a quarter of a mile, he was so far behind the rest of the field that he probably couldn't even see the other horses. His jockey finally conceded defeat and pulled him up. I was baffled. As a rule I would have expected such a terrible performance from a horse who had previously won for $10,000 and now was entered with a $1500 pricetag. He had to be a virtual basket case. I was doubly annoyed because the winner of the race was a logical horse, one whom I would have bet if I had not been hypnotized by the blinking lights on the tote board. Where had that money come from?

Obviously, I was not the only person at Barrington who was playing the board-watching game. As I had lingered in the vicinity of the $50 window, observing the fluctuation of the odds, many other horseplayers were lingering with me. And when I made my move and started punching out $50 tickets, rubberneckers were looking over my shoulder to see what the smart money was doing. The board-watchers like me had started the stampede and then had been swept up in it. This same phenomenon would recur throughout the week. There were frequent dramatic plunges in horses' odds, but there was no consistent correlation between the nature of the betting action and the outcome of the race. Still, these last-minute betdowns were always eye-catching, and I could never decide whether to bet on the basis of logic or larceny. I habitually zigged when I should have zagged, as I did just a couple hours after the Von Rincon debacle.

7 BARRINGTON

ABOUT 5½ FURLONGS. (1.05⅗) CLAIMING. Purse $1,800. 3-year-olds and upward, non-winners of three races since September 22, 1976. Weight, 3-year-olds, 118 lbs. Older, 122 lbs. Non-wineers of two races since June 13, allowed 2 lbs. Two races since April 13, 4 lbs. Two races in 1977, 6 lbs. Claiming price $1,500.

Doggonit Honey
Own.—Smith David D
B. g. 6, by Doggonit—Honey Torch, by Wild Honey
$1,500 Br.—Moorer Betty (N.Mex)
Tr.—Smith David A
122
St. 1st 2nd 3rd Amt.
1977 8 2 1 2 $2,452
1976 16 0 3 2 $1,499

8Sep77- 6Nmpfst *6½f 1:25⅗ 3+Clm 1500 1 1 1³ 1³½ 1³½ 1⁴ Martinez A V b 122 3.50 82-21 DoggontHony122⁴JumpnJckFlsh122⁵Clown'sPrncss122²½ Handily 8
4Sep77- 3Nmpfst *6½f 1:26⅖ 3+Clm 1500 1 1 1hd 1hd 1hd 1½ Martinez A V b 122 2.80 77-20 Doggonit Honey 122½ Nashver's Boy 117⁵ Silver Call 122⁵ Driving 7
11Jun77- 2Poc fst 6f :23⅘ :48 1:14⅘ 3+Clm 1500 1 2 3½ 5³½ 7⁷½ 6¹¹ Martinez A V b 122 3.30 70-17 Linda's Ken 122¾ Yura Dancer 122³½Unbendable122²¾ Brief speed 10
4Jun77- 2Poc fst *6½f :22 :46⅗ 1:18⅘ 3+Clm 1500 2 1 3²½ 2²½ 2³½ 3⁴¾ Pasquarelli R 122 2.40 75-16 Star Rise 117¾ Ribots Flinger122¹DoggonitHoney122¾ Weakened 10
29May77- 5Poc fst 6f :22⅘ :47⅘ 1:16 3+Clm 1500 9 10 9⁸½ 6⁷ 5⁶ 3⁵½ Pasquarelli R b 118 6.10 70-22 Magic Fire 117¾ Oscar's Tower122¹½DoggonitHoney118²½ Rallied 10
22May77- 3Poc fst 6f :23⅕ :47⅖ 1:15⅖ 3+Clm 1500 6 8 6⁷ 5⁴¾ 3²½ 2½ Pasquarelli R b 118 3.90 77-15 ThreeBidders118½DoggonitHoney118¾Pokehtilhgo118¹ Full of run 10
10May77- 6Poc fst 5½f :23⅗ :47⅗ 1:08 3+Clm 1500 3 3 2¹½ 3³ 3⁴ 4⁵½ Pasquarelli R b 122 33.70 79-21 Freedom Threat 122³NotOldDan122¹DirectUnion117¹½ Weakened 10
3May77- 1Poc fst 5½f :24⅗ :50 1:11⅗ 3+Clm 1500 4 4 7⁵¾ 6⁷½ 7⁷½ 7⁷ Berberena J b 122 19.90 60-29 Santiam Moon 122nk Amdor 122¹ Law's Lou 117¹ Steadied 10

Mickey's Choice *
Own.—Williams Charlotte
B. m. 7, by Bolero—Mito Miss, by Mito
$1,500 Br.—Collins I J (Ky)
Tr.—Williams Charlotte
114
St. 1st 2nd 3rd Amt.
1977 3 0 0 1 $210
1976 12 1 0 1 $1,345

8Sep77- 2Nmpfst *5f :59⅗ 3+Clm 1500 3 8 8⁵¾ 7⁸½ 5⁴½ 3¹ Bennett D J b 115 23.40 75-21 HildyB.117¾WhiteyTheGhost122nkMickey'sChoic115⁵ Closed well 8
1Sep77- 1Nmpfst *5f :59⅕ 3+Clm 1500 2 7 7⁵½ 6⁷ 5⁵ 5⁴ Saul D b 117 25.60 74-24 Unbendable 120¹½ Hildy B. 119¾ Sadie's Idol 119¹½ Outrun 8
22Aug77- 2MF sly *5f 1:05⅗ 3+Clm 1500 4 8 8⁶¾ 8¹⁷ 8¹⁴ 8⁹¾ Parker R M b 114 21.70 76-19 Marvel 119¹ Lynn's Pleasure 114hd WhiteyTheGhost119¹½ Trailed 8
17Sep76- 5GBF sly *6½f 1:29⅗ 3+Clm 1500 4 7 7⁶½ 6⁹ 7¹⁴ 7²⁹ Polion J b 117 33.90 28-21 GoldMemories122¹²OurSecondHolme114²BrillintDrm122¾ Outrun 8
4Sep76- 4Nmpfst *5f :57 3+Clm 1500 7 8 8¹⁰ 8¹³ 8¹³ 8¹² Konan J M b 119 35.60 77-14 Nick Saponara 120⁷ Presto Pronto123¹½PeaceBullitin122¾ Outrun 8
24Aug76- 6MF fst *5f 1:03⅗ 3+Clm 1500 7 7 8⁹½ 7¹⁰ — — Konan J M b 119 15.40 — — Pirate Deb 117¹½ Bamette 120³ Westfield 118² Lost rider 8
28Jly76- 7GM fst 5f :23 :47⅘ 1:01⅕ 3+Clm 1500 10 7 9⁹½ 9¹¹ 7⁷ 7⁵¾ Keeler T J⁵ b 112 23.90 76-22 Bay Sallie 117hd Gal Chaser 122¹½ Mr. Cee Roe 122¹ Wide 10
15Jly76- 7GM fst 7½f :24⅕ :48⅘ 1:35⅗ 3+Clm 1500 3 6 6⁷ 5⁷½ 6¹¹ 7²⁰ Sullivan D b 118 26.40 59-21 Skipper's Son 122nk Quick Hanna117¹⁰OttoRussell122⁴ No factor 7

Festive Clarion *
Own.—Barnhart W
B. g. 6, by Moon Age—Whirling Duchess, by Whirling Home
$1,500 Br.—Bennett Bill (Can)
Tr.—Cesarini Joseph
115
Turf Record: St. 1st 2nd 3rd — 3 0 0 2
St. 1st 2nd 3rd Amt.
1977 14 2 3 2 $3,349
1975 2 0 0 0

7Sep77- 9Nmpfst *1⅛ 1:55⅘ 3+Clm 1500 2 4 4⁴ 5⁸ 5¹⁶ 8²⁴ Pasquarelli R b 122 2.30 44-20 Star Mike 118⁴ Seaman's Ghost 120¹⁵ Quillo King 118² Tired 8
3Sep77- 6Nmpfst *6½f 1:26⅕ 3+Clm 1500 7 2 5⁵½ 5¹¾ 4² 3nk Pasquarelli R b 122 *1.80 78-23 StayingPower120hdLuckyDr.Yeagle118nkFestiveClrion122¹ Rallied 8
1Sep77- 6Nmpfst *6½f 1:26⅗ 3+Clm 1500 3 4 3² 2¹½ 2³ 2hd Vergara F b 120 11.10 76-24 Bobby's Quest119hdFestiveClarion120noSummerNot120²½ Gamely 8
20Aug77- 5MF fst *6½f 1:28 3+Clm 1500 8 1 1¹ 1½ 2¹½ 3³½ Buisson R b 122 13.40 83-15 Hot Stove 122²½ Dr. Hecker 118¹ Festive Clarion 122⁵ Weakened 8
14Aug77- 7Commy 7f :23⅗ :48 1:29 3+Clm 1500 10 8 9⁹ 6¹⁴ 6⁷ 5⁸¾ Brosnan J A⁷ b 112 3.30 71-17 Snooky Bart 116hd Larry's Jeepful 122nk Count Loral114⁸ Evenly 10
2Aug77- 5Comfst 1 :48 1:14⅖ 1:43 3+Clm 1500 9 8 8⁹ 8⁷½ 6⁴½ 4¹ Keeler T J b 119 6.40 75-17 Summer Day S. 119¾ Cherrico 116hd Miss PenT.104hd Closed well 10
23Jly77- 7Comfst 7f :23⅗ :48 1:26⅘ 3+Clm 1500 4 3 3⁵ 3⁶ 3⁶½ 2⁶ Baker E J b 119 7.80 85-13 Perilous Path 111⁶ Festive Clarion 119hd Hugess 109¹½ Steadied 10
10Jly77- 2Comfst 6½f :23⅗ :47 1:21⅘ 3+Clm 2000 3 10 6¹⁵ 6¹⁵ 5¹⁸ 5⁶½ Vergara F b 122 10.80 76-15 Saturday Hero 115¹½ Miss Cachos 117² Vics Host 115½ Outrun 10

A. Happy Day *
Own.—George H A
Ch. g. 10, by Itsa Great Day—Lady Rippey, by Rippey
$1,500 Br.—Manfuso J A (Md)
Tr.—George Harry A
120
St. 1st 2nd 3rd Amt.
1977 7 2 1 0 $2,757
1976 14 1 3 1 $2,454

Entered 12Sep77- 7 GBF
1Aug77- 2Rkmfst 6f :22 :45 1:11⅘ 3+Clm 2500 8 10 10²⁸ 10³³ 10³⁴ 9²⁰ Ernst P b 122 118.20 65-20 Doc Moody 122⁵½ Klaxon 117³ Payne Quelu 119nk No factor 10
18Jun77-10Poc sly 1 :48⅗ 1:14⅕ 1:40⅗ 3+Clm 2500 9 9 9¹³ 9¹⁴ 9¹³ 9¹⁷ Masia A b 122 9.90 75-14 Domour 119½ Palpitador 119²½ Ask George 122¾ Outrup 9
11Jun77-10Poc fst 1 :47⅗ 1:13⅘ 1:41⅗ 3+Clm 2500 9 10 10¹⁵ 10¹⁴ 9¹³ 8¹³ Masia A b 122 3.70 73-17 Sevell 122¾ Whispers Quietly 117¹¾ StrangeDancer122⁵ No factor 10
28May77-10Poc fst 1 :48⅗ 1:14⅘ 1:43⅕ 3+Clm 2500 4 9 8⁹ 6⁹ 5⁴½ 2¾ Masia A 122 3.60 77-18 Old Nap 117¾ A.HappyDay122nkLooseConnection122½ Closed well 9
14May77-10Poc fst 1 :48⅘ 1:15⅘ 1:43⅘ 3+Clm 2000 7 10 9⁸¾ 7⁵ 4¹½ 1³ Masia A b 122 *2.40 75-19 A. Happy Day 122³ StrangeDancer122³½FortPoint119¹ Drew clear 10
6May77- 4Poc gd 6f :23⅕ :48⅕ 1:15 3+Clm 1500 1 2 5⁶ 4⁵ 3³ 1⁴½ Masia A b 118 2.50 80-21 A. Happy Day 118⁴½ Ravenous 118hdSwissBounce118½ Ridden out 9
28Apr77- 9Poc fst 6f :23 :47⅗ 1:14⅘ 3+Clm 2000 9 10 10⁹ 10⁸¾ 8⁹½ 5¹³ Masia A b 122 13.20 70-25 Happy Gal117⁶BosunsFalcon115⁴SnowSpy122² Passed tired ones 10
28Apr77-Disqualified from purse money.
12Nov76- 4Poc fst 1 :49⅗ 1:15⅗ 1:43⅕ 3+Clm 2000 4 8 7⁷¾ 3² 3½ 2hd Rivera F b 116 *1.70 78-21 Chionia Man 116hd A. Happy Day 116¹½ Asian Ways 122nk Gamely 10

Staying Power *
Own.—Delmolino D
Ch. g. 8, by Sensitivo—Byzantine Empress, by Royal Charger
$1,500 Br.—Torf Mrs L (Fla)
Tr.—Delmolino Dante
122
St. 1st 2nd 3rd Amt.
1977 7 2 0 0 $1,617
1976 18 1 4 2 $2,457

9Sep77- 7Nmpfst *6½f 1:26⅖ 3+Clm 1500 3 8 8¹¹ 7⁸½ 5⁶ 4⁴¾ Creedon R b 122 5.20 72-22 Blue Suede Shoes 120¾ Im Gonna Whirl 120¹½ Danta120²½ Rallied 8
3Sep77- 6Nmpfst *6½f 1:26⅕ 3+Clm 1500 2 4 7⁷½ 6²¾ 2½ 1hd Creedon R b 120 6.40 78-23 StayingPower120hdLuckyDr.Yegle118nkFestiveClrion122¹ Driving 8
23Aug77- 1MF fst *6½f 1:30⅕ 3+Clm 1500 3 3 5⁷ 4⁸ 4³ 1nk Creedon R b 118 15.90 76-19 Staying Power 118nk Li'l Urge 115¾ Otto Russell 118nk Driving 8
18Jun77- 2Poc sly 1 :48⅗ 1:15⅕ 1:41⅗ 3+Clm 1500 10 5 4²½ 4²½ 4⁷ 7¹³ Rivera F b 122 53.80 74-14 Ginny's Beau 122²½ Telli B. 119⁴½ Mr Brick Jr 122⁴¾ Tired 10
11Jun77- 2Poc fst 6f :23⅘ :48 1:14⅘ 3+Clm 1500 5 10 10⁷½ 8⁸ 8⁸½ 8¹² Rivera F b 122 23.80 69-17 Linda's Ken 122¾ Yura Dancer 122³½ Unbendable 122²¾ No factor 10
7Jun77- 1Poc gd *3½f :22⅘ :38⅘ 3+Clm 1500 9 9 9⁹ 8⁹½ 7⁹½ Olcott W b 122 263.10 82-09 I Must Believe 122¾ Make Ends Meet117³Mr.H.B.122nk No factor 9
2Jun77- 6Poc fst 5½f :23⅗ :47⅕ 1:07 3+Clm 1500 9 9 9¹² 9¹³ 9¹² 9¹⁷ Boudreau R b 122 141.80 72-19 Beauvan 122nk Jovial Indian 122⁶ Unbendable 122nk Trailed 9
23Oct76- 5Poc fst 1 :48⅘ 1:15⅘ 1:43⅗ 3+Clm 1500 4 8 7¹⁴ 8¹¹ 8¹³ 8¹⁵ Whitemen P b 119 7.10 60-24 FuryFlight117¹¾Nde'sFvor122¹¾Pennyporkpie116no Showed little 10

Summer Not
Own.—Henry Mary Sue
Ch. g. 9, by Summer Tan—Lets Go Modern, by High Bandit
$1,500 Br.—Wiedemann Mr-Mrs J A (Ky)
Tr.—Henry Mary Sue
120
St. 1st 2nd 3rd Amt.
1977 21 2 1 5 $2,898
1976 20 4 0 4 $4,257

Entered 10Sep77- 7 NMP, finished 3
3Sep77- 9Nmpfst *1⅛ 1:55⅗ 3+Clm 1500 6 1 2³½ 4⁷½ 7¹⁷ 8²⁴ Heim K b 120 7.50 45-23 Torullo 118¹½ Steep Slopes 117¹⁰ Golden Feathers 121¹½ Tired 8
1Sep77- 6Nmpfst *6½f 1:26⅗ 3+Clm 1500 1 1 1hd 3¹½ 3⁴ 3hd Konan J M b 120 9.60 76-24 Bobby'sQuest119hdFestiveClarion120noSummerNot120²½ Checked 8
23Aug77- 6MF fst *6½f 1:29⅗ 3+Clm 1500 8 2 6⁵½ 6¹¹ 5¹¹ 5¹² Heim K b 122 10.30 67-19 Yura Dancer 122²¾ Tupelo Honey 117¹½ GoodSusie117⁶ No factor 8
20Aug77- 8MF fst *6½f 1:29⅕ 3+Clm 1500 4 3 4³ 3⁴ 4⁶ 5⁶½ Heim K b 122 11.40 74-15 Small Miracle 117nk Tupelo Honey 117²½ Good Susie 117²½ Tired 8
12Aug77-10Comfst 7f :24⅕ :48⅘ 1:28⅘ 3+Clm 1500 7 2 3² 2¹½ 3⁶ 3⁵½ Heim K b 122 16.60 75-22 Quarter Flip 119½ Iron Bucket 113⁵ Summer Not122¹½ Weakened 9
31Jly77- 6Comfst 6½f :24 :47⅘ 1:21 3+Clm 1500 7 4 7⁹½ 7¹¹ 4⁷ 3⁶½ Ramos W b 119 24.70 77-16 Black Donnelly 119⁵ Ben Said 119¹½ Summer Not 119¹½ Late bid 8
22Jly77-10Comfst 7f :24⅖ :48 1:27⅖ 3+Clm 1500 7 7 9⁹¾ 9¹⁹ 8¹⁷ 7²¹ Adams J R b 119 32.30 67-14 Star Sky 112⁶ Black Donnelly 119¾ Summer Day S.122³ No factor 9
16Jly77- 4Comfst 6½f :24⅖ :48 1:20 3+Clm 1500 4 3 5⁴½ 6⁹½ 8¹⁸ 8¹⁷ Adams J R b 119 41.80 72-08 Larry's Jeepful 119⁶ Shirt Tail 122hd Val's Slipper110hd No factor 10
LATEST WORKOUTS Aug 9 Com 3f gd :39⅗ b Jly 15 Com 2f fst :25⅘ b

Kiowa Lou
Own.—Harvey D
Dk. b. or br. g. 4, by Pierlou—Kiowa Girl, by Blue Gay
$1,500 Br.—Ensio P (Can)
Tr.—Rice Sean
120
St. 1st 2nd 3rd Amt.
1977 16 2 0 0 $2,447
1976 6 1 0 1 $1,225

6Sep77- 6Nmpfst *6½f 1:26⅗ 3+Clm 1500 3 3 4⁶½ 3² 1² 1⁵ Long D b 118 16.90 76-26 Kiowa Lou 118⁵ Jet Romulus 120½ Wasp's Nest 118³ Driving 8
19Jun77- 5Poc fst 1 :48⅕ 1:14⅖ 1:42⅕ 3+Clm 1500 4 7 8¹³ 7¹⁰ 5⁷½ 4⁸½ Long D b 119 17.70 75-15 Battery 122⁷ Carriacou 119¾ Jack And Game 117½ Rallied 9
14Jun77- 8Poc fst 5½f :23⅗ :47⅗ 1:08⅗ 3+Clm 1500 7 10 10¹² 9¹⁴ 7⁹ 5²½ Long D b 122 50.70 79-20 Ama Squirt 122nk Charlie Phillips 122¹½ Clever Hare 122¾ Rallied 10
10Jun77- 5Poc fst 5½f :23⅗ :47⅗ 1:06⅘ 3+Clm 1500 10 9 10¹² 9¹¹ 6⁸½ 6¹⁰ Long D b 119 35.90 80-15 Ramentum 111⁸ Clown's Princess 116¹½ Ethera 120½ No factor 10
4Jun77- 8Poc fst 1 :49 1:14⅖ 1:41⅕ 3+Clm 1500 4 7 7⁴ 6⁵ 4⁵½ 5⁶¾ Greco R L b 122 35.40 81-16 Golden Feathers 117nk Oso Speedy 119¹½ Oondooroo 122⁵ Outrun 10
31May77- 9Poc fst 5½f :24⅕ :48⅗ 1:08⅗ 3+Clm 1500 3 10 10⁶¾ 10⁸¾ 8⁶ 4⁸½ Long D b 122 38.40 71-23 Brik 122³ Stone Gate 122³½ Ocnap 117² Rallied 10
19May77- 9Poc fst 5½f :23⅗ :47⅗ 1:07 3+Clm 1500 6 8 8⁷½ 8⁸½ 8⁷½ 5¹¹ Long D b 122 26.60 78-10 SirW.R.Javelin122²PrincessQueen117³Esther'sPet117¹½ No factor 9
14May77-10Poc fst 1 :48⅘ 1:15⅘ 1:43⅘ 3+Clm 1750 4 6 8⁸½ 8⁶½ 9⁸¾ 9¹⁶ Rowan D⁷ b 112 30.80 59-19 A. Happy Day 122³ Strange Dancer 122³½ Fort Point 119¹ Outrun 10

Palmdale *
Own.—Lynch Charlotte

B. g. 9, by Donut King—Desert, by Heliopolis
$1,500 **Br.—Winchell V H (Cal)**
Tr.—Bertone Nicholas

122

Turf Record					St.	1st	2nd	3rd	Amt.
St. 1st 2nd 3rd				1977	16	2	0	1	$2,530
2	0	0	0	1976	24	1	1	6	$3,824

6Sep77- 6Nmp	fst	*6½f			1:26⅗	3+ Clm 1500	8	6	67½	54½	46	59¼	Brown L W Jr^5	b	117	2.70	67–26	Kiowa Lou 118^5	Jet Romulus 120½	Wasp's Nest 118^3	No threat	8
3Sep77- 9Nmp	fst	*1$\frac{1}{16}$			1:55⅖	3+ Clm 1500	5	6	45½	36½	3^{10}	6^{17}	Brown L W Jr^5	b	117	11.40	52–23	Torullo 118$1\frac{1}{4}$	Steep Slopes 117^{10}	Golden Feathers 121$1\frac{1}{4}$	Tired	8
25Aug77- 8MF	fst	*6½f			1:29⅖	3+ Clm 1500	6	8	57½	52¼	12½	11½	Brown L W Jr^5	b	115	3.10	80–17	Palmdale 115$1\frac{1}{2}$	Coosaw Kookeroo 122$1\frac{1}{2}$	Port's Son 118^{hd}	Driving	8
19Aug77- 5MF	fst	*6½f			1:30⅕	3+ Clm 1500	1	1	3^4	44½	45½	35½	Brown L W Jr	b	120	*3.60	70–25	Yura Dancer 122^4	Mardie's Boy 120$1\frac{1}{2}$	Palmdale 120^{nk}	No mishap	8
3Aug77-10Rkm	fst	1$\frac{1}{16}$	:46⅗	1:11⅘	1:46⅘	3+ Clm 2500	8	4	4^{13}	7^{18}	10^{24}	10^{25}	Diaz O C	b	117	70.80	51–18	DownAmong 116$2\frac{1}{4}$	RoadToStardom 119^4	NobleEncounter 122^5	Tired	10
20Jly77-10Rkm	fst	1$\frac{1}{16}$	:47⅗	1:13	1:47⅕	3+ Clm 2500	1	3	31½	67½	7^{14}	7^{16}	Diaz O C	b	117	11.70	58–19	Woulda Coulda 114^5	Johnny Champ 117¾	Steelfa 115no	Tired	8
13Jly77- 2Rkm	fst	1$\frac{1}{16}$	:48⅖	1:14	1:49⅗	3+ Clm 2500	6	2	2½	2^{hd}	2^{hd}	64¾	Alvarado A	b	117	25.70	57–21	Great Wonder 117^1	Steelfa 114^{nk}	Old Penny 117¾	Weakened	10
6Jly77- 5Rkm	fst	6f	:22⅗	:46	1:11⅖	3+ Clm 2500	2	7	77½	7^{10}	7^{14}	5^{13}	Alvarado A	b	117	70.60	74–16	Ronnie's Dream 117^5	IsraeliJet 114^3	MoonAttraction 117^{hd}	No factor	7

As I analyzed this race, I looked at the chart of each horse's previous start and noted the conditions under which he had been entered. This was the information I gathered:

Doggonit Honey: Nonwinners of two races since September.
Mickey's Choice: Nonwinners of a race since November.
Festive Clarion: Nonwinners of three races in 1976–77.
A. Happy Day: Raced at Rockingham.
Staying Power: Nonwinners of three races since September.
Summer Not: Nonwinners of three races in 1977.
Kiowa Lou: Nonwinners of three races since September.
Palmdale: Nonwinners of three races since September.

The favorite, Doggonit Honey, was stepping up in class, from "nonwinners of two races since September" to "nonwinners of three races since September." Her ascent was as significant as that of a horse of a major track who moves from $4000 to $5000 company. Kiowa Lou, however, had just won by five lengths against "nonwinners of three races since September." For my friend Mark, who was fully attuned to the importance of class at Barrington, Kiowa Lou deserved an automatic bet because she had already won under today's conditions. I recognized the strength of her credentials, but I also watched the odds board. I saw that Doggonit Honey was getting strong support, opening at 9 to 5 and dropping to even money. A. Happy Day, the Rockingham shipper, was holding firm at 5 to 2. But Kiowa Lou's price was drifting up steadily to 8 to 1. There was no smart money on her. I passed the race.

SEVENTH RACE
GBF
SEPTEMBER 13, 1977

ABOUT 6 ½ FURLONGS. (1.21) CLAIMING. Purse $1,800. 3-year-olds and upward, non-winners of three races since September 22, 1976. Weight, 3-year-olds, 118 lbs. Older, 122 lbs. Non-wineers of two races since June 13, allowed 2 lbs. Two races since April 13, 4 lbs. Two races in 1977, 6 lbs. Claiming price $1,500.

Value of race $1,800, value to winner $1,000, second $335, third $185, fourth $80, balance of starters $50 each. Mutuel pool $52,551.

Last Raced	Horse	Eqt.A.Wt PP St	¼	½	Str	Fin	Jockey	Cl'g Pr	Odds $1
6Sep77 6Nmp1	Kiowa Lou	b 4 120 7 1	4¹	4¹	3¹½	1¹¹½	Long D	1500	8.30
1Aug77 2Rkm9	A. Happy Day	b 10 120 4 7	8	6¹½	2hd	2¹½	Rivera F	1500	2.90
10Sep77 7Nmp3	Summer Not	b 9 120 6 2	2¹½	1hd	1hd	3hd	Heim K	1500	22.40
9Sep77 7Nmp4	Staying Power	b 8 122 5 4	5¹½	5½	5³	42½	Creedon R	1500	6.60
8Sep77 6Nmp1	Doggonit Honey	b 6 122 1 3	1¹½	2³	4¹	52½	Martinez A V	1500	1.00
7Sep77 9Nmp8	Festive Clarion	b 6 115 3 5	6½	7½	6¹	6¾	Saul D	1500	6.30
6Sep77 6Nmp5	Palmdale	b 9 122 8 6	3²	3½	7¹½	72½	Brown L W Jr	1500	19.60
8Sep77 2Nmp3	Mickey's Choice	7 119 2 8	7¹	8	8	8	Bennett D J	1500	23.20

OFF AT 4:17 EDT. Start good, Won driving. Time, 1:32⅕ Track fast.

$2 Mutuel Prices:

7-KIOWA LOU	18.60	8.20	4.40
4-A. HAPPY DAY		4.60	3.80
6-SUMMER NOT			5.60

dk b or br. g, by Pierlou—Kiowa Girl, by Blue Gay. Trainer Rice Sean. Bred by Ensio P (Can).

KIOWA LOU reserved close up moved readily from between horses when roused leaving backstretch and outfinished A. HAPPY DAY. The latter settled after a half, was forced to come widest on final turn and could not stay with winner late. SUMMER NOT disputed pace and held gamely, STAYING POWER finished evenly. DOGGONIT HONEY tired from his early effort. PALMALE had some early foot.

Owners— 1, Harvey D; 2, George D J; 3, Henry Mary Sue; 4, Delmolino D; 5, Smith David D; 6, Barnhart W; 7, Lynch Charlotte; 8, Williams Charlotte.

Trainers— 1, Rice Sean; 2, George Donald J; 3, Henry Mary Sue; 4, Delmolino Dante; 5, Smith David A; 6, Cesarini Joseph; 7, Bertone Nicholas; 8, Williams Charlotte.

Overweight: Mickey's Choice 5 pounds.

Scratched—Political Football (22Aug77 6MF1); Star Mike (7Sep77 9Nmp1); Crackers and Pops (5Sep77 9Nmp8); Rocade (10Sep77 6Nmp4).

After watching a standout win and pay $18.60, I felt like a fool, and realized that I had succumbed to the same paranoid thinking which I see in so many horseplayers and hold in utter contempt. Such bettors believe that the game is controlled by an omniscient, omnipotent group known as "They." If a horse's odds drop sharply, "They" are betting. If a horse gets no action, "They" don't like him. If a winner is disqualified, "They" must have bet the second-place finisher. I shared this notion until I started writing about horses, interviewed jockeys and trainers, and saw that racetrack insiders do not constitute a monolithic power bloc. They are individuals who vary greatly in terms of temperament, competence, and character, and getting eight of them to agree on what to have for lunch, let alone to prearrange the outcome of a race, would be impossible.

The next day I made an effort to acquaint myself with the reality of racing at Barrington, as opposed to the popular conspiratorial view of it. In the morning I went to the stable area and visited one of the leading trainers on the Massachusetts fair circuit, Iva Mae Parrish, who had broken into the business in 1937. I walked with her down the shed row as she looked at her horses and surveyed a veritable catalog of equine ailments.

"This is Intensive Care. He's got knee troubles. I give him different medications and get in there and massage his knees." She walked to the next stall and patted the head of its occupant. "This is Red Light Lady. She was in terrible shape when I got her last month. She wasn't breathing right until I smoked her head out and cleared up her sinuses." Mrs. Parrish walked on. "This is Hook N Hurry. He's got knee troubles, too. You know, I've got twenty horses here and I have one who ain't got no problems and he just hasn't had time to develop them yet. These horses are a lot like children. You have to give them attention because they can't think for themselves or take care of themselves. I've had so many horses over the years that I can usually tell what's wrong when I see them walk or breathe. But then, you've got to work with them. You've got to get in the stall and get down there and work on their legs. It's not easy, but there's money in it if you do it right."

Mrs. Parrish did not exactly sound like one of those sinister, scheming backstretch insiders I had envisioned. After talking with her, I went to that den of iniquity, the jockeys' room, to interview John L. Smith, the track's leading rider. He told me he had just canceled his mounts for the rest of the day; he was suffering from a troublesome ulcer which was undoubtedly a product of the occupation he had chosen eleven years earlier. Smith talked about the special demands and hazards of riding at a track like Barrington.

"I like the bull rings," he said. "The turns are a lot sharper than at other tracks, and you have to make sure you don't go wide. You've got to get a position at the first turn. There's not much else to it. You ride here with your heart, not your head."

Of course, all the jockeys at Barrington knew what Smith did— that the way to win is to come out of the gate fast and get to the lead on the rail before the first turn. When several half-ton animals are trying to occupy the same space at the same time, the results are sometimes catastrophic. The horse who gets into the winning position on the rail is, very often, the one ridden by the jockey most willing to take risks.

"I've had twelve spills to be exact," Smith said. "At Blue Bonnets I broke my arm and broke my leg in two spots when a horse broke down and fell on top of me. At Green Mountain I broke my ankle when my horse broke his leg. I broke my ankle another time. . . ."

And with all that, Smith considered himself lucky. He has seen much worse. He had been scheduled to ride in the race that a few years earlier had produced Barrington's worst carnage. But he was fortunately watching from the jockeys' room when three horses spilled their riders at the start, ran down the stretch, and then, inexplicably, reversed their direction. They headed back up the stretch, right at the horses and jockeys who were driving to the finish line. "It sounded like shotguns going off," Smith remembered. "It was real bad. One of the jockeys who was in that race is like a vegetable now."

If it was improbable that a grandmotherly trainer would be a party to any illegalities, so did it seem unlikely that a jockey willing to risk life, limb, and ulcer to win races would also conspire to lose them. Reality seemed to clash headlong with all the myths that envelop racing at Barrington, and I looked forward to giving Charlie a lecture on the subject of paranoia.

Charlie arrived at Barrington for a one-day visit on Sunday the eighteenth, and we had barely settled into our seats before the first race when I let him have it. "I can't believe that a horseplayer as good as you could swallow all that nonsense about fixed races here," I said heatedly. "And I'm really mad that I've lost more than a thousand bucks because you told me to come up here and bet on the hot horses."

Charlie looked disbelieving. "Every time I've been up here I've cashed six or seven bets a day. You must be doing something wrong. I can't believe that things are so much different this year." He launched into the familiar recitation of previous years' larceny, but I turned a deaf ear and started to analyze the daily double, using normal, sane handicapping procedures.

1 BARRINGTON

ABOUT 6 ½ FURLONGS. (1.21) CLAIMING. Purse $1,600. 3-year-olds and upward, non-winners of two races in 1976–77. Weights, 3-year-olds, 118 lbs.; older, 122 lbs. Non-winners since June 18, allowed 2 lbs.; in 1977, 4 lbs. Claiming Price $1,500.

Superado Tip — B. g. 5, by Superado—Toi Reward, by Quick Reward — $1,500 — Br.—Walton M (Tex) — Tr.—Hargrove Bill — 118
Own.—Hargrove Anna & B

	St.	1st	2nd	3rd	Amt.
1977	3	0	0	0	$106
1976	17	0	2	3	$1,660

10Sep77- 1Nmp	fst	*6½f			1:26⅕	3↑Clm 1500	6	5	4^{6}	$5^{6\frac{1}{2}}$	5^{9}	$6^{8\frac{3}{4}}$	Gaffney R	b 122	6.50	70-21	Tiny Chance 114^{1} Yaguajay 122^{2} Red Bee Opal 122^{2}	No mishap	8
16Jun77- 4Poc	fst	6f	:23⅗	:47⅖	1:14	3↑Clm 1500	10	9	9^{12}	9^{13}	7^{11}	7^{11}	Greco T	b 122	16.30	74-14	C'Est Simone 117$^{2\frac{3}{4}}$ Kollegiate Kid 122$^{2\frac{1}{2}}$ [D]My Girl Kel117^{3}	Wide	10
16Jun77-Placed fifth through disqualification																			
9Jun77- 5Poc	sly	6f	:23	:47⅗	1:14⅖	3↑Clm 1500	5	7	$8^{6\frac{1}{2}}$	$9^{6\frac{3}{4}}$	$10^{8\frac{1}{2}}$	8^{13}	Greco T	b 122	5.50	70-17	Belford Bonnie S.117^{nk}CressetRooster122$^{4\frac{3}{4}}$WaTawnKo122$^{3\frac{1}{2}}$	Dull	10
6Nov76- 3Poc	gd	6f	:23⅖	:48⅕	1:15⅘	3↑Clm 2000	1	1	$6^{8\frac{1}{2}}$	$6^{6\frac{3}{4}}$	$7^{4\frac{1}{2}}$	$4^{2\frac{1}{2}}$	Long D	b 116	2.40	73-21	Tall Tankard 116¾ Tomar Star 117$^{1\frac{1}{2}}$ Petite Embers 115^{nk}	Rallied	8
20Sep76- 8Poc	gd	*6½f	:22⅘	:47⅗	1:20⅕	3↑Allowance	9	10	$9^{8\frac{1}{2}}$	6^{9}	$6^{6\frac{1}{2}}$	$6^{4\frac{3}{4}}$	Tutela J	b 117	4.30	67-27	GenuineTigerEye106½Maranath122^{3}YewAmzedUs115^{no}	No factor	10
15Aug76- 8GM	fst	7½f	:24	:48⅗	1:34	3↑Spec'l Wt	7	6	6^{8}	$6^{6\frac{1}{2}}$	$6^{5\frac{1}{2}}$	$3^{5\frac{1}{2}}$	Tutela J	b 122	*1.50	82-14	First Mike 117^{5} Kaleidoscopic 117^{nk} Superado Tip 122^{1}	Rallied	7
4Aug76- 7GM	fst	7½f	:24	:48⅖	1:35⅖	3↑Alw 1500s	7	7	7^{11}	7^{12}	$5^{3\frac{1}{2}}$	2^{nk}	Tutela J	b 117	*.80	80-20	At A Glance 119^{nk} Superado Tip 117$^{1\frac{1}{2}}$ Fort Point 117$^{3\frac{1}{2}}$	Bore out	7
25Jly76- 3GM	fst	7½f	:23⅗	:48⅕	1:34⅗	3↑Allowance	1	7	5^{8}	5^{9}	5^{6}	$4^{2\frac{1}{2}}$	Hanks M	b 118	7.70	81-14	Stew Pan 114½ First Mike 109½ Admiral's Josie 114$^{1\frac{1}{2}}$	Stride late	9

Charged Up — B. g. 5, by Gentle Art—Swift Charger, by Tulyar — $1,500 — Br.—Shady Lane Farm (Fla) — Tr.—Shetron Leonard T Jr — 118
Own.—Shetron L T Jr

	St.	1st	2nd	3rd	Amt.
1977	5	0	0	1	$368
1976	4	1	0	0	$1,520

12Sep77- 1GBF	fst	*6½f			1:31⅕	3↑Clm 1500	6	8	7^{13}	7^{12}	5^{14}	$4^{7\frac{3}{4}}$	Masia A	b 119	8.40	41-28	Grand Request 120^{nk} Little Tracer 119½ Diver Duecer117^{7}	Evenly	8
4Sep77- 5Nmp	fst	*6½f			1:26⅕	3↑Clm 2000	8	7	$5^{3\frac{1}{2}}$	$7^{4\frac{3}{4}}$	$7^{9\frac{1}{2}}$	7^{15}	Masia A	b 118	10.60	63-20	ImGonnaWhirl120$^{2\frac{1}{2}}$BentonRod118½LedingContender118^{3}	Outrun	8
20May77- 9Poc	fst	5½f	:23⅗	:47⅖	1:07⅘	3↑Clm 1500	5	6	$5^{3\frac{1}{2}}$	6^{6}	$7^{4\frac{1}{2}}$	6^{4}	Corriveau R	b 116	*1.70	81-13	Miss Van 111$^{3\frac{3}{4}}$DukeofRenwick119^{nk}PerfectInvestment114^{no}	Dull	10
6May77- 3Poc	gd	6f	:23⅖	:48⅕	1:16	3↑Clm 1500	6	8	$3^{3\frac{1}{2}}$	3^{2}	$2^{1\frac{1}{2}}$	$3^{1\frac{3}{4}}$	Corriveau R	b 122	3.00	73-21	Night Flit 122$^{1\frac{1}{2}}$ Yo Ho Mat 122^{nk} Charged Up 122^{1}	Weakened	10
29Apr77- 3Poc	fst	5½f	:24⅖	:49⅖	1:09⅖	3↑Clm 1500	3	5	$5^{1\frac{3}{4}}$	$5^{4\frac{1}{2}}$	$4^{4\frac{1}{2}}$	$4^{4\frac{1}{2}}$	Corriveau R	b 116	13.00	72-26	Hooze Irving 116^{1} Miss Van 113½ Strange Dancer 122^{3}	Hung	10
30Aug76- 5Rkm	fst	6f	:22⅖	:46⅗	1:13	3↑Clm 3500	6	7	$7^{7\frac{1}{4}}$	$6^{8\frac{1}{2}}$	8^{8}	7^{10}	Capalbo P	b 110	52.90	69-23	Game Of Luck 115$^{1\frac{3}{4}}$ BreedsHill112^{hd}StickyMarty117$^{4\frac{3}{4}}$	No factor	9
6Mar76- 1Suf	gd	6f	:22⅘	:47	1:15⅘	Clm 2500	10	3	3^{6}	2^{6}	$2^{4\frac{1}{2}}$	1^{nk}	Capalbo P	b 114	4.40	62-30	Charged Up 114^{nk} Divine Quest 109^{3} BostonBrahmin114¾	Just up	10
13Jan76- 1Crc	fst	6f	:23	:47	1:13⅗	Clm 3500	8	10	$11^{7\frac{1}{2}}$	11^{9}	$8^{7\frac{1}{4}}$	$6^{7\frac{3}{4}}$	Rodriguez D P7	b 109	28.70	77-17	Let Emat It 119no Fearless Invader 116$^{4\frac{1}{2}}$Tojocuke116^{2}	No factor	12

LATEST WORKOUTS Aug 24 CT 4f gd :51⅗ b

Reason to Sing * — Dk. b. or br. m. 7, by Aristocratic—Chante Princesse, by Blue Prince — $1,500 — Br.—Walker W F (Md) — Tr.—Roy Joseph H Sr — 118
Own.—Roy Mrs P

	St.	1st	2nd	3rd	Amt.
1977	4	0	0	0	$180
1976	7	0	0	0	

Entered 17Sep77- 2 GBF

10Sep77- 1Nmp	fst	*6½f			1:26⅕	3↑Clm 1500	3	7	8^{11}	7^{12}	$7^{9\frac{1}{2}}$	$7^{8\frac{1}{2}}$	Wiseheart L	b 119	6.20	69-21	Tiny Chance 114^{1} Yaguajay 122^{2} Red Bee Opal 122^{2}	No factor	8
4Sep77- 5Nmp	fst	*6½f			1:26⅕	3↑Clm 2000	6	6	$6^{5\frac{1}{2}}$	$6^{4\frac{3}{4}}$	$4^{3\frac{1}{2}}$	4^{6}	Wiseheart L	b 120	46.70	72-20	ImGonnaWhirl120$^{2\frac{1}{2}}$BentonRod118½LedingContender118^{3}	Rallied	8
23Aug77- 2MF	fst	*6½f			1:29⅕	3↑Clm 1500	2	7	3^{4}	$3^{\frac{1}{2}}$	5^{14}	6^{22}	Savage J	b 122	23.60	59-19	Tom Caribou 122$^{2\frac{1}{2}}$ Don't Trouble 118^{7} April Jewel 117$^{1\frac{1}{2}}$	Tired	7
19Aug77- 2MF	fst	*6½f			1:32⅖	3↑Clm 1500	7	8	2^{hd}	2^{1}	7^{12}	7^{16}	Vergara F	b 117	9.40	49-25	Bank On Taber 122^{1} Lucky Mat 122^{1} Oyarsa 112^{1}	Early speed	8
24Nov76- 6CT	fst	6½f	:24	:48⅖	1:22⅖	3↑Clm 1500	1	3	4^{6}	$8^{5\frac{3}{4}}$	$9^{8\frac{1}{2}}$	8^{14}	Thornton J	b 111	73.90	63-27	Love Those Gloves 118$^{4\frac{1}{2}}$DixieClover111^{hd}David'sNeill110^{nk}	Tired	10
23Oct76-10CT	fst	6½f	:24⅕	:48⅘	1:23⅘	3↑Clm 1500	5	9	6^{7}	8^{11}	7^{9}	7^{12}	Garcia M A	b 111	65.20	58-28	Madison Mantle 114^{2} Col Amber 114^{3} Loving Gate 117no	Outrun	10
16Oct76- 2CT	fst	4½f	:22⅖	:47⅘	:55	3↑Clm 1500	6	9		$8^{9\frac{1}{2}}$	$7^{8\frac{1}{2}}$	7^{9}	Woodson R H	b 116	45.30	74-12	GrouchyNurse112$^{2\frac{1}{2}}$She'sSmsher114^{no}NightPrincess114^{nk}	Outrun	9
2Oct76- 5CT	sly	4½f	:23⅕	:48	:54⅘	3↑Clm 1500	1	9		$9^{9\frac{3}{4}}$	10^{10}	10^{16}	Woodson R H	b 116	35.60	68-09	WltzingGirl117$^{2\frac{1}{2}}$Techer'sPrid114^{1}Empror'sDlight118$^{1\frac{1}{2}}$	No factor	10

Gambler's Green ✻ B. h. 8, by Raffle Ticket—China Cat, by Rippey
$1,500 Br.—Crest Farm (N.Y.) Tr.—Smith William W 119
Own.—Roberti B
St. 1st 2nd 3rd Amt. 1977 4 0 1 1 $525 1976 11 1 2 4 $2,880

14Sep77- 4GBF gd *6½f 1:33⅕ 3+Clm 1500 7 4 1½ 1½ 2½ 24½ Trenger G b 118 18.20 34-30 Mini Monarch115½Gambler'sGreen118noBentonRoad1221 Gamely 8
9Sep77- 5Nmpfst *5f :58⅗ 3+Clm 1500 8 5 31½ 44 45 47½ Trenger G b 118 3.50 73-22 Give 'em Steel 1224½ Tipsey Parson 1182½ Raki 118½ Weakened 8
5Sep77- 5Nmpfst *5f :57⅗ 3+Clm 1500 2 6 52¾ 35½ 37 36 Trenger G b 118 5.20 80-20 Jet's Puppy 1151½ SweetBoy1224½Gambler'sGreen1183 No mishap 8
24Aug77- 7MF fst *5f 1:04⅖ 3+Allowance 4 8 79¾ 717 713 712 Bonneau M b 118 18.40 80-16 Nade'sDelight1222KmsinWind1242ShortFoot1131½ Squeezed back 8
21Aug76- 5MF fst *6½f 1:28 3+Clm 1500 8 6 2½ 2½ 54½ 710 Maeda T b 122 *2.10 77-10 My Rock 120½ Flower World 1102 Lucky Dr. Yeagle 1202 Stopped 8
31Jly76- 1LD fst 5f :23 :47⅘ 1:01⅕ 3+Clm 2000 7 4 2½ 3½ 1hd 11 Maeda T b 120 3.40 81-20 Gambler's Green1201TusconTundy120noChieflyPoetic1202 Driving 12
19Jly76- 9LD fst 5f :22⅘ :47⅖ 1:01⅕ 3+Clm 1500 9 3 22½ 22½ 24 3nk Maeda T b 120 *1.90 81-17 AllToWin115hdTinyMrtini120hdGmbler'sGrn1201½ Closed willingly 10
12Jly76- 1LD fst 5f :23 :47⅘ 1:00⅗ 3+Clm 2000 1 3 1hd 1hd 1hd 23 Maeda T b 120 2.00 81-21 Espea's Wac 1153 Gambler's Green 1203 Five Grand120no Gamely 10

Be Alike Blk. m. 7, by Ampose—Two Alike, by Bolinas Boy
$1,500 Br.—Kramer A (Fla) Tr.—Pyefinch Harry 115
Own.—Pyefinch Mr-Mrs H
St. 1st 2nd 3rd Amt. 1977 1 0 0 1 $140 1976 19 0 3 2 $1,560
Entered 17Sep77- 1 GBF

6Sep77- 1Nmpfst *6½f 1:29⅘ 3+Clm 1500 1 3 1hd 11 32 35¾ Deboise M b 119 9.20 56-26 Scotch Clown 1223 Command Wind 1222¾BeAlike1192 Weakened 8
4Oct76- 2BD fst *6½f 1:30 3+Clm 1500 3 3 56½ 67 87¾ 88½ Deboise M b 120 6.60 62-24 Stickout119nkSprkingBurgundy118noSevernRiver1191¾ No factor 8
26Sep76- 2BD fst *6½f 1:31⅗ 3+Clm 1500 2 1 1½ 1hd 21½ 34½ Deboise M b 115 *.70 60-29 Little Brave 1181½ DOrphaned 1133 Be Alike 115½ Impeded 8
26Sep76-Placed second through disqualification
19Sep76- 9GBF fst *6½f 1:28⅘ 3+Clm 1500 6 6 31 45½ 511 616 Maeda T b 113 12.50 48-31 Hy Land And Sea 1181¾ Golden Feathers 1195 Nahigh 1177 Tired 8
13Sep76- 2GBF fst *6½f 1:29⅗ 3+Clm 1500 7 4 53½ 51¾ 31 21 Maeda T b 119 5.20 57-24 Irish Bonita 1101 Be Alike 1191 Pied's Rival 122¾ Wide 8
3Sep76- 2GM fst 7½f :23⅘ :47⅗ 1:35 3+Clm 1500 6 5 46 58½ 510 78 Keeler T J5 b 114 8.50 74-17 Sunland Sam 1222 Stickout 1223½ Sparking Burgundy119hd Tired 7
13Aug76- 3GM sly 7½f :25 :50⅘ 1:37⅕ 3+Clm 1500 1 4 22½ 21½ 45 46½ Keeler T J5 b 112 4.70 64-23 Wink Prince122hdItsaNewDawn1174Knave'sBeau1222½ Weakened 8
6Aug76- 9GM fst 5f :22⅘ :47⅘ 1:01 3+Clm 1500 3 8 96¾ 77½ 75 65½ Rivera F b 117 15.80 78-18 Jumpin Jo-Ann 1171½YvetteB.Good117½StormyAce1172 No factor 9

Leading Contender Dk. b. or br. g. 4, by Pollux—Bootfull, by Roman Sandal
$1,500 Br.—Kennedy R A (Can) Tr.—Martin Thomas P 120
Own.—Beaton Alice M
Turf Record St. 1st 2nd 3rd 1 0 0 0
St. 1st 2nd 3rd Amt. 1977 10 0 3 1 $1,317 1976 20 0 0 2 $1,671
Entered 17Sep77- 1 GBF

8Sep77- 4Nmpfst *6½f 1:27⅘ 3+Clm 1500 7 6 79 410 46 22½ Gaffney R b 120 3.60 69-21 Social Graces1172½LeadingContender120½MoonAriel1201½ Gamely 8
4Sep77- 5Nmpfst *6½f 1:26⅕ 3+Clm 1500 5 8 89½ 86¾ 55 33 Konan J M b 118 2.60 75-20 ImGonnaWhirl1202½BentonRod118½LedingContender1183 Rallied 8
23Aug77- 8MF fst *5f 1:06⅕ 3+Clm 2000 7 7 63½ 67½ 44½ 23 Konan J M b 122 *1.40 80-19 SomthinToSy1173LdingContndr1221½SlipprvLss117¾ Forced wide 7
3Jly77- 4Comfst 6½f :24 :47⅘ 1:21 3+Clm 2000 2 8 913 915 813 78¾ Creedon R b 116 33.90 75-13 Sign A Tip 122hd World Fare 117¾ R. Scott 1222½ Outrun 9
22Jun77- 2Suf fst 1 :47⅘ 1:13 1:40⅕ Clm 2500 6 3 32 46½ 917 914 Sisum T b 114 51.90 62-23 DarlinNail1143Michael'sDrem1144QuiteAPrize114¾ Close quarters 10
15Jun77- 2Suf fst 1 :47⅘ 1:12⅘ 1:39⅗ 3+Clm 2500 4 8 811 815 717 716 Sisum T b 114 7.30 62-17 Gay Parisi 1121 Darlin Nail 1144½ Trey Lea 1144½ Outrun 8
28May77- 1Suf fst 6f :22⅗ :45⅗ 1:11⅘ 3+Clm 2500 3 12 1213 1220 922 78¾ Sisum T b 114 18.50 73-15 SingleHitch1142Michael'sDream117noRunningTed1141½ No factor 12
22May77- 1Suf fst 6f :22⅗ :46⅗ 1:12⅘ Clm 2500 4 10 88½ 76¾ 77½ 47½ Sisum T b 118 4.60 69-16 Big Job 1182½ More Cricket 1183 My Wonderment1182 Late gain 11

Tiny Chance B. m. 5, by Chancero—Tiny Fib, by Fabricator
$1,500 Br.—Caple J R (Fla) Tr.—Cesarini Joseph 119
Own.—Bitman A
St. 1st 2nd 3rd Amt. 1977 20 1 0 2 $1,723 1976 8 0 0 0 $537

10Sep77- 1Nmpfst *6½f 1:26⅕ 3+Clm 1500 5 6 67 34 33½ 11 Tillotta N5 b 114 10.20 78-21 Tiny Chance 1141 Yaguajay 1222 Red Bee Opal 1222 Driving 8
5Sep77- 4Nmpfst *5f :58⅕ 3+Clm 1500 3 7 64½ 56 34½ 34 Tillotta N b 117 12.00 79-20 ShortLanding1172½MaintenanceMan1151½TinyChance1176 Rallied 8
20Aug77- 6MF fst *5f 1:05⅗ 3+Clm 2000 5 7 56 613 612 69¾ Pasquarelli R b 117 16.10 78-15 Fearless Foz 1225 No Trust 1161½ Thor's Clown 119½ Outrun 8
2Jly77- 7Comfst 6½f :24⅕ :48⅗ 1:21⅘ 3+Clm 2000 5 5 68½ 59½ 918 1014 Vergara F b 117 55.20 66-15 Nurse Farley 1175 Alfie O 1221 Easter Comet 1171½ Tired 10
3Jun77- 2Poc fst 5½f :24⅖ :49⅖ 1:10 3+Clm 1500 10 9 74½ 74 106½ 95¾ Fussell W 117 101.80 68-23 SundialDale1221½CinnamonBrandy117nkChickenKing1221½ Outrun 10
29May77- 5Poc fst 6f :22⅘ :47⅘ 1:16 3+Clm 1500 10 9 75¾ 87¾ 1013 1016 Whitemen P 113 28.20 59-22 Magic Fire 1173¾ Oscar'sTower1221½DoggonitHoney1182½ Outrun 10
22May77- 3Poc fst 6f :23⅕ :47⅖ 1:15⅗ 3+Clm 1500 1 3 46 44½ 44 42½ Whitemen P 113 *2.90 76-15 ThreeBidders118½DoggonitHoney118¾Pokehtilhgo1181 Weakened 10
30Apr77- 2Poc fst 5½f :24⅕ :49 1:10⅕ 3+ⒻClm 1500 6 7 106½ 95½ 95¾ 63 Pasquarelli R 119 65.00 70-26 Fanny Lark 119¾ Rhythm Maid 119½ Joyful Desire 122½ Outrun 10

Double Arc B. f. 3, by Flaneur II—Noor's Arc, by Noureddin
$1,500 Br.—Potter Mrs J E (Mass) Tr.—Potter Norman 111
Own.—Potter Joan E
St. 1st 2nd 3rd Amt. 1977 12 M 1 4 $1,123 1976 0 M 0 0

10Sep77-10Nmpfst *1$\frac{1}{16}$ 1:57⅕ 3+Clm 1500 3 4 68 615 717 720 Long D b 114 8.20 40-21 Wall Mount 122hd Silver Call 1172 Miss Rose Lee 1193½ Tired 8
6Sep77- 1Nmpfst *6½f 1:29⅘ 3+Clm 1500 3 7 815 813 87½ 59½ Long D b 115 9.30 53-26 Scotch Clown 1223 Command Wind 1222¾ Be Alike 1192 Outrun 8
23Aug77- 3MF fst *6½f 1:30⅗ 3+Md 2000 4 6 47½ 412 411 315 Martinez A V b 112 8.30 61-19 I'm In Trouble 1225 Dassie 11710 Double Arc 1121 No mishap 7
20May77- 4Poc fst 1 :49⅘ 1:15⅗ 1:42⅘ 3+Md 1500 6 4 42 43 33½ 35¾ Boudreau R b 112 2.70 74-13 Spirit Of Shiloh 1172 Jaded Jane1173¾DoubleArc1121½ Weakened 10
13May77- 7Poc fst 1 :49⅘ 1:16⅘ 1:45 3+Md 1500 9 9 96½ 56 46½ 36 Boudreau R b 109 3.80 63-24 Lively Brook 1226 Gregorian Twist 117no DoubleArc1093½ Rallied 10
3May77- 2Poc fst 1 :50⅕ 1:18⅗ 1:47⅗ 3+Md 1500 10 7 52½ 3½ 3nk 2nk Boudreau R b 114 3.30 56-29 Nervabello 122nk Double Arc 1143 Ken Dynomite 1225 Wide 10
22Apr77- 7Poc fst 1 :49⅘ 1:16⅕ 1:43⅗ 3+Md 1500 5 9 912 66 413 322 Boudreau R 114 16.20 53-20 Sage Mars 12218 Quick Fizzle1143½DoubleArc1141½ Pinched back 10
31Mar77- 3FD fst 170 :49⅘ 1:16 1:47⅗ 3+Md 2000 9 5 87½ 811 811 814 Pruden K 111 9.00 57-19 Laurels Scholar 1161 Dandy Kid 1204½ Swan Duel 1111 No factor 9

2 BARRINGTON

5 FURLONGS. (1.01) CLAIMING. Purse $1,500. 3-year-olds and upward, non-winners of two races in 1976–77. Weights, 3-year-olds, 118 lbs.; older, 122 lbs. Non-winners since June 18, allowed 2 lbs.; in 1977, 4 lbs. Claiming Price $1,500.

Arro Aura Ch. m. 6, by Arrogate—May's Got It, by His Babu
$1,500 Br.—Klein Patricia M (Ohio) Tr.—Sparling Arthur E 119
Own.—Sparling A E
St. 1st 2nd 3rd Amt. 1977 15 1 3 3 $2,618 1976 18 0 3 2 $3,538

2Sep77- 9Pen sly 6f :23⅘ :46⅘ 1:12⅘ Clm 2000 2 5 32 710 718 723 Soto J b 115 59.20 59-19 Misty Tex 1166½ Charlie Spares 106no Native Serenade 1133 Tired 7
26Aug77- 9Pen gd 6f :22⅗ :46⅗ 1:13 Clm 2000 3 8 88½ 815 1118 1116 Soto J b 113 178.70 65-20 Sunday Presents 1162 Rex De Cursus 1132 StarQueen1081 Outrun 12
21Aug77- 1Pen fst 5½f :22⅗ :46⅗ 1:06⅘ Clm 2000 7 6 1110 1117 1115 1111 Donlon J R b 111 75.70 74-19 Millfleet 113½ Airtime 1132 Leigh Quest 1192½ No factor 12
4Aug77- 8Pen fst 5½f :22⅗ :46⅗ 1:05⅘ Clm 2000 4 10 1113 1111 1115 1018 Fussell W b 113 93.20 74-13 Mr. Pinter 1131 Airtime 1132 Chats Dream 1191 No factor 11
22Jly77- 5Pen fst 6f :23 :46⅘ 1:12⅘ Clm 2000 4 8 65¾ 88 913 913 Hakes D7 b 104 49.60 69-20 Seatrain 1163 Haircut 1162 Honky Mary 111hd Outrun 9
15Jly77- 9Pen fst 6f :22⅘ :46⅗ 1:12⅘ 3+ⒻClm 2500 1 9 105½ 69 914 910 Popara D E5 b 111 32.50 73-14 FoxieDealer113½MakeMineMeal1061CincinntiRose1131 No factor 12
17Jun77- 5Poc fst 5½f :24 :48 1:08 3+Clm 1500 9 6 42½ 33½ 33 31½ Martinez A V b 117 *2.00 83-14 Meep Meep 118nk Hold True 1181 Arro Aura 1172 No mishap 9
12Jun77- 5Poc fst 5½f :23⅘ :48 1:08⅕ 3+Clm 1500 1 2 63½ 52 2½ 3nk Martinez A V b 117 *1.60 83-17 Fort Point 122nk Strong George B. 122hd ArroAura1172½ Steadied 10
LATEST WORKOUTS ●Jly 19 Pen 4f gd :51 h

Raki Ch. g. 5, by Mystic II—Rakibu, by Ribot
$1,500 Br.—Scott Mrs M duPont (Va) Tr.—Grace Karen 118
Own.—Cimini Hazel
St. 1st 2nd 3rd Amt. 1977 9 0 2 1 $1,046 1976 4 1 1 0 $1,665
Entered 17Sep77- 2 GBF

9Sep77- 5Nmpfst *5f :58⅗ 3+Clm 1500 1 8 74½ 611 66¾ 37 Bennett D A b 118 6.20 74-22 Give 'em Steel 1224½ Tipsey Parson 1182½ Raki 118½ Rallied 8
3Sep77- 2Nmpfst *5f :59⅗ 3+Clm 1500 4 7 810 714 711 78 Vergara F b 118 *1.70 68-23 Windy Cop 120nk Nabra 1181 Slippery Lass 1154 Outrun 8
19Aug77- 6MF fst *5f 1:06⅕ 3+Clm 1500 2 3 56 614 613 59¾ Trenger G b 118 2.60 73-25 Miss Joker 115¾ Ocnap 1196 Imposer 1201½ Bore out start 8
19Jun77- 4Poc fst 5½f :23⅕ :47⅘ 1:08⅘ 3+Clm 2000 6 6 67 65 54½ 62¾ Ernst P 122 *1.40 79-15 In The Vogue 1181¾ Stogey Jack 122¾ Mi Everett 122nk Dull 10
9Jun77- 8Poc sly 6f :23 :47⅘ 1:14 3+Clm 2000 10 8 31½ 33 32 22 Ernst P 122 9.40 83-17 Nosey Guy 1222 Raki 122½ Reyoro 1221¾ Gamely 10
2Jun77- 8Poc fst 5½f :23⅘ :48⅘ 1:09 3+Clm 2000 2 3 3½ 32 2½ 2no Berberena J 122 9.90 79-19 Dashing Prince 122no Raki 122no Foxy Vixen 117hd Just missed 10
27May77- 8Poc fst 6f :23⅗ :48 1:14⅕ 3+Clm 2500 4 6 2hd 21 22½ 55½ Berberena J 122 80.40 78-22 Admiral Fox 1223 Ky. Knobs 1221 Stogey Jack 122¾ Speed, tired 9
12May77- 9Poc fst 6f :23 :47⅕ 1:14⅘ 3+Clm 2000 8 10 1013 1013 911 715 Berberena J 122 38.00 66-22 MinstrelClown1224½Doc'sEstrBunny1221½TokyoJo122½ No factor 10

Mystery Hill B. f. 3, by Inkosana—Maggie's Act, by Bill The King

$1,500 Br.—Smith D D (SC) Tr.—Roberts James E — 111

Own.—Roberts L

St. 1st 2nd 3rd Amt. | 1977 2 M 0 0 $40 | 1976 0 M 0 0

9Sep77- 2Nmpfst *6½f 1:27⅕ 3↑Clm 1500 1 6 714 716 722 822 Sullivan D 120 23.40 51-22 Phantom Pilot 1209 Little Kicker 1171½ Billy Sox 122¾ Outrun 8

25Aug77- 1Rkmfst 6f :23 :47⅕ 1:14 3↑Md 2500 12 10 78½1118112611129 Smith J A5 109 69.40 45-20 Royal Apron 1151½ LittleMole1155½PolishedSilver1052¾ No factor 12

LATEST WORKOUTS Aug 22 Rkm 4f fst :49 h Aug 11 Rkm 5f gd 1:06 b Aug 1 Rkm 5f fst 1:04⅕ bg Jly 27 Rkm 5f fst 1:02⅗ b

Hallumore * Ch. m. 7, by Hallursan—More Contrary, by More Sun

$1,500 Br.—Leone J A (Mass) Tr.—Liebenow Carl — 115

Own.—Nestler W Jr

St. 1st 2nd 3rd Amt. | 1977 2 0 0 0 $110 | 1976 5 0 0 0 $190

8Sep77- 1Nmpfst *5f :59⅗ 3↑Clm 1500 3 2 31½ 31 21 43½ Vergara F b 119 3.20 74-21 Just B Speed 122½ Zipper's Zip 122½ April Jewel 1192¼ Weakened 8

25Aug77- 2MF fst *5f 1:05⅕ 3↑Clm 1500 2 7 85¾ 821 816 68¾ Vergara F b 115 15.10 80-17 AntiochTamao124¾Jet'sPuppy1181ZueCanBee1225 Knocked back 8

30ct76- 1BD fst 5f 1:02⅕ 3↑Clm 1500 7 6 65½ 69 69¼ 613 Bovaird J b 115 33.30 72-23 Abby's Mermaid1225¾Westfield1181½QueenofMarkets1175 Outrun 7

25Sep76- 3BD fst 5f 1:02⅕ 3↑Clm 1500 6 8 86½ 814 812 716 Bovaird J b 115 13.70 69-22 Steam Away 1132½ Trinity River 122no Trajabit 1226 No factor 8

18Sep76- 2GBF fst 5f 1:02⅗ 3↑Clm 1500 1 5 31 43 43½ 46½ Kastel F b 122 5.20 85-20 Count Frenchy 1221 Six Below 1192¾ ChantStar1222¾ Best others 7

4Sep76- 1Nmpfst *5f :57⅗ 3↑Clm 1500 4 3 55½ 510 512 512 Kastel F b 117 40.40 74-14 Hessy's Baby 1153¾ Fighting Judge 1224 Facetiae 1193½ Evenly 8

27Aug76- 2MF fst *5f 1:05 3↑Clm 1500 1 1 56½ 614 — — Contrada G b 118 7.60 — — Little Jay Jay 1184½ Karrie K 1201½ Nabsent 1181¾ Eased 7

8Nov75- 7GM fst 5f :23⅘ :49 1:02⅗ 3↑Clm 1500 7 10 108¼1011101410 14 Sullivan D b 122 51.00 61-29 Hilda'sDoll1192¼TurntoNative122nkNoPlasticSddle1222 No factor 10

Nolowblows * Dk. b. or br. m. 8, by Uppercut—Goosander, by Merganser

$1,500 Br.—Lytle J B (Ga) Tr.—Coopee Dennis — 115

Own.—Coopee D

St. 1st 2nd 3rd Amt. | 1977 1 0 0 0 $80 | 1976 15 1 2 3 $2,860

13Sep77- 1GBF fst 5f 1:03⅗ 3↑Clm 1500 3 4 65 512 413 48 Bonneau M 114 6.10 80-31 LittleBrownie1223Shn'sSwthrt1191½Bobby'sTurn1193½ No mishap 8

5Sep76- 9GM fst 5f :23⅗ :48 1:00⅘ 3↑Clm 1500 10 9 96¾ 97¾ 97¾ 55 Shewell J5 114 3.40 79-11 PromptAttntion1192JumpinJo-Ann1191BmBliss'19hd Raced wide 10

26Aug76- 5GM fst 5f :22⅘ :47⅗ 1:00⅘ 3↑Clm 1500 2 9 105½107½ 73 53¾ Shewell J5 112 6.70 80-21 Everfast 117¾ Thistle Bridge 122½ Conway Silver 1171 Wide str. 10

31Jly76- 3LD fst 5f :22⅗ :48⅕ 1:01 3↑Clm 1500 3 3 56½ 66½ 35 22¼ McCrea R 112 2.30 80-20 Conn'sCookng1152¼Nolowblows1121¾MllrdCov1204½ Finished fast 7

17Jly76- 4LD fst 5f :23 :47⅕ 1:00⅕ 3↑ⒻClm 2000 1 2 43 44½ 42½ 32½ Ho G 117 3.80 83-20 YourCopy1191CinnmonBrndy1171½Nolowblows1171¾ Lacked rally 6

10Jly76- 4LD fst 5f :23 :47⅖ 1:00⅘ 3↑Clm 1500 4 5 66 55½ 54½ 3½ Cravo R 115 41.80 82-19 Mack McCoy 120½ Play the Devil 114hd Nolowblows 1154¾ Rallied 7

24Jun76- 5LD fst 5f :22⅕ :46⅘ 1:00⅖ 3↑ⒻClm 2000 1 8 812 913 918 919 Lapensee M 117 30.60 66-19 Mt. Boo Boo 115hd Pluck's Doll117¾SuccessfulLiving1175 Outrun 10

28May76- 5Suf fst 6f :23 :46 1:12⅗ Clm 2500 6 11 1118122012301225 Giovanni J 113 109.10 53-21 Willie Pay 1162¾ Good Profit 117½ Seton Hi' 14nk No factor 12

Back River * Dk. b. or br. g. 8, by Staysail—Dover Girl, by Billings

$1,500 Br.—Bishop C S (Mass) Tr.—Martino Phyllis — 118

Own.—Martino Phyllis

Turf Record St. 1st 2nd 3rd: 1 0 0 0

St. 1st 2nd 3rd Amt. | 1977 1 0 0 0 $30 | 1976 2 0 1 0 $240

22Aug77- 8MF sly *6½f 1:30⅗ 3↑Clm 1500 1 2 55¾ 716 821 835 Gaffney R 124 16.00 40-19 Sindical II 1202¾ Foxy Vixen 1153 Benton Road 1181½ Tired 8

29May76- 1GM fst 5f :22⅕ :46⅘ 1:00⅕ 3↑Clm c-1500 7 8 63¾ 54¾ 33½ 2½ Pruden K 122 1.50 86-13 Bakers Miss 117½ Back River 1224 Amber Tamber 122½ Gamely 10

31Jan76- 3Suf fst 6f :22⅘ :46⅘ 1:12⅘ Clm 2500 10 7 108¼101210101012 Bradfield W 115 88.40 67-18 Wings of Victory 118no Sir R 1141½ Rush a Bet 1192½ Outrun 10

28Dec75- 2Suf gd 6f :23 :47⅕ 1:13⅘ 3↑Clm 2750 5 9 11131116111310 13 Bradfield W 114 76.50 59-29 Tribel City 1145 Spring Market1111ⒹFamousCross109½ No factor 11

15Dec75- 5Suf fst 6f :22⅘ :46⅕ 1:12⅖ 3↑Clm 2750 6 11 111411121120 1014 Bradfield W 118 12.60 65-26 Sherry's Bully 1161½ Hep's Choice 1164¾HardButFair116no Outrun 12

8Dec75- 7Suf fst 6f :23 :47⅕ 1:13⅕ 3↑Clm 2750 7 11 121212111113119¾ Bradfield W 113 19.50 65-26 Fenity's Rule 1142½Dagmar'sBoy1121½ChairmanBaker1141 Outrun 12

16Nov75- 2Suf fst 6f :23 :47 1:14⅗ 3↑Clm 2500 7 6 88 912 918 910 Kelly E 116 26.60 59-27 Wings of Victory 118nkHep'sChoice118½IdolHand1161¾ No factor 9

2Nov75- 3Suf fst 6f :22⅗ :46⅗ 1:14⅕ 3↑Clm 2500 4 8 811 916 98¾ 85¼ Kelly E 117 66.90 65-25 Ed n Mert 114½ Mandrake Ernesto 114½ Ah Netta 111½ Outrun 9

Bev's Junior B. g. 6, by Jacksorbetter—Beverly G, by Wild Honey

$1,500 Br.—Salvaggi M (Mass) Tr.—Salvaggi M — 113

Own.—Salvaggi A

St. 1st 2nd 3rd Amt. | 1977 7 0 0 0 $280 | 1976 11 1 0 3 $1,190

10Sep77- 5Nmpfst *5f :58⅕ 3↑Clm 1500 4 7 78¼ 719 818 820 Boucher E Jr5 115 45.70 63-21 Royal Work 1208 Unbendable 1221 Short Landing 1191½ Outrun 8

5Sep77- 6Nmpfst *5f :58⅖ 3↑Clm 2000 5 8 88½ 813 612 58¼ Boucher E Jr5 115 35.70 74-20 ⒹLegend Star117hdHopefulSteve1202¾MissBonnet114½ No factor 8

5Sep77-Placed fourth through disqualification

1Sep77- 2Nmpfst *5f :59⅕ 3↑Clm 1500 6 6 75¾ 712 78 69 Konan J M 118 40.60 69-24 Gold Memories 1122½ Gypsy Rover 1201¼ Rainy Star 1183 Outrun 8

27Aug77- 2MF fst *6½f 1:29⅕ 3↑Clm 1500 5 7 710 716 815 829 Konan J M 118 14.50 52-17 Virginia Way 118½ Emp 1224 Lord Medford 118nk Outrun 8

26Aug77- 5MF fst *5f 1:05⅗ 3↑Clm 1500 3 8 812 819 813 716 Polion J 122 14.00 70-14 Cesere's Image 1154FortDillon1203ApacheRunner1133¾ No factor 8

23Aug77- 4MF fst *5f 1:05⅕ 3↑Clm 1500 1 4 810 816 714 617 Polion J 122 15.00 71-19 FearlessFoz12210Pagod'sOdyssey1172½PuertoBello1201 No speed 8

20Aug77- 1MF fst *5f 1:05⅕ 3↑Clm 1500 5 3 64¾ 611 78¼ 711 Polion J 120 20.90 77-15 Bobby's Quest 115½SpotOfInk113½Shane'sSweetheart1158 Outrun 8

4Oct76- 4BD fst 5f 1:03⅘ 3↑Clm 1500 7 3 73¾ 35 2½ 11½ Konan J M 122 5.80 77-24 Bev's Junior 1221½ Wino's Alibhai 119½ Tatgol 1191½ Drew clear 8

Hallumore, in the second race, looked like the key to the daily double. He had stalked a pair of speedballs in his most recent start at the Northampton Fair. Now he was entered against a field of plodders and seemed likely to get the lead on the rail. I was trying to choose from among the evenly matched horses in the first race when I glanced up from my *Racing Form* and looked at the tote board. Be Alike, who appeared no better or worse than the other contenders, had been the tepid early favorite at 5-to-2 odds. Suddenly his price dropped to 9 to 5 in one flash. On the next blink of the board he was 6 to 5. And on the next flash, 4 to 5. This was it! I sprinted toward the betting area, hastily debated what to do, and then went to the daily-double window and bet a $100 combination on Be Alike and Hallumore. When I got back to my seat for the race, Be Alike was 3 to 5.

7th Day. WEATHER CLOUDY. TEMPERATURE 75 DEGREES.

FIRST RACE

GBF

SEPTEMBER 18, 1977

ABOUT 6 ½ FURLONGS. (1.21) CLAIMING. Purse $1,600. 3–year–olds and upward, non–winners of two races in 1976–77. Weights, 3–year–olds, 118 lbs.; older, 122 lbs. Non–winners since June 18, allowed 2 lbs.; in 1977, 4 lbs. Claiming Price $1,500.

Value of race $1,600, value to winner $910, second $300, third $150, fourth $80, balance of starters $40 each. Mutuel pool $23,741.

Last Raced	Horse	Eqt.A.Wt	PP	St	¼	½	Str	Fin	Jockey	Cl'g Pr	Odds $1
6Sep77 1Nmp3	Be Alike	b 7 115	5	1	1^5	1^5	1^7	1^5	Maeda T	1500	.70
10Sep77 1Nmp1	Tiny Chance	b 5 119	7	2	4^{1}_{2}	4^{1}_{2}	3^4	2^{1}_{2}	Creedon R	1500	5.30
14Sep77 4GBF2	Gambler's Green	b 8 118	4	3	2^{1}_{2}	2^2	2^{1}_{2}	3^2	Trenger G	1500	6.30
12Sep77 1GBF4	Charged Up	b 5 120	2	5	6^2	6^{1}_{2}	6^{hd}	4^{hd}	Savage J	1500	8.10
10Sep77 1Nmp7	Reason to Sing	b 7 120	3	7	5^{1}_{2}	5^5	5^{1}_{2}	5^1	Wiseheart L	1500	22.50
10Sep77 1Nmp6	Superado Tip	b 5 118	1	4	3^{1}_{2}	3^{1}_{2}	4^{hd}	6^{nk}	Greco T	1500	22.60
8Sep77 4Nmp2	Leading Contender	b 4 121	6	6	7^4	7^5	7^8	7^{10}	Gaffney R	1500	4.70
10Sep77 10Nmp7	Double Arc	b 3 116	8	8	8	8	8	8	Smith J L	1500	32.60

OFF AT 1:36, EDT. Start good, Won easily. Time, 1:30⅕ Track fast.

Official Program Numbers\

$2 Mutuel Prices:

5–BE ALIKE	3.40	2.80	3.00
7–TINY CHANCE		4.60	3.40
4–GAMBLER'S GREEN			4.00

Blk. m, by Ampose—Two Alike, by Bolinas Boy. Trainer Pyefinch Harry. Bred by Kramer A (Fla).

BE ALIKE set pace with a length lead and won as much the best. TINY CHANCE rallied mildly to earn the placing. GAMBLER'S GREEN raced nearest winner but lacked a late response. CHARGED UP was no threat with a belated gain. LEADING CONTENDER showed little.

Owners— 1, Pyefinch Mr–Mrs H; 2, Bitman A; 3, Roberti B; 4, Shetron L T Jr; 5, Roy Mrs P; 6, Hargrove Anna & B; 7, Beaton Alice M; 8, Potter Joan E.

Trainers— 1, Pyefinch Harry; 2, Cesarini Joseph; 3, Smith William W; 4, Shetron Leonard T Jr; 5, Roy Joseph H Sr; 6, Hargrove Bill; 7, Martin Thomas P; 8, Potter Norman.

Corrected weight: Gambler's Green 118 pounds. **Overweight:** Charged Up 2 pounds; Reason to Sing 2; Leading Contender 1; Double Arc 5.

Scratched—Four Cuckoos (5Sep77 1Nmp3), Diver Duecer (12Sep77 1GBF3); Brother to Foi (9Sep77 1Nmp3); Moon Ariel (12Sep77 6GBF4).

This was not one of those Barrington races that I had talked about with John L. Smith, in which all the jockeys are whipping and driving feverishly to get to the rail first. Be Alike was five lengths on top a few strides out of the gate, and it became readily apparent that he was not going to be challenged. As the horse turned into the stretch, Charlie laughed and said, "This is the way it always used to be. Do you still think I'm crazy?" I did not.

I had a chance now to recoup all of my previous losses for the meeting. I waited eagerly for the daily-double payoffs to be announced, and was pleased to hear that the combination with Hallumore was paying $17.60. Moments later the announcer said that the daily double with Nolowblows would be worth $11.

Impossible! Nolowblows had finished a lackluster fourth in his only start of the year. He had never been first, second, or third at the first call of any race in his past performances. He was 15 to 1 in the morning line. How could the daily-double payoff be only $11? There was only one possible answer, and Charlie did not have to tell me what it was. When Nolowblows was bet down to 3-to-2 favoritism, I wagered enough on him to cover my investment in the double. And then I

watched the race with the surest sense of foreknowledge that I have
ever felt at a racetrack.

SECOND RACE

GBF

SEPTEMBER 18, 1977

5 FURLONGS. (1.01) CLAIMING. Purse $1,500. 3–year–olds and upward, non–winners of two races in 1976–77. Weights, 3–year–olds, 118 lbs.; older, 122 lbs. Non–winners since June 18, allowed 2 lbs.; in 1977, 4 lbs. Claiming Price $1,500.

Value of race $1,500, value to winner $885, second $275, third $140, fourth $80, balance of starters $40 each. Mutuel pool $27,455.

Last Raced	Horse	Eqt.A.Wt.PP St	¼	¾	Str	Fin	Jockey	Cl'g Pr	Odds $1
13Sep77 1GBF4	Nolowblows	8 115 5 2	12½	15	18	18	Brown L W Jr	1500	1.50
9Sep77 2Nmp8	Mystery Hill	3 111 3 4	3hd	3hd	2hd	21	Saul D	1500	21.60
9Sep77 5Nmp3	Raki	b 5 118 2 6	6hd	62	51	34½	Trenger G	1500	2.40
10Sep77 5Nmp8	Bev's Junior	6 113 7 1	5hd	53½	64	42½	Boucher E Jr	1500	15.50
22Aug77 8MF8	Back River	8 122 6 5	21½	23	32	51½	Sullivan D	1500	8.40
8Sep77 1Nmp4	Hallumore	b 7 117 4 3	41½	43	4hd	62	Vergara F	1500	3.80
2Sep77 9Pen7	Arro Aura	b 6 119 1 7	7	7	7	7	Greco T	1500	9.30

OFF AT 2:10 EDT Start good, Won ridden out. Time, 1:03⅕ Track fast.

$2 Mutuel Prices:

6–NOLOWBLOWS	5.00	3.60	2.20
4–MYSTERY HILL		12.40	4.80
2–RAKI			2.60

dl: b or br. m, by Uppercut—Goosander, by Merganser. Trainer Coopee Dennis. Bred by Lytle J B (Ga).

NOLOBOWS set pace with a cmfortable lead and won under mild urging. MYSTERY HILL rallied mildly. RAKI passed tired ones. BEV'S JUNIOR outlasted others. BACK RIVER weakened. HALLUMORE was outrun.

Owners— 1, Coopee D; 2, Roberts L; 3, Cimini Hazel; 4, Salvaggi A; 5, Ward Louise; 6, Nestler W Jr; 7, Sparling A E.

Trainers— 1, Coopee Dennis; 2, Roberts James E; 3, Grace Karen; 4, Salvaggi M; 5, Stockdale Van; 6, Liebenow Carl; 7, Sparling Arthur E.

Overweight: Back River 4 pounds; Hallumore 2.

Scratched—Spanish Caper (29Nov76 3FL5); Tapboc (9Sep77 4Nmp5); Mickey's Choice (13Sep77 7GBF8); Slippery Lass (12Sep77 1GBF5); Native Tongue (17Jun77 5Poc6).

$2 Daily Double 5–6 Paid $11.00. Daily Double Pool $75,658.

Nolowblows went to the front immediately, while none of the other
jockeys seemed to be beating their mounts into a bloody pulp. Nobody
ever challenged Nolowblows, of course, and he coasted to the finish
line eight lengths in front. Could anything be more brazen?

I learned the answer to that question the next day. My old nemesis
Von Rincon, the horse who had started my troubles at Barrington six
day earlier, was entered in the sixth race. It pained me just to look at
the running line and the comment for the most recent race in his past
performances:

8¹⁵   8²¹   —   —   **Pulled up sore**

It pained me even more when I watched him make a miraculous
physical recovery and win with ease at 5 to 1. I turned around and
headed straight toward the airport. I had lost $1540 at the Barrington
Fair, and had also lost the last vestiges of my innocence.

6

Making Figures

For most horseplayers, making figures would be a tedious, laborious process, a necessary evil at best. For me it is an art that represents the creation of order out of chaos. When I made the decision to spend the winter at Gulfstream Park and started looking at the *Racing Form* past performance for the Florida tracks, I saw only an impenetrable mass of names and data. But when I had constructed a set of figures, I understood the nature of the tracks' racing surfaces; I recognized the strongest and weakest classes of horses; I could evaluate the relative ability of individual animals. The figures gave me an overall understanding of the sport, and they eventually became the primary source of my success at Gulfstream.

The procedure I used for making figures in Florida can serve as a model for horseplayers who want to become speed handicappers. I explained my method in *Picking Winners*, but I placed more emphasis on the theoretical underpinnings of the figures than on the step-by-step construction of them. Ever since the book was published I have been getting letters and phone calls from readers asking for clarification, including one from a man who wanted to know if the figures could be adapted for use at a dog track in Tampa, and another from an ex-nun who needed help with her figures at Cahokia Downs.

While I may be able to clarify the process of making figures, I cannot simplify it. Speed handicapping demands such a commitment of time and effort that it is incompatible with being a casual racing fan. Some horseplayers may be tempted to look for shortcuts—such as buying speed charts or track variants that are the products of someone else's labor—but this doesn't work. Just as a racecar driver has to tinker under the hood and get to know his own vehicle before he can drive it perfectly, a horseplayer has to understand the derivation and meaning of the figures in order to use them properly.

Step One: Speed Ratings

A speed figure has two components. One is the *speed rating*, which translates a horse's time into a number. In my system, for example, a horse who runs six furlongs in 1:12 gets a rating of 78. The second component is the *track variant,* a number which is added to or subtracted from the rating to compensate for the effect of the track condition on the time. If the horse who ran in 1:12 did it over a slow track with a variant of +13, he would earn a figure of 91.

When I closeted myself in my handicapping room to prepare for the trip to Florida, my first task was to construct a chart that would assign ratings to the times of races and would enable me to compare horses' performances at different distances. If a horse who had run six furlongs in 1:10 was meeting a rival who had run seven furlongs in 1:22⅗, I had to know which one was superior. Even though I knew nothing about Gulfstream yet, I felt I had learned the answer from past experience. In fact, when I meet my Maker and He asks me what great truths I have discovered in my time on earth, I will cite my speed-rating chart for six and seven furlongs:

SIX FURLONGS		SEVEN FURLONGS	
1:08	134	1:21	125
1:08-1	131	1:21-1	123
1:08-2	128	1:21-2	121
1:08-3	125	1:21-3	118
1:08-4	122	1:21-4	116
1:09	120	1:22	113
1:09-1	117	1:22-1	111
1:09-2	114	1:22-2	109
1:09-3	111	1:22-3	106
1:09-4	108	1:22-4	104
1:10	106	1:23	102
1:10-1	103	1:23-1	100
1:10-2	100	1:23-2	97
1:10-3	97	1:23-3	95
1:10-4	94	1:23-4	93
1:11	92	1:24	90
1:11-1	89	1:24-1	88
1:11-2	86	1:24-2	86

SIX FURLONGS		SEVEN FURLONGS	
1:11-3	83	1:24-3	83
1:11-4	81	1:24-4	81
1:12	78	1:25	79
1:12-1	75	1:25-1	77
1:12-2	72	1:25-2	74
1:12-3	70	1:25-3	72
1:12-4	67	1:25-4	70
1:13	64	1:26	67
1:13-1	61	1:26-1	65
1:13-2	59	1:26-2	63
1:13-3	56	1:26-3	60
1:13-4	53	1:26-4	58
1:14	50	1:27	56
1:14-1	47	1:27-1	54
1:14-2	44	1:27-2	51
1:14-3	42	1:27-3	49
1:14-4	39	1:27-4	47
1:15	36	1:28	44

The chart shows that a horse who runs six furlongs in 1:10 earns a rating of 106. He is the equal of a horse who runs seven furlongs in 1:22⅗, also a 106. These ratings are the product of years of research and tinkering. They had their genesis when I analyzed the results of hundreds of $3000 claiming races in Maryland and found that the average winning time of six-furlong races was 1:13, while the seven-furlong average was 1:26⅕. Then I compiled statistics on races in New York and found, excitedly, that a group of horses who averaged 1:13 for six furlongs would also cover the longer distance in 1:26⅕. I now knew that 1:13 in some sense "equaled" 1:26⅕, but it was a brilliant Harvard classmate who showed me how to make use of this information.

Sheldon Kovitz's interest in speed handicapping antedated mine, and he patiently pointed out to me that even though 1:13 equaled 1:26⅕, that did not mean I could compare times at six and seven furlongs simply by adding or subtracting 13⅕ seconds. Horses who ran six furlongs considerably faster than 1:13 would cover the extra furlong faster, too. And plodders who ran six furlongs in 1:16 might run an additional eighth of a mile in something like 14 seconds.

Sheldon also made the observation—which seems axiomatic to me now but came as a revelation then—that a fifth of a second is more significant at a short distance than at a long distance. I finally grasped this concept by formulating an analogy with human runners. A hundred-yard-dash man who is one second faster than an opponent is overwhelmingly superior. But a miler who is one second faster than his competition has a very narrow advantage.

With his extensive background in mathematics, Sheldon had no difficulty conceiving a way to measure the relative importance of a fifth of a second at different distances. A horse who ran six furlongs in 1:13 was covering the distance in 365 fifths of a second. Therefore one-fifth of a second represented 1/365, or .28 percent, of the entire race. For the horse who ran seven furlongs in 1:26⅕, one-fifth of a second was 1/431, or .23 percent, of his race. So Sheldon decided that a fifth of a second would equal 2.8 points at six furlongs, and 2.3 points at seven furlongs, with the decimal point shifted one place for the sake of convenience.

If I arbitrarily decided that six furlongs in 1:13 was a rating of 64,* I could construct an entire speed chart from that starting point, adding or subtracting 2.8 points for each fifth of a second and rounding off the numbers:

1:12	78.0	=	78
1:12-1	75.2	=	75
1:12-2	72.4	=	72
1:12-3	69.6	=	70
1:12-4	66.8	=	67
1:13	64.0	=	64
1:13-1	61.2	=	61
1:13-2	58.4	=	58

The beauty of Sheldon's ratings is the way his theory is confirmed by reality. The upper end of my chart on page 120 says that six furlongs in 1:09 has the same rating as seven furlongs in 1:21⅖. An analysis of the results of such fast races will disclose that horses do cover the last furlong in an average of 12⅖ seconds. The relationship between six and seven furlongs in my chart has proved valid at every track where the races are run around one turn.

Unfortunately, there is no such neat, universal relationship between the times of sprint races and route races. A class of horses which averages six furlongs in 1:13 at Bowie will run a mile and one-sixteenth in 1:46⅗. A class which averages 1:13 at Monmouth will

* These ratings differ from the ones in *Picking Winners.* My six-furlong ratings are 16 points lower than in the earlier book, and the seven-furlong ratings are 15 points lower, so that 1:13 doesn't precisely equal 1:26⅕ any more. These alterations are largely cosmetic, a product of my compulsive tinkering with my figures; but the principles behind the ratings have not changed.

go the longer distance in 1:48⅗. On Aqueduct's inner dirt course, six furlongs in 1:13 equals a mile and one-sixteenth in 1:47⅗. In order to make a speed chart for the route races at Gulfstream, I had to learn how fast different classes of horses ran at different distances. If, for example, a broad group of horses averaged 1:13 for six furlongs, 1:26⅕ for seven furlongs, and 1:48 for a mile and one-sixteenth, I would have a sound basis for constructing my speed chart.

I waited to perform the necessary calculations until the coldest, most dismal day in December, when there was nothing better to do than sit indoors with my figures. I took a large sheet of poster paper and ruled it off into vertical columns for all the common classes of races at Gulfstream. I drew horizontal lines to separate the chart into sections for six furlongs, seven furlongs, and a mile and one-sixteenth. On another sheet of poster paper I made a similar chart for races limited to three-year-olds. Then I went through all the Gulfstream results from the previous season, looking at the class and the final time of each race and transcribing that time into the appropriate grid. If the race was limited to fillies and mares, I subtracted three-fifths of a second from the final time, compensating for the fact that females typically run that much slower than open competition. Finally, I averaged the times for each class and distance. A portion of my statistics looked like this:

	$3500 claimers	$5000 claimers	$6000–7500 claimers	$10,000 claimers
	1:12	1:11-3	1:11-2	1:11
	1:12-2	1:11	1:11-2	1:11
	1:12	1:12	1:11-1	1:11
	1:11-3	1:11-3	1:11-3	1:11-2
	1:11-4	1:11-3	1:12-1	1:10-3
	1:12	1:11-2	1:11	1:11
	1:12	1:12	1:10-4	1:10
SIX FURLONGS	1:12-2	1:12-2	1:10-4	1:11-1
	1:12-1	1:11	1:11	1:10
	1:12-4	1:10-3	1:11-3	1:10-3
	1:11-1	1:11	1:11	1:11-1
	1:12	1:10-2	1:10	**average**
	1:11-1	1:11-2	1:11-3	**1:10-4**
	average	1:11-2	**average**	
	1:12	1:11-3	**1:11-3**	
		average		
		1:11-2		

	$3500 claimers	$5000 claimers	$6000–7500 claimers	$10,000 claimers
SEVEN FURLONGS	1:25-4	1:25-4	1:24-3	1:24
	1:25-1	1:24-2	1:23-1	
	1:25-2	1:24-2	1:25-1	
	1:24-3	average	1:23-1	
	1:25-2	1:24-4	1:23-4	
	1:24-3		1:22-4	
	1:24-1		average	
	1:25-1		1:23-4	
	1:24-4			
	average			
	1:25			
1¹/₁₆ MILES	1:46-4	1:47-1	1:45-3	1:45-3
	1:48	1:47-1	1:45-4	1:46-2
	1:47-3	1:47	1:46-1	1:45-3
	1:46-4	1:46	1:45-3	1:44.3
	1:47-4	1:47-1	1:44-4	average
	1:46-2	1:48-1	1:46-2	1:45-3
	1:46-3	1:45-3	1:45-1	
	1:48	average	average	
	1:47-3	1:46-4	1:46	
	1:48			
	1:47-2			
	1:48			
	1:45-1			
	average			
	1:47-1			

The data for $3500 claiming races made perfect sense. The average winning time at six furlongs was 1:12, a rating of 78. At seven furlongs it was 1:25, a rating of 79. The average winning time at a mile and one-sixteenth was 1:47⅕. So on a Gulfstream speed chart, 1:47⅕ should probably have a value around 78 or 79.

I was perplexed by the $5000 and $6000–7500 averages, because they defied logic. The cheaper horses had run faster than the higher-class horses at six furlongs. But at seven furlongs, the $6000–7500 animals were a full second faster. Such discrepancies can arise whenever averages are based on a small sampling, and when this happens I prefer to trust my common sense rather than the statistics. In order to create a larger sampling that yielded more realistic results, I lumped the $5000 and $6000–7500 groups together. These were their averages:

Six furlongs	1:11-2
Seven furlongs	1:24-1
1$\frac{1}{16}$ miles	1:46-2

Now the data made sense. Six furlongs in 1:11$\frac{2}{5}$ has a rating of 86. Seven furlongs in 1:24$\frac{1}{5}$ is an 88. So the equivalent of these times, 1:46$\frac{2}{5}$, should have a rating around 86–88 on the speed chart I would construct.

In a 1$\frac{1}{16}$-mile race run in 1:47$\frac{1}{5}$, the average for $3500 claimers, one-fifth of a second would represent $\frac{1}{535}$, or about .19 percent, of the entire race. So in a speed chart, each fifth of a second would be worth 1.9 points. Starting with the assumption, based on the $3500 averages, that a mile and one-sixteenth in 1:47$\frac{1}{5}$ should have a rating of 79, I constructed a tentative speed chart in this fashion:

1:42	128.3 =	128	1:45-3	94.1 =	94
1:42-1	126.4 =	126	1:45-4	92.2 =	92
1:42-2	124.5 =	125	1:46	90.3 =	90
1:42-3	122.6 =	123	1:46-1	88.4 =	88
1:42-4	120.7 =	121	1:46-2	86.5 =	87
1:43	118.8 =	119	1:46-3	84.6 =	85
1:43-1	116.9 =	117	1:46-4	82.7 =	83
1:43-2	115.0 =	115	1:47	80.8 =	81
1:43-3	113.1 =	113	1:47-1	79.0 =	79
1:43-4	111.2 =	111	1:47-2	77.1 =	77
1:44	109.3 =	109	1:47-3	75.2 =	75
1:44-1	107.4 =	107	1:47-4	73.3 =	73
1:44-2	105.5 =	106	1:48	71.4 =	71
1:44-3	103.6 =	104	1:48-1	69.5 =	70
1:44-4	101.7 =	102	1:48-2	67.6 =	68
1:45	99.8 =	100	1:48 3	65.7 =	66
1:45-1	97.9 =	98	1:48-4	63.8 =	64
1:45-2	96.0 =	96	1:49	61.9 =	62

Perfect! The chart assigned a rating of 87 to 1:46$\frac{2}{5}$, and the $5000–7500 averages had indicated that this time should have a value in the 86–88 range. There was other evidence of my chart's validity. The average for $10,000 claimers at six furlongs was 1:10$\frac{4}{5}$, a rating of 94. The average winning time for a small sampling of $10,000 claimers at a route was 1:45$\frac{3}{5}$—also a rating of 94. I was now satisfied that I had a chart which would enable me to compare with precision the times of races at Gulfstream's different distances. I had fashioned a little bit of order out of chaos.

Now I had to do the same for Calder Race Course, because most of the horses at Gulfstream would be coming from there. So I took some fresh sheets of poster paper and the results of several months of races at Calder and repeated the whole process. These were some of the relevant average winning times:

	$3500 claimers	$6500–7000 claimers	$15,000–$20,000 claimers
Six furlongs	1:13-3	1:12-4	1:12-1
Seven furlongs	1:27-2	1:26-4	1:25-4
1¹⁄₁₆ miles	1:48-4	1:48-2	—

I stared at these data with disbelief. They had to be wrong. I knew from my time-honored equation, $1:13 = 1:26\frac{1}{5}$, that cheaper horses will run the last eighth of a mile of a seven-furlong race in 13⅕ seconds. But in the Calder averages, $3500 claimers needed 13⅘ seconds to cover the seventh furlong. And for the best claiming horses at the track, there was a 13⅗-second difference between the averages for six and seven furlongs.

I was immobilized for days by this discovery; I didn't know how to proceed. I even telephoned Sheldon and tried to coax him out of retirement. But finally I thought of a way to test the validity of my Calder averages. I went through all the result charts again and looked at the seven-furlong races whose six-furlong fractions were in the vicinity of 1:13. I listed the times in which the final furlong of these races had been run. And I found that the average time for the seventh furlong was 13⅘ seconds.

As they ran farther, horses did tire and slow down more at Calder than at other tracks. I could only speculate that this phenomenon was due to the unusual nature of the racing surface, which consists of a synthetic track covered with sand. But whatever the reason, I knew that my seven-furlong chart was not as universally accurate as I had thought, and I would have to construct a new one for Calder. I followed the same basic procedure I had used for Gulfstream. Six furlongs in 1:13⅗, the average winning time for $3500 claimers at Calder, has a rating of 56. So the other $3500 averages, 1:27⅖ for seven furlongs and 1:48⅘ for a mile and one-sixteenth, should also have a value in the vicinity of 56.

The speed charts for seven furlongs and a mile and one-sixteenth were easy to make. But Calder also offers races at other distances—

six-and-a-half furlongs, one mile, and a mile and 70 yards—which are not run often enough to provide a meaningful set of average times. For these distances I had to construct speed charts that were based on theory and common sense.

If a horse who runs six furlongs in 1:13⅗ requires 13⅘ seconds to travel an additional furlong, he will need 6.9 seconds to go half a furlong. So six furlongs in 1:13⅗ should equal 6½ furlongs in 1:20.5, or a point midway between 1:20⅖ and 1:20⅗ on the speed chart.

Similarly, the knowledge that cheap horses run half a furlong in 6.9 seconds enabled me to make ratings for one mile, as well as the bastard distance of a mile and 70 yards. If the basic $3500 claimer runs a mile and one-sixteenth in 1:48⅘ seconds, the equivalent time at a mile ought to be 1:41.9. When a horse goes a mile and 70 yards, he is covering $\frac{70}{110}$ of the distance between 1 mile and $1\frac{1}{16}$ miles. And $\frac{70}{110}$ of 6.9 seconds comes to 4⅖ seconds. Adding this to the mile time of 1:41.9, I concluded that the mile-and-70 equivalent is 1:46.3. After all these calculations, I finally had a Calder speed chart:

CALDER SPEED RATINGS

6 furlongs		6½ furlongs		7 furlongs		1 mile		1 mile, 70 yards		$1\frac{1}{16}$ miles	
1:11	92	**1:18**	88	**1:25**	85	**1:39**	86	**1:44**	79	**1:46**	83
1:11⅕	89	1:18⅕	85	1:25⅕	82	1:39⅕	84	1:44⅕	77	1:46⅕	81
1:11⅖	86	1:18⅖	83	1:25⅖	80	1:39⅖	82	1:44⅖	75	1:46⅖	79
1:11⅗	83	1:18⅗	80	1:25⅗	78	1:39⅗	80	1:44⅗	73	1:46⅗	77
1:11⅘	81	1:18⅘	78	1:25⅘	76	1:39⅘	78	1:44⅘	71	1:46⅘	75
1:12	78	**1:19**	75	**1:26**	73	**1:40**	76	**1:45**	69	**1:47**	73
1:12⅕	75	1:19⅕	73	1:26⅕	71	1:40⅕	74	1:45⅕	67	1:47⅕	71
1:12⅖	72	1:19⅖	70	1:26⅖	69	1:40⅖	72	1:45⅖	65	1:47⅖	69
1:12⅗	70	1:19⅗	68	1:26⅗	66	1:40⅗	70	1:45⅗	63	1:47⅗	68
1:12⅘	67	1:19⅘	65	1:26⅘	64	1:40⅘	68	1:45⅘	62	1:47⅘	66
1:13	64	**1:20**	63	**1:27**	62	**1:41**	66	**1:46**	60	**1:48**	64
1:13⅕	61	1:20⅕	60	1:27⅕	59	1:41⅕	64	1:46⅕	58	1:48⅕	62
1:13⅖	59	1:20⅖	58	1:27⅖	57	1:41⅖	62	1:46⅖	56	1:48⅖	60
1:13⅗	56	1:20⅗	55	1:27⅗	55	1:41⅗	60	1:46⅗	54	1:48⅗	59
1:13⅘	53	1:20⅘	53	1:27⅘	53	1:41⅘	58	1:46⅘	52	1:48⅘	57
1:14	50	**1:21**	50	**1:28**	50	**1:42**	56	**1:47**	50	**1:49**	55
1:14⅕	47	1:21⅕	48	1:28⅕	48	1:42⅕	54	1:47⅕	48	1:49⅕	53
1:14⅖	44	1:21⅖	45	1:28⅖	46	1:42⅖	52	1:47⅖	46	1:49⅖	51
1:14⅗	42	1:21⅗	43	1:28⅗	43	1:42⅗	50	1:47⅗	44	1:49⅗	50
1:14⅘	39	1:21⅘	40	1:28⅘	41	1:42⅘	48	1:47⅘	43	1:49⅘	48
1:15	36	**1:22**	38	**1:29**	39	**1:43**	46	**1:48**	41	**1:50**	46
1:15⅕	33	1:22⅕	35	1:29⅕	36	1:43⅕	44	1:48⅕	39	1:50⅕	44
1:15⅖	30	1:22⅖	33	1:29⅖	34	1:43⅖	43	1:48⅖	37	1:50⅖	42
1:15⅗	28	1:22⅗	30	1:29⅗	32	1:43⅗	41	1:48⅗	35	1:50⅗	41
1:15⅘	25	1:22⅘	28	1:29⅘	30	1:43⅘	39	1:48⅘	33	1:50⅘	39
1:16	22	**1:23**	25	**1:30**	28	**1:44**	37	**1:49**	31	**1:51**	37

Step Two: Par Figures

Having created my speed charts for Calder and Gulfstream, I was ready to go to work on the second important component of the figures: the track variant. The condition of a racetrack changes from day to day—sometimes subtly, sometimes dramatically—and it can determine the times of races even more than the ability of the animals. A horse who runs six furlongs in 1:13 at Calder may be superior to one who runs in 1:11 at Gulfstream. And that 1:11 horse may actually be faster than another who runs in 1:10 over the same track the next day. A speed handicapper has to measure the influence of the track before he can understand the true meaning of horses' times.

The only way I know to judge the inherent speed of a racetrack is to compare the way horses run over it with the way they *ought* to run over it. For example, I know that the average seven-furlong $3500 claiming race at Calder is run in 1:27⅗. If I saw several such races on the same afternoon run in 1:28, I would think that the track was three-fifths of a second slower than normal. This observation can be expressed in terms of speed ratings as well. If the average rating for the class is 57, and horses are winning in 1:28, a rating of 50, the track seems to be seven points slow.

To calculate track variants in this way, I needed to know the average winning rating for all the classes in Florida. In my earlier research for the speed charts, I had already compiled the winning times for every class and distance at Calder and Gulfstream. Now I could translate these times into speed ratings, lumping together the results at all distances to form a single average. These were my computations for $12,500 claiming races at Gulfstream:

$12,500 Claiming—Gulfstream

Distance	Winning Time	Rating
6f	1:10-1	103
6f	1:10-2	100
6f	1:11-1	92
6f	1:10-2	100
7f	1:23-2	97
7f	1:23	102
7f	1:23-2	97
1¹/₁₆m	1:45-3	94
		Average = 98

The average $12,500 claiming race for older horses at Gulfstream was won with a rating of 98. By performing similar computations, I found that races for the same class at Calder were won with an average rating of 72. In most other classes as well, horses ran about 26 points faster over Gulfstream's hard, sun-baked track than over Calder's tiring, sandy surface.

I wanted to be able to compare the two tracks easily, rather than make a mental adjustment of 26 points every time a Calder horse faced a Gulfstream horse. I needed a set of figures that were interchangeable from track to track.

To make such figures I had to use the same standard of reference from races at both tracks, instead of comparing Gulfstream results with the Gulfstream average winning figures and Calder results with the Calder averages. In the $12,500 claiming category, I could say that the *par figure* was 85 (the average of Gulfstream's 98 and Calder's 72). So on a typical day at Gulfstream, when $12,500 claiming races were being won with ratings of 98, the track was 13 points faster than par. The variant was −13. And on a typical day at Calder, when $12,500 claimers ran 13 points slower than par, the variant would be +13. I could construct accurate daily track variants once I had a set of par figures derived from the average results at Calder and Gulfstream.

FLORIDA PAR FIGURES

Older horses			*Younger horses* (Two-year-olds at Calder and Three-year-olds at Gulfstream)		
$3500	Claiming	68	$5000	Claiming	56
$5000	"	72	$6000–7500	"	63
$6000–7500	"	77	$10,000	"	68
$10,000	"	80	$12,500	"	73
$12,500	"	85	$15,000	"	77
$15,000	"	87	$18,000–20,000	"	79
$18,000–20,000	"	88	Maiden $5000		55
$25,000–30,000	"	91	Maiden $7500		58
Maiden $5000		65	Maiden $10,000–12,000		65
Maiden $10,000		74	Maiden $15,000		66
Maiden special weight		80	Maiden $20,000		71
Nonwinners of a race other than maiden or claiming		86	Maiden special weight		75
			Nonwinners of a race other than maiden or claiming		84
Allowance race with $8500 purse		97	Other allowance races		87
			Adjustment for all races limited to fillies and mares		−8

Step Three: Track Variants

With the above par-figure chart, I was finally ready to begin calculating the track variants and the figures that would be my principal handicapping tools in Florida. Because I wanted to arrive at Gulfstream with a two-month accumulation of figures, I went back to the Calder results for mid-November and started making my daily variants. These were the results on November 18:

Race	Distance	Class	Time
1.	6f	Maiden $5000 (2-year-olds)	1:14-4
2.	6f	Maiden $10,000 (2-year-old fillies)	1:14-3
3.	6f	Maiden $5000 (2-year-olds)	1:14-3
4.	(Turf)	—	—
5.	7f	Maiden special weight (older)	1:27
6.	6f	$7000 Claiming (older)	1:13
7.	6f	$10,000 Claiming (2-year-old fillies)	1:14-3
8.	7f	Allowance, 2-year-old nonwinners of two races other than maiden or claiming	1:26-4
9.	6f	Allowance, older fillies, $8500 purse	1:12-2
10.	6f	$3000 Claiming (older fillies)	1:14-1

As inscrutable as these data might appear to a casual horseplayer, I could measure the inherent speed of the Calder track on November 18 by consulting my par-figure chart (p. 129) and my speed-rating chart (p. 127). The second race, for example, was a $10,000 claiming event for maiden two-year-old fillies. The par figure for this class is 57 (65, minus 8 points because it is limited to females). The winner was timed in 1:14⅗, which, according to my Calder speed chart, has a rating of 42. So the second race was run 15 points slower than par. I analyzed the entire card in this fashion:

Race	Par Figure	Speed Rating	Difference
1.	55	39	16
2.	57	42	15
3.	55	42	13
4.	(Turf)	—	—
5.	80	62	18
6.	77	64	13
7.	60	42	18

Race	Par Figure	Speed Rating	Difference
8.	87	64	23
9.	89	72	17
10.	60	47	13
			—
		Average difference = 16	

The average race on November 18 at Calder was run 16 points slower than the par for its class. So the track variant was +16; I would add this amount to the speed rating of every horse in order to compensate for the condition of the track. The filly who won the second race in 1:14⅗, a rating of 42, had earned a figure of 58. I transcribed the winning figures onto a line in my notebook in this fashion:

Date	Variant	1	2	3	4	5	6	7	8	9	10
Nov 18	+16	55	58	58	T	78	80	58	80	88	63

Whenever I encountered a horse who had raced on November 18, I could refer to this line and learn what his figure was. If he had won the first race, I could see at a glance that his figure was 55. If he had been beaten in this field, I had to subtract a number of points that depended on the margin of his defeat and the distance of the race. Years ago Sheldon had employed some sophisticated mathematics to devise a table that converted beaten lengths into figures, and it had stood the test of time:

Beaten-lengths Adjustment Chart

Margin	5 Fur.	6 Fur.	7 Fur.	Mile	1$^1/_{16}$	1⅛	1½
neck	1	1	1	0	0	0	0
½	1	1	1	1	1	1	1
¾	2	2	2	1	1	1	1
1	3	2	2	2	2	2	1
1¼	4	3	3	2	2	2	1
1½	4	4	3	3	3	2	2
1¾	5	4	4	3	3	3	2
2	6	5	4	4	3	3	2
2¼	7	6	5	4	4	4	3
2½	7	6	5	4	4	4	3
2¾	8	7	6	5	5	5	3
3	9	7	6	5	5	5	3
3¼	9	8	7	6	5	5	4

Beaten-lengths Adjustment Chart (Cont.)

Margin	5 Fur.	6 Fur.	7 Fur.	Mile	1¹/₁₆	1¹/₈	1¹/₂
3½	10	9	7	6	6	6	4
3¾	11	9	8	7	6	6	4
4	12	10	8	7	7	6	5
4¼	12	10	9	8	7	7	5
4½	13	11	9	8	8	7	5
4¾	14	11	10	9	8	8	5
5	15	12	10	9	8	8	6
5½	16	13	11	10	9	9	6
6	18	15	12	11	10	9	7
6½	19	16	13	12	11	10	8
7	20	17	14	13	12	11	8
7½	22	18	15	13	13	12	9
8	23	20	17	14	13	13	10
8½	25	21	18	15	14	13	10
9	26	22	19	16	15	14	11
9½	28	23	19	17	16	16	11
10	29	24	20	18	17	17	12
11	32	27	23	20	18	18	13
12	35	29	25	21	20	20	14
13	38	32	27	23	22	22	15
14	41	34	29	25	23	23	16
15	44	37	31	27	25	25	17

If a horse had been beaten by 5½ lengths in the six-furlong first race on November 18, I would refer to the chart and see that his margin of defeat equaled 13 points. So I would subtract 13 from the winner's figure of 63 and give the horse a figure of 50.

Step Four: Track-to-Track Comparisons

After I had compiled about a month of figures at Calder, I was ready to tackle the problem which had confounded me ever since I discovered speed handicapping. I wanted to learn how to evaluate horses who shipped from one racing circuit to another—in this case, the horses who would be coming from New York to Florida for the winter.

I had a reliable set of figures for the New York tracks, but comparing them with my Florida numbers was like comparing apples with oranges. I had figures for different groups of horses who ran in different times over different tracks with different contours, and I had no idea what would constitute a logical basis for comparing them. I had been able to make a single set of figures for Calder and Gulfstream because I could properly assume that the horses in any class at one track were equal to the horses in the same class at the other. The $12,500 claimers at Gulfstream were the very same horses who had been $12,500 claimers at Calder and now had been vanned four miles up Hallandale Beach Boulevard.

But I could not assume that each class of horses in New York was equal in ability to the same class in Florida. The fields for maiden-special-weight races at the New York tracks are often very strong because so many well-bred young horses from fashionable stables launch their careers in them. These events are surely not comparable to Florida's maiden-special-weight races, which are usually populated by chronic losers. Such differences might exist at every class level, confounding any attempt to compare horses at different tracks.

As perplexing as the problem was, I knew it could be solved, because I had spoken with one horseplayer who had done it. Len Ragozin is a New Yorker who became so proficient as a speed handicapper that he graduated from betting horses to owning them. Ragozin makes figures for several eastern tracks, employs a trainer at each of them, and moves his horses from spot to spot as if they were chess pieces. He might ship a $10,000 claimer from Aqueduct to Keystone because he knows the Pennsylvania horses in that class are running weak figures. Once, in a brilliant stroke, he claimed a horse named Rare Joel out of a $5000 maiden race at Garden State. A month later he ran the animal in a $16,000 race for New York–breds at Belmont Park—and won by nine lengths. This was no accident. Obviously, figures that compare the ability of horses at different tracks could be immensely valuable.

After pondering the matter for weeks, I finally conceived a possible way to make such figures. I would assume, tentatively, that horses of a given claiming price have similar ability, regardless of where they run. Even though the ability of maidens, allowance horses, and stakes horses might vary considerably from track to track, there could not be an enormous difference between a $10,000 claimer in New York and a $10,000 claimer in Florida. I could learn how the two areas differed by comparing my par figures for the classes of older claiming horses:

	Florida	New York	Difference
$3500	68	—	—
$5000	72	80	8
$6000–7500	77	84	7
$10,000	80	88	8
$12,500	85	91	6
$15,000	87	95	8
$18,000–20,000	88	98	10
$25,000–30,000	91	99	8

My New York par figures averaged eight points higher than the Florida par figures. If the horses had comparable ability, if a $10,000 claimer in the South was as good as a $10,000 claimer in the North, I could simply add eight points to all my Florida figures and make them interchangeable with New York. Fortunately, there was a way to test this solution empirically. A vanguard of horses had already come from Aqueduct and started running at Calder. Because I now had figures for both tracks, I could compare each horse's numbers in New York and Florida and see if there was any consistent relationship between them. A portion of my data looked like this:

Horse	New York figure	Florida figure	Difference
Le Punch	77	67	10
But Never Sunday	72	63	9
Fame International	86	75	11
Pretty Frisky	77	75	2
Unchallenged	91	80	11
Know It All James	95	85	10
Smashing Native	95	92	3
		Average difference	= 8

When a New York horse ran in Florida, his figure dropped—on the average—by eight points. I was ecstatic. I could make the figures interchangeable by upgrading my Florida numbers eight points. The par figures on page 129 would be increased by eight: the par for a typical $5000 claiming race would be 80 instead of 72, bringing it in line with New York. The variants would be increased by eight points: a +13 track at Calder would now be a +21. And all the figures would be eight points higher. Redoing much of my earlier work was only a minor annoyance, because I knew I was bringing my figures closer to perfection.

Step Five: The Projection Method

There was one step yet to be taken. I had made my initial figures at Calder by comparing the par for a class with the horses' actual performance. This is the way most speed handicappers operate, but the procedure is, in fact, rather crude. Although the average $5000 claiming race is won with a figure of 80, one field might draw a group of weaklings who record a 60; another might have a standout who demolishes his opposition and earns a figure of 95. A track variant based on the premise that every $5000 race should have a figure of 80 is rooted in shaky ground.

Horses rarely perform as neatly as they did at Calder on November 18, when every race was run about 16 points slower than the par for its class. Bewildering days like January 21 at Gulfstream are far more commonplace. This is the way the results that day compared with the par figures:

Race	Par Figure	Speed Rating	Difference
1.	64	45	Slow by 19
2.	81	53	Slow by 28
3.	68	57	Slow by 11
4.	81	83	Fast by 2
5.	77	59	Slow by 18
6.	(Turf)	—	—
7.	(Turf)	—	—
8.	92	83	Slow by 9
9.	(Turf)	—	—
10.	71	63	Slow by 8

It is difficult to draw any conclusions from such a hodgepodge of results, when one race suggests that the track is 28 points slow and another indicates that it is two points fast. Averaging such divergent figures might produce a track variant that bears no relation to reality.

I use par times only at the start of a season, when I have no other basis for making track variants. But after I have compiled two or three weeks of figures, I begin to use what I term the *projection method*. I analyze the results of each race, look at the previous figures that the horses in it have run, and estimate what the winning figure should have been. Then I compare my estimate with the speed rating that the winner actually ran, and that forms the basis for my track variant. Mankind has not devised a more accurate way to judge the condition of a racetrack.

To make my track variant for the confusing day of January 21, I studied the result chart for each race as well as the past performances of the top finishers.

FIRST RACE

FIRST RACE
Gulfstream
JANUARY 21, 1977

6 FURLONGS. (1.07⅗) CLAIMING. Purse $4,000. 3-year-olds. Weights 122 lbs. Non-winners of two races since December 15, allowed 2 lbs. Two races since November 15, 4 lbs. A race since December 1, 6 lbs. Claiming Price $5,000. (Florida Breds Preferred.)

Value of race $4,000, value to winner $2,508, second $760, third $320, fourth $160, balance of starters $36 each. Mutuel pool $38,459.

Last Raced	Horse	Eqt.A.Wt	PP	St	¼	½	Str	Fin	Jockey	Cl'g Pr	Odds $1
13Jan77 1Crc4	Sixty Five Roses	b 3 116	3	3	2½	1hd	12	11	Rivera M A	5000	2.70
23Dec76 1Crc2	Westwood P. O.	3 116	1	5	1hd	21½	21½	21	Hernandez R	5000	2.90
18Jan77 2GP7	Pride King	3 116	7	2	41½	34	32	32½	MacBeth D	5000	3.50
25Dec76 4Crc6	Sweet N Clean	b 3 111	4	7	62	43	43	41½	Bailey J D	5000	4.90
11Jan77 2Crc7	Haz Raz	3 116	11	1	101	83	53	53	Danjean R	5000	86.00
	Simple Life	3 115	8	6	7½	7hd	71½	6¾	St Leon G	5000	20.20
	Fancy Persuasion	3 111	2	4	5hd	5½	6½	71¼	Capodici J	5000	18.30
24Dec76 3Crc4	Beck O' Luv	b 3 115	6	8	9½	6½	83	83¾	Perret C	5000	7.70
14Jan77 2Crc12	Streakin Agen	3 116	10	10	81	104	94	912	Beuviere L	5000	160.10
17Nov76 2Crc7	Hidden Promise	3 114	9	9	11	11	105	106	Solomone M	5000	18.80
18Jan77 2GP12	Bag o' Flower	b 3 116	5	11	31	9½	11	11	Smith A Jr	5000	42.60

OFF AT 1:16 EST. Start good, Won driving. Time, :23⅖, :47⅘, 1:14⅖ Track fast.

Official Program Numbers

$2 Mutuel Prices:				
	4–SIXTY FIVE ROSES	**7.40**	**3.80**	**2.80**
	1–WESTWOOD P. O.		**3.60**	**2.80**
	8–PRIDE KING			**2.80**

B. c, by Chieftain—Happy Request, by Requsted. Trainer Vargas Armand. Bred by Hasam Farms Inc (Fla).

SIXTY FIVE ROSES vied for command from the outset moved to a clear lead in midstretch and proved best. WESTWOOD P. O. alternated for command to early stretch could not keep pace with winner in midstretch but continued on gamely. PRIDE KING raced forwardly and was gaining slowly at the finish. SWEET N CLEAN bumped with BECK O LUV at the start and lacked the needed stretch response. BECK O LUV bumped with SWEET N CLEAN at the start. BAG O FLOWER was squeezed back at the start rushed along the inside to reach contention leaving the backstretch but had nothing left.

Owners— 1, Vargas A; 2, C & S Stable; 3, Elias Bros Farm; 4, Kern H & L; 5, Sinclair D A; 6, Larkin H; 7, Korhumel N F; 8, Davis J E; 9, Broic Helen; 10, Sibley Marion; 11, Hinton T L.

Trainers— 1, Vargas Armand; 2, Metcalf Raymond F; 3, Mayberry Brian A; 4, Edmundson S M; 5, Draper Manley; 6, Geiger Larry; 7, Viera Christine; 8, Butler Cy; 9, Broic Danny; 10, Shuman Hanford B Jr; 11, Armbrister Carl.

Overweight: Simple Life 4 pounds; Beck O' Luv 4; Hidden Promise 3.

Westwood P. O. was claimed by Prime Acres Inc; trainer, MacFarlane Ralph S; Pride King was claimed by Willowbrook Stable; trainer, Morguelan Steven L.

Scratched—Doctor Dyn-O-Mite (11Jan77 2Crc5); Dazzling Debbie (3Jan77 2Crc2); Mike's Hope (4Nov76 3Key8); Nanna Lee (13Jan77 7Crc8); The Spud Stud (18Jan77 2GP11); Ellie's Dream (3Jan77 2Crc7); Swift Bernie (10Jan77 6Crc4).

Sixty Five Roses — **B. c. 3, by Chieftain—Happy Request, by Requsted** — **$5,000** — **Br.—Hasam Farms Inc (Fla)** — **Tr.—Vargas Armand** — **116**
Own.—Vargas A

	St.	1st	2nd	3rd	Amt.
1977	1	0	0	0	$210
1976	6	1	0	0	$2,690

13Jan77- 1Crc	fst	7f	:22⅘	:46	1:27⅕	Clm 5000	6	5	41¾	22	22	46	Rivera M A 60		117	12.10	74–17	Desoto Prince 1203½ Certainty 1072 Mr. V. C. 117½	Bumped	9
30Dec76- 6Crc	fst	6f	:23	47	1:15	Clm 7500	7	2	41½	53½	811	812	Diaz P G 38		119	20.90	66–19	Northern Park 112½ First Brinks Edge105nk[D]EndRise1161½	Tired	8
26Nov76- 5Crc	fst	1$\frac{1}{16}$	:49⅘	1:15⅖	1:49⅖	Clm c-7000	7	4	64¼	64¼	66¼	615	Bailey J D	b	113	2.80	60–15	Emerald Pit 1173½ Fastex 1171½ Set n' Hope 117½	Tired	8
18Oct76- 7Crc	fst	6f	:23⅕	:46⅗	1:14⅘	Clm 9000	8	9	87	911	814	66	Bailey J D	b	115	5.10	73–19	Born Mean 120¾ Earlgroll 114½ Bupers Spin 117¾	Outrun	9
8Oct76- 5Crc	fst	6f	:23⅗	:47⅖	1:15	Md 10000	8	4	63¾	53¾	23	1½	Bailey J D	b	118	*1.70	78–17	Sixty Five Roses 118½ Seebrullah 1181½ Tom Blitz 109¾	Driving	10
18Sep76- 3Crc	fst	6f	:23⅗	:47⅕	1:13⅗	Md Sp Wt	8	6	73¼	78¾	79	86¾	Lopez R D		118	75.50	78–13	FameInternational1183NativeVelvet118noMiniStyls118¾	No factor	11
6Sep76- 3Crc	fst	6f	:23⅖	:47⅖	1:14	Md Sp Wt	5	8	106	1013	1114	1011	Lopez R D		118	12.60	72–18	FrindlyPrincss1153MostAmbitious118nkSlvrSpngld1152	No factor	12

LATEST WORKOUTS **Dec 23 Crc 3f fst :38⅖ b** **Nov 23 Crc 4f fst :50⅖ b**

Westwood P. O. — **B. g. 3, by Currock—Whizdale, by Hillsdale** — **$5,000** — **Br.—Oxford Farm (Fla)** — **Tr.—Metcalf Raymond F** — **116**
Own.—C & S Stable

	St.	1st	2nd	3rd	Amt.
1976	6	M	2	0	$1,470

23Dec76- 1Crc	fst	6f	:23⅗	:47⅖	1:14⅕	Md 5000	12	1	2½	22	22	21½	Riera R Jr 64	118	2.60	80–17	First BrinksEdge1111½WestwoodP.O.1186OhWhatFun1181	Gamely	12
13Dec76- 2Crc	fst	6f	:23⅖	:47⅗	1:14	Md 7000	12	1	67½	712	712	412	Riera R Jr 43	118	13.90	71–17	Chosen Few 1163 Time For Love 1154 Stangley 1184½	Ducked in	12
26Nov76- 1Crc	fst	6½f	:23⅕	:47⅕	1:20⅗	Md 5000	4	6	61¾	67½	37	29	Romero P 53	118	34.70	79–15	MythMaster1189WestwoodP.O.1181½EasterMoon1182	Best others	12
3Nov76- 1Mth	fst	6f	:22⅖	:46⅕	1:12⅘	Md 6500	4	5	2hd	22½	34½	714	Perret C	116	5.80	62–18	Queen of Tenn. 1153½ Delightful Sam 118no Manidevo 113½	Tired	10
21Oct76- 1Mth	gd	6f	:23⅖	:48⅕	1:14⅕	Md 7000	3	6	21	65¼	78½	814	Romero P	118	40.90	55–26	Hail To the Prince 1185 Cannonball Joe 1186Koorshum111¾	Tried	12
31Aug76- 3Tim	fst	*6½f	:24⅕	:49	1:21⅖	Md 9000	2	3	54¾	56	79¼	614	Marrone A	120	15.70	63–19	Parsenn 1173 Unacceptable 118no Yore Ly'in Eyes1096	No factor	7

LATEST WORKOUTS **Jan 18 Hia 5f fst 1:02 b** **Dec 18 GP 4f fst :50 b** **Dec 8 GP 4f fst :49⅖ b** **Nov 23 GP 5f fst 1:03 b**

Westwood P. O. came into this race with the top figure of 64, compared with a figure of 60 for Sixty Five Roses. For Sixty Five Roses to win, he had to improve or Westwood P.O. had to deteriorate. There is every reason to believe that Sixty Five Roses ran a better figure than he did in his previous start. He had been bumped in that race. And he had been running seven-eighths of a mile, tiring near the end. The shorter six-furlong distance would help him.

If Westwood P. O. ran his figure of 64 again, Sixty Five Roses would have run a 66 to beat him by one length. (According to my beaten-lengths adjustment chart, a length at six furlongs equals two points.) So I projected a figure of 66 for the first race at Gulfstream. Sixty Five Roses actually ran in 1:14⅗, a rating of 45. Before proceeding to the second race, I summarized the data in this fashion:

Race	Projected Figure	Speed Rating	Difference
1.	66	45	Slow by 21

SECOND RACE

SECOND RACE **6 FURLONGS. (1.07⅘) MAIDEN CLAIMING. Purse $6,000. 3-year-olds. Weights 120 lbs. Claiming Price $40,000 for each $2,500 to $35,000 allowed 2 lbs. (Preference to horses which have not started for $15,000 or less).**

Gulfstream

JANUARY 21, 1977

Value of race $6,000, value to winner $3,732, second $1,140, third $540, fourths $168 each, balance of starters $36 each. Mutuel pool $73,107.

Last Raced	Horse	Eqt.	A.	Wt	PP	St	¼	½	Str	Fin	Jockey	Cl'g Pr	Odds $1
1Jan77 $^{3}Crc^{2}$	G's Brandy	b	3	116	8	2	4^{1}	$3^{1\frac{1}{2}}$	$1^{\frac{1}{2}}$	1^{1}	Thornburg B	35000	2.10
14Jan77 $^{1}Crc^{2}$	Bobs A Prince		3	116	12	1	$2^{\frac{1}{2}}$	1^{hd}	2^{2}	$2^{\frac{1}{2}}$	Gallitano G	35000	10.70
	Li'l Indian		3	120	11	3	6^{1}	6^{2}	$3^{\frac{1}{2}}$	3^{5}	Saumell L	40000	7.20
22Dec76 $^{2}Crc^{10}$	[DH] Jonah Boy		3	120	1	4	3^{1}	$5^{1\frac{1}{2}}$	5^{1}	4	Duffy L	40000	29.40
	[DH] Handy Mac		3	116	3	7	7^{hd}	8^{2}	8^{3}	4^{hd}	Fell J	35000	10.60
4Oct76 $^{4}Bel^{9}$	Distinctive's Boy	b	3	120	7	5	$1^{\frac{1}{2}}$	$2^{\frac{1}{2}}$	$4^{\frac{1}{2}}$	$6^{2\frac{1}{2}}$	Baltazar C	40000	10.10
	Lavish Lad		3	116	9	11	5^{1}	4^{hd}	6^{2}	$7^{\frac{1}{2}}$	Ramos A	35000	11.40
17Jan77 $^{3}GP^{4}$	Noble Irishman	b	3	120	2	8	$8^{\frac{1}{2}}$	$7^{1\frac{1}{2}}$	7^{hd}	$8^{1\frac{1}{2}}$	Rivera M A	40000	3.20
13Dec76 $^{3}Lrl^{9}$	Rinerhorn		3	116	5	6	11^{3}	11^{2}	9^{3}	9^{6}	Lindberg G	35000	41.90
6Jan77 $^{5}Crc^{10}$	On The Set	b	3	116	6	10	10^{1}	$9^{\frac{1}{2}}$	$10^{\frac{1}{2}}$	$10^{\frac{1}{2}}$	Perret C	35000	23.60
	Schuyler Lake		3	116	4	9	9^{hd}	11^{3}	11^{4}	11^{5}	Breen R	35000	12.90
	Bosoni	b	3	116	10	12	12	12	12	12	Solomone M	35000	34.70

[DH]—Dead heat.

OFF AT 1:42 EST. Start good, Won driving. Time, :23, :47⅘, 1:13⅘ Track fast.

$2 Mutuel Prices:

8–G'S BRANDY	**6.20**	**3.80**	**3.20**
12–BOBS A PRINCE		**7.20**	**4.80**
11–LI'L INDIAN			**5.40**

B. c, by Dance To Market—Dulia, by Dunce. Trainer Scruton Arnold Sr. Bred by Green G (Fla).

G'S BRANDY, away alertly, came along the outside to gain command in midstretch and slowly increased the margin. BOBS A PRINCE vied for command to midstretch, then could not stay with the winner. LI'L INDIAN reached sharp contention in midstretch and was gaining slowly at the finish. HANDY MAC improved his position to finish in a dead heat with JONAH BOY. The latter raced forwardly but lacked needed closing response while finishing on even terms with HANDY MAC. NOBLE IRISHMAN was outrun. RINERHORN was steadied out of tight quarters along the backstretch.

Owners— 1, Shelly Maude; 2, Merlo Thomas; 3, Jaclyn Stable; 4, Shefry Farms; 5, Torsney J M; 6, Allen Herbert; 7, Copper Stable; 8, Crown Stable; 9, Obre Mrs H; 10, Elberon Farms; 11, Wright Ernest B; 12, Chianelli A.

Trainers— 1, Scruton Arnold Sr; 2, Edmundson Samuel M; 3, Croll Warren A Jr; 4, Moerman G C; 5, Schulhofer Flint S; 6, Jacobs Eugene; 7, Plett J F; 8, Lepman Budd; 9, Field Kenneth; 10, Bond J Bowes; 11, Weipert J J; 12, Mullin William.

Scratched—Vorhees Diplomat (17Jan77 $^{3}GP^{10}$); Slick Sheikh (18Sep76 $^{9}Mth^{9}$); Brenners Park (6Jan77 $^{5}Crc^{8}$); Three O Five; Arezzo (16Oct76 $^{3}Crc^{5}$); Destin To Burn (11Jan77 $^{6}Crc^{2}$).

G's Brandy — **B. c. 3, by Dance To Market—Dulia, by Dunce** — **$35,000** — **Br.—Green G (Fla)** — **Tr.—Scruton Arnold Sr** — **116**

Own.—Shelly Maude

	St.	1st	2nd	3rd	Amt.
1977	1	M	1	0	$1,080
1976	3	M	1	0	$1,200

1Jan77- 3Crc fst 7f :23 :47 1:27 Md Sp Wt 7 3 $5^{3\frac{1}{4}}$ $5^{2\frac{1}{2}}$ $1^{\frac{1}{2}}$ 2^{1} Romero P 78 b 120 3.70 80–18 Buckfan 115^{1} G's Brandy $120^{\frac{1}{2}}$ Jungle Adam 120no Game try 9

22Dec76- 2Crc fst 6f :22⅗ :46⅖ 1:13⅖ Md Sp Wt 7 5 2^{2} 2^{2} 3^{2} 2^{1} Romero P 74 118 28.10 85–14 Be Gallant 118^{1} G's Brandy 118^{nk} Mills Bill 118^{2} Good try 11

4Dec76- 2Crc fst 6f :22⅖ :46 1:13⅖ M[illegible] Sp Wt 11 2 $6^{3\frac{3}{4}}$ 5^{5} $6^{9\frac{1}{2}}$ 8^{11} MacBeth D 48 118 73.70 75–12 Times Square $118^{\frac{3}{4}}$ Tuxson 118no L' Epouvantail 118^{nk} No mishap 12

20Nov76- 2Crc fst 6f :23⅕ :47⅗ 1:14⅖ M[illegible] Wt 8 4 2^{1} $2^{\frac{1}{2}}$ 4^{3} $7^{8\frac{1}{4}}$ MacBeth D b 118 38.80 73–15 Ole Spats $118^{2\frac{1}{2}}$ Swinging Knight 118^{hd} Native Velvet $118^{\frac{3}{4}}$ Tired 11

LATEST WORKOUTS **Jan 19 GP 4f f[illegible] b** **Jan 13 GP 4f fst :49⅖ b** **Dec 18 GP 5f fst 1:02 b** **Nov 27 GP 4f fst :53 b**

Bobs A Prince — **Ch. g. 3, by Bold Bob—Royal J V, by Royal Note** — **$35,000** — **Br.—Triple M Farm (Fla)** — **Tr.—Edmundson Samuel M** — **116**

Own.—Merlo Thomas

	St.	1st	2nd	3rd	Amt.
1977	1	M	1	0	$900
1976	0	M	0	0	

14Jan77- 1Crc fst 6f :22⅘ :46⅘ 1:14⅕ Md 18000 10 3 $5^{4\frac{3}{4}}$ 3^{2} $3^{2\frac{1}{2}}$ $2^{1\frac{1}{2}}$ Gallitano G 68 116 19.60 80–13 Short Memory $116^{1\frac{1}{2}}$ Bobs A Prince 116^{1} JuanDavid$116^{1\frac{1}{2}}$ Gamely 12

LATEST WORKOUTS **Jan 13 Crc 3f fst :37 b** **Jan 8 Crc 5f fst 1:02⅕ b** **Dec 27 Crc 5f fst 1:02 b** **Dec 17 Crc 6f fst 1:16⅗ b**

G's Brandy had run figures of 78 and 74 in his last two starts, but today he scored by only a length over Bobs A Prince, who had earned a 68 in his racing debut. Because young horses customarily benefit from experience, Bobs A Prince might well have improved sharply to finish so close, while G's Brandy duplicated his recent 78.

Race	Projected Figure	Speed Rating	Difference
2.	78	53	Slow by 25

THIRD RACE

THIRD RACE	1 $\frac{1}{16}$ MILES. (1.40⅕) CLAIMING. Purse $5,800. Fillies, 3–year–olds. Weights 122 lbs.

Gulfstream

JANUARY 21, 1977

Non–winners of two races since December 1, allowed 2 lbs. Two races since November 15, 4 lbs. Two races since November 1, 6 lbs. Claiming Price $10,000 for each $500 to $9,000 allowed 2 lbs. (Races where entered for $7,500 or less not considered.)

Value of race $5,800, value to winner $3,612, second $1,160, third $522, fourth $290, balance of starters $36 each. Mutuel pool $90,959.

Last Raced	Horse	Eqt.A.Wt PP St	¼	½	¾	Str	Fin	Jockey	Cl'g Pr	Odds $1
12Jan77 4Crc1	Time For Love	b 3 116 7 3	2¹	2½	2½	1hd	11½	Barrow T	10000	5.20
14Dec76 2Crc8	Cartersville Miss	3 114 8 4	1²	11½	1¹	2½	2²	Gomez A	9000	42.50
14Jan77 2Crc6	George's Pick	3 112 1 2	3¹	51½	3½	3³	3¾	Lopez R D	9000	7.30
28Dec76 2Crc2	Am Home	b 3 116 2 1	6³	6³	4²	4²	41½	Breen R	10000	10.00
14Jan77 2Crc11	Go Streak Go	b 3 112 3 6	7³	7hd	7½	6²	51½	MacBeth D	9000	60.50
11Jan77 5Crc4	Funglint	b 3 116 10 10	10	9½	8²	5hd	6²	Garrido J	10000	3.00
11Jan77 5Crc11	Marfox	b 3 107 4 7	91½	10	10	7hd	7¹	Harbacek D5	9000	a-6.20
4Jan77 2Crc4	Best Vitriol	b 3 116 6 8	5½	4hd	5hd	8³	82½	Rivera M A	10000	3.30
11Jan77 5Crc8	Maxi Class	3 111 9 9	8²	8⁴	9hd	10	9²	O'Connell J5	10000	a-6.20
7Jan77 10Crc2	Sal Sal	b 3 115 5 5	41½	3½	6²	9hd	10	Perret C	9000	4.30

a–Coupled: Marfox and Maxi Class.

OFF AT 2:08, EST. Start good, Won driving. Time, :23⅗, :48⅘, 1:15, 1:42⅗, 1:49⅗ Track fast.

$2 Mutuel Prices:

7–TIME FOR LOVE	12.40	6.60	5.40
8–CARTERSVILLE MISS		30.00	12.60
2–GEORGE'S PICK			5.40

Ch. f, by Ky Pioneer—Final Belle, by Bolinas Boy. Trainer Viera Christine. Bred by Talbot Mr–Mrs W G (Ky).

TIME FOR LOVE pressed the pace from the outset, gained the advantage in midstretch and proved best. CARTERSVILLE MISS moved to command early but could not stay with winner in final sixteenth. GEORGE'S PICK raced along the inside, loomed a serious threat in midstretch but could not sustain the bid. AM HOME raced forwardly and had no apparent mishap. FUNGLINT was outrun. MARFOX was never a serious threat. BEST VITRIOL lacked a stretch response. MAXI CLASS failed to reach contention. SAL SAL was jostled around soon after the start, had speed for a half, then gave way.

Owners— 1, Katz & Weiland; 2, Merrill F H; 3, Parchment & Satz; 4, Sandera Farm; 5, Divito J P; 6, Fuchs J; 7, Frazier J A; 8, Caserta Tony; 9, Frazier & Pendray J C & Sons Inc; 10, Le Petit Stable.

Trainers— 1, Viera Christine; 2, Merrill Frank H; 3, Parchment Basil V; 4, Sanders Greg; 5, Divito Jim P· 6, Hebert Leo; 7, Tortora Emanuel; 8, Bowles C F; 9, Tortora Emanuel; 10, Delk Danny Sr.

Overweight: Cartersville Miss 2 pounds; Sal Sal 3.

During the previous few days, the mile-and-one-sixteenth races at Gulfstream had made no sense to me. They seemed to be faster than they should have been, relative to the times of sprints, and I suspected that there must be some temporary aberration in the condition of the track.

I saw that if I took the result of the third race at face value, many of the horses in it were going to be credited with the best figure of their lives—a figure that I did not trust. Many speed handicappers follow their usual procedures mechanically and accept the results of their calculations even when they defy common' sense. But I would rather assign no figure to a race than use an erroneous one that could cost me money. So I decided to ignore the third race in the computation of my track variant.

FOURTH RACE

FOURTH RACE
Gulfstream
JANUARY 21, 1977

6 FURLONGS. (1.07⅘) MAIDEN CLAIMING. Purse $6,000. 3-year-olds. Weights 120 lbs. Claiming Price $40,000 for each $2,500 to $35,000 allowed 2 lbs. (Preference to horses which have not started for $15,000 or less).

Value of race $6,000, value to winner $3,732, second $1,140, third $540, fourth $300, balance of starters $36 each. Mutuel pool $65,161. Perfecta Pool $81,509.

Last Raced	Horse	Eqt.	A.	Wt	PP	St	¼	½	Str	Fin	Jockey	Cl'g Pr	Odds $1
	White Rammer		3	120	11	2	$4^{1\frac{1}{2}}$	2^{hd}	2^{5}	1^{1}	Saumell L	40000	1.90
	Bio Grey		3	116	6	4	$1^{1\frac{1}{2}}$	$1^{1\frac{1}{2}}$	$1^{\frac{1}{2}}$	2^{9}	Manganello M	35000	16.80
	Never Guilty		3	116	3	5	5^{3}	4^{2}	3^{2}	3^{3}	Gomez A	35000	14.60
	Sir Judge		3	120	5	9	$7^{\frac{1}{2}}$	6^{hd}	5^{3}	$4^{1\frac{1}{2}}$	Aviles O B	40000	7.30
	Cash Or Credit		3	120	4	6	2^{1}	3^{2}	4^{2}	5^{2}	Perret C	40000	5.70
	Squadron Castle		3	116	7	11	9^{2}	$8^{1\frac{1}{2}}$	$6^{1\frac{1}{2}}$	6^{2}	Salinas S	35000	45.10
17Jan77 ^{3}GP^{11}	Speedy Catch		3	116	9	10	10^{8}	10^{10}	$8^{\frac{1}{2}}$	7^{1}	Solomone M	35000	11.10
22Dec76 ^{2}Crc^{5}	Indian Mountain		3	120	2	7	$6^{\frac{1}{2}}$	7^{3}	9^{3}	8^{1}	MacBeth D	40000	4.00
11Nov76 ^{4}CD^{5}	East Union	b	3	116	10	1	3^{hd}	5^{3}	7^{1}	9^{3}	Gavidia W	35000	8.50
	Mohawk Drive		3	120	8	8	8^{3}	$9^{1\frac{1}{2}}$	10^{14}	10^{11}	Cedeno M	40000	37.70
	Lugano		3	120	12	3	12	12	12	11^{7}	Miceli M	40000	80.20
	Dad's Sugar		3	116	1	12	11^{10}	11^{8}	11^{2}	12	Barrow T	35000	28.80

OFF AT 2:38 1/2 EST. Start good, Won driving. Time, :22, :46⅕, 1:11⅗ Track fast.

$2 Mutuel Prices:				
	11-WHITE RAMMER	5.80	4.00	3.00
	6-BIO GREY		12.20	9.20
	3-NEVER GUILTY			6.00

$2 PERFECTA 11-6 PAID $99.00.

Ch. c, by Jim J—Been Taken, by Tom Fool. Trainer Croll Warren A Jr. Bred by Bryand Mr-Mrs J C H (Va).

WHITE RAMMER well placed early improved position from the outside on the turn to challenge in midstretch and under brisk left handed pressure was drawing clear at the finish. BIO GREY sprinted to a clear lead early responded when challenged in midstretch but was outfinished. NEVER GUILTY prominent early had no apparent mishap. SIR JUDGE was outrun. CASH OR CREDIT had speed to head of stretch. INDIAN MOUNTAIN showed little. EAST UNION was finished after a half. LUGANO bore out badly along the backstretch.

Owners— 1, Bryant J C H; 2, Crimson King Farm; 3, Wilson M; 4, S & F Farm; 5, Stoll Mr-Mrs J; 6, Wettach M; 7, Hoffman Mrs P B; 8, Lake Don; 9, Bromagen G S & W; 10, Horner Earl & Ellie; 11, Briardale Farm; 12, Beardsley Mrs M & Pillsbury J.

Trainers— 1, Croll Warren A Jr; 2, Salmen Peter W Jr; 3, Merrill Frank H; 4, Kelley Walter A; 5, Bond J Bowes; 6, Field Kenneth; 7, Prater R W; 8, Richards Robert J Jr; 9, Kelley Thomas W; 10, Gallagher R J; 11, Armstrong K D; 12, Simmons John P.

Overweight: Dad's Sugar 5 pounds.

Scratched—Real Flyer (17Jan77 ^{3}GP^{2}); Pac; Joe Gural (7Jan77 ^{2}Crc^{2}); No Bluffing; Back First; Senate.

Indian Mountain　Ch. c. 3, by Jim J—Lorgnette II, by High Hat
Own.—Lake Don　$40,000　Br.—Moore Marie A (Ky)　Tr.—Richards Robert J Jr　65　120
St. 1st 2nd 3rd Amt.　1976 2 M 0 0 $300
22Dec76- 2Crc fst 6f :22⅘ :46⅘ 1:13⅘ Md Sp Wt 3 9 $3^{2\frac{1}{2}}$ $3^{2\frac{1}{2}}$ 4^{5} $5^{4\frac{1}{2}}$ St Leon G 118 5.60 82-14 Be Gallant 118^{1} G's Brandy 118^{nk} Mills Bill 118^{2} Weakened 11
13Dec76- 4Crc fst 7f :23⅘ :47⅕ 1:27 Md Sp Wt 3 3 1^{2} $1^{1\frac{1}{2}}$ $1^{\frac{1}{2}}$ $4^{4\frac{1}{2}}$ Bohenko P 118 41.10 77-17 Highland Jim 118^{1}PoorMan'sBluff118^{nk}Satan'sThunder118^{3} Tired 12
LATEST WORKOUTS　Jan 11 GP 6f fst 1:16⅖ b　Dec 30 GP 4f fst :49⅖ b　Dec 1 GP 3f fst :37⅘ bg

White Rammer　Ch. c. 3, by Jim J—Been Taken, by Tom Fool
Own.—Bryant J C H　$40,000　Br.—Bryand Mr-Mrs J C H (Va)　Tr.—Croll Warren A Jr　120
St. 1st 2nd 3rd Amt.　1977 0 M 0 0　1976 0 M 0 0
LATEST WORKOUTS　Jan 19 GP 4f fst :48 h　Jan 14 GP 4f fst :48 hg　Jan 10 GP 5f fst 1:01 hg　Jan 6 GP 4f fst :49 b

I had scored one of my first triumphs of the Gulfstream season on White Rammer, and I knew that a Jimmy Croll first-time starter was eligible to run a powerful race. The fact that he and Bio Grey had routed the rest of the field by nine lengths suggested that their figure had been very big. But how big? The only horse in the race with any established form was Indian Mountain, and he had been beaten by 19½ lengths. If he had duplicated his previous figure of 65, that would make White Rammer a 113 and my future-book choice to win the Kentucky Derby. I doubted he was that good. There was not enough evidence on which to base a projection for the fourth race.

FIFTH RACE

FIFTH RACE
Gulfstream
JANUARY 21, 1977

6 FURLONGS. (1.07⅘) CLAIMING. Purse $6,500. Fillies, 3-year-olds. Weights 122 lbs. Non-winners of two races since December 15, allowed 2 lbs. Two races since November 15, 4 lbs. A race since December 1, 6lbs. Claiming Price $16,000 for each $1,000 to $14,000 allowed 2 lbs. (Races where entered for $12,500 or less not considered.)

Value of race $6,500, value to winner $4,067, second $1,235, third $585, fourth $325, balance of starters $36 each. Mutuel pool $122,203.

Last Raced	Horse	Eqt.	A.Wt	PP	St	¼	½	Str	Fin	Jockey	Cl'g Pr	Odds $1
20Dec76 5Crc9	Ladies Dont		3 116	8	3	1½	1hd	13	12½	Barrow T	16000	4.40
7Jan77 5Crc3	Helga Behaves	b	3 116	5	11	11hd	81½	42	22½	Bailey J D	16000	6.50
31Dec76 6Crc4	Attention Now	b	3 116	11	5	51	3hd	32	32	Hidalgo D	15000	9.00
14Oct76 2Mth6	Impulsive Decision	b	3 116	12	2	21½	26	23	41	Cedeno M	16000	63.50
25Dec76 3Crc6	Hey Dolly A.	b	3 114	7	10	101	6hd	51½	5½	Breen R	14000	38.10
18Oct76 3Mth3	Brave London Lady		3 116	9	4	91½	9hd	6½	65	Perret C	16000	6.90
21Sep76 9Bel2	Sun Bank	b	3 116	4	9	6½	72	72	71	Saumell L	16000	6.90
7Jan77 5Crc5	Glen's Bunny		3 113	10	1	7hd	113	102	81½	Crews W	14000	42.70
7Jan77 5Crc1	Branded Woman		3 118	1	6	42	4½	81	9¾	Brumfield D	16000	3.50
8Nov76 6Mth4	Bold Slam		3 116	3	8	8½	101	114	10nk	Miceli M	16000	16.00
10Nov76 8Crc7	Linda Love Lane	b	3 114	2	7	3hd	52	9hd	115	Perna R	15000	5.40
27Dec76 2Crc4	Pamtorin	b	3 115	6	12	12	12	12	12	Rodriguez J	15000	19.40

OFF AT 3:06, EST Start good, Won handily. Time, :23⅕, :47⅕, 1:13⅖ Track fast.

$2 Mutuel Prices:			
8-LADIES DONT	10.80	6.80	5.00
5-HELGA BEHAVES		7.60	5.40
11-ATTENTION NOW			5.40

B. f, by Pass Catcher—New Woman, by Staunchness. Trainer Kaelin Forrest. Bred by Elsam Farm (Fla).

LADIES DONT vied for command with IMPULSIVE DECISION to head of the stretch disposed of that one and won in hand. HELGA BEHAVES unhurried early improved position between hoses in stretch run. ATTENTION NOW well placed was gaining slowly at the finish. IMPULSIVE DECISION raced wide, dueled for command to head of stretch then weakened. BRAVE LONDON LADY outfinished the others. SUN BANK raced wide on turn and into stretch. BRANDED WOMAN had no apparent excuse. LINDA LOVE LANE gave way when outrun early.

Owners— 1, Peltier H Jr; 2, Brauer D R; 3, Steil J; 4, Heller C; 5, Al-Bar Stable & Baron; 6, Lohn & Pierce; 7, Rose Betty; 8, Underwood Ruth & Werner; 9, Le Petit Stable; 10, Posen E L; 11, Gaston Linda T & Stutts G R; 12, Cohen & Rodriguez.

Trainers— 1, Kaelin Forrest; 2, Brauer Donald R; 3, Julian George; 4, Fox M H; 5, Padovani Mario; 6, Pierce J H Jr; 7, Moncrief Marvin L; 8, Rose Harold J; 9, Delk Danny Sr; 10, Puglisi Anthony; 11, Stutts C R; 12, Rodriguez Jose T.

Overweight: Hey Dolly A. 2 pounds; Glen's Bunny 1; Pamtorin 1.

Scratched—Coopers Block (14Jan77 1Crc8); Dragon High (7Jan77 5Crc9); Merrie's Nail (7Jan77 5Crc8); Bagger's Delight (7Jan77 5Crc2); Her Grace Sarah (20Dec76 5Crc3); Holiday Mood (25Sep76 6Crc8).

Ladies Dont — **B. f. 3, by Pass Catcher—New Woman, by Staunchness**
Own.—Peltier H Jr — **$16,000** — **Br.—Elsam Farm (Fla)** — **Tr.—Kaelin Forrest** — **116**

	St.	1st	2nd	3rd	Amt.
1976	8	1	1	1	$5,045

20Dec76- 5Crc	fst	7f	:23	:47	1:27⅕	ⒻClm 20000	9	3	916	917	916	99¼	Barrow T	59 116	29.00	71-16	Lady Lib 119½ Stephens' Grad116hdHerGraceSarah118¾ No factor	10
27Nov76- 6CD	my	6f	:23	:48	1:14⅖	ⒻAllowance	8	7	915	914	817	718	Barrow T	121	2.30e	56-36	Haley Baby 11613 Twice Foolish 121nk MaggieMar116¾ No factor	9
13Nov76- 7CD	fst	6f	:22⅗	:46⅖	1:13⅗	ⒻAllowance	2	4	2½	23½	78	911	Barrow T	119	3.80	67-29	Plain and Fancy 122½ Like Ducks117hdPocketPrincess122no Tired	12
6Nov76- 7CD	fst	6f	:22⅕	:45⅗	1:12⅘	ⒻAllowance	10	3	66	34	34	23¾	Barrow T	116	27.20	78-25	Grey Glitter 1143¾ Ladies Dont 116hd Work Sheet 114hd Gamely	12
18Sep76- 8Lat	fst	6f	:22⅗	:45⅘	1:11⅖	ⒻClipsetta	4	6	1220	1121	1016	1023	Fann B	114	17.80	68-17	Historic Site 1231 Sagittarius Gal 1162½ Careless Moment 1167	12
3Sep76- 2Del	fst	6f	:22⅘	:46⅗	1:11⅖	ⒻMd Sp Wt	8	1	12½	11½	12½	12½	Barrow T	118	3.30	88-14	LdisDont1182½FollowThRinbow1189OnlyAMmory118¾ Ridden out	8
3Aug76- 1Atl	fst	5f	:22⅖	:45⅗	:58	ⒻMd Sp Wt	4	5	44¼	22	35	39	Barrow T	119	14.10	97-13	Angel's Singing 1194 Spring Visit 1195LadiesDont1192 Weakened	6
17Jly76- 4Del	fst	5½f	:22⅕	:47⅕	1:07	ⒻMd Sp Wt	2	4	21	41½	44½	66½	Barrow T	118	16.80	76-16	NonSoPrtty118nkDncofthHors1181½PcktPrncss1182½ Speed, tired	12

LATEST WORKOUTS Jan 8 Hia 5f fst 1:01 h Dec 29 Hia 3f fst :36 b

Helga Behaves Dk. b. or br. f. 3, by Ambehaving—Helga, by Needles
$16,000 Br.—Meadowbrook Farm Inc (Fla) **116** Turf Record St. 1st 2nd 3rd 1 0 0 0 | St. 1st 2nd 3rd Amt. 1977 1 0 0 1 $900 1976 12 1 2 4 $8,236
Own.—Brauer D R Tr.—Brauer Donald R
7Jan77- 5Crc fst 6f :23 :46⅘ 1:13⅘ ⒻClm 15000 3 7 78¼ 48 58 32¼ Bailey J D 68 b 116 4.60 82-15 BrndedWomn1142Bgger'sDelight119nkHelgBhvs116½ Swerved late 9
14Dec76- 5Crc sly 7f :23⅗ :47⅕ 1:26⅗ ⒻClm 12500 6 1 42½ 23 2hd 2½ Bailey J D 83 116 4.20 82-17 DoMeProud116½HelgaBehves1162MissQuickTrigger1126 Bore out 8
1Dec76- 7Crc sly 6f :23 :46⅗ 1:13 ⒻClm 12500 9 10 117¼ 89½ 46½ 44 St Leon G 73 119 8.80 84-19 Hope Beach 111½ Do Me Proud116noBelindaMyLove1163½ Rallied 11
18Nov76- 7Crc fst 6f :23⅕ :47⅕ 1:14⅗ ⒻClm c-10000 4 9 107¼ 99 88 51¼ Baltazar C b 117 *1.20 79-17 JollyJoll114hdTouchThSky120nkPicnninyPigtil114no Finished well 10
29Oct76- 6Crc fm *1 Ⓣ 1:41⅗ ⒻClm 12500 10 7 85¼ 98¼ 108¾ 1011 Baltazar C b 118 *2.40 70-13 Snooty Hooty 1163 Liray 1121 A Saint I Aint 1141¼ Wide 10
30Sep76- 5Crc fst 6f :23⅖ :47⅘ 1:14⅖ ⒻClm 12500 8 3 76 76 64½ 31 St Leon G b 120 *1.30e 80-23 Bonnie Meil 1141Bagger'sDelight114hdHelgaBehaves120no Rallied 8
18Sep76- 5Crc fst 6½f :23⅖ :47⅗ 1:20 ⒻClm 16000 8 7 96¾ 86¼ 65¾ 35½ Lopez R D b 114 3.30e 85-13 Her GraceSarah1164½WinningNews1171HelgaBehaves114½ Rallied 9
2Sep76- 8Crc fst 6f :23⅕ :47⅖ 1:14⅖ ⒻClm 12500 3 8 98¾ 98¾ 62¾ 32 St Leon G b 117 3.00 79-19 Najia 1071 Hello Goodie 1091 Helga Behaves 117½ Altered course 11
23Aug76- 1Crc fst 6f :24 :48⅗ 1:14 ⒻMd 12500 1 5 53½ 53½ 32 1nk Baltazar C b 118 *1.50 83-19 Helga Behaves 118nk Foreign Coin 1141½ Here Here 114½ Driving 8
16Aug76- 1Crc fst 6f :23⅗ :47⅗ 1:14⅖ ⒻMd 12500 4 7 73¾ 44 42½ 3½ Baltazar C b 118 *2.20 80-15 Vit's Charger 113½ Picki Patti 118hd Helga Behaves 1181½ Rallied 9
LATEST WORKOUTS Jan 18 GP 4f fst :49⅖ b Dec 29 GP 3f fst :37 b Dec 10 GP 5f fst 1:02⅗ b Nov 30 GP 3f fst :37⅗ b

Attention Now B. f. 3, by Turma-Now—Miss Attentive, by Adaris
$15,000 Br.—Knisely D F (Fla) **116** Turf Record St. 1st 2nd 3rd 1 0 0 0 | St. 1st 2nd 3rd Amt. 1976 10 2 2 2 $9,872
Own.—Steil J Tr.—Julian George
31Dec76- 6Crc fst 7f :23⅗ :48 1:28 ⒻAllowance 7 2 53½ 86¼ 64¾ 44¼ Harbacek D5 72 b 111 28.60 72-22 HereHere1221½NorthernBrand1192½Stephens'Grad116nk No threat 9
16Dec76- 7Crc fm *1 Ⓣ 1:42 ⒻClm 19000 2 4 63¼ 88½ 68 64¾ Harbacek D5 b 106 4.60 74-23 Snooty Hooty 114½ Hope Beach 111nk Diplomat Lady 1182 Tired 10
2Dec76- 3Crc sly 1 :49 1:14⅘ 1:41⅖ ⒻClm 15000 1 2 1½ 11 13 13½ Harbacek D5 75 b 113 *1.50 82-13 AttentionNow1133½FightableLdy112noASintIAint1149 Ridden out 6
22Nov76- 6Crc fst 1 :48⅕ 1:13⅘ 1:41⅕ ⒻClm 15000 7 4 46 46 36 28 Harbacek D5 b 115 *1.70 75-16 FrindlyPrincss1128 DH ASintIAint114 DH AttntionNow115hd Rallied 8
22Nov76-Dead heat
10Nov76- 8Crc fst 6f :23 :47 1:12⅘ ⒻAllowance 7 1 66½ 77¼ 68 48 Harbacek D5 b 111 13.10 81-18 Desoto Princess 1163 Appetizer1202½SwankyLady1202½ Mild rally 8
1Oct76- 6Crc sly 7f :23⅖ :47⅕ 1:27⅕ ⒻClm 18000 7 1 1hd 31½ 53 33 Harbacek D5 b 105 4.30 77-18 WinningNews1171½HerGrcSrh1161½AttntionNow105½ Came again 7
22Sep76- 1Crc fst 6f :23⅖ :47⅘ 1:14⅖ ⒻMd 15000 8 2 62½ 43½ 23 11 Harbacek D5 b 113 4.10 81-16 Attention Now 1131 Here Here 114½ Umbrage 1184 Driving 10
23Jly76- 3Crc sly 6f :23 :47⅖ 1:14 ⒻMd 18000 6 2 42¼ 52¾ 45 37 Perna R b 114 2.70 76-18 Beach Ruler 1115 Dina Carolyn 1182 Attention Now 114nk Rallied 10
26Jun76- 9Crc fst 5f :22⅖ :46⅗ 1:00 ⒻTa Wee 3 4 95¼ 1110 109 67¼ Perna R 111 148.00 88-11 Feudalism 117½ Informatory 1173 Azure Main 111¾ Finished well 11
16Jun76- 2Crc fst 5f :23⅕ :48⅖ 1:01⅖ ⒻMd 12500 4 5 41 42 2½ 21 Perna R 118 *2.30 87-16 Mypsy Feet 1181 Attention Now 1183½ DH Fleet Isis 118 Gamely 12

The most recent figure of Ladies Dont, a 59, was untrue. The stable (or someone) knew it when it disregarded her ninth-place finish at 29-to-1 odds and bet her down to 4 to 1. But I didn't know what her figure might be, because she had done her previous racing in Delaware and Kentucky. Helga Behaves, the second-place finisher, had run 68–83–73 in her last three starts; she was hardly a paragon of consistency. Attention Now, the third-place finisher, looked like a more reliable barometer. If she had repeated her last figure of 72, Helga Behaves would have run a 78 to beat her by 2½ lengths, and Ladies Dont would have won with an 84. That seemed plausible.

Race	Projected Figure	Speed Rating	Difference
5.	84	59	Slow by 25

EIGHTH RACE

EIGHTH RACE
Gulfstream
JANUARY 21, 1977

6 FURLONGS. (1.07⅘) ALLOWANCE. Purse $6,500. 3-year-olds which have not won a race other than Maiden or Claiming. Weights 122 lbs. Non-winners of $6,100 since October 15, allowed 3 lbs. $5,400 twice since November 1, 5 lbs. $4,300 twice since October 1, 8 lbs.

Value of race $6,500, value to winner $4,045, second $1,300, third $650, fourth $325, balance of starters $36 each. Mutuel pool $128,364.

Last Raced	Horse	Eqt.	A.	Wt	PP	St	¼	½	Str	Fin	Jockey	Odds $1
20Nov76 4Aqu7	Iron Constitution		3	114	8	2	21½	22	1hd	11	Fell J	3.40
24Sep76 8AP4	Brach's Hilarious		3	115	1	3	52	42	3½	22	Perret C	15.00
22Dec76 2Crc1	Be Gallant	b	3	114	4	5	3hd	3hd	43	31	MacBeth D	4.70
9Dec76 9Crc3	Satan's Poppy	b	3	114	7	1	11	1½	21	41	Manganello M	3.20
18Dec76 3Crc3	DH Rocket Punch		3	114	3	6	4hd	54	53	5	Fires E	a-2.10
10Nov76 8CD7	DH Coined Silver	b	3	114	2	9	76	61½	62	52½	Brumfield D	6.10
12Jan77 9Crc7	Ky. Slim	b	3	116	9	8	9	82	73	71½	Barrow T	50.30
2Oct76 5Crc1	Strong As Steel		3	114	6	7	8½	9	84	810	Scocca D	23.10
24Sep76 8AP5	Restless Rascal		3	114	5	4	61½	73	9	9	Gavidia W	a-2.10

DH—Dead heat.
a-Coupled: Rocket Punch and Restless Rascal.

OFF AT 4:28 EST. Start good, Won driving. Time, :22⅖, :46, 1:11⅗ Track fast.

$2 Mutuel Prices:				
	7-IRON CONSTITUTION	8.80	6.00	4.40
	2-BRACH'S HILARIOUS		11.40	6.80
	4-BE GALLANT			4.60

Gr. c, by Iron Ruler—Water Cress, by Hail to Reason. Trainer Root Thomas F Sr. Bred by Evans T M (Va).

IRON CONSTITUTION prominent from the start gained command from between horses in midstretch never far back reached sharp contention in midstretch from the outside cut could not gain in final eighth while besting the others. SATAN'S POPPY set the pace to midstretch then steadily gave ground when displaced. ROCKET PUNCH lacked the needed closing response and finished on even terms with COINED SILVER. The latter bumped and forced to inside at the start was gaining slowly at the finish. RESTLESS RASCAL showed little.

Owners— 1, Mangurian H T Jr; 2, Brach Helen; 3, Coschi & Dell; 4, Crimson King Farm; 5, Reineman R L Stable Inc; 6, Whitney C V; 7, Kaelin Betty; 8, Rosso W P; 9, Reineman R L Stables Inc.

Trainers— 1, Root Thomas F Sr; 2, Divito Peter J; 3, Robbins Charles L; 4, Salmen Peter W Jr; 5, Bollero Joseph M; 6, Poole George T; 7, Kaelin Forrest; 8, Semler Gene W; 9, Bollero Joseph M.

Overweight: Brach's Hilarious 1 pound; Ky. Slim 2.

Scratched—Highland Jim (13Dec76 4Crc1); Bill Campbell (9Dec76 9Crc11); Brach's Honey (15Jan77 6GP5).

Iron Constitution — Gr. c. 3, by Iron Ruler—Water Cress, by Hail to Reason
Own.—Mangurian H T Jr — Br.—Evans T M (Va) — Tr.—Root Thomas F Sr — 114
St. 1st 2nd 3rd Amt. — 1976 5 1 0 0 $6,060

20Nov76- 4Aqu fst 6f :22⅘ :46⅕ 1:12 Allowance 6 2 31 34½ 59½ 711 Cruguet J 68 115 3.90 72-17 SmashingNative1152½Postscript1151¼ImpressiveBlend115hd Tired 7
13Nov76- 6Aqu fst 7f :23⅕ :46⅗ 1:24⅖ Allowance 6 4 21 21 34 47¾ Cruguet J 86 117 11.80 71-19 CruiseOnIn1173SmshingNtive1174½GoldenReserv117nk Weakened 8
21Jly76- 8Aqu fst 6f :22⅖ :46⅗ 1:12⅖ Tremont 1 4 22 31½ 66 711 Day P 61 115 3.00 70-22 Turn of Coin 1151¾ ToTheQuick122hdJudgeJohnBoone1222¼ Tired 7
30Jun76- 4Aqu fst 5½f :22⅕ :45⅖ 1:03⅗ Md Sp Wt 1 3 11½ 11½ 11 1¾ Hernandez 95 122 8.10 95-10 IronConstitution122¾BrodwyForli1225¾HighIndLight1222¼ Driving 8
23Jun76- 4Bel fst 5½f :22⅘ :46⅘ 1:05 Md Sp Wt 2 2 1½ 2hd 36 715 Vasquez J 122 *1.40 75-12 Crow Country 122hd Lynn Davis 1227 Judge Mauck 122¾ Tired 8
LATEST WORKOUTS Jan 16 GP 6f sly 1:15 h — Jan 6 GP 6f fst 1:14⅗ h — ●Jan 2 GP 5f fst 1:00 h — Dec 29 GP 4f fst :49 b

Be Gallant — Dk. b. or br. c. 3, by Gallant Romeo—Apple Pan Dowdy, by Bold Commander
Own.—Coschi & Dell — Br.—Lyman Mrs C B (Pa) — Tr.—Robbins Charles L — 114
St. 1st 2nd 3rd Amt. — 1976 1 1 0 0 $3,600

22Dec76- 2Crc fst 6f :22⅘ :46⅖ 1:13⅖ Md Sp Wt 1 2 65½ 45½ 22 11 MacBeth D 76 118 25.00 86-14 Be Gallant 1181 G's Brandy 118nk Mills Bill 1182 Driving 11
LATEST WORKOUTS Jan 13 GP 3f fst :35⅗ h — Jan 7 GP 5f fst 1:03 b — Dec 13 GP 5f fst 1:02⅖ b — Dec 8 GP 5f fst 1:03 b

Satan's Poppy — Ch. c. 3, by Crimson Satan—Crimson Poppy, by War Relic
Own.—Crimson King Farm — Br.—Crimson King Farm (Ky) — Tr.—Salmen Peter W Jr — 114
St. 1st 2nd 3rd Amt. — 1976 3 1 0 2 $5,725

9Dec76- 9Crc fst 6f :22⅖ :45⅗ 1:12⅗ Allowance 7 4 2hd 12 22 37 Manganello M 74 120 9.50 83-14 Herecomesthbrid1175ModlSilor1202Stn'sPoppy120nk Speed; tired 12
23Nov76- 7CD fst 6f :22 :45⅘ 1:12⅖ Allowance 1 3 42 2½ 1hd 35½ Manganello M 122 3.40 78-29 Kodiack 1224½ Weque 1171 Satan's Poppy 122no Weakened 11
15Nov76- 4CD fst 6f :22⅕ :46⅗ 1:14⅘ Md Sp Wt 7 3 14 14 14 14¾ Manganello M b 122 *1.80 72-33 Satan's Poppy 1224¾CaribePirate1223½MapleMousse1221½ Driving 12
LATEST WORKOUTS Jan 18 GP 4f fst :50 b — Jan 10 GP 6f fst 1:15 h — Jan 3 GP 6f fst 1:16 b — Dec 28 GP 5f fst 1:02 b

Rocket Punch — B. c. 3, by Reflected Glory—Stew Zoo, by Sunrise Flight
Own.—Reineman R L Stable Inc — Br.—Clark & Jones (Ky) — Tr.—Bollero Joseph M — 114
St. 1st 2nd 3rd Amt. — 1976 6 1 2 3 $8,940

18Dec76- 3Crc fst 6f :23 :46⅖ 1:12⅘ Allowance 1 8 34 33 31½ 31 Anderson J R 86 120 3.10 88-14 Dee Dee's Ruler 120hd Model Sailor1201RocketPunch1201 Rallied 8
28Oct76- 5Kee fst 6f :22⅕ :45⅖ 1:11 Allowance 3 9 53½ 63¾ 21½ 31 Brumfield D 118 *1.50e 86-21 Marve 113hd Governor's Pardon 1121 Rocket Punch 1181 Hung 9
16Oct76- 5Kee fst 6f :21⅘ :44⅘ 1:10⅕ Allowance 6 4 53½ 31½ 32 36½ Gavidia W 118 3.50 84-13 SwoonSwept1126Governor'sPardon112½RocketPunch1182 Rallied 7
16Sep76- 4AP fst 6f :22⅗ :46⅗ 1:12⅕ Md Sp Wt 3 6 3½ 3nk 1hd 1½ Fires E 120 2.20 82-18 Rocket Punch 120½ Barely Safe 1202½ Solo Singer 120½ Driving 9
8Sep76- 1AP fst 6f :22⅕ :45⅗ 1:12 Md Sp Wt 10 3 53 32 32½ 21¼ Patterson G 120 *1.00 82-12 Lightning Barb 1201¼ Rocket Punch 120hd Dravir 120¾ Gamely 10
19Aug76- 1AP fst 6f :21⅘ :45 1:10⅖ Md 25000 8 6 53¾ 34 35 22 Snyder L 119 10.70 89-13 Brach's Honey 1192 Rocket Punch1194SocietyScion119hd Gamely 10
LATEST WORKOUTS Jan 18 GP 5f fst 1:02 b — Jan 11 GP 5f fst 1:02 b — Jan 6 GP 5f fst 1:03 b — Dec 29 GP 4f fst :49 b

6

Neither Iron Constitution nor Brach's Hilarious had raced recently, but the third-, fourth-, and fifth-place horses had. Be Gallant (with a figure of 76), Satan's Poppy (74), and Rocket Punch (86) finished a length apart. If Be Gallant and Satan's Poppy had repeated their figures, with Rocket Punch going off form, the winner would have earned an 83 for beating them by three lengths. If, on the other hand, Be Gallant and Satan's Poppy had improved sharply, with Rocket Punch duplicating his 86, Iron Constitution's number would be a 98.

Either interpretation was possible. But Iron Constitution had run a 95 at Aqueduct, and he had trained steadily and sharply for this race. I decided to estimate that he had earned a 95 again.

Race	Projected Figure	Speed Rating	Difference
8.	95	83	Slow by 12

TENTH RACE

TENTH RACE
Gulfstream
JANUARY 21, 1977

7 FURLONGS. (1.20⅘) CLAIMING. Purse $4,600. 3-year-olds. Weights 122 lbs. Non-winners of two races since December 15, allowed 2 lbs. Two races since December 1, 4 lbs. Two races since November 1, 6 lbs. Claiming Price $7,500 for each $250 to $7,000 allowed 2 lbs. (Races where entered for $6,000 or less not considered.)

Value of race $4,600, value to winner $2,886, second $874, third $368, fourth $184, balance of starters $36 each. Mutuel pool $48,038. Perfecta Pool $85,641.

Last Raced	Horse	Eqt.	A.	Wt	PP	St	¼	½	Str	Fin	Jockey	Cl'g Pr	Odds $1
17Jan77 ^{6}GP^{9}	Tudor's Decision	b	3	118	10	2	9^{2}	4^{½}	1^{½}	1^{2}	Saumell L	7500	2.60
4Dec76 ^{9}Lrl^{5}	Flash's Memory	b	3	112	8	5	1^{1½}	1^{2}	2^{3}	2^{4½}	MacBeth D	7000	5.90
7Jan77 ^{10}Crc^{4}	Cool Faith	b	3	116	5	8	5^{½}	5^{½}	4^{2}	3^{1½}	Saumell F	7500	9.80
10Jan77 ^{6}Crc^{2}	End Rise	b	3	116	12	3	2^{hd}	3^{3}	3^{½}	4^{3½}	Haldar A	7500	7.00
13Jan77 ^{6}Crc^{7}	Ms. Finstad	b	3	115	1	12	12	10^{6}	8^{2}	5^{2}	Solomone M	7500	7.20
13Jan77 ^{1}Crc^{5}	Storm Lake Man	b	3	112	11	4	6^{1}	7^{3}	6^{1}	6^{nk}	Lopez R D	7000	66.80
11Jan77 ^{2}Crc^{2}	Willie Russ	b	3	116	6	6	3^{½}	2^{hd}	5^{3}	7^{2}	Rivera M A	7500	5.50
11Jan77 ^{5}Crc^{12}	Squaw Woman	b	3	107	9	1	4^{3}	6^{2}	7^{hd}	8^{¾}	Cardone E	7000	16.10
16Dec76 ^{6}Crc^{9}	Reflected Back	b	3	116	7	7	7^{½}	8^{hd}	9^{4}	9^{3}	Gavidia W	7500	5.20
4Jan77 ^{1}Crc^{5}	Calouchi		3	112	4	11	10^{3}	9^{hd}	10^{10}	10^{14}	Capodici J	7000	34.70
10Jan77 ^{2}Crc^{8}	Spoofery	b	3	112	2	10	11^{½}	11	11	11	Rodriguez J A	7000	109.20
11Nov76 ^{1}Mth^{1}	Sinology	b	3	109	3	9	8^{hd}	—	—	—	Cedeno M	7000	27.10

Sinology, Pulled up.

OFF AT 5:22 EST. Start good, Won driving. Time, :22⅘, :46⅗, 1:13⅕, 1:26⅖ Track fast.

$2 Mutuel Prices:				
	10–TUDOR'S DECISION	**7.20**	**4.00**	**3.80**
	8–FLASH'S MEMORY		**8.80**	**6.60**
	5–COOL FAITH			**5.60**

$2 PERFECTA 10–8 PAID $44.20.

Gr. c, by Tudor Grey—Valley Of Decision, by Determine. Trainer Simmons John P. Bred by S H L Enterprises (Ky).

TUDOR'S DECISION in hand early circled rivals on second turn to gain command in midstretch and was clear at the finish. FLASH'S MEMORY set pace to midstretch then gave way to winner. COOL FAITH could not gain on top pair while besting others. END RISE had no apparent excuse. MS. FINSTAD was never prominent. WILLIE RUSS had speed to head of stretch. REFLECTED BACK showed little. SINOLOGY appeared to lose her action on turn and was pulled up.

Owners— 1, D A J Stable; 2, Siegel Jan; 3, Canet O; 4, Batthyany Countess Margit; 5, Wien L; 6, Willis Mrs P; 7, Galbut & Osman & Tendrich; 8, Gonzalez H B; 9, Deets C R; 10, Shaver J; 11, CashmanE C; 12, Triple T Stable.

Trainers— 1, Simmons John P; 2, Mayberry Brian A; 3, Canet Oswaldo; 4, Sarmiento Guillermo; 5, Caple H R; 6, Viera Christine; 7, Kurland Jeff; 8, Rosenthal Maurice J; 9, Kelley Thomas W; 10, Hall Kenneth G; 11, Fabry William A; 12, Felix Ronald A.

Corrected weight: Tudor's Decision 118 pounds. **Overweight:** Ms. Finstad 4 pounds; Sinology 2.

Scratched—Ed's Favor (4Dec76 ^{9}Lrl^{8}); Babebear (18Jan77 ^{2}GP^{10}); Morlaine (14Jan77 ^{1}Crc^{6}); Refreshing Road; Northern Park (10Jan77 ^{6}Crc^{5}); Prince Renato (18Jan77 ^{2}GP^{9}).

Tudor's Decision
Own.—D A J Stable

Gr. c. 3, by Tudor Grey—Valley Of Decision, by Determine
$7,500 **Br.—S H L Enterprises (Ky)**
Tr.—Simmons John P

120

Turf Record	St.	1st	2nd	3rd		St.	1st	2nd	3rd	Amt.
	1	0	0	0	1977	2	0	0	0	$111
					1976	15	4	3	1	$15,677

17Jan77- 6GP	fm	*1$\frac{1}{16}$ Ⓣ			1:50⅕	Clm 30000	8	8	8^{9}	8^{11}	9^{18}	9^{31}	Saumell L	b	113	27.50	25–40	Funny Joke 112^{1½} Big Bearing 114^{5½} Blazing Judge 116^{10}	Outrun	10
4Jan77- 5Crc	fst	1$\frac{1}{16}$	:49⅘	1:15⅕	1:48⅖	Clm 11500	1	5	4^{5}	3^{1}	4^{1½}	5^{2¾}	Saumell L	b	113	*1.70	77–19	Kentucky Honey 116^{hd} Pica Pica 107^{1} Great Business114^{1½}	Tired	7
20Dec76- 1Crc	fst	1^{70}	:46	1:15	1:46⅕	Clm 9000	5	6	4^{4½}	1^{2}	1^{4}	1^{5}	Saumell L	b	112	6.30	84–16	Tudor's Decision112^{5}PicaPica117^{nk}RxfortheBlues112^{2}	Ridden out	10
10Dec76- 6Crc	fst	6½f	:23	:45⅘	1:19⅖	Clm 10500	1	9	8^{8}	6^{12}	6^{8½}	6^{6}	Lopez R D	b	113	14.70	88–14	Black Native 119^{1} Born Mean 109^{hd} Doc Reboz 114^{4}	No factor	9
15Nov76- 6Crc	fst	1^{70}	:48⅖	1:14	1:45⅖	Clm 11500	8	6	6^{8½}	5^{8½}	4^{9}	4^{11}	Lopez R D	b	112	7.20	77–18	Breton Sailor 112^{4} Asian Emperor 114^{6} FrostyFlorida115^{½}	Outrun	8
3Nov76- 3Crc	fst	6f	:24	:48	1:14⅕	Clm 7500	4	5	6^{3¼}	5^{2¾}	3^{½}	1^{2}	Lopez R D	b	122	3.50	82–19	Tudor'sDecision122^{2}SolitryKnight112^{no}Tht'sTboo113^{6}	Drew clear	7
14Oct76- 5Crc	fst	1	:50⅕	1:16	1:43⅕	Clm 5000	8	3	2^{1½}	1^{2}	1^{2}	1^{6}	Lopez R D	b	115	*1.30	73–21	Tudor'sDecision115^{6}HurricaneWnd115^{3}MicheRod102^{2}	Ridden out	8
2Oct76- 5Crc	fst	1	:49⅕	1:14	1:40⅗	Clm 11500	1	6	8^{5½}	7^{10}	7^{9}	6^{8¼}	Lopez R D	b	111	14.40	78–14	Strong As Steel 112^{1} Utility Tax 112^{5} Frosty Florida 110^{2}	Outrun	8
22Sep76- 5Crc	fst	7f	:24⅗	:48⅘	1:27⅘	Clm 10500	4	5	4^{1}	2^{1}	2^{hd}	3^{2½}	Amato V	b	110	22.70	74–16	UtilityTx112^{1½}ThrlingThoughts110^{1}Tudor'sDcson110^{no}	Weakened	8
2Sep76- 3Crc	fst	7f	:23⅘	:48	1:28⅘	Md 7500	5	6	4^{3¼}	4^{3}	1^{hd}	1^{2½}	Lopez R D	b	118	*1.50	72–19	Tudor's Decision 118^{2½} Robello 115^{nk} Cool Faith 118^{½}	Driving	11

Cool Faith
Own.—Canet O

B. c. 3, by Cool Moon—Boyera, by Boucheron
$7,500 **Br.—Meadowbrook Farm Inc (Fla)**
Tr.—Canet Oswaldo

116

	St.	1st	2nd	3rd	Amt.
1977	1	0	0	0	$300
1976	11	1	1	1	$3,864

7Jan77-10Crc	fst	1^{70}	:50⅗	1:15	1:47⅕	Clm 7000	6	5	4^{3½}	3^{3}	3^{3½}	4^{3¾}	Saumell F		114	10.10	75–15	Emerald Pit 117^{¾} Sal Sal 111^{1} King Bolt 116^{2}	Lacked rally	10
1Dec76- 5Crc	fst	7f	:23⅗	:47⅗	1:27⅘	Clm 6500	4	6	7^{4}	6^{5½}	3^{4½}	2^{3}	St Leon G	b	116	3.90	74–22	Steady 115^{3} Cool Faith 116^{nk} Marfox 114^{1½}	Rallied	8
27Nov76- 2Crc	fst	7f	:23⅖	:47⅖	1:28	Clm 5000	9	1	6^{6}	7^{6}	7^{7½}	4^{2}	St Leon G	b	117	*2.40	74–15	Ⓓ Near Par 115^{½} Count Rix 112^{1½} Brown Toast 117^{hd}	Rallied	9
16Nov76- 5Crc	fst	6f	:23⅕	:47⅗	1:15⅕	Clm 5000	2	10	8^{7¼}	8^{8}	7^{6¼}	4^{3}	Marquez C	b	120	2.20	74–16	Lavendar Jade 114^{1}FamousDeb104^{1½}HighCostO'Livin117^{½}	Rallied	10
27Oct76- 7Crc	fst	6f	:23⅗	:47⅗	1:14⅖	Clm 7500	1	11	11^{7}	11^{8}	8^{4¼}	7^{2}	Marquez C	b	116	23.00	79–15	Dimond'sWinnr120^{no}NotMBoy114^{1½}SolitryKnight110^{no}	No threat	11
1Oct76- 1Crc	sly	6f	:24	:48⅖	1:15	Md 5000	3	9	6^{2¼}	3^{3½}	2^{1}	1^{hd}	Baltazar C	b	120	*2.10	78–18	Cool Faith 120^{hd} Willie Russ 120no Sonex 115^{1}	Driving	12
20Sep76- 1Crc	fst	6f	:23⅖	:47⅗	1:14⅘	Md 7500	5	8	8^{3¾}	7^{5¾}	6^{7½}	5^{5}	Marquez C	b	118	3.60	74–16	Von Rincon 114^{1½} Doc Reboz 114^{½} Not Me Boy 115^{3}	No threat	12
2Sep76- 3Crc	fst	7f	:23⅘	:48	1:28⅘	Md 7500	1	10	6^{4¾}	6^{5½}	3^{nk}	3^{2¾}	Rivera M A	b	118	4.40	69–19	Tudor's Decision 118^{2½} Robello 115^{nk} Cool Faith 118^{½}	Rallied	11
25Aug76- 2Crc	fst	6f	:23⅘	:48⅕	1:14⅗	Md 7500	2	8	7^{4¾}	7^{7¾}	4^{6}	5^{8½}	Rivera M A	b	118	8.90	71–17	Dimond'sWinnr118^{4}Tudor'sDcision118^{1½}AmriHro114^{hd}	No mishap	9
11Jun76- 4Mth	fst	5f	:22	:47	1:00	Md 18000	7	11	11^{17}	11^{16}	11^{14}	8^{16}	Delahoussaye E	b	116	30.30	70–25	French Eagle 118^{3½} CrunchBird114^{2½}Mr.RedWing118^{5½}	No factor	11

LATEST WORKOUTS Jan 15 Hia 7f fst 1:27 h

Tudor's Decision had earned a figure of 73 running a mile and one-sixteenth on the main track. He might fare better at today's seven-furlong distance. Cool Faith, who finished third, was a consistent animal who had run 63–66–64 in his last three starts. If he repeated the 66 figure of his last seven-furlong effort, Tudor's Decision would have run a 79 to defeat him by 6½ lengths.

Race	Projected Figure	Speed Rating	Difference
10.	79	63	Slow by 16

Now I assembled all the data into one chart:

Race	Projected Figure	Speed Rating	Difference
1.	66	45	Slow by 21
2.	78	53	Slow by 25
3.	—	—	—
4.	—	83	—
5.	84	59	Slow by 25
6.	(Turf)	—	—
7.	(Turf)	—	—
8.	95	83	Slow by 12
9.	(Turf)	—	—
10.	79	63	Slow by 16

Averaging the numbers in the right-hand column, I found that the average race was run 20 points slower than it should have been. The track variant for Gulfstream Park on January 21 was +20. And it made sense. It yielded plausible results even in races where my projections had been wrong by several points. The figure for the second race would be a 73 instead of the 78 I had anticipated. I had based my estimate on the premise that the runnerup, Bobs A Prince, was going to improve sharply in the second start of his career. In fact, he had improved only moderately, but the result was still logical. In the eighth race, Iron Constitution had earned a figure of 103, much better than I had expected, but it was conceivable that a field of good young horses would run so well. I inscribed the day's results into my notebook with confidence:

Date	Variant	1	2	3	4	5	6	7	8	9	10
Jan 21	+20	65	73	—	103	79	T	T	103	T	83

Even when I have complete faith in the accuracy of a track variant, I like to monitor the subsequent performances of the horses who ran on that day to make certain that they verify the figures I have given them. I had to wait little more than a week to test—and to profit from—my January 21 figures. These were the past performances for the seventh race on February 2:

7 GULFSTREAM — 6 FURLONGS GULFSTREAM (Start / Finish)

6 FURLONGS. (1.07⅘) ALLOWANCE. Purse $6,500. 3-year-olds which have not won two races. Weight, 122 lbs. Non-winners of $6,100 allowed 3 lbs. $5,400, 5lbs. $4,900, 8 lbs. (Florida breds peferred) Winner preferred.

Golden Gossip — Ch. c. 3, by Golden Ruler—Hot Gossip, by Correspondent
Own.—Greer J L — Br.—Polk A F Jr (Ky) — Tr.—Jolley Leroy — **114**
St. 1st 2nd 3rd Amt. — 1976 5 1 1 2 $12,777
24Aug76- 2Sar fst 6f :22⅕ :45⅗ 1:12 Clm 50000 3 1 14 16 15 2¾ Maple E 76 b 117 *1.40 79-16 Plantaris 119¾ Golden Gossip 117½ Prize Native 1172 Gave way 7
7Jly76- 8Aqu sly 5½f :22 :45⅖ 1:04⅘ Juvenile 2 1 12½ 11½ 3½ 35 Baeza B 81 b 119 1.60e 84-14 To The Quick 119hd Turn of Coin 1135GoldenGossip119½ Used up 5
9Jun76- 8Hol fst 5f :21⅗ :44⅘ :57⅘ Westchester 4 7 78 713 712 611 McHargue D G b 120 2.00 80-14 Mr.DveyNy120nkColdCourge120hdGryMoonRunnr1204½ Poor start 7
9Jun76-Run in two divisions 7th & 8th races.
23Apr76- 7Kee fst 4½f :22⅗ :45⅘ :52 Lafayette 5 1 12 2½ 33¼ Baeza B b 119 *.60 92-06 United Holme 1192 Marve 1191¼ Golden Gossip 119hd Weakened 5
14Apr76- 5Kee fst 4½f :22⅖ :46⅕ :51⅘ Allowance 1 2 16 15 17 McHargue D G b 112 *1.20 96-05 Golden Gossip 1127 Windsong Lady114¾CoinedSilver1126 Driving 5
LATEST WORKOUTS Jan 31 Hia 4f fst :50⅖ b Jan 21 Hia 6f fst 1:19 b Jan 10 Hia 5f fst 1:02 bg Jan 3 Hia 5f fst 1:04⅖ b

Boldtrapsky — B. c. 3, by Bold Reasoning—Lechiguanas, by Forli
Own.—Parrish M — Br.—Lakeside Ranch (Ky) — Tr.—Nash Joseph S — **119**
Turf Record St. 1st 2nd 3rd 2 1 0 0 — St. 1st 2nd 3rd Amt. — 1976 2 1 0 0 $7,154
25Jly76♦4MLaffitte(Fra) gd*5½f 1:04⅘ Ⓣ Prix Robert Papin(Gr.1) 1021 Piggott L 123 5.25 — — BlushingGroom123¾ RivrDn1218 SunnySpring123¾ Bumped badly 12
20Jly76♦7Evry(Fra) gd*6f 1:13⅗ Ⓣ Prix de Noirval(Mdn) 14 Piggott L 123 *1.20 — — Boldtrapsky 1234 Picketer 1233 Slide Easy 1232 Led thruout 9
LATEST WORKOUTS Jan 18 Hia 5f fst 1:03⅗ b Jan 15 Hia 3f fst :36⅗ b

Fleet Beam — B. c. 3, by Fleet Nasrullah—Moonbeam, by Tim Tam
Own.—Calumet Farm — Br.—Calumet Farm (Ky) — Tr.—Veitch John M — **114**
St. 1st 2nd 3rd Amt. — 1976 5 M 0 0 $540
13Sep76- 4Bel fst 6f :22⅕ :45⅕ 1:10 Md Sp Wt 5 6 54½ 57½ 510 613 Day P 62 122 12.40 79-11 Postscript 1223 Quill Prince 1223 Preferred Position1224½ Evenly 9
28Aug76- 1Sar gd 6f :22⅖ :45⅘ 1:11 Md Sp Wt 5 4 1hd 2½ 22½ 67¾ Hernandez 63 122 7.00 77-12 Bartender'sPride1221¼PreferredPosition1224IndianQuil122½ Tired 7
14Aug76- 1Sar fst 6f :22⅕ :45⅗ 1:11⅗ Md Sp Wt 2 12 55 44¼ 53 95¼ Ruane J 66 122 13.80 77-11 Something Rotten1222SmashingNative122nkCorruptor122hd Tired 12
7Aug76- 5Sar sly 6f :22⅗ :46⅖ 1:12⅕ Md Sp Wt 7 6 89 715 1019 1024 Cordero A Jr b 122 4.20 55-17 Winterlock 1223 Drums and Fife 1229 Gun Blast 115hd Outrun 10
24Jly76- 3Aqu fst 5½f :22⅗ :46⅖ 1:05 Md Sp Wt 5 6 57 57½ 57 45¾ Cordero A Jr b 122 *1.80 82-14 Star Spangled 1221¾ Mon Fu 1222 Winterlock 1222 No threat 8
LATEST WORKOUTS Jan 26 Hia 4f fst :48 h Jan 20 Hia 5f fst 1:00⅖ h ●Jan 15 Hia 4f fst :47 hg Jan 11 Hia 6f fst 1:14⅖ h

Present Memories — Ch. c. 3, by Olden Times—Mighty Funny, by Jester
Own.—Seltzer E D — Br.—Seltzer E (Ky) — Tr.—Trotsek Harry E — **114**
St. 1st 2nd 3rd Amt. — 1977 1 0 0 0 $65 — 1976 6 1 1 0 $5,885
12Jan77- 9Crc fst 6½f :23 :47⅕ 1:20⅖ Allowance 5 2 2½ 1hd 2½ 52½ Arroyo H 74 120 12.80 87-18 CaribePirate120½Dr.DvidArbuse116noNshu'sSong120½ Weakened 7
27Dec76- 9Crc fst 6f :22⅘ :46⅕ 1:13 Clm 30000 4 7 84½ 913 98¼ 85½ Arroyo H 77 115 63.00 82-19 Feudalism 114½ EditorialComment1161GreatSpeed1121½ No room 9
23Nov76- 7CD fst 6f :22 :45⅘ 1:12⅖ Allowance 8 7 85¾ 58 99½ 79¾ Arroyo H 117 64.40 74-29 Kodiack 1224½ Weque 1171 Satan's Poppy 122no Tired 11
11Nov76- 6CD fst 6f :22⅖ :46⅗ 1:13⅗ Clm 20000 2 6 2hd 1hd 2½ 22¼ Arroyo H 117 3.80 76-23 MarketBagger1082¼PresentMemories117nkSquw'sLst115¾ Gamely 8
28Oct76- 5Kee fst 6f :22⅕ :45⅖ 1:11 Allowance 6 5 66 88¼ 812 813 Lopez T 118 24.30 74-21 Marve 113hd Governor's Pardon 1121RocketPunch1181 No factor 9
30Sep76- 4AP fst 6f :22⅗ :46 1:11⅗ Md Sp Wt 4 3 1½ 11 11½ 11¼ Arroyo H 120 6.90 85-16 Present Memories 1201¼ Solo Singer 1201½ Dravir 120½ Driving 9
16Sep76- 4AP fst 6f :22⅗ :46⅗ 1:12⅕ Md Sp Wt 7 8 52 42¼ 66¼ 67½ Arroyo H 120 16.80 74-18 Rocket Punch 120½ Barely Safe 1202½ Solo Singer 120½ Tired 9
LATEST WORKOUTS Feb 1 Hia 4f fst :49⅖ b Jan 19 Hia 3f fst :38⅖ b Dec 25 Hia 4f sly :52 b Dec 21 Hia 4f sly :49 b

Buckfan — B. c. 3, by Buckpasser—Dance Fan, by Dedicate
Own.—Woldenberg M M — Br.—Mereworth Farm (Ky) — Tr.—Davis Duke — **114**
Turf Record St. 1st 2nd 3rd 1 0 0 0 — St. 1st 2nd 3rd Amt. — 1977 2 1 0 0 $3,670 — 1976 5 M 0 1 $1,290
8Jan77- 5Crc fst 1$\frac{1}{16}$:48⅘ 1:13⅖ 1:47⅖ Allowance 1 5 58½ 611 610 59¾ Delguidice R Jr5 77 115 7.10 75-16 Wine Treasure 120nk BigBearing1161½Satan'sThunder1207 Outrun 8
1Jan77- 3Crc fst 7f :23 :47 1:27 Md Sp Wt 4 8 87¼ 76 53 11 Delguidice R Jr5 80 115 19.60 81-18 Buckfan 1151 G's Brandy 120½ Jungle Adam 120no Going away 9
20Dec76- 2Crc fm *1$\frac{1}{16}$ Ⓣ :47⅕ 1:12⅕ 1:46⅕ Md Sp Wt 4 7 79½ 914 511 66¼ Delguidice R Jr5 b 113 18.30 78-14 Satan's Thunder 118hd Liege Lord 1183FunnyHumor1151 No rally 10
26Nov76- 3Crc fst 6½f :22⅖ :45⅘ 1:19⅗ Md Sp Wt 9 4 77½ 713 713 711 Baltazar C b 118 7.40 82-15 Nashua'sSong1182¼L'Epouvantil1183¼MiniStyls1181 Showed little 9
17Nov76- 3Crc fst 1$\frac{1}{16}$:49⅗ 1:15⅖ 1:48⅗ Md Sp Wt 1 3 44 64½ 48½ 410 Baltazar C 118 2.70 69-17 Fair Sport 1181 Mark Four 1181 Here Here 1158 Weakened 8
3Nov76- 1Crc fst 1 :48⅗ 1:14 1:40⅗ Md Sp Wt 3 5 59 512 49½ 310 MacBeth D 118 6.40 76-19 Sir Sir 1188 Twin Double 1182 Buckfan 1185 Rallied 9
4Aug76- 3Crc fst 6f :23⅘ :48 1:13⅗ Md Sp Wt 8 6 54¼ 67½ 713 712 Acosta G 118 5.60 73-20 Bold Thomas1182ShapeOfFame1183½Salman1182½ Bothered early 11
LATEST WORKOUTS Jan 29 GP 5f sly 1:01⅖ h Jan 24 GP 6f fst 1:15 h Jan 19 GP 4f fst :49⅖ b Jan 7 Crc 4f fst :48⅗ h

White Rammer — Ch. c. 3, by Jim J—Been Taken, by Tom Fool
Own.—Bryant J C H — Br.—Bryant Mr-Mrs J C H (Va) — Tr.—Croll Warren A Jr — **114**
St. 1st 2nd 3rd Amt. — 1977 1 1 0 0 $3,732 — 1976 0 M 0 0
21Jan77- 4GP fst 6f :22 :46⅕ 1:11⅗ Md 40000 11 2 42½ 21½ 2½ 11 Saumell L 103 120 *1.90 81-29 White Rammer 1201 Bio Grey 1169 Never Guilty 1163 Driving 12
LATEST WORKOUTS Feb 1 GP 3f fst :39 b Jan 27 GP 5f fst :59⅖ h Jan 19 GP 4f fst :48 h Jan 14 GP 4f fst :48 hg

Be Gallant — Dk. b. or br. c. 3, by Gallant Romeo—Apple Pan Dowdy, by Bold Commander
Own.—Coschi & Dell — Br.—Lyman Mrs C B (Pa) — Tr.—Robbins Charles L — **114**
St. 1st 2nd 3rd Amt. — 1977 1 0 0 1 $650 — 1976 1 1 0 0 $3,600
21Jan77- 8GP fst 6f :22⅖ :46 1:11⅗ Allowance 4 5 32½ 32½ 41½ 33 MacBeth D 96 114 4.70 78-29 IronConstitution1141Brach'sHilarious1152BeGllnt1141 No mishap 9
22Dec76- 2Crc fst 6f :22⅗ :46⅖ 1:13⅖ Md Sp Wt 1 2 65½ 45½ 22 11 MacBeth D 76 118 25.00 86-14 Be Gallant 1181 G's Brandy 118nk Mills Bill 1182 Driving 11
LATEST WORKOUTS Jan 30 GP 4f fst :49⅗ b Jan 13 GP 3f fst :35⅗ h Jan 7 GP 5f fst 1:03 b Dec 13 GP 5f fst 1:02⅖ b

Shape Of Fame — Dk. b. or br. c. 3, by The Pruner—Stay Out Front, by Currock
Own.—Devries Mrs D & Fett D — Br.—Devries Dorothy (Fla) — Tr.—Sarner Jerome J Jr — **114**
Turf Record St. 1st 2nd 3rd 2 0 0 0 — St. 1st 2nd 3rd Amt. — 1977 1 0 0 0 $36 — 1976 12 1 3 3 $9,680
24Jan77- 7GP fm *1 Ⓣ 1:40⅘ Allowance 6 3 42 98½ 912 914 Perret C b 114 20.70 63-28 Stn'sThunder1141UnionMnifest114¾Dr.DvidArbus1141 Forced out 10
17Dec76- 8Crc fm *1$\frac{1}{16}$ Ⓣ 1:47⅘ Allowance 10 3 32½ — — — Marquez C b 120 41.50 — — KntckyFrnchmn120½SonnyCollns1201½UnonMnfst1201 Lost rider 10
10Dec76- 8Crc fst 170 :48⅖ 1:13⅖ 1:45⅕ Allowance 4 4 63¾ 45½ 56½ 77¼ Marquez C 74 b 120 25.20 82-14 Dreaming Of Moe 114¾ Wine Treasure 1172 BigBearing1093 Tired 10
27Nov76- 3Crc fst 1 :48⅖ 1:14⅖ 1:42⅖ Md Sp Wt 6 5 36 41¾ 3nk 1½ Marquez C b 118 3.90 77-15 Shape Of Fame 118½ Recitalist 1181 Union Manifest 1181 Driving 7
20Nov76- 2Crc fst 6f :23⅕ :47⅗ 1:14⅖ Md Sp Wt 1 6 63½ 64 74¼ 64¾ Vergara O b 118 3.40 76-15 Ole Spats 1182½ Swinging Knight 118hd Native Velvet118¾ Outrun 11
25Aug76- 5Crc fst 7f :24⅖ :48⅖ 1:28 Md Sp Wt 1 2 1½ 2hd 12 2¾ St Leon G b 118 *1.10 75-17 Millwood Road 118¾ Shape Of Fame 1184 Sir Sir 1181½ Tired 7
14Aug76- 3Crc fst 6f :23⅗ :47 1:12⅗ Md Sp Wt 9 2 42½ 33 33½ 26 Ramos A b 118 *.30e 84-11 Haworthia 1186 Shape Of Fame 118hd Misty Jungle 113¾ Gamely 10
4Aug76- 3Crc fst 6f :23⅘ :48 1:13⅗ Md Sp Wt 5 4 42¼ 22 23 22 Salinas J b 118 3.30 83-20 Bold Thomas 1182 Shape Of Fame1183½Salman1182½ Second best 11
17Jly76- 3Crc fst 6f :23⅕ :47⅗ 1:13⅗ Md Sp Wt 3 5 32 33 43 36½ Baltazar C b 118 *.80e 78-17 Quavering Spear 1185½DestinToBurn1181ShapeOfFame118¾ Tired 12
26Jun76- 2Crc fst 5½f :22⅘ :47⅕ 1:07⅖ Md Sp Wt 3 3 2hd 2½ 23 35 Baltazar C b 118 8.10 88-11 Basic Rhythm 1185 In Theory 118no Shape Of Fame 1181½ Evenly 12
LATEST WORKOUTS ●Jan 17 Crc 6f fst 1:16 b Jan 11 Crc 5f fst 1:02 b Jan 6 Crc 4f fst :51⅖ b Dec 25 Crc 5f fst 1:05 b

Bask Ch. c. 3, by Hawaii—Flail, by Bagdad
Br.—Clay Ward Agency Inc (Ky)
Tr.—Bollero Joseph M
Own.—R L Reineman Stable Inc **114**

	St.	1st	2nd	3rd	Amt.
1977	1	0	0	0	$36
1976	8	1	2	0	$7,320

25Jan77- 7GP fst 7f :22⅗ :46 1:24⅘ Allowance 6 10 106½ 109¾ 1025 1038 MacBeth D b 117 33.80 42–19 Nashua's Song117½Haworthia1171Cornucopian1171 Swerved start 10
28Oct76- 5Kee fst 6f :22⅕ :45⅖ 1:11 Allowance 4 1 11½ 1hd 67½ 919 Gavidia W b 118 *1.50e 68–21 Marve 113hd Governor's Pardon 1121 Rocket Punch1181 Stopped 9
12Oct76- 5Kee fst 6½f :22⅗ :45⅖ 1:16⅗ Allowance 8 2 15 14 12½ 23¼ Gavidia W b 118 16.30 91–14 Golden Trade 1183¼ Bask 118nk Natural Drive 1152 Second best 12
23Sep76- 1AP fst 6f :22⅘ :46⅕ 1:11⅗ Md Sp Wt 3 6 1½ 14 15 16 Snyder L b 120 8.80 85–15 Bask 1206 Dravir 120½ Exploratory 120hd Ridden out 10
8Sep76- 4AP fst 6f :22⅕ :45⅗ 1:11⅕ Md Sp Wt 6 5 41 31½ 69½ 814 Patterson G b 120 9.20 73–12 Oui Henry 1201¼ [D]Barely Safe 1201½ Arthur S. 1201¾ Tired 9
8Sep76-Placed seventh through disqualification
23Aug76- 3AP fst 6f :22⅖ :46⅖ 1:11⅘ Md Sp Wt 9 3 33 22½ 2½ 45¾ Snyder L 119 *1.80e 78–14 Windy City Butch 119nk Cornucopian 119½ Hinkston 1195 Tired 9
29Jly76- 5AP sly 5½f :22⅖ :47 1:06⅖ Md Sp Wt 10 5 42¼ 2hd 41 78¼ Snyder L 118 3.50 75–19 Drone's Reward 1182½ Coldwater 118no Unkie Jer 1181½ Tired 11
13Jly76- 2AP fst 5½f :22⅕ :46⅕ 1:05 Md Sp Wt 10 6 33 21½ 1½ 25 Snyder L 118 7.60 85–13 Bob's Dusty 1185 Bask 1181¼ Iron Crow 118nk Weakened 11
3Jly76- 1AP fst 5½f :22⅗ :46⅘ 1:06 Md Sp Wt 10 9 61¼ 44½ 45 912 Snyder L 118 *2.40 73–16 Castle Call 1182¼ Bold Ryan 1182 Iron Crow 118nk Tired 12
LATEST WORKOUTS Jan 31 GP 4f fst :48 b Jan 23 GP 4f fst :50⅖ b Jan 18 GP 5f fst 1:02 b Jan 12 GP 5f fst 1:02 b

Big Daddy Bryan Dk. b. or br. g. 3, by Irongate—Ankola, by Our Love II
Br.—Hash V E (Ky)
Tr.—Warren Fred
Own.—Rainbow Farm **114**

	St.	1st	2nd	3rd	Amt.
1977	2	0	0	1	$700
1976	7	1	1	1	$3,463

14Jan77- 2Crc fst 6f :23⅕ :47⅗ 1:14⅗ Clm 6500 9 3 31 2hd 1½ 33 Bove T 60 b 120 3.60 77–13 BragginRights1201Vit'sCharger1162BigDaddyBryn1201 Weakened 12
5Jan77- 5Crc fst 6f :23 :47 1:13⅖ Clm 9000 2 4 46½ 34 33 45¾ Bove T 67 b 114 8.10 80–14 Myth Master 1163 So Rash 1162 Mister Rockie 114¾ No mishap 7
7Dec76- 1Crc fst 6½f :23⅘ :48⅖ 1:23 Md c-5000 12 1 1hd 12 13 12 Baltazar C 47 b 118 *1.20 76–19 Big Daddy Bryan 1182 Enkidu 1185 Mac Cat 1181½ Driving 12
17Nov76- 2Crc fst 6f :22⅘ :47⅗ 1:14⅕ Md 7000 4 4 1hd 12 1hd 22½ Diaz J R7 b 107 4.10 79–17 So Rash 1182½ Big Daddy Bryan 107hd Hand Combat1142 Gamely 12
8Nov76- 1Crc fst 6f :23⅕ :47⅖ 1:14⅘ Md 7500 4 5 1hd 2hd 56 79 Baltazar C b 118 4.30 70–22 Gene Ramsey 114nk Doc Cosens Dol 1183 Calouchi 1183½ Tired 11
2Aug76- 3Crc sly 6f :23⅖ :47⅗ 1:14⅗ Md 15000 2 7 74½ 712 815 821 Gaffglione R b 118 8.40 59–18 Fast Warrior 1143½ Janco's Jim 1181 Grange II1182½ Showed litle 9
30Jun76- 3Crc fst 5½f :22⅖ :47⅕ 1:08⅖ Md 15000 2 5 47½ 511 813 910 Baltazar C b 118 3.80 78–16 Mr. Precipitator 1181HurryOnAdmiral118nkJudgeRoot118no Tired 12
21Jun76- 3Crc fst 5½f :22⅘ :48 1:08⅕ Md 15000 2 4 15 13 11½ 34½ Baltazar C b 118 8.00 84–19 AmericaBehave1181Backdouble1163½BigDaddyBryn1183 Faltered 8
3Jun76- 5Crc fst 5f :23⅗ :48⅘ 1:02⅖ Md 15000 2 6 2hd 22 57 64¾ Baltazar C 120 15.70 78–18 Alison'sBoy120½HurryOnAdmirl1201FourthMrtn1161½ Speed, tired 12
LATEST WORKOUTS Jan 25 Crc 3f fst :37 b Jan 4 Crc 3f fst :37 b Dec 31 Crc 4f fst :49 b Dec 20 Crc 5f fst 1:01⅕ h

Time To B. c. 3, by Turn-To—Sherry R, by Eight Thirty
Br.—Peckham & Sparks (Ky)
Tr.—Pickard Oral C
Own.—King J D & Jaunich H J **114**

	St.	1st	2nd	3rd	Amt.
1976	2	1	0	0	$3,000

25Jun76- 7Mth fst 5½f :22⅗ :46⅘ 1:06⅕ Allowance 5 6 63¼ 611 611 59½ Miceli M 117 7.60 76–20 Ali Oop 117no Fleet Busher 1174½ Harve's Dude 1203 No rally 7
9Mar76- 3GP fst 3f :22⅘ :34⅕ Md Sp Wt 8 3 2½ 1no Fires E 120 *3.20 90–10 Time To 120no Polemicist 1201½ Model Sailor 1201 Just up 14
LATEST WORKOUTS Jan 20 GP 5f fst 1:02 b Jan 10 GP 6f fst 1;16 b Jan 5 GP 4f gd :52 b Dec 27 GP 6f sly 1:16⅗ b

This was the race which had been the third part of the Kid's three-horse parlay, the race which forced him to decide whether to bet $660 on the exacta of White Rammer and Be Gallant. The two horses had earned figures of 103 and 96, respectively, on January 21, and they towered over this field. Golden Gossip looked superficially formidable, but now that I had New York figures which were comparable to Florida, I could see that the 76 he had earned the previous season at Saratoga would not make him even a marginal contender. Of the other challengers, Buckfan had the best figure, but the 80 he ran in his next-to-last start would not put him close to the leaders. If White Rammer and Be Gallant had not dominated this field, I would have returned to my data for January 21 and reconsidered the track variant. As it turned out, this was not necessary.

SEVENTH RACE
Gulfstream
FEBRUARY 2, 1977

6 FURLONGS. (1.07⅘) ALLOWANCE. Purse $6,500. 3-year-olds which have not won two races. Weight, 122 lbs. Non-winners of $6,100 allowed 3 lbs. $5,400, 3 lbs. $4,900, 8 lbs. (Florida breds preferred) Winner preferred.

Value of race $6,500, value to winner $4,103, second $1,235, third $585, fourth $325, balance of starters $36 each. Mutuel pool $88,300. Perfecta Pool $113,368.

Last Raced	Horse	Eqt.	A.	Wt	PP	St	¼	½	Str	Fin	Jockey	Odds $1
21Jan77 ^{4}GP^{1}	White Rammer		3	114	6	5	$3^{1\frac{1}{2}}$	2^{1}	$1^{1\frac{1}{2}}$	1^{2}	Saumell L	1.30
21Jan77 ^{8}GP^{3}	Be Gallant	b	3	114	7	8	$5^{1\frac{1}{2}}$	4^{4}	3^{3}	$2^{1\frac{1}{2}}$	MacBeth D	3.90
25Jun76 ^{7}Mth^{5}	Time To		3	114	11	2	2^{hd}	3^{3}	$2^{1\frac{1}{2}}$	$3^{3\frac{1}{2}}$	Fires E	16.70
8Jan77 ^{5}Crc^{5}	Buckfan	b	3	114	5	10	11	10^{6}	7^{5}	4^{1}	Delguidice R Jr	38.60
12Jan77 ^{9}Crc^{5}	Present Memories		3	114	4	7	$4^{\frac{1}{2}}$	$5^{1\frac{1}{2}}$	$5^{1\frac{1}{2}}$	5^{1}	Arroyo H	21.50
13Sep76 ^{4}Bel^{6}	Fleet Beam		3	114	3	9	7^{hd}	6^{3}	$6^{1\frac{1}{2}}$	$6^{5\frac{1}{2}}$	Adams L	27.90
24Jan77 ^{7}GP^{9}	Shape Of Fame		3	114	8	1	$8^{1\frac{1}{2}}$	8^{hd}	$8^{\frac{1}{2}}$	$7^{\frac{3}{4}}$	Riera R Jr	61.40
25Jly76 ^{4}MLa^{10}	Boldtrapsky		3	122	2	11	9^{2}	$7^{1\frac{1}{2}}$	9^{5}	8^{2}	Brumfield D	5.40
24Aug76 ^{2}Sar^{2}	Golden Gossip	b	3	114	1	4	1^{5}	1^{2}	4^{hd}	9^{5}	Capodici J	4.00
25Jan77 ^{7}GP^{10}	Bask	b	3	114	9	3	$6^{1\frac{1}{2}}$	$9^{\frac{1}{2}}$	10^{5}	10^{4}	Gavidia W	27.20
14Jan77 ^{2}Crc^{3}	Big Daddy Bryan	b	3	114	10	6	10^{3}	11	11	11	Bove T	62.10

OFF AT 4:02 1/2, EST Start good, Won driving. Time, :21⅕, :44⅗, 1:09⅖ Track fast.

$2 Mutuel Prices:				
	6–WHITE RAMMER	4.60	2.80	2.40
	7–BE GALLANT		3.40	3.00
	11–TIME TO			4.40

$2 PERFECTA 6–7 PAID $14.60.

Ch. c, by Jim J—Been Taken, by Tom Fool. Trainer Croll Warren A Jr. Bred by Bryant Mr–Mrs J C H (Va).

WHITE RAMMER allowed to settle in stride came between horses at head of stretch to gain command drew clear and proved best. BE GALLANT raced forwardly reached sharp contention in midstretch and was gaining slowly on the winner at the finish. TIME TO a sharp factor from the outset was giving ground slowly at the finish. BUCKFAN steadily improved position in the drive without posing serious threat to winner. SHAPE OF FAME raced wide on the turn. BOLDTRAPSKY was never prominent. GOLDEN GOSSIP rushed to a long early lead and had nothing left for stretch run. BASK bore out badly on the turn.

Owners— 1, Bryant J C H; 2, Coschi & Dell; 3, King J D & Jaunich H J; 4, Woldenberg M M; 5, Seltzer E D; 6, Calumet Farm; 7, Devries Mrs D & Fett D; 8, Parrish M; 9, Greer J L; 10, R L Reineman Stable Inc; 11, Rainbow Farm.

Trainers— 1, Croll Warren A Jr; 2, Robbins Charles L; 3, Pickard Oral C; 4, Davis Duke; 5, Trotsek Harry E; 6, Veitch John M; 7, Sarner Jerome J Jr; 8, Nash Joseph S; 9, Jolley Leroy; 10, Bollero Joseph M; 11, Warren Fred.

Corrected weight: Boldtrapsky 122 pounds.

White Rammer defeated Be Gallant by two lengths, running six furlongs in 1:09⅖. The speed rating for the race was 114, and I made the track variant for the day −11. White Rammer earned a figure of 103 for his victory, providing a perfect confirmation of my January 21 variant and figures.

I get special satisfaction from winning money on bets like the White Rammer–Be Gallant exacta and others which are the fruit of my labors with the figures. I was raised to believe in the Protestant Ethic; I accepted the premise that academic study and hard work are both virtuous and rewarding. The hucksters of racing books and systems like to advertise that they have a simple, effortless way to win at the track; most horseplayers listen to these blandishments while rejecting speed handicapping because it requires so much time and effort. But they don't understand what the game is all about. I enjoy speed handicapping precisely because of the time and effort it demands. After spending weeks to prepare for my trip to Florida, after losing sleep to worry about the technical nuances of the figures, after devoting part of every day to the construction of my track variants, I deserved my rewards. And the rewards were not just monetary.

Epilogue

During the final three months of 1977, I played the horses in a desultory fashion, making occasional trips to Laurel and occasional wagers with bookmakers, as much for entertainment as for profit. On December 31 I tabulated my results for the year. If I had been engaged in a nonmonetary activity, or one which did not permit me to keep score in some fashion, I would have looked back on 1977 with mixed emotions; I remembered all the disappointments, failures, and traumas too vividly. But even if my memories were equivocal, the bottom line was not. I had made a profit of $50,664.

I had achieved my first great year as a horseplayer by following the advice Charlie had given me twelve months earlier. I had become a specialist. From the hundreds of factors which influence the outcome of horse races, I had identified two or three which could make me a winner.

Speed figures had for years given me an overall understanding of the game and provided me with my best betting opportunities. But in 1977 I learned that the most profitable use of figures comes when a horse is shipped from one track to another. I amassed nearly half my total winnings on Carolina Horn (shipped from Charles Town to Pimlico), Just John (Atlantic City to Monmouth), Talc (Aqueduct to Pimlico), and L'Alezane (Woodbine to Saratoga).

The track bias at Pimlico accounted for almost all the rest of my profits. I had recognized the existence of biases at Pimlico and other tracks in previous years, but in 1977 I finally learned how to capitalize on such conditions. I was able to disregard all my other convictions about handicapping, to concentrate single-mindedly on the bias, and to bet aggressively on nearly every race.

The combination of factors I employ does not constitute a universally applicable Secret of Beating the Races. It is merely an approach that is right for me. I happen to love poring over fine print and esoteric figures hour after hour. I would not enjoy scrutinizing all the horses in all the races at a track and making notes about their physical condition, even though that is a valid way to beat the races, too. I could not win using Charlie's methodology. Nor could he win using mine. So when a budding horseplayer asks me how to win money at the track, I do not necessarily recommend that he emulate me. I suggest that he take an inventory of his own skills, identify the methods he has used with the greatest success, and concentrate on refining them.

A horseplayer's choice of methods is less important than the discipline with which he employs them. I won in 1977 because I matured as a gambler during the course of the year. Even if I do not possess Charlie's brand of superhuman patience and composure, I was able to sidestep most of the psychological pitfalls which had regularly tripped me up in the past. When I was winning, I resisted overconfidence or megalomania. I kept my emotional balance even during the most dizzying moments of the Pimlico season. And in my encounters with adversity, I suffered only two serious lapses of equanimity and self-control: after the disqualification at Gulfstream, which was forgiveable; and during the last week at Saratoga, which was not. The end of the Saratoga debacle demonstrated that I had merely suppressed—rather than conquered—my tendencies toward self-destructive irrationality at the betting windows.

Saratoga reminded me of something else: the impermanence and fragility of success at the racetrack. Before that meeting began, I was tempted to think that I could never lose again. After it I knew that past triumphs are no guarantee of future successes.

One night in Saratoga I went to the Turf Bar for dinner and happened to sit with Mannie Kalish, who for decades has been one of the most successful, distinguished horseplayers in New York. Kalish began to talk wistfully about the old Saratoga racing strip, which had been a deep, slow bog until it was rebuilt in 1972. On this old Saratoga track, Kalish employed some of the classic handicapping methods which textbooks of the past described as "condition factors." He looked for horses who had raced recently; horses who had been running in routes and now were entered in sprints; horses who had made a previous start over the Saratoga track. Kalish knew that on a tiring surface, such horses would have an important edge in fitness over their rivals. He made money with this approach for many years. And then one day he woke up to find that the game had changed, and that he would have to adapt in order to survive.

I know that some day I will have to do the same. I cannot stop the passage of time and the evolution of the sport and continue to live in 1977 forever. I may have caught a glimpse of the future in Saratoga, where—for reasons I do not understand—visual skills were more important than analytical abilities. I may have to adopt some of the methods of the "trip handicappers" and incorporate them into my own approach.

In order to win in the future I will surely have to change my itinerary and travel to new tracks where I can use my handicapping methods more profitably. I cannot count on Pimlico's bias to provide an annual source of easy money. As 1978 began, I was looking forward to a winter at Hialeah, where a large-scale invasion of New York stables guaranteed an excellent, competitive season of racing. I was considering a trip in the fall to the Meadowlands in New Jersey, where a biased track, a regular influx of out-of-state horses, and an unsophisticated clientele might create conditions that were ideal for me.

When I first started to dream about becoming a successful horse-player, I had thought that one great winning year would represent a permanent breakthrough. Like achieving manhood, it would be irreversible. But after finally experiencing that year, I realized that I still could not proclaim, "I beat the races," using the present tense as if it were an unchanging condition. In 1978 I would have to study the *Racing Form* just as much and work to develop new handicapping skills, understand new racetracks, and fight the same old battles with fate and with my emotions.

How to Read the *Daily Racing Form*

The *Daily Racing Form*'s past performances are marvels of conciseness, superior to any comparable publication in the world. In little more than an inch of space, they tell a handicapper almost everything he could want to know about a horse, such as Timothy K.

Timothy K. — **Dk. b. or br. c. 3, by Bushido—Mirabilis, by Owen Tudor**
Own.—Fall Cecilia E — **Br.—Fisher Susan B (Mich)** — **Tr.—Fall James M**

106^{7}

Turf Record	St.	1st	2nd	3rd
	3	0	0	1

	St.	1st	2nd	3rd	Amt.
1977	21	2	3	3	$19,575
1976	11	M	0	0	$543

26Nov77- 3Lrl	my	1	:46	1:11⅘	1:38⅘	Clm 25000	1	2	2^{3}	$2^{1\frac{1}{2}}$	2^{3}	2^{1}	McCarron C J	b	116	6.00	78-24	Simplified 116^{1} Timothy K. $116^{2\frac{1}{2}}$ Stammer 114^{4}	Gamely	5
20Nov77- 8Key	fst	6f	:22⅖	:45⅖	1:12⅗	3↑Allowance	5	10	$8^{8\frac{3}{4}}$	8^{10}	$7^{6\frac{3}{4}}$	$10^{8\frac{1}{2}}$	Fall M^{10}	b	107	44.50	70-24	Happy Dorimar 122^{hd} MightySong $115^{1\frac{1}{4}}$ PleasureTrap 113^{2}	No speed	10
5Nov77- 9Lrl	gd	1	:46⅗	1:12⅗	1:38⅗	3↑Allowance	4	7	7^{8}	$7^{7\frac{3}{4}}$	5^{8}	6^{11}	Fall M^{10}	b	106	'6.00	69-20	PennsburyManor $122^{2\frac{1}{2}}$ Parnis $112^{3\frac{1}{4}}$ ThunderO'Shay 112^{3}	No mishap	10
24Oct77- 9Lrl	fst	1	:47	1:12⅗	1:39	3↑Allowance	1	7	$10^{6\frac{3}{4}}$	$10^{7\frac{3}{4}}$	11^{12}	10^{10}	Fall M^{10}	b	106	8.10	68-25	ZeroLunch $107^{1\frac{1}{4}}$ TurnToFright 113no TdSchoonmkr 114no	Slow start	11
29Sep77- 8Bow	fst	$1\frac{1}{16}$	:47⅘	1:12⅘	1:47⅕	3↑Allowance	7	3	$3^{2\frac{1}{2}}$	3^{1}	$3^{1\frac{1}{2}}$	$5^{2\frac{1}{4}}$	Fall M^{10}	b	106	7.10	68-24	John Alden $114^{1\frac{1}{4}}$ What A Tele 114^{nk} Sea Defier 113^{nk}	Brushed	7
25Sep77- 7Key	sly	1^{70}	:47⅕	1:12⅘	1:43⅗	3↑Allowance	8	3	4^{4}	$4^{2\frac{1}{2}}$	$2^{1\frac{1}{2}}$	$3^{1\frac{3}{4}}$	Fall M^{7}	b	106	6.80	80-21	Eastern Monarch $117^{1\frac{1}{2}}$ Epic Quest 106^{nk} Timothy K. 106^{1}	Evenly	8
11Sep77- 4Del	fst	$1\frac{1}{16}$	:46⅘	1:11⅗	1:45	3↑Allowance	4	1	$1^{1\frac{1}{2}}$	1^{1}	1^{1}	1no	Fall M^{5}	b	109	10.60	84-16	Timothy K. 109no Influencer 114^{11} Malevolent $114^{1\frac{1}{2}}$	Driving	6
2Sep77- 6Atl	yl	*1 Ⓣ			1:41⅗	3↑Allowance	3	3	3^{3}	2^{2}	2^{3}	$3^{4\frac{1}{2}}$	O'Connell J	b	109	7.90	74-25	Royal Owen $115^{4\frac{1}{2}}$ Doctrinaire 114^{hd} Timothy K. $109^{2\frac{1}{2}}$	Evenly	7
20Aug77- 4Del	fst	1^{70}	:47⅗	1:13⅖	1:44	Allowance	5	4	$2^{2\frac{1}{2}}$	2^{1}	$5^{4\frac{1}{4}}$	$5^{6\frac{3}{4}}$	Gilbert R B	b	115	2.90	70-20	Influencer $110^{2\frac{3}{4}}$ Basically 115^{nk} Just Talk 114^{hd}	Tired	6
11Aug77- 8Del	fst	$1\frac{1}{16}$	:46	1:11⅘	1:45⅗	3↑Allowance	8	4	4^{8}	3^{1}	$1^{\frac{1}{2}}$	$2^{2\frac{1}{2}}$	Gilbert R B	b	112	11.00	78-14	John Alden $112^{2\frac{1}{2}}$ Timothy K. $112^{\frac{1}{2}}$ Double Recipe 107^{4}	Gamely	9

LATEST WORKOUTS **Dec 9 Lrl 3f gd :39⅖ b** **●Nov 18 Lrl 4f fst :47⅖ h** **Nov 13 Lrl 6f fst 1:19⅗ b** **Oct 14 Lrl 5f gd 1:03 h**

Breeding Line

Dk. b. or br. c. 3, by Bushido—Mirabilis, by Owen Tudor

The top line of Timothy K.'s past performances tells his color, sex, age, sire, dam, and maternal grandsire. He is a dark bay or brown colt, three years old, by Bushido out of Marabilis, whose sire was Owen Tudor.

The colors of thoroughbred horses are bay (b.), brown (br.), black (blk.), chestnut (ch.), gray (gr.), and roan (ro.).

A male thoroughbred is a colt (c.) until he reaches the age of five and becomes a horse (h.) A female is a filly (f.) until she turns five and becomes a mare (m.). A gelding (g.) is a castrated male of any age. A ridgling (rig.) is a male with one or both testicles absent from the sac.

Overall Record

	Turf Record				St.	1st	2nd	3rd		Amt.
St.	1st	2nd	3rd	1977	21	2	3	3		$19,575
3	0	0	1	1976	11	M	0	0		$543

The figures in the upper-right-hand corner of Timothy K.'s past performances summarize his record for the last two years. In 1977 he started twenty-one times, with two wins, three seconds, and three thirds, and earned $19,575. In 1976, he had not yet won a race; hence the "M" (for "maiden") on that line. Next to his overall record is his lifetime turf record. Timothy K. has made three starts on the grass and finished third once.

Date and Track

26Nov77- 3Lrl

The first item in the past-performance line is the date of a horse's race. Timothy K. made his most recent start on November 26, 1977. He was running in the third race at Laurel. These are the abbreviations for American tracks:

AC	(Agua) Caliente, Mexico		Cen	Centennial Race Tr'k, Colo.
Aks	Ak-Sar-Ben, Omaha, Neb.		Cka	Cahokia Downs, Illinois
Alb	Albuquerque, N. Mexico		Cls	Columbus, Nebraska
AP	Arlington Park, Illinois		Com	Commodore Downs, Pa.
Aqu	Aqueduct, New York		Crc	Calder Race Course, Fla.
AsD	Assiniboia D'ns, Win'g, Can.		CT	Charles Town, W. Va.
Atl	Atlantic City, N. Jersey		Cwl	Commonwealth, Ky.
Ato	Atokad Pk., S. Sioux C., Neb.			Formerly Miles Park
BB	Blue Bonnets, Canada		DeD	Delta Downs, La.
BD	Berkshire Downs, Mass.		Del	Delaware Park, Delaware
Bel	Belmont Park, New York		Det	Detroit, Michigan
Beu	Beulah Park, Ohio		Dmr	Del Mar, California
BF	Brockton Fair, Mass.		ElP	Ellis Park, Kentucky
Bil	Billings, Montana		EP	Exhibit'n Pk., B.C., Can.
BM	Bay Meadows, California		EvD	Evangeline Downs, La.
BmF	Bay Meadows Fair, Cal.		FD	Florida Downs, Fla.
Boi	Boise, Idaho		FE	Fort Erie, Canada
Bow	Bowie, Maryland		Fer	Ferndale, California
CD	Churchill Downs, Ky.		FG	Fair Grounds, N. Orleans, La.
CDA	Coeur d'Alene, Idaho		FL	Finger Lakes, Can'gua, N.Y.
Ceg	Calgary, Alberta, Can.		Fno	Fresno, California

Fon	Fonner Park, Nebraska	Rui	Ruidoso, New Mexico
FP	Fairmount Park, Illinois	SA	Santa Anita Park, Cal.
GBF	Great Barrington, Mass.	Sac	Sacramento, California
GF	Great Falls, Montana	Sal	Salem, Ore. (Lone Oak)
GG	Golden Gate Fields, Cal.	San	Sandown P'k., B.C., Can.
GM	Green Mountain, Vermont	Sar	Saratoga Springs, N.Y.
GP	Gulfstream Park, Florida	SFe	Santa Fe, New Mexico
Grd	Greenwood, Can.	ShD	Shenand'h Downs, W. Va.
GS	Garden State Park, N.J.	Sol	Solano, California
Haw	Hawthorne, Illinois	Spt	Sportsman's Park, Ill.
Hia	Hialeah Park, Fla.	SR	Santa Rosa, California
Hol	Hollywood Park, Cal.	Stk	Stockton, California
HP	Hazel Park, Michigan	StP	Stampede Park, Alberta, Can.
JnD	Jefferson Downs, La.	Suf	Suffolk Downs, Mass.
Jua	Juarez, Mexico	Sun	Sunland Park, New Mex.
Kee	Keeneland, Kentucky	Tdn	Thistledown, Ohio
Key	Keystone Race Track, Pa.	Tim	Timonium, Maryland
LA	Los Alamitos, California	TuP	Turf Paradise, Arizona
LaD	Louisiana Downs, La.	Was	Washington Park, Ill.
LaM	La Mesa P'k., Rat'n, N. Mex.	Wat	Waterford Park, W. Va.
Lat	Latonia, Kentucky	Wey	Weymouth Fair, Mass.
Lbg	Lethbridge, Alberta, Can.	WO	Woodbine, Canada
LD	Lincoln Downs, R.I.	YM	Yakima Meadows, Wash.
Lga	Longacres, Washington		
LnN	Lincoln State Fair, Neb.		
Lrl	Laurel Race Course, Md.		**HUNT MEETINGS**
MD	Marquis Downs, Can.		
Med	Meadowlands, N.J.	Aik	Aiken, S. Carolina
Mex	Mexico City, Mexico	AtH	Atlanta, Roswell, Ga.
MF	Marshfield Fair, Mass.	Cam	Camden, S. Carolina
MP	Miles Park, Kentucky	Clm	Clemmons, N. Carolina
Mth	Montmouth Park, N.J.	Fal	Fair Hill, Maryland
Nar	Narragansett Park, R.I.	Fax	Fairfax, Reston, Virginia
Nmp	Northampton, Mass.	FH	Far Hills, New Jersey
NP	Northlands Park, Canada	Gln	Glyndon, Maryland
OP	Oaklawn Park, Arkansas	GN	Grand Nat'l, Butler, Md.
Pen	Penn National, Pa.	Lex	Lexington, Kentucky
Pim	Pimlico, Maryland	Lig	Ligonier, Pennsylvania
PJ	Park Jefferson, S.D.	Mal	Malvern, Pennsylvania
Pla	Playfair, Washington	Mid	Middleburg, Virginia
Pln	Pleasanton, California	Mon	Monkton, Maryland
PM	Portland Meadows, Ore.	Mtp	Montpelier, Virginia
Pmf	Portl'nd M'd'ws Fair, Ore.	Oxm	Oxmoor, Kentucky
Poc	Pocono Downs, Pa.	Pro	Prospect, Kentucky
Pom	Pomona, California	PW	Percy Warner, Tennessee
PR	Puerto Rico (El Com'te)	RB	Red Bank, New Jersey
Pre	Prescott Downs, Ariz.	SH	Strawberry Hill, Virginia
RaP	Raceway Pk., Toledo, O.	SoP	Southern Pines, N.C.
RD	River Downs, Ohio	Try	Tryon, North Carolina
Reg	Regina, Canada	Unl	Unionville, Pennsylvania
Ril	Rillito, Arizona	War	Warrenton, Virginia
Rkm	Rockingham Park, N.H.	Wel	Wellsville, Pennsylvania

Track Condition and Distance

my 1

Timothy K.'s last start was on a muddy track at the distance of one mile. The designations for track conditions are fast (fst), frozen (fr), good (gd), slow (sl), sloppy (sly), muddy (my), and heavy (hy). Turf courses are described as hard (hd), firm (fm), good (gd), soft (sf), or yielding (yl).

Distances less than one mile are listed in furlongs; Timothy K.'s next-to-last start was at six furlongs (6f). An asterisk preceding the distance indicates an approximate distance. The symbol Ⓣ following it denotes a race on the turf.

Fractional Times

:46   1:11⅘ 1:38⅘

The times in Timothy K.'s past-performance line are those for the leader at different stages of the race. The leader ran the first half-mile in 46 seconds, three-quarters of a mile in 1:11⅘, and the mile in 1:38⅘.

In races shorter than a mile, the times listed are those for the quarter-mile, the half-mile, and the finish.

Class

Clm 25000

Timothy K.'s last race was a $25,000 claiming event. If he had been claimed out of the race, the price would have been preceded by the letter "c."

A $25,000 claiming race for maidens would be abbreviated Md25000. A starter-handicap, open to horses who have run for a claiming price of, say, $10,000 or less would be designated Hcp 10000s.

"Allowance," obviously, indicates an allowance race, which can be just about any kind of nonclaiming event. "Md Sp Wt" means maiden special weight—a nonclaiming race for horses who have never won. A stakes race would be described by its name—"Ky Derby" for instance.

The symbol **3↑** preceding the class reveals that the race was limited to three-year-olds and up. Ⓕ means a race for females only, Ⓢ a race for state-breds.

Post Position and Running Line

$$1 \quad 2 \quad 2^3 \quad 2^{1\frac{1}{2}} \quad 2^3 \quad 2^1$$

The first of these figures is Timothy K.'s post position in his last start: he broke from post one. The rest of the numbers describe the way he ran at different stages of the race. After a quarter-mile, he was in second position. After a half-mile, he was second, three lengths behind the leader. After six furlongs, he was still second, 1½ lengths behind. Entering the stretch he was second by three lengths again. He finished second by a length.

The post position, stretch call, and finish always appear in the same place in the past-performance lines. The meaning of the other calls varies according to the distance of the race. In sprints, the *Racing Form* shows a horse's position at the break, the quarter-mile and the half-mile. But in races from one mile to a mile and one-eighth, the call at the break is replaced by the horse's position after a quarter-mile. The next two numbers indicate his position after a half-mile and six furlongs.

Jockey

McCarron C J

Timothy K. was ridden in his last start by Christopher J. McCarron. If a ^{5}, ^{7}, or ^{10} appeared by the rider's name, it would indicate that he was an apprentice, with a weight allowance of 5, 7, or 10 pounds.

Blinkers and Weight

b 116

Timothy K. wore blinkers in his last start. He carried 116 pounds. His weight in today's race is shown by the boldface **106⁷** which appears next to his turf record. He is scheduled to carry 106 pounds and be ridden by an apprentice with a seven-pound weight allowance.

Odds

6.00

In his last start, Timothy K. went to the post at 6 to 1. An asterisk preceding the price would mean that he was the favorite. The letter "e" following the odds would mean that he had been part of a stable entry.

Speed Rating and Track Variant

78–24

The *Racing Form* computes its own speed rating and track variant, although they are a bit crude by sophisticated speed-handicapping standards. The *Form* establishes a rating of 100 for the track record for each distance, and subtracts 1 point for each fifth of a second slower than the record that a horse runs. Laurel's one-mile record is 1:34⅘. Timothy K. ran in 1:39. (He lost by one length to a horse who won in 1:38⅘, and a length is roughly equal to a fifth of a second.) He missed the track record by 22 fifths of a second. So his speed rating is 100 minus 22, or 78.

The *Form* takes the number of fifths of a second by which each winner on a card missed the track record and averages them to produce a track variant. On the day Timothy K. ran at Laurel, the winners ran an average of 24 fifths slower than the track record. The higher the variant is, the slower the track would appear to be. The trouble with this method is that it fails to take into account the quality of horses competing on a given day. A high track variant can be produced by slow horses rather than a slow racing surface.

Company Line

Simplified 116¹ Timothy K. 116²⅟₂ Stammer 114⁴

Simplified was the winner of Timothy K.'s last race. He carried 116 pounds, and he won by one length, which we already saw in Timothy K.'s running line. Timothy K. was 2½ lengths ahead of the third horse, Stammer, who carried 114 and finished four lengths ahead of the fourth horse.

Comment and Size of Field

Gamely 5

The *Racing Form*'s comment on Timothy K.'s last performance is "Gamely." Although this is not terribly edifying, comments which say "Blocked" or "Impeded" can be very important. The numeral 5 at the end of the past-performance line shows the number of horses in the field.

Workouts

LATEST WORKOUTS Dec 9 Lrl 3f gd :39⅖ b

The bottom line of a horse's past performances will usually show his last four workouts. Timothy K.'s most recent work was at Laurel on December 9. He went three furlongs on a good track in 39⅖ seconds. The letter "b" means he was breezing, going rather easily; "h" would have indicated that he had run handily, with his rider urging him a bit; "g" indicates the horse broke from the starting gate.

Reading Charts

THIRD RACE
Laurel
NOVEMBER 26, 1977

1 MILE. (1.34⅗) CLAIMING. Purse $9,000. 3-year-olds. Weights, 122 lbs. Non-winners of two races since October 1, allowed 3 lbs. A race, 6 lbs. Claiming price $25,000; for each $2,500 to $20,000, 2 lbs. (Races where entered for $18,500 or less not considered).

Value of race $9,000, value to winner $5,400, second $1,980, third $1,080, fourth $540. Mutuel pool $62,157. Exacta Pool $79,819.

Last Raced	Horse	Eqt.	A.	Wt	PP	St	¼	½	¾	Str	Fin	Jockey	Cl'g Pr	Odds $1
8Nov77 ^{6}Lrl^{2}	Simplified	b	3	116	3	1	$1^{1\frac{1}{2}}$	1^{3}	$1^{1\frac{1}{2}}$	1^{3}	1^{1}	Passmore W J	25000	2.60
20Nov77 ^{8}Key^{10}	Timothy K.	b	3	116	1	3	2^{2}	2^{2}	2^{1}	2^{2}	$2^{2\frac{1}{2}}$	McCarron C J	25000	6.00
5Nov77 ^{5}Lrl^{3}	Stammer	b	3	114	5	2	$3^{3\frac{1}{2}}$	3^{5}	3^{6}	3^{4}	3^{4}	Lindberg G	20000	3.50
24Oct77 ^{5}Lrl^{2}	Sea Defier	b	3	116	4	5	5	5	4^{4}	4^{5}	4^{10}	Hinojosa H	25000	2.00
3Nov77 ^{3}Lrl^{1}	Ocean Deep	b	3	119	2	4	4^{hd}	$4^{\frac{1}{2}}$	5	5	5	Moyers L	25000	3.80

OFF AT 1:30, EST. Start good, Won driving. Time, :23⅕, :46, 1:11⅘, 1:38⅘ Track muddy.

$2 Mutuel Prices:				
	3-SIMPLIFIED	7.20	3.60	3.80
	1-TIMOTHY K.		5.60	4.20
	5-STAMMER			4.00

$2 EXACTA 3-1 PAID $46.20.

dk b or br. g, by Aristocratic—Snow Flyer, by Snow Boots. Trainer Hacker Beverly P. Bred by Parker J C (Pa).

SIMPLIFIED broke alertly to gain the early lead, was well handled making the pace then had enough left to hold back TIMOTHY K. The latter, forwardly placed from the outset, rallied outside the winner leaving the furlong grounds and was slowly gaining late. STAMMER, slightly wide while within striking distance from the outset, finished without mishap. SEA DEFIER was not a serious threat. OCEAN DEEP showed little.

Owners— 1, Fourbros Stable; 2, Fall Cecilia E; 3, Helmore Farm; 4, Schneider H G; 5, Christiana Stable.

Trainers— 1, Hacker Beverly P; 2, Fall James M; 3, Adams Robert L; 4, Field Thomas E; 5, Clark Henry S.

Overweight: Stammer 2 pounds.

Scratched—Zero Launch (14Nov77 ^{8}Lrl^{3}).

Charts are summaries of individual races from which the information in past-performances lines is drawn. They are mostly self-explanatory, except for the running line. The charts show a horse's position and the number of lengths he was ahead of the horse behind him, rather than the margin by which he trailed the leader. At the finish call of Timothy K.'s race, the chart says $2^{2\frac{1}{2}}$, meaning that he was second, 2½ lengths in front of the third-place horse, Stammer.

A Glossary
of Some Common
Racing Terms

ALLOWANCE RACE. A nonclaiming race which has conditions to determine the horses who are eligible to enter. For example, an allowance race might be open to horses who have never won three races in their career.

BOX. To play an exacta (or triple) by taking all the possible combinations of certain horses. A box of numbers 2, 5, and 6 in the exacta would actually be six different combinations: 2–5, 2–6, 5–2, 5–6, 6–2, 6–5.

CLAIMING RACE. The most common type of race in America. Horses are entered for a specific pricetag, and they may be purchased (claimed) before the race by any owner or trainer at the track. The effect of the claiming system is to keep the competition in a race fairly equal.

DAILY DOUBLE. A form of wagering that requires the bettor to pick the winners of the first two races.

EXACTA. A form of wagering that requires the bettor to pick the first and second finishers in a race in order. Also known as a *perfecta*.

FURLONG. One-eighth of a mile.

HANDICAP. A type of race in which the entrants are assigned weights which will theoretically equalize their chances of winning. The racing secretary who assigns the weights is said to handicap the race. As a verb, *handicap* has come to be applied generally to the process of analyzing an event and predicting its outcome.

MAIDEN. A horse (of either sex) who has never won a race.

PARLAY. A bet on two or more races in which all the proceeds from the first wager are carried over onto the second horse, and so on.

ROUTE. A race of a mile or longer.

SPRINT. A race shorter than a mile.

STAKES RACE. A race in which owners must post an entry fee to start their horses. Stakes are generally the highest-class races.

TRACK BIAS. The tendency of a racing surface to favor horses with certain post positions or running styles.

TRACK VARIANT. A numerical measurement of the inherent speed of a racing surface.

TRIPLE. A form of wagering that requires the bettor to pick the first, second, and third finishers in a race in order. Also known as a *trifecta*.

YEARLING. A one-year-old horse.